GREECE AT THE CROSSROADS

GREECE AT THE CROSSROADS

The Civil War and Its Legacy

Edited by

John O. Iatrides
and
Linda Wrigley

The Pennsylvania State University Press
University Park, Pennsylvania

Library of Congress Cataloging-in-Publication Data

Greece at the crossroads : the civil war and its legacy / edited by
    John O. Iatrides and Linda Wrigley.
        p.   cm.
    Revised papers presented originally at a conference organized by the Lehrman
Institute and held in the Vilvorde Conference Center in Copenhagen, Denmark,
June 3–5, 1987.
    Includes bibliographical references and index.
    ISBN 0-271-01410-5 (cloth). — ISBN 0-271-01411-3 (pbk.)
    1. Greece—History—Civil War, 1944–1949—Congresses.
I. Iatrides, John O.   II. Wrigley, Linda.   III. Lehrman Institute.
DF849.52.G74   1995
949.507—dc20   94-27072
                                                                          CIP

Published by The Pennsylvania State University Press,
University Park, PA 16802-1003

It is the policy of The Pennsylvania State University Press to use acid-free paper for
the first printing of all clothbound books. Publications on uncoated stock satisfy the
minimum requirements of American National Standard for Information Sciences—
Permanence of Paper for Printed Library Materials, ANSI Z39.48–1992.

Contents

Preface

The end of the cold war and the cooling of ideological passions make possible a more detached and balanced examination of the major episodes of the East-West conflict. At the same time, the increased availability of source materials, both government and private, reveals a more complex reality than earlier interpretations described, particularly with respect to the role of the two superpowers, which in certain of these episodes was less decisive than previously thought.

One such episode is the Greek civil war, a critical turning point in the history of that nation and, according to some historians, in the shaping of America's containment policy. The study of the Greek civil war is important, therefore, to our understanding not only of the contemporaneous and subsequent developments in that country but also of the dynamics of Balkan forces and the intricacies of American and Soviet perceptions and tactics in the early days of the East-West confrontation.

For Greece, the end of the Second World War brought to the surface new and dynamic social forces and unveiled a national schism of unprecedented ferocity. The deeper roots of this state of affairs can be traced to the bankruptcy of the interwar political institutions that had spawned the dictatorship of Ioannis Metaxas in August 1936. When the dictator suddenly died in January 1941, and the country in short order suffered complete military defeat at the hands of the German invaders and occupation by the Axis forces a few months later, the regime's collapse not only created a power void but set in motion the struggle for a new, postwar political order and legitimacy whose outcome was bound to determine the country's longer-term future. The simmering crisis was greatly aggravated by the paralysis imposed upon the Greek polity by the harsh enemy occupation, many instances of collaborationism, and by the highly politicized resistance movements that mobilized, indoctrinated, and armed large numbers of followers propounding radical views.

In the fall of 1944, at the moment of liberation from the German occupiers, Greece stood "at the crossroads" and in need of a new constitutional and social order. At least in principle, the political paths open before the populace ranged across the entire ideological compass: from a dictatorship of the Left or the Right to a moderate socialist, progressive democratic, or rigidly conservative regime; from a republican to a monarchist form of government. The final choice could have been made on the basis of a passionate but peaceful electoral contest to determine the nation's will. But the factions that vied for influence over the state promoted their particular agendas with a vehemence, exclusiveness, and mistrust that destroyed any chance for genuine compromise and reconciliation. Before long the political tug of war turned into full-scale civil war.

Moreover, the contest for legitimacy and control over the nation's future could not be waged on a purely Greek stage. As in other periods of its development, Greece was buffeted by powerful external forces that sought to harness the feuding factions, as well as the Greek state itself, to their own particular interests. In turn, in their desperate effort to defeat their domestic foes, Greek leaders eagerly solicited foreign assistance, guidance, and patronage. In the end, the indigenous struggle for power became enmeshed not only in age-old Balkan feuds—which have re-ignited with renewed ferocity today—but also came to be viewed as a major battleground of the cold war, pitting the British and the Americans against the Soviet-dominated Communist-bloc countries to the north of Greece. External factors thus exerted considerable influence over the course and final outcome of the Greek civil war and had much to do with the political path Greece was to follow beyond the decade of the 1940s.

The chapters in this volume represent a systematic attempt to examine the domestic and external forces that were actively involved in the Greek crisis of the late 1940s. Specifically, they consider the political options available to postwar Greece by identifying the principal actors promoting such options and analyzing their programs and tactics, their strengths and weaknesses. These chapters also highlight the close interaction between domestic, regional, and global levels of conflict as they relate to the political development of Greece. It should be noted that because the involvement of Britain and the United States in Greek affairs during the 1940s has been the subject of a large number of previous studies, mostly in English, a detailed analysis of the development of British and American policy toward Greece is not attempted here.

The chapters in this book originated as papers presented at a conference held at the Vilvorde Conference Center in Copenhagen, Denmark, June 3–5, 1987, and most were subsequently extensively revised. The conference was organized under the aegis of the Lehrman Institute in New York City. Nicholas X. Rizopoulos, then the Institute's executive director, not only conceived of the conference but worked tirelessly to secure the necessary funding both for the conference itself and subsequently for the publication of these essays. The editors are also indebted to him for his invaluable editorial advice and his unflagging interest in this project.

The conference in Copenhagen was funded in part by grants from the Smith Richardson Foundation and the Lynde and Harry Bradley Foundation, and by generous contributions from John D. Soutter and Daniel Yergin. Lars Baerentzen contributed enormously to the success of the conference, handling the arrangements in Copenhagen with efficiency and good cheer. Finally, the publication of this volume was made possible by an additional grant from the Lynde and Harry Bradley Foundation and by a second contribution from Daniel Yergin. The editors speak for all the conference participants and writers represented in this volume when they express their heartfelt thanks to those whose contributions made this project possible.

Terms and Abbreviations

Terms and abbreviations used frequently in the main text are defined here. Source abbreviations appearing only in the footnotes are not included.

AKE — Agrotikon Komma Elladas (Agrarian Party of Greece)

ASKE — Agrotiko Sosialdemokratiko Komma Elladas (Agrarian Social-Democratic Party of Greece)

BLO — British Liaison Officer (attached to resistance groups)

BMM — British Military Mission to resistance groups

EA — Ethniki Allilengii (National Solidarity), EAM's welfare organization

EAM — Ethniko Apeleftherotiko Metopo (National Liberation Front), the largest wartime resistance organization comprised of leftists-republicans and Communists

EDA — Eniaia Demokratiki Aristera (United Democratic Left), leftist coalition party of the 1950s and 1960s

EDES — Ethnikos Demokratikos Ellinikos Dyndesmos (National Republican Greek League), major wartime resistance group commanded by the onetime republican officer Napoleon Zervas, who in his fight with EAM/ELAS gradually moved to the royalist camp

EEAM — Ethniko Ergatiko Apeleftherotiko Metopo (National Workers' Liberation Front), EAM's wartime labor arm

EEE — Ethniki Enosis Ellados (National Union of Greece), small right-wing wartime resistance group

EKKA — Ethniki kai Koinoniki Apeleftherosi (National and Social Liberation), republican wartime resistance group under Col. Dimitrios Psarros destroyed by ELAS in October 1943 ("First Round"); Psarros was murdered by Communists in April 1944

ELAS — Ethnikos Laikos Apeleftherotikos Stratos (National People's Liberation Army), the military arm of EAM and the largest group of armed resistance

ELD	Enosi Laikis Demokratias (Union of People's Democracy), small socialist party in the EAM coalition until 1945
EPON	Eniaia Panelladiki Organosi Neon (United Panhellenic Organization of Youth), EAM's wartime youth organization
ERGAS	Ergatikos Antifasistikos Syndesmos (Workers' Antifascist League), leftist labor organization
"First Round"	Fighting precipitated by ELAS against its rivals in the resistance during the fall and winter of 1943. Has been viewed as the first attempt by the Communists to seize power by force
GSEE	Geniki Synomospondia Ellinon Ergaton (General Confederation of Greek Workers)
IDEA	Ieros Desmos Ellinon Axiomatikon (Sacred League of Greek Officers), secret rightist society of officers
KKE	Kommounistiko Komma Elladas (Communist Party of Greece)
Liberal Party (Komma Fileleftheron)	Centrist party founded by Eleftherios Venizelos in the 1910s
Mountain Brigade (also Rimini or Third Brigade)	Army unit formed in Spring 1944 in the Middle East in the aftermath of mutinies in the Greek armed forces and the purging of leftist elements
OEEC	Organization of European Economic Cooperation
OPLA	Omades Prostasias Laikou Agona (Teams for the Protection of the People's Struggle), wartime EAM/ELAS security and terror group
PEEA	Politiki Epitropi Ethnikis Apeleftherosis (Political Committee of National Liberation), shadow government established by EAM in the liberated areas in March 1944
Populist (People's) Party (Laikon Komma)	Rightist-royalist party
"Second Round" (*Dekemvriana*)	Fighting in Athens area in December 1944 between ELAS and government troops, primarily British; has been viewed as the Communists' second attempt to seize power by force
Security Battalions (Tagmata Asfaleias)	Greek military units authorized by the collaborationist government of John Rallis to help the German occupation forces suppress resistance activity

SKE	Sosialistikon Komma Elladas (Socialist Party of Greece)
SOE	Special Operations Executive, British wartime intelligence and sabotage agency
"Third Round"	The civil war of 1946–49
UNRRA	United Nations Relief and Rehabilitation Administration
UNSCOB	United Nations Special Committee on the Balkans
Varkiza Agreement	Signed on February 12, 1945, near Athens, between the government and EAM/ELAS, ending the December fighting in the capital and providing for the disarming and dissolution of ELAS and for measures to resolve the political crisis
X	A small wartime royalist clandestine organization whose principal target was leftist resistance activists

1

Greece at the Crossroads, 1944–1950

John O. Iatrides

The Second World War swept through most of Europe like a terrible maelstrom, killing, uprooting, and destroying virtually everything in its path. When it was over, countless millions were dead, crippled, or emaciated; others had been driven from their homes, their lives shattered. Beyond the human losses, the material and economic devastation was no less appalling. Whole cities lay in ruins, industrial plants, agricultural machinery, and transportation and communication networks were destroyed or pillaged, and all but the most primitive economic activity was at a standstill. Public treasuries and personal wealth were gone, looted or spent in the desperate struggle to stay alive. Victors or vanquished, most of Europe's nations found themselves ravaged, destitute, and with little hope of early recovery.

Beyond the death toll and the physical losses that could be seen and counted, the war amounted to an assault on Europe's traditional institutions of authority, power, and social order. Long-established concepts of legitimacy came under attack from a variety of forces demanding radical change. The need for such change was most obvious in the defeated states of the Axis and its accomplices, where the wartime regimes now had to be formally and fully dismantled and purged. Under the control of the victorious Allies, new political forces had to be nurtured and new governmental institutions fashioned.

However, even in countries that had fought on the winning side, the prewar political and social establishment had been shaken to its foundations. Especially where the war had brought defeat and enemy occupation, a sense of national collapse and humiliation often tended to alienate the public from its traditional political leadership. The spectacle of passive submission or, worse, of collaboration with the foreign occupiers, gave rise to feelings of hatred of fellow countrymen who had remained in office, whatever their motives. Significantly, resistance against the Axis occupation forces was largely the work of the hitherto powerless, of those who had felt oppressed or exploited by the prewar political elites. In fact, in most cases, wartime resistance was as much a struggle for empowerment and public recognition as it was a continuation of the fight against the foreign enemy. Even Britain, which suffered severe human losses and material destruction but was spared the ordeal of defeat and occupation of the homeland, did not entirely escape the winds of change: the war's end would usher in an era of major political and economic reform.

In short, with the exception of the few who managed to remain neutral, the war left Europe's states not only ravaged and ruined but with their power structures shaken or discredited. For most, a return to the prewar political institutions and practices was simply impossible: economic reconstruction would have to go hand in hand with sweeping political, economic, and social reform.

If the desire for a new institutional order was felt across much of the continent, its practical consequences varied dramatically from country to country. In East Central Europe and most of the Balkans the collapse of the Nazi-imposed regimes was followed by a new era of oppression and terror. By 1948, relying on the presence of the Red Army to suppress all opposition, the Soviet Union had imposed on these "liberated" states puppet regimes whose "socialist revolution" was designed to turn them into pliant appendages of Moscow's new empire. In Yugoslavia, Tito's Communist-led Partisans copied Stalin's revolution by establishing their own brand of single-party dictatorship and exterminating tens of thousands of their enemies. Whether largely homegrown, as in Yugoslavia and Albania, or imposed by Soviet military force, as in Bulgaria, Czechoslovakia, Hungary, Poland, and Romania, these new political systems created a wasteful, unproductive, and corrupt economic order, suppressed basic freedoms, and suffocated the human spirit. The full measure of the regression and misery they caused became apparent only after 1989, when, deprived of Moscow's propping, they were brought down by—mostly peaceful—popular revolt.

Where Soviet power did not reach, and where democratic tradition had been strong, the cause of social change and reform fared much better. Thus, a victorious but economically exhausted Britain sought to answer the call for better conditions for the masses through the humane but austere socialism of the Labour Party. In the Low Countries and Scandinavia, progressive governments experimented with other variations of social-democratic reforms designed to redistribute wealth for the benefit of the lower classes, expand public services of every kind, and generally create the modern welfare state.

In France, the road to recovery was made more difficult by the bitter legacy of the collaborationist Vichy regime, the burdens of an already collapsing overseas empire, and the presence of a powerful newcomer to the political center ring: the Communist Party. Their impressive resistance record, their superior grass-roots organization, and their image as the defenders of the underprivileged had turned the French Communists into a formidable political force. In addition, at the time of liberation, they still had access to weapons with which they could have intimidated their domestic opponents. Nevertheless, despite their popularity and potential for bold action, in the immediate postwar period the leaders of the French Communist Party remained cautious and ambivalent on the central issue of imposing sweeping social and political reform by force. While paying lip service to Communist dogma, they seemed more eager to earn for themselves legitimacy within the existing political order of the Fourth Republic than to become the instrument of genuine revolution. Whatever their deeper motives, they behaved as if they could not bring themselves to resort to sweeping violent action. As a result of its tactics and its willingness to collaborate with bourgeois groups in a series of largely ineffective coalition governments, the French Communist Party under Maurice Thorez and Jacques Duclos lost much of its luster and managed to alienate its more radical followers. After 1947, it also became a casualty of the cold war when European Communists were accused by their domestic adversaries of being "antinational" and little more than Moscow's willing tools.

Similarly, in postwar Italy, a strong Communist movement under

Palmiro Togliatti, who for a while appeared to enjoy Stalin's personal favor and support, had the opportunity to dominate the national debate concerning the country's future. The Communist Party led the effort to exorcise the demons of the Fascist past and sparred with other budding leftist groups over political and economic reform. With the apparent approval of Moscow, the Italian Communists confined their efforts to lawful political activity. Even after 1948, when they fomented labor unrest against the Marshall Plan and its underlying capitalist ideology, they appeared to have no intention of seizing power by force. Like their French comrades, who also vociferously opposed American influence in postwar European reconstruction, they soon found themselves accused of antinational motives and banished from their country's political councils.

Thus, even in the presence of strong Communist and leftist parties, those states that did not fall behind Stalin's iron curtain managed to confront their postwar problems, including constitutional issues of critical importance, with remarkably little political violence. Except in Spain and Portugal, where right-wing dictatorships continued to muzzle political opposition, a strong leftist-populist movement appeared to be ascendant across the continent, demanding to share power with the traditional elites. Yet, despite much tension and instability, in the end lawful discourse and compromise rather than revolutionary confrontation was the chosen path.

To be sure, American influence over governmental activity in Western Europe was also instrumental in discouraging revolutionary initiatives and truly radical social reforms. Europe's state of economic collapse and political division, combined with the specter of a Soviet military giant seemingly bent on further expansion, afforded the United States a unique opportunity to play a decisive role in shaping the continent's political future. To ensure the success of its ambitious recovery program, the Truman administration urged the Europeans to engage in constructive regional cooperation, encourage stability, and, above all, promote a political climate free of radical departures from traditional liberal-capitalist norms. As a consequence, the principal beneficiaries of American economic and political support were those moderate and centrist groupings that were ready to introduce extensive reforms while shunning revolutionary solutions. However, in the long run, for all of Washington's controlling influence, it was the Western Europeans' own spirit of pragmatism that defined the course to be followed and ensured the success of the continent's recovery program. Identifying their self-interest with the

Truman administration's resolve to keep Western Europe free of Soviet influence, they opted for reformist policies devoid of doctrinaire socialist content.

On Europe's southeastern fringe, Greece was to prove the exception to the rule, the one country that, buffeted by the turbulence spawned by the world war, could not find peaceful solutions to its festering political problems. Less than two years after its liberation from the Nazi hordes the nation was drawn into a full-scale civil war that greatly compounded the human suffering and material losses sustained during the Axis occupation.

Partly because—at least initially—the Greek insurgents acted in self-defense against an officially sanctioned "white terror," and because they were in the end crushed militarily, their long-term political goals remain to this day a matter of contentious interpretation and factious debate. Moreover, the presence of Communist regimes throughout the Balkans, and their considerable involvement in the Greek crisis, created the impression that the Greek civil war was fomented from abroad. This was the Athens government's own official position, as well as the centerpiece of the Truman administration's arguments and decision in March 1947 to ensure the insurgents' defeat through the promulgation of the Truman Doctrine.

After mid-1946, the insurgents' once-independent bands came under the firm control of the Greek Communist Party (KKE), which now appeared ready to advocate the radical transformation of the nation's social order and international orientation. Moreover, increasingly the insurgents' actions left little doubt that they intended to achieve their goals through the use of armed force. And while the Greek Communists did solicit support from foreign comrades, including Stalin, they launched the insurrection on their own initiative and not at the instigation of others. Therefore, in the final analysis, the Greek crisis of 1946–49 has to be viewed as the result of a Communist-inspired revolution domestically conceived. That is how the leaders of the insurgency viewed their struggle at the time, generally labeling it a people's revolution (*laiki epanastasi*) whose immediate goal, a people's democracy (*laiki demokratia*), would be the first major step on the road to "true socialism" (i.e., communism).

This said, the exact reasons why, of all the parts of Europe that remained beyond Soviet domination, only Greece experienced the horrors of revolutionary violence are not easy to explain. To be sure, there had developed in recent Greek history seemingly irreconcilable cleavages, instances of social unrest, acts of politically inspired violence, all contributing to a widespread popular mistrust of traditional governmental authority. Yet, Greece's plight was hardly unique. Indeed, in the turbulent interwar years, many other European nations had fared far worse.

In August 1936, a fascist-like dictatorship had been imposed on Greece by Ioannis Metaxas with the connivance of King George II, himself returned to his throne by fraudulent means the previous year and personally unpopular. A harsh police state had thereupon been established that repressed all political debate and exiled its opponents, while saving its harshest measures for the members of the KKE. Before it was officially toppled by the invading German armies in the spring of 1941, the Metaxas dictatorship had intensified the nation's divisions by adding to the assortment of victims across the Greek political spectrum who now waited for the chance to take their revenge on their former tormentors and share in the control of the state. The Greeks' surprising victories against Mussolini's troops, which attacked through Albania in October 1940, had momentarily turned Metaxas into a national hero. But when he died suddenly in January 1941, he left behind an inept and demoralized government to face defeat at the hands of the unstoppable Germans. Accompanied by a coterie of mostly Metaxist or monarchist political figures, and protected by the retreating British forces, the king fled first to Crete and then to Cairo, where his government would wait out the war.

Under Emmanuel Tsouderos, a prominent banker, and, later, George Papandreou, a liberal politician, the Greek government in exile tried in vain to preserve a semblance of unity and discipline among the fractious politicians and the unruly officers who made their way to the Middle East. In Allied councils, ultimate responsibility for sustaining the Greek government, and for controlling the resistance movement that developed in occupied Greece, rested with the British political and military authorities, which were themselves divided as to the proper course of action in Greek affairs.

As the day of liberation approached, opposition to the monarchy and, in particular, to the return of King George II, reemerged as the one national issue on which virtually all political groups could agree. Old-fashioned republicanism, now mixed with a strong element of populism, was on the rise within Greece, as well as among the Greek civilian and military groups in the Middle East.

The trend toward populism and the demand for social change were particularly evident among those who had come as refugees from Asia

Minor in the 1920s, among radical republicans, and among workers and farmers. The willingness of a considerable number of Greeks to collaborate in various ways with the occupation forces or to enrich themselves through black-market activity at the expense of their compatriots deepened class hatreds and gave rise to demands, voiced largely by leftists, for the severe punishment after liberation of all those guilty of such antinational conduct. But the demand for social justice went unheeded. In the immediate post-liberation period, feuding politicians, royalist as well as republican, could not see beyond their mutual suspicions and narrow partisan interests. Reverting to their prewar tactics, they succeeded in stalemating each other and obstructing the road to recovery, thus alienating further a general public already mistrustful of its traditional leaders. Nor had the war undone the country's blatantly uneven distribution of wealth. Islands of ostentatious luxury, especially in Athens, remained amid a sea of extreme poverty and suffering, fueling feelings of hatred toward the numerically small upper class among the destitute masses and the refugees. The ever-inflexible and overly centralized state bureaucracy, combined with the all-pervasive patronage and nepotism found in all state-run enterprises, added to the public's sense of impotence and alienation, especially among those living away from Athens, creating a deep divide between the capital and the rest of the country.

In sum, there can be no question that, in the aftermath of the Second World War, Greece found itself physically devastated and with a large segment of its population destitute, frustrated, and alienated from its traditional political leaders. Yet for all their enormity, the ills of the Greek state and society, and the frailty of the nation's institutions, were not in themselves sufficient to spark a violent revolution. Unless deliberately harnessed to such a cause, the prewar cleavages and the widespread feelings of frustration and alienation would have more likely perpetuated political instability, and the nation would have continued its spasmodic search for compromise, stability, and social reform.

There is undoubtedly an important connection to be made between the wartime resistance in Greece and the civil war that ensued. The KKE, which commanded the organized insurrection in 1946, had been the genius and driving force behind the largest of the resistance organizations, EAM (National Liberation Front), and its powerful military arm, ELAS (National People's Liberation Army). The backbone of the so-called Democratic Army—which the insurgents fielded in late 1946—including most of its military commanders, consisted of veterans of ELAS, while former EAM cadres provided key support services. Initially, most of the Democratic Army's weapons had belonged to the wartime ELAS. Once again, however, a powerful wartime resistance movement under Communist control and easy access to quantities of weapons were not unique to Greece; such conditions existed in Italy and France but did not produce a Communist revolution after the war's end.

In nearby Yugoslavia, Tito's Communist guerrillas, taking advantage of their military strength, mercilessly attacked their domestic opponents under cover of the resistance struggle and seized control of the country on the heels of the retreating Germans. On the other hand, in Greece the Communists (who were in contact with their Yugoslav comrades) made no concerted effort to exploit their popularity and military superiority in order to impose their own regime before the Papandreou government and British troops returned. To be sure, in the fall of 1943, ELAS units had clashed with rival resistance bands in an attempt to remove from the field groups hostile to EAM. British liaison officers finally managed to impose a cease-fire, and the warring factions accepted an agreement based on separate areas of operational responsibility. And in the spring of 1944, units of the Greek army and navy in the Middle East mutinied and had to be suppressed by force. Yet these isolated acts of violence, in which Communists were involved, resulted from localized antagonisms and friction rather than from a decision of the KKE to impose its will on postwar Greece. Reluctantly, and succumbing to fear of political isolation and to British pressure, the KKE subordinated itself to the authority of the Papandreou government, which despite its apparent liberal-republican character remained hostile to the Communists. In the late summer of 1944, abandoning their "provisional government" in the regions under EAM/ELAS control, the Communists joined a revamped government of "national unity" as a very junior partner. Thus, in the weeks immediately preceding and following liberation the KKE formally shared responsibility for the government's actions without being able to influence them in any appreciable way. More important, the KKE placed ELAS under direct British military authority at the very moment when Prime Minister Winston Churchill, whose hostility toward EAM/ELAS had become all too apparent, was preparing to dispatch British troops to Athens in an effort to neutralize the Greek Left's political influence in the postwar balance of forces. Finally, the central question of King George's return to Greece had not been resolved in a manner that would be reassuring to the leftists and radical republicans.

As a consequence of these developments, and even though the king remained in London, the liberation of Greece in October 1944 saw the reestablishment in Athens of a predominantly anticommunist government escorted by British troops, the continuation in office of a staunchly anticommunist civil service, and the preservation of the police and security forces that the occupation regime had employed to hunt down leftists. Liberation also permitted the reemergence of pre-Metaxas political groups, at least in the person of their leaders, almost all of whom viewed the Communists with open hostility and demonstrated no particular desire to see the wartime collaborators punished.

The Communists' uneasy coexistence with their adversaries broke down in early December 1944 when Papandreou, frightened by the continuing leftist influence in the countryside, where the resistance organizations remained the dominant force, ordered ELAS disarmed and disbanded. In the tense and devious negotiations that followed, the prime minister received the full backing of Britain's embassy and military authorities in Athens. The Communists and their allies in EAM, who now left the government in protest, saw the move to disarm ELAS as an attempt to deprive them of their most potent weapon and to banish them from the political arena. When a Communist-organized mass demonstration in the center of Athens was fired upon by a panicky police, causing many deaths, fighting broke out in and around the city, pitting ELAS units against the meager government security forces, various paramilitary anticommunist groups, and the British troops. After more than a month's murderous street fighting, in the last days of the *Dekemvriana* revolt British reinforcements from Italy drove ELAS out of Athens and forced it to eventual capitulation. While retreating, ELAS took hostages, including prominent Athenians, many of whom perished under barbarous conditions.

In mid-February 1945, a peace agreement arranged by the British authorities and Archbishop Damaskinos, whom Churchill had first opposed but finally promoted as regent, was signed by the principal political factions at Varkiza, outside Athens. The Varkiza Agreement provided for the disarming and disbanding of ELAS, the restoration of civil authority, a plebiscite on the issue of the king's return, and national elections for a constituent parliament. For all its flaws, the agreement offered hope for a peaceful resolution of the most contentious political issues and for an eventual national reconciliation. However, the most important consequence of the *Dekemvriana* and of the Varkiza Agreement was the discrediting of EAM/ELAS, and especially of the KKE, in the eyes of most moderates, who blamed the Communists for the recent violence. With its popularity sharply diminished and with ELAS essentially disarmed and disbanded, the entire leftist coalition of the occupation years became the target of persecution by resurgent rightist forces, which the Athens government either could not or would not restrain. The Communist Party stood alone, its wartime political allies alienated and divided, its followers harassed, imprisoned, and demoralized. The parliamentary elections of March 1946, which the KKE and other leftists chose to boycott, produced a clear victory for the conservative-royalists of the Populist (People's) Party. In September of the same year, a plebiscite, from which many Communists and leftists abstained, returned King George to his throne by a substantial margin: the previously unpopular monarchy had come to be viewed by many Greeks as the symbol of "nationalism" and a tangible barrier against the threat of communism.

Under these turbulent conditions, and as the country's economic crisis persisted, in a series of decisions taken during the winter of 1946–47 the leadership of the Greek Communist Party moved toward a full-scale rebellion. In its public pronouncements the KKE maintained that it had been forced to resort to radical action, and that its aim was the destruction of "monarcho-fascism," the punishment of collaborators, the protection of the people's liberties and civil rights, and the promotion of equality and justice for all. More doctrinaire issues and matters of tactics were discussed in closed meetings of the KKE Central Committee's political bureau, whose deliberations and records remained closely guarded secrets.

Whatever its long-term vision, the KKE could not hope to succeed except through the overthrow of the established political order: the days of possible compromise, peaceful reform, and broad coalition governments were long gone. In the face of the virulent anticommunism that permeated the entire Greek state apparatus and much of society, the KKE had to choose between virtual oblivion and revolution. At a time when its political leverage was at its nadir, and when its much more powerful counterparts in Italy and France were straining to remain within the law, the Greek Communist Party chose revolution. Moreover, it did so at a time—certainly by mid-1947—when its domestic opponents were united in their determination to suppress the KKE, and when the United States, through the Truman Doctrine and the Marshall Plan, had committed its boundless economic resources, military strength, and prestige to the containment of communism generally and to the defeat of the Greek Communists in particular.

Politically inspired violence is, of course, a common occurrence in to-day's world. Especially in recently created states, political institutions and social traditions often fail to confine to a peaceful process the contin-uous struggle for predominance among competing factions. Where civil society is in fact a patchwork of ethnic or tribal groups, and where a fundamental consensus regarding national priorities and methods of conflict resolution has never developed, violence frequently determines who governs. As a result, armed forces rather than civilian groups remain the key factor in the political life of many states. In addition, the unstable international order, in which states seek to enhance their position by creating client governments elsewhere, along with the overabundance of modern weapons of every kind, contribute to the frequency of violent eruptions. In such cases the objective of political violence is to either overthrow or preserve a particular government and to intimidate or elim-inate its opponents. Often the crisis is short-lived, involves small minori-ties of militants, and its impact upon society is minimal: change is con-fined to the very top and is a matter of the emergence of new personnel rather than of new principles.

By contrast, genuinely revolutionary violence is a much more pro-found event, one that engulfs the nation in an all-pervasive turbulence and whose effects continue to be felt long after the fighting has stopped. Like a massive volcanic eruption, it brings to the surface forces hitherto suppressed and, if successful, violently rearranges the entire political landscape. It is accompanied by the strong emotional involvement of most of the population, convincing the leaders on both sides of the armed conflict that their cause is the public's cause, and that their victory will safeguard the nation's vital interests. Thus, while revolutionaries struggle to overthrow the existing order and replace it with one they deem superior and better serving the nation's needs, defenders fight to preserve that order and retain their privileged position in it. For both sides the stakes are much higher than the simple question of who gov-erns. The success or failure of the revolution will determine not only the character and composition of governmental authority, but also the institutions and social values that will henceforth predominate, the kind of life an individual will be permitted to lead, or indeed, for the losers, whether life within the state will be possible at all.

In short, in addition to an ideological compass and plan of action, revolution requires a strong popular base of support and the ability to draw from it a sizeable armed force with which to challenge the incumbent government's military might. The insurgents are not simply a dissident military faction temporarily in rebellion, but a largely new and irregular force of political activists (some of whom may have had military experience) who take up arms in the cause of radical change that only force can achieve. As in any war, basic military skills, discipline, and organization are important. Yet, whether the revolution succeeds depends on the insurgents' leadership in which, typically, political and military roles are virtually indistinguishable. Propagating the revolution's goals in a manner that produces the willing support of the largest possible segment of the public and inspires confidence in a successful outcome requires political sophistication to understand the nation's mood and the international climate. Securing the materiel to conduct major military operations, and organizing an effective system of transportation and distribution in the face of the government's countermeasures, requires a great deal more than determination and ideological zeal. Fighting successfully an adversary who is far superior in troop strength, better equipped and supplied, and led by trained professionals is possible only when the insurgents' own commanders can counter with unorthodox tactics and constant improvisation that demoralize and sap the strength of the government's troops. Above all, the success of an armed revolution depends on its leaders' sense of timing. If they strike prematurely, their forces are likely to be defeated before they can reach their optimum strength; if they wait too long, the struggle will lose its momentum or the opposition may have grown too powerful to crush.

The Greek civil war of 1946–49 amounted to a genuine revolution. In retrospect, it was a revolution that might have succeeded but for its timing. Its ideological program was based on simple Marxist-Bolshevik concepts crudely adapted to fit the postwar Greek crisis. However, having built during the years of occupation a strong popular base through EAM and its ancillary organizations and a powerful armed force, the KKE could not bring itself to launch its violent struggle at the time of liberation when virtually no serious obstacles stood in the way. Instead, it temporized and held its ideological program in abeyance, hoping to earn for itself acceptance as a legitimate political movement, albeit one opposed to the reestablishment of the pre-Metaxas regime. After liberation it allowed itself to be outmaneuvered by its domestic opponents and their

British patrons when it employed force, in December 1944, in the country's only area where its opponents were militarily superior: Athens. Yet two years later, when virtually all its tangible assets had vanished, the KKE finally decided to take the road to revolution. Thus, the crucial questions: Why only then? What domestic and external conditions provided the setting for the rebellion? What were the KKE's vision and internal dynamics that caused it to set and reset its sights throughout the 1940s? At a broader level: Who were the revolution's domestic opponents, and what was their political program? Who were its foreign benefactors and its enemies, and what were their motives and tactics? Finally, what were the revolution's long-term consequences for Greece's political and social development?

Much in this complex period of recent Greek history remains unexplored or inadequately analyzed. In particular, for all their prominence, the leaders on both sides of the civil war are still for the most part shadowy figures, their personalities and calculations unclear. Opposition to the perceived Communist threat made strange bedfellows of Greece's more prominent political personalities. For example, in 1944 the one-time self-proclaimed Socialist George Papandreou became the spearhead of the anti-Left coalition; and such leading republican officers as Napoleon Zervas and Nikolaos Plastiras made their peace with the monarchy in order to fight against the Left. Sophocles Venizelos, son of the throne's nemesis in earlier decades, ended up a favorite of the palace. Moreover, while the two main prewar parties, the Liberal and the Populist (People's), continued their rivalry after 1944, with the king's return their disputes had lost all ideological content, and they focused instead on a rehash of personal grievances and petty recriminations going as far back as 1915. While disagreeing on the division of spoils and the privileges of power, they were united in their opposition to the new populist forces of the Left. As for actually combating the revolution, they simply expected Britain and, later, the United States, to provide both the means and the plan for action.

The perceptions, intent, and tactics of the KKE leadership throughout the decade of the 1940s are even more difficult to explain than those of its opponents. In part, the problem stems from the continuing lack of reliable primary sources and the party's traditionally secretive ways. It is compounded by the collective decision-making within the KKE's highest councils, which in turn obscures the role played by particular individuals, as well as by the popular assumption that the party was susceptible to direct manipulation by "higher authority" within the international Communist movement.

So far, our knowledge of such external influences remains episodic at best, allowing much room for widely divergent accounts and interpretations. In particular, it would be important to determine whether, prior to 1946, the KKE's decision to refrain from open revolutionary action was in response to specific Soviet directives—or at least to the party's own assumptions concerning Moscow's wishes. Similarly, after 1946, the party's decision to launch an armed insurrection cannot be properly scrutinized without adequate and concrete evidence as to the material assistance and political support it expected to receive from abroad, and the basis for such expectations. On the eve of Greece's liberation, in purely military terms the party did possess the necessary strength to carry out an armed revolution. But once ELAS had been disbanded and the wholesale persecution of leftists had intensified, the Communists would never again have the means to defeat their opponents, even though the government's forces remained disorganized, demoralized, and poorly equipped all through 1945–47. By their own estimates, to succeed, the Communists needed a combat strength of about 50,000 (approximately the size of ELAS in 1944), which after 1946 could be armed and sustained only with the active support of friendly neighboring regimes, presumably acting with Moscow's approval. Yet at its peak, in 1948, the strength of the Communists' Democratic Army was little more than half that number, and most of its troops were poorly armed. By the time the KKE had issued a call to its followers to join the insurrection in mid-1947, many Communists, including ELAS veterans, were already under confinement; and the government's strict police measures—under general martial law—prevented those living in urban centers from traveling to the mountains. As a rule, recruitment was to prove an insurmountable obstacle to the Democratic Army. Also, the quantities of arms and other war materiel the Communists needed, including heavier weapons and mechanized equipment, never materialized. Moreover, as soon as the Democratic Army switched from guerrilla tactics to static warfare in December 1947, its defeat became simply a matter of time. Cornered in the mountains of northwest Greece and exhausted, it fought its last desperate battles in the summer of 1949, when it was totally annihilated by government forces now fully supported by American material aid and tactical advice. One is left to wonder, therefore, whether the revolution was not in fact launched on a faulty assessment of the domestic and international situation and on the basis of promises or expectations that were not fulfilled.

On the political level, one can only speculate about the KKE leaders' perceptions of Soviet postwar strategies regarding the Balkans, of the British and American commitment to prevent a Communist victory in Greece, and of the practical consequences of the emerging cold war. Finally, it is not at all clear why, after 1945, the KKE leaders could believe that they continued to enjoy enough public support at home to ensure the success of a Communist-directed revolution. Or did they simply trust that, eventually, foreign backing would be sufficient to overwhelm their opponents and open for them the road to power?

Again, so long as the behavior of the Greek Communist leadership of the 1940s escapes systematic investigation, definitive answers to these questions will remain elusive. And while no single factor can be viewed as decisive, it is tempting to conclude that one key difference between the KKE's failure to actively pursue revolutionary objectives during the war and the subsequent move toward revolution—indeed, the main difference between the Greek Communists and their French and Italian counterparts—is to be found in the party leadership.

During the Second World War, the KKE was led by George Siantos, Secretary of the party's Central Committee and a veteran trade unionist. A man of little formal education and no international experience, he grew up poor among the tobacco workers of central Greece and served in the army during the turbulent ten-year period (1912–22) of the Balkan wars, the First World War, and Greece's disastrous invasion of Asia Minor. He was a dedicated Communist and party loyalist better known for his practical approach to the everyday issues of class struggle than for his mastery of refined Communist doctrine. His own deep roots bound him to the nation's struggle for liberation and self-aggrandizement and made him sensitive to the mood and simple aspirations of the underprivileged among his compatriots. He was conditioned by the strains and vicissitudes of the Greek Communist movement, itself very much a byproduct of Greece's Anatolian disaster, and of the KKE's efforts to become something more than a foreign-dominated political conspiracy. He appeared suspicious of his party's patrons abroad, and in the months immediately before and after liberation in 1944 he may have lacked the resolve to pursue the cause of the proletarian revolution by force. Cautious by nature, fearful of the party's domestic adversaries, and intimidated by Britain's power and traditionally dominant role in Greece, he was anxious to avoid risks that might damage the party's postwar standing as a legitimate political movement. As a stand-in for the imprisoned party Secretary General, Nikos Zahariadis, during the turbulence of 1944–45 Siantos may have also felt that he did not have the authority to lead the party into revolutionary battle.

By contrast, Zahariadis, the party's undisputed leader all through the 1930s and 1940s, was the quintessential cadre of international communism. Born and raised in the polyethnic environment of Asia Minor with no emotional attachment to the Greek state, and an activist from his youth, he fled to the Soviet Union, joined the Bolsheviks in the last days of the Russian civil war, and received special training in schools for professional party leaders. Sent to Greece for the first time in 1923, he quickly became a leader of the KKE's clandestine youth organization. Arrested for agitating in favor of an independent Macedonia (whose establishment would have deprived Greece of most of the territory newly acquired in the Balkan wars), he escaped and remained a fugitive until 1929, when the party sent him back to Moscow for further training. He was dispatched to Greece again in 1931 with instructions to discipline the badly splintered and ineffective party leadership and bring it into line with Comintern directives. On orders from the Kremlin he was named Secretary General and quickly established firm personal control over the party. Imprisoned by the Metaxas dictatorship in 1936, he remained in jail until 1942, when the German occupation authorities sent him to the concentration camp at Dachau. Freed by the advancing Allied armies, he returned to Greece in May 1945 and immediately took charge of the party's direction once again. He remained first and foremost a professional revolutionary in the service of international communism. He had little understanding of the political climate in Greece especially after the *Dekemvriana,* and viewed the situation entirely through the prism of dogmatic conviction. He thus spurned the pragmatism of Siantos (whose sudden death in 1947 remains something of a mystery) and later denounced him as a traitor, an enemy of the proletariat, and even as an agent of the British.

It was Zahariadis, Stalin's man in Greece, who set the timetable of the KKE's march toward armed insurrection. He bossed and manipulated his comrades in the Central Committee, claiming to have access to higher Communist authority in Belgrade, Sofia, and Moscow. It was Zahariadis who directed communications with the neighboring regimes, and with Stalin himself, in an effort to secure their endorsement and full support for the cause of a Communist-led revolution in Greece. It was he who, in 1948, forced the party hierarchy to side with Stalin in his attack on Tito, thus depriving the Democratic Army of its principal foreign supporters and hastening its collapse. And it was Zahariadis who orchestrated the denunciation and disgrace of Markos Vaphiadis, the Democratic Army's military commander, demoralizing further an already sorely tested insurgency while setting the stage for the terrible internal split that would plague the KKE for decades to come. Moreover, in ordering the party to take up arms against the Athens government, Zahariadis appears to have acted without clear Soviet authorization, perhaps believing that Stalin could not possibly fail to come to the aid of a revolution launched by a Communist leader whom Moscow had trained and guided throughout his adult life. Whatever Zahariadis' reasoning, he—more than any other individual—led the rebellion and directed its course to the bitter end. In the process, he wrecked the powerful mass movement that Siantos and his comrades built up during the Second World War. Years later, renouncing the doomed revolution he had led, and blaming him for bringing disaster to their movement, Zahariadis' comrades would declare him a renegade and an enemy of the KKE. The architect of revolution had met the fate of his creation.

In the wake of the Second World War, Greece stood at a historic crossroads. For the first time in its modern history, a full complement of powerful forces extending from the revolutionary Left to the reactionary Right was ready to fight for the right to set the future course of the nation's political, economic, and social development. And while the elements struggling for control of the state were fundamentally autochthonous, foreign patrons would be called upon to ensure victory. In the end, the level of foreign intervention on each side would spell the difference between winners and losers in the Greek crisis.

The essays collected in this volume represent new and authoritative attempts to analyze the main forces, domestic and external, that brought the nation to such a crossroads and determined the outcome of the ensuing violent confrontation. They also shed important light on the long-term impact of the upheaval on the nation's institutions and civil society.

If the Greek civil war of the late 1940s was largely the result of Communist initiatives, the conditions that set the stage for that crisis were many and complex; some can be properly traced to a much earlier period of the country's turbulent history. As George Th. Mavrogordatos demonstrates in his chapter, "The 1940s Between Past and Future," Greece, for all its vaunted ethnic homogeneity, had suffered from chronic cleavages, polarization, and political fragmentation. After the First World War, traditionally personalized and parochial politics had been further aggravated by frustrated irredentist dreams and, following the 1922 Anatolian debacle, the influx of more than a million destitute refugees from Asia Minor. A controversial institution from its establishment in the nineteenthth century, the Greek monarchy (since 1863 the royal family had been of Danish-German extraction) continued to divide and to inflame partisan passions. At critical moments of the country's development, foreign intervention had played one Greek faction against another, which had resulted in officially sanctioned lawlessness and violence. The institutions of government came to be viewed as mere instruments for partisan politics and personal aggrandizement, to be seized and manipulated by whatever means possible, thus preventing the emergence of a consensus on how the nation should solve its fundamental domestic and international problems. The two dominant parties, dating from the period of the First World War, were the Liberals, molded by the dynamic personality and bold tactics of Eleftherios Venizelos, and the Populists (or People's Party), who, led by Dimitrios Gounaris and Panayiotis Tsaldaris, represented the forces of "Antivenizelism" and tended to identify their political fortunes with those of the monarchy. Although the Liberals are often considered to have been the progressive reformers of the day, while the Populists are usually described as staunch conservatives, the distinction is (and was) more a matter of appearances than of substance: beyond the fundamental disagreements between Venizelists and Antivenizelists concerning Greece's entry into the First World War, in the 1920s and 1930s the nation's politics revolved largely around personal vendettas rather than concrete issues of social policy. The vast majority of Greek voters had become prisoners of two political cults: they were Venizelists or Antivenizelists, republicans or monarchists.

When both Venizelos and Tsaldaris died in 1936, their followers were left leaderless and without a social program. The resulting political paralysis, exacerbated by violent international developments and by the Great Depression, gave a definite boost to the fortunes of the Communists. In the January 1936 elections, while receiving only 5.76 percent of the popular vote, the Communists won enough seats in the new parliament to emerge as potential power brokers. This situation did not in the least signify that communism was suddenly a threat to traditional Greek institutions and society. Nevertheless, given the Liberal-Populist impasse in the parliament, the attention accorded the Communists gave Gen. Ioannis Metaxas, onetime chief of staff and head of a small party of ultranationalist royalists, the excuse he needed to request the king's authorization to dissolve parliament "temporarily" and establish what was soon to become a personal dictatorship. Disdainful of Greek politicians, King George II gave his consent, providing the Metaxas regime with the appearance of legitimacy. While most of the KKE's leadership was quickly jailed, many other republican politicians remained passive, thus allowing Metaxas to consolidate his power. The ensuing paralysis of all normal political activity, which the Axis invasion and occupation further prolonged for an additional four years, temporarily silenced but did not resolve the republican-royalist split; on the contrary, as the day of liberation approached, this "national schism" threatened to lead to widespread violence. Thus, as Mavrogordatos convincingly argues, the crisis of the 1940s must be understood as the extension of the cleavages of the interwar period. With the collapse of the Venizelist camp, its more radical republican elements moved to the left and joined the wartime resistance movement EAM. The civil war finally brought the traditional national schism to an end, as Left and Right replaced Venizelism and Antivenizelism and opened the way to eventual national integration.

During the years of the Axis occupation, except for those who actually collaborated with the enemy, most of the bourgeois politicians—both in Athens and in Cairo, where the government in exile had been established—remained largely inactive or argued endlessly about the future of the monarchy while waiting for the war to end. However, in the mountains of Greece, but also in the towns and villages, a new mass political movement was taking shape. Largely guided by the KKE, and working through a broadly leftist coalition, EAM applied itself to the immediate tasks of resisting the occupation forces and providing a rudimentary relief system for the most needy. Smaller resistance organizations, including EDES and EKKA, were sponsored by non-Communists. In the process, these movements appeared intent on replacing the bankrupt prewar political system or, at the very least, on subjecting it to radical change once the country had been set free again.

The origins, structure, and achievements of the leftist mass movement are reviewed in Hagen Fleischer's chapter, "The National Liberation Front (EAM), 1941–1947: A Reassessment." Originally the product of spontaneous resistance at the grass-roots level, EAM was soon shaped by the Communists and their Socialist allies into a powerful political weapon. EAM and its various auxiliary organizations, especially its military arm, ELAS, satisfied a need of Greeks from all walks of life not only to resist the occupiers by the modest means initially available, but to provide as well a populist structure of local organization and a support network untainted by the stigma of collaboration with the enemy. For countless Greeks this was an exhilarating experience and a political awakening such as the nation had not had since the struggle for independence against the Turks more than a century earlier. And although there were a number of other resistance organizations in the field, including ELAS's principal rival, the ostensibly republican but ultimately fiercely anticommunist EDES, it was the populist activism of the Communist-led EAM that attracted by far the largest following. Unquestionably, as Fleischer argues, the main reason for EAM's popularity was the perception that it represented a truly progressive force that, after liberation, would restructure the country's entire political and social system, beginning with the abolition of the monarchy, the dismantling of the vestiges of the Metaxas dictatorship, and the punishment of wartime collaborators and black-marketers.

For all its promise to bring about radical change, this wartime mass movement was not intended by the vast majority of its supporters to become the instrument of Communist revolution. Despite occasional clashes with rival resistance organizations, and its determination to monopolize the national effort, EAM's reform program did not go beyond fairly unexceptional social-democratic themes and a harsh brand of populist justice. It emphasized its purely patriotic character and avoided clear-cut Marxist slogans and any suggestion that it was linked to international communism. As a result, although it owed much to the KKE, the wartime EAM was not a Communist organization. Nor was ELAS, whose bands were commanded by old-time republican as well as Communist officers, a Communist army. In fact, under Siantos's leadership, the KKE had been careful to keep its long-term goals carefully concealed. Following the December 1944 fighting in Athens and the Varkiza Agreement, ELAS was in any event disarmed and dismantled; EAM itself became virtually an empty shell, having been abandoned by its non-Communist cadres. By 1947, when the KKE openly challenged the Athens government with a full-scale insurrection, EAM as a cohesive political force no longer existed, and a conspiratorial network and a fighting force—now entirely dominated by the Communists—had to be established virtually from the ground up. Thus, Fleischer is particularly effective in depicting EAM as partly the Communists' creature, sometimes their partner, and ultimately their victim.

Until 1946, the KKE had remained restrained and ambivalent on both its long-term strategy and its day-to-day tactics. It had reluctantly joined the "government of national unity" under Papandreou just as the Axis occupation was ending, only to plunge into an armed confrontation with Papandreou and his British backers in Athens unprepared and without a clear program other than the determination to preserve its wartime gains and its share of political power. After the *Dekemvriana,* deprived of its popularity and much of its organizational base, hunted down by the authorities and various right-wing bands, the KKE leadership went through a period of self-doubt and confusion before Zahariadis, released from Dachau, reasserted his personal authority and guided it toward open civil war. Ole L. Smith, in his chapter, "Communist Perceptions, Strategy, and Tactics, 1945–1949," relying on admittedly spotty evidence, traces the process through which the party moved during 1945–46 from basically defensive tactics to full-scale armed insurrection. In his carefully constructed narrative, decisions are shown to have been taken gradually, as the unfolding domestic and international events were discussed and analyzed, as dissenters were silenced, and as Zahariadis made his views known with increasing firmness. There are indications that as early as January or February 1946, i.e., before the first postwar parliamentary elections in March 1946, which the KKE boycotted, Zahariadis was already leaning in the direction of armed struggle while publicly expressing preference for parliamentary solutions. During that period, contacts with the neighboring Communist regimes, especially Tito's, became far more regular and substantive: their primary purpose was to solicit assistance of every kind. Similar approaches and appeals were directed to the Soviet Union and to Stalin personally. One is compelled to assume that, before the spring of 1947, when Zahariadis declared the party to be in revolt against the Athens government, he had received serious promises of support from abroad; otherwise the decision to fight appears incongruous, especially for one trained to obey orders from his ideological mentors. However, the details of any such promises remain essentially unknown; indeed, to this day the party leadership's internal decision-making process is less than adequately understood. Smith reasons that the KKE opted for armed confrontation in response to the escalating right-wing terror, that Tito and Stalin endorsed the decision to

launch a full-scale insurrection, and that, unaware of the Truman administration's commitment to defeat communism in Greece, Zahariadis and
his comrades believed that military victory was attainable. On the other
hand, in the absence of concrete evidence to the contrary, one may reasonably conclude instead that Zahariadis and his comrades deceived
themselves into believing that their Balkan neighbors and the Soviet
Union would eventually provide the tools needed for a military victory.
If that is the case, the Greek Communists wrote their own ticket to disaster and afforded their enemies the opportunity to remove them from any
position of influence they might have enjoyed as a result of their role in
the wartime resistance.

It is one of the ironies of postwar Greek political developments that
the traditional Right, which in many ways had the least legitimate claim
to represent the national will, nevertheless emerged dominant. That it
did so—given the disarray within the ranks of the Left and the Center—
largely by default does not reduce the significance of that occurrence.
The Populists, the Right's largest party during the 1930s, were the country's principal conservative group, and the backbone of monarchism.
Thanks to their close ties to the palace, most right-wing politicians had
escaped harassment by the royalist Metaxas regime, with which they
were thus linked in the public mind, and continued to hold senior positions in the civil service, the armed forces, and state-controlled agencies.
To make matters worse, individual Populists had served in the wartime
collaborationist governments and had staffed their security forces, which
had hunted down the leftist resistance organizations with weapons provided by the Germans. Therefore, in the eyes of most Greeks, the Right
remained the pillar of authoritarianism and political oppression that liberation was supposed to remove and destroy once and for all. It hardly
needs saying that the Right, whether represented by the Populist Party
or by various factions outside it, had no reform program of its own, drew
much of its support from the wave of anticommunist reaction that swept
Greece in the wake of the *Dekemvriana,* and was regarded with disdain
if not open hostility by British and American officials as well. Even Prime
Minister Churchill, who had struggled hard to preserve the Greek monarchy, had no use for the vast majority of politicians who supported it.

But if at the moment of liberation the Right stood largely discredited
and despised, it had not been deprived of its principal political assets. As
David H. Close demonstrates in his chapter, "The Changing Structure of
the Right, 1945–1950," the prewar Right continued to control the civil

service, the security forces, and the courts. Following the violence of December 1944, hitherto clandestine right-wing gangs and paramilitary organizations launched a wave of "white terror" directed indiscriminately against the Left. Under the prevailing climate of mutual suspicion, lawlessness, and intimidation the Communists led a broad spectrum of leftist groups in boycotting the parliamentary elections of March 1946. Predictably, the result was a clear victory for the Populists and their allies, and legitimation of the Right's control of the state machinery. Under Prime Minister Constantine Tsaldaris, the new government successfully promoted the return of George II (in the plebiscite of September 1946), now seen no longer as the unpopular and discredited king but as the national symbol of order and political stability, as well as the guarantor of Anglo-American support against communism. Focusing his attention on the Populists, Close shows their dogma to have been a blend of adulation of the crown and of the national church, of highly personalized clientelistic party politics, mostly in central and southern Greece, of hypernationalist and anticommunist rhetoric, and of a marriage of convenience with the very wealthy who wished to remain so. They benefited from the authoritarian measures necessitated by the conditions of civil war, when the security forces dominated the state apparatus and when freedom of expression was all but banned. They remained genuinely unpopular and proved themselves incompetent and unable to govern. As a result, they were compelled to share office with the Liberals in coalition governments imposed upon them by British and American officials who exercised ultimate control of the Greek state. In the aftermath of the civil war the Populists faded and disappeared, despised by most Greeks, abandoned by the increasingly assertive palace, and humiliated by one of their own, Marshal Alexander Papagos, who launched his own conservative party. But if, as Close shows, the Populists squandered and lost the power they enjoyed in the mid- and late 1940s, under new leaders the Right would continue to determine the nation's course for years to come.

Although in the wake of the Second World War a variety of forces stood ready to compete for supremacy, the playing field before them was hardly level. From the outset, the opponents of the leftist-populist movement represented by EAM enjoyed a decisive advantage. As already noted, in the post-liberation governments centrists and moderates were not totally excluded from high office. On the contrary, at the insistence of the Americans, in September 1947 Themistocles Sophoulis was named Prime Minister, and other prominent Liberals held important positions in the coalition cabinets of the civil war years, creating the appearance of a broadly representative government. Although during most of this same period martial law was in force, and there were severe restrictions on citizens' basic civil rights, at the formal level the system of government appeared to be constitutional, fundamentally democratic, and even "progressive" by the standards of the day. What is more striking, however, is the degree to which the system's formal appearances differed from reality.

This discrepancy between the constitutional framework and the principle of government accountability, on the one hand, and the manner in which governmental power was exercised in practice, on the other, is the subject of Nicos C. Alivizatos's chapter, "The Executive in the Post-Liberation Period, 1944–1949." To some extent, this discrepancy between democratic trappings and undemocratic substance was the result of continued application of those restrictive and authoritarian decrees inherited from the Metaxas dictatorship and the occupation period that served only too well the purposes of those who were now in power. Despite the pressing need to make a clean break with the prewar state institutions and practices, no early revision of the constitution and legal framework was contemplated. And by refusing to challenge the legality of Metaxist measures, the Greek court system became in effect the tool of right-wing partisan politics.

However, the more fundamental reason for the discrepancy between appearance and reality, and for the resulting undemocratic character of the governing process, was the usurpation of power by decision makers who acted without constitutional authorization and whom the nation had not elected to office. These included senior and middle-level officers of the armed forces and the police, the king and palace officials, and, especially during the late 1940s and early 1950s, American advisers in Athens. Thanks to the influence exercised by these extraconstitutional centers of power, the decline of parliamentary government became a chronic feature of Greek political life, and the military, who saw themselves as the nation's guardians, in a symbiotic relationship with the Right and the Americans, determined the essence of government policy. In Alivizatos's perceptive analysis, this rule by extraconstitutional means paved the way for the military junta of 1967–74.

There is a natural tendency to view the Greek civil war as a conflict between irreconcilable forces struggling to either seize or retain control of the state. Even when attention is paid to the conflict's ideological underpinnings, the issues dividing the two camps are too often examined purely in their political context. Yet politics, and especially the politics of revolution and counterrevolution, is in the last analysis mostly about economic resources and their distribution. Particularly in societies where material resources are scarce and the level of economic development is low, the struggle for political power and for control of the state turns into a contest whose outcome will determine how the nation's resources are to be utilized and how wealth is to be acquired and distributed. Thus, ultimately, the KKE-instigated insurrection symbolized both a rejection of Greece's past economic realities and an attempt to seize the state in order to restructure the national economy and redistribute wealth in accordance with revolutionary dogma.

The economic dimension of Greece's postwar crisis is examined by Stavros B. Thomadakis in his chapter, "Stabilization, Development, and Government Economic Authority in the 1940s." Of course, given the desperate struggle for political power and the violence of the civil war, there could be no clear focus on purely socioeconomic issues. Nor could there be serious consideration of the various strategies for economic development advocated by different factions, especially those of the Left. Inevitably, formulas for major economic reform fell victim to political violence.

Undoubtedly, the success of EAM's mobilization efforts during the enemy occupation had been due in large measure to the emphasis placed on relief measures and on the promise of a radical reorganization of the nation's postwar economy calculated to improve living conditions for the masses. However, after liberation the Athens government failed to offer a serious program of long-term economic development, limiting its efforts to the practical goals of currency stabilization, combating speculation, and securing infusions of foreign aid. After the Varkiza Agreement of February 1945, the widespread persecution of the Left aggravated further the traditional antagonism between a conservative state bureaucracy and the nation's workers and resulted in the subjugation of trade unions to government authority. Moreover, as a consequence of the sharp political divisions, recommendations for radical reform coming from the Left fell on deaf ears. Thomadakis argues that one such recommendation that was ignored was to seek solutions to Greece's problem of chronic economic weakness through an ambitious program of industrial development. In his view, such a program was realistic and, indeed, necessary. However, once the civil war had begun in earnest, the most the government and its British and American advisers appeared anxious to achieve was to meet the immediate needs of the faltering Greek economy and, in time, restore it to its pre-1940 levels. One might add that under the best of circumstances, and given Greece's underdevelopment and limited resources, rapid industrialization might have been realistically contemplated only if a massive infusion of foreign capital and technology were forthcoming. But in the late 1940s, Britain could not, and the United States would not, support such an ambitious scheme, especially when it was espoused by those whom London and Washington perceived as belonging to the enemy camp in the developing cold war. The goal of the Western allies was to defeat the Communist insurgency and bring about a measure of political stability, not to help Greece become a modern industrial state.

The postwar crisis in Greece was first and foremost a domestic affair. It erupted against a background of a deep internal political schism that paved the way for the KKE's decision in 1946 to revolt. But the civil war did not occur in a vacuum. For a moment at least, the emerging East-West confrontation gave the appearance of centering on developments in Greece, which assumed an importance they did not truly deserve. Thus the Communist insurgency and the attempts to suppress it came to be regarded as one of the first major battles of the cold war.

The Soviet connection to the crisis is explored in Peter J. Stavrakis' chapter, "Soviet Policy in Areas of Limited Control: The Case of Greece, 1944–1949," which views the subject primarily from Moscow's perspective. This is a critically important topic about which no significant documentary sources are available, forcing one to speculate about Stalin's Greek policy on the basis of broader Soviet initiatives in the immediate postwar period. Greek and Balkan Communist sources, which have provided us with most of what we know about the Soviet factor, are fragmentary and one-sided.

Stavrakis shows Stalin's Greek policy to have been largely opportunistic—a mixture of pragmatic caution and occasional expansionist tendencies. He argues that, in the short run, Stalin saw in the KKE's strength an asset that might prove useful in undermining Britain's traditional influence in Greece and the Near East. He did not regard the control of Greece as essential to the Soviet Union's security considerations, and his interest in the Greek Communist movement itself may have been minimal at best: the KKE was not invited to join the Cominform when it was established in the fall of 1947. Nevertheless, in Stavrakis' analysis Stalin could not fail to regard the reemergence in Greece of a strongly anticommunist regime attached to Britain as a threat to Soviet interests in the Balkans and the eastern Mediterranean. Had the Greek Communists succeeded in bringing down the Athens government on their own, Stalin would almost certainly have compelled them to attach their country to Moscow's orbit. In this manner, without actually instigating or even endorsing a revolutionary uprising, and having taken no risks in his growing confrontation with Britain and the United States, Stalin could have achieved the same goals he pursued much more aggressively, and with success, across Eastern Europe. His ambivalence about boosting the fortunes of the Greek Communists may also have resulted in part from his suspicion that they were more likely to fall under the control of Tito, whose ambitious schemes in 1946–47 Stalin would not tolerate.

We may never know Stalin's precise plans concerning the postwar situation in Greece. While Moscow temporized and possibly sent Delphic responses to Zahariadis' appeals for material assistance and endorsement, the KKE took matters into its own hands. Encouraged primarily by the Yugoslavs, and expecting its own resources to suffice at least for the start of the struggle, it moved toward a show of force. In the civil war that ensued, the Soviet Union remained very much on the sidelines, loudly condemning the Athens government for its "undemocratic" ways and praising the insurgents' cause, but doing nothing to ensure a Communist victory. On the contrary, by precipitating his much-publicized quarrel with Tito and expelling the Yugoslavs from the Cominform, Stalin added to the burdens of the Greek Communists and speeded up the collapse of their insurrection, which was cut off from its main supply and training bases in Yugoslavia. Moreover, as Stalin had apparently feared, the open threat of a Communist takeover in Greece, and the appearance that Britain was wavering in its continuing support for the Athens government, brought the United States rushing onto the scene. The civil war in Greece contributed significantly to the Truman administration's perception that the Soviet Union, acting directly or through proxies, posed a serious threat to the security interests of the United States that had to be confronted with all available means, including military power. Thus the Greek civil war, in which Moscow was involved indirectly or marginally, if at all, emerged briefly as a major episode in the early years of the cold war. And American action in support of the Athens regime doomed the Greek Left to defeat and banishment.

There is ample proof that in the aftermath of the Second World War the Yugoslav Communists egged on their Greek comrades to seize power.

Exploiting ties established between Tito's wartime Partisans and ELAS, as well as the autonomist aspirations of the Slav-speaking element among Greek Communists, the Belgrade government hoped to harness the KKE to its own ambitious cause. The success of a Communist revolution in Greece would have eliminated the principal base from which Britain and the United States, already in serious dispute with Tito over Trieste and other points of friction, might choose to attack it. In addition, a Communist regime in Athens, or even one controlling only Greece's northern regions, would have represented the crowning achievement of Tito's scheme to establish a Balkan federation under his aegis. It is therefore ironic that his encouragement and support of the Greek Communists, and his dream of a Communist federation for the Balkans, brought Stalin's wrath down on Tito's head. When, in 1948, Zahariadis took Stalin's side against the "heretic" Tito, the Yugoslavs had no reason to continue their assistance to the Greek insurgents. By stopping the flow of weapons and supplies to the KKE's Democratic Army and in due course closing the border, Tito deprived the Greek Communists of the essentials needed to carry on their struggle.

The impact of Belgrade's involvement in the Greek civil war on Tito's relations with Moscow is examined by Ivo Banac in "The Tito-Stalin Split and the Greek Civil War." Banac details the close attention the Yugoslav Communist leadership paid to developments in Greece and regards its endorsement of the KKE's insurrection as concrete and crucial. Indeed, he argues that the civil war was at least as much the result of Yugoslav pressures as of Zahariadis' own initiatives. However, Tito's plans for a Belgrade-dominated Balkan federation and, in particular, the Kremlin's suspicion that the Yugoslavs were about to occupy Albania, infuriated Stalin, who felt personally insulted and challenged. Rather than endorsing the Communist uprising in Greece, the Soviet leader is described as angry at the Yugoslavs for promoting what he perceived as a reckless and dangerous initiative. Ever sensitive to broader strategic considerations and to all possible threats to Soviet security, Stalin ordered the Yugoslavs to end their involvement in the Greek civil war, which he feared would cause the United States and Britain to take countermeasures elsewhere in Eastern Europe. When the Yugoslavs, who had been resisting Soviet attempts to penetrate their state bureaucracy, refused to oblige, they were unceremoniously expelled from the Cominform, thus causing the first major crack in the supposedly monolithic Soviet bloc. In Banac's carefully constructed analysis, instead of ensuring the success of the

Communist revolution in Greece, Tito actually contributed to its defeat by increasing its symbolic importance for both sides in the East-West confrontation.

Yugoslavia's involvement in the Greek civil war went beyond material assistance to the KKE's Democratic Army. As Evangelos Kofos shows in "The Impact of the Macedonian Question on Civil Conflict in Greece, 1943–1949," it extended to the manipulation of minority groups in northern Greece, and particularly the Slavo-Macedonians. A relatively small but militant minority residing along Greece's northern region, the Slavo-Macedonians were closely linked to kindred elements in the other neighboring Balkan states. Traditionally, many among them had not regarded themselves as Greeks, were hostile to the authorities in Athens, and looked either to Belgrade or to Sofia for help in realizing their dream of political autonomy. In the 1920s and 1930s their cause had been overshadowed by the twists and turns of international communism and by the never-ending quarrels of Balkan governments. During the Second World War, the Slavo-Macedonians in Greece, who had been subjected to harsh assimilationist measures under the Metaxas dictatorship, had formed their own resistance bands and had cooperated closely with Tito's Partisans. After 1945, Tito's considerable influence in the Balkan region and the establishment of a Macedonian republic within the new Yugoslavia had caused them to look to Belgrade for the achievement of their separatist goals. Moreover, since the KKE could not hope to succeed without Yugoslav support, it was compelled to accommodate itself, however nervously, to the machinations of Tito's Slavo-Macedonian protégés circulating in its midst.

But not for long. After the summer of 1948, when the KKE leadership sided with Moscow in the Stalin-Tito break, Zahariadis removed Tito's loyalists from positions of authority in the insurrection, and the Slavo-Macedonians of Greece found themselves once again the pawns in someone else's struggle for power. Zahariadis produced his own Slavophones and, in keeping with the current Cominform stand, sought to promote the notion of a distinct Macedonian nation that would lay claim to Greek Macedonia. This was a desperate and destructive move for which the Greek Communist movement would pay a heavy price: the defeat of the Democratic Army in 1949 would banish the Communists from the nation's political arena. Their full rehabilitation would have to await the self-destruction of the Colonels' junta twenty-five years later.

In sum, for a brief moment following the last days of the Second World

War, Greece entered a critical turning point in its turbulent history as a range of constitutional, political, economic, and social options appeared to be open before it. As these essays make clear, the contestants spanned the ideological compass: from Stalinists to monarchists, from radical reformers to defenders of the prewar order, with all manner of moderates and centrists between. The stage seemed set for a protracted contest in which all factions would compete for public approval and the right to determine the nation's future. However, two developments conspired to prevent such a struggle from remaining within the domestic political arena. First, already by 1945 the issues at hand had been reduced by a grotesquely distorting division into "nationalist" and "antinationalist." Genuine political discourse thus became impossible. Second, unsure of their strength and determined to destroy their opponents by any means, both camps looked to outsiders for support in an armed confrontation. The result was a bloody civil war whose outcome permitted the winners and their foreign patrons to settle all national disputes according to their particular narrow agenda. After 1950, domestic and foreign policy developments brought about considerable change in Greek politics and society. Yet only in the mid-1970s, after the collapse of the military dictatorship, was the nation able once again to stand at a crossroads and set its new course, this time peacefully, in accordance with the popular will.

2

The 1940s Between Past and Future

George Th. Mavrogordatos

The purpose of this essay is to develop and connect two arguments that served as mere epilogues elsewhere. The first, from my book on the interwar period, links that era to the 1940s.[1] The second, from an article on the National Schism as a crisis of national integration, goes further by alluding to the traumatic events of the 1940s as the resolution of that crisis.[2]

In the concluding paragraph of *Stillborn Republic,* I argue that the Metaxas dictatorship did not destroy the seeds planted in 1935–36. In the wake of this forced interval, and during the Axis occupation that followed, the radicalized Republicanism born of the March 1935 coup

1. George Th. Mavrogordatos, *Stillborn Republic: Social Coalitions and Party Strategies in Greece, 1922–1936* (Berkeley and Los Angeles: University of California Press, 1983). Hereafter cited as *Stillborn Republic.*

2. "O Ethnikos Dihasmos os Krise Ethnikes Olokleroses" (The national schism as a crisis of national integration), in George Th. Mavrogordatos, *Meletes kai Keimena gia ten Periodo 1909–1940* (Studies and documents on the period 1909–1940) (Athens: Sakkoulas, 1982), 39–53. Also published in D. G. Tsaousis, ed., *Hellenismos—Hellenikoteta* (Hellenism—Greekness) (Athens: Hestia, 1983). Hereafter cited as "Ethnikos Dihasmos."

and the ensuing repression would combine with the hegemonic project of the Communist Party (KKE) in a formidable popular movement: the National Liberation Front (EAM) and its army (ELAS). For their part, the political heirs of Venizelism continued to be plagued by the dilemma of 1935–36 for almost four decades, while the bogey that had been dubbed then "Venizelo-communism" remained the central myth of the Royalist Right. Let us now examine more closely these "seeds" that the Metaxas dictatorship froze but did not extirpate.

The Situation Frozen in 1936

The most portentous developments concerned Venizelism in general and its backbone, the Liberal Party, in particular. In the wake of the monarchy's restoration, which was a direct consequence of the disastrous coup of March 1935, the Venizelist bloc faced a novel strategic dilemma: whether to form a common *bourgeois* front with Antivenizelism around the Crown and against the Left, or to form a common *Republican* front with the Left against the monarchy and its Antivenizelist supporters. In either case, the historical interclass alliance between the entrepreneurial bourgeoisie and specific popular strata that was Venizelism would not survive—and its disintegration would undermine the bourgeois order even further. Under the first option—which Eleftherios Venizelos apparently chose, bequeathing his choice to his successors—a massive defection of Venizelist popular support to the Left could no longer be contained once the betrayal of Republicanism had irrevocably emptied the alliance of its last remaining historical content. Under the second, the bourgeoisie as a whole would rally around Antivenizelism and the Crown, and Venizelism would unwittingly be transformed into a radical popular movement sharing an essentially common mass audience with the Communists. Either choice would spell the end of the Liberal project for bourgeois hegemony.

This agonizing strategic dilemma was inextricably linked to an unprecedented crisis of leadership, produced by the probably insoluble problem of succession to a charismatic leader. Venizelos escaped from Greece in the wake of the disastrous coup in March 1935 and formally resigned as the Liberal Party leader for the fifth and last time. His death, exactly one year later, precluded his staging a comeback as on previous occasions.

It was precisely his last comeback, in 1928, that had forced Georgios Kaphandaris, the best possible choice as his successor to the leadership of the Liberal Party, to break irrevocably with the party. The same thing had happened with several other aspiring leaders. By the summer of 1935, only the vacuous but cunning Themistocles Sophoulis remained to grab the now vacant nominal leadership, thanks mainly to the support of Dimitrios Lambrakis, publisher of the daily *Eleftheron Vema,* in his first successful performance as kingmaker of the Venizelist camp.

Nevertheless, Sophoulis, as nominal party leader, was insecure from the outset and was bound to remain so to the very end. The formation of a committee of three, consisting of Stylianos Gonatas and Constantinos Gotsis, with Sophoulis as chairman, was forced upon him after the January 1936 elections and the earlier release from jail of Gonatas, whose claims to the leadership stemmed from his membership in the previous party triumvirate established in 1933 (Venizelos, Sophoulis, Gonatas). On the other hand, the absent Venizelos clearly remained the ultimate source of authority for the Liberal Party, as he proved in November 1935 by abruptly dictating the recognition by the party of the monarchy's restoration. With Venizelos's sudden death, in March 1936, it appeared that the Liberal Party, emancipated from its founder at last, might turn to Kaphandaris and offer him the leadership. However, to regain the protection of charismatic legitimacy, Sophoulis swiftly invited Sophocles Venizelos, the deceased statesman's son, to participate in the party committee with himself and Gonatas. Although henceforth protected from an external threat, Sophoulis soon faced internal challenges, as the younger Venizelos began taking initiatives on his own, while Gonatas sought to establish the tutelage of the committee over the leader. Things came to a head at the last party caucus to be held before the dictatorship, on 2 July 1936. The resolution finally adopted clearly registered the failure to resolve a conflict of authority (and personality) that was to plague the party for years to come.[3]

The situation confronting Antivenizelism and the People's Party, in particular, in 1936 was even worse. In contrast to the Liberal Party, its historic rival, whose crisis of leadership was at least plastered over and whose dominance of Venizelism as a whole remained unchallenged, the People's Party was not only practically leaderless, but also split. Several splits had been produced even before the monarchy's restoration by an

3. *Stillborn Republic,* 84–85.

underlying strategic dilemma that both logically and temporally preceded that which plagued Venizelism later. It was a dilemma between the prospect of an Antivenizelist Republic, in which the People's Party rule could be perpetuated by patronage and gerrymandering if not fraud, and the dictates of the party's royalist tradition, which required restoration of the monarchy by all means and at the earliest opportunity. That opportunity finally presented itself when Venizelism was crushed militarily in March 1935. For the People's Party leader, Panagis Tsaldaris, it was his long-awaited hour of triumph,[4] but his victory was a Pyrrhic one. Ioannis Metaxas rushed to raise the banner of restoration in a new bid for the leadership of the Antivenizelist bloc. Once Metaxas had been neutralized through government pressure and fraud in the June 1935 elections, Georgios Kondylis seized his own long-awaited opportunity by becoming head of the coalition of Antivenizelist officers and People's Party defectors that was to impose the restoration by force and fraud. Caught in the web of evasive tactical maneuvers that had served him so well in the past, Tsaldaris was dragged along until he was finally pushed aside, without offering any resistance. It may be conjectured that he preferred the preservation of the Republic but was more concerned about the unity of his party and his bloc, both as a political force and as a civil-military coalition. And yet he failed dismally on both counts. As the elections of January 1936 would show, Antivenizelism was split down the middle politically, while its military arm had emancipated itself from civilian leadership, making it possible for Metaxas to stage a spectacular comeback as dictator after twelve frustrating years as a hapless party leader.

Between March and November 1935, the People's Party was abandoned by many diehard royalists, led by Ioannis Rallis, Georgios Stratos, and Ioannis Theotokis (who eventually founded his own National People's Party), but it also lost its sincerely Republican wing led by Pericles Rallis. When Panagis Tsaldaris died in May 1936, the badly decimated and divided party was simply not prepared to elect a new leader, despite its new statutes. Instead, at the end of June, in the last party caucus to be held before the dictatorship, an executive committee of five was elected (Constantine Tsaldaris, Petros Mavromihalis, Stephanos Stephanopoulos, Vasileios Sagias, and Petros Rallis), with Charalambos Vozikis, hitherto chairman of the party's administrative council in the

---

4. See, for example, D. K. Svolopoulos, *Panagis Tsaldaris* (Athens: Pyrsos, 1946), 151.

chair.[5] This makeshift arrangement was to leave the People's Party effectively leaderless for an entire decade until April 1946, when Constantine Tsaldaris was elected the party's third leader (following his namesake and the founder, Dimitrios Gounaris).

Speaking of leadership in the case of the People's Party, and Antivenizelism in general, one must go back to their own charismatic legacy: that of King Constantine. Following his death in 1922, Constantine's charisma may be said to have been reabsorbed by the monarchy and the dynasty as such, with its established order of succession. To the extent, however, that this charisma was not familial but personal and that Constantine had been in effect a charismatic party leader and not simply a king, in a uniquely personal fusion, George II was not his successor. In this sense, succession was hardly possible, not only because Constantinism had never been identified with a single party, organization, or group, but with several, but also because any political heir would perforce constitute a challenge to the royal heir and explode the original fusion. Republican Antivenizelism briefly appeared to offer a possible resolution of the problem, through a total break with the royalist past and hereditary monarchy. The forced restoration in 1935, however, ultimately resolved the contradiction in favor of George II and the monarchy. Consequently, already in 1936, and for years to come, the leaderless People's Party and Antivenizelism in general were bound to recognize in effect the King himself as their supreme leader.

In sharp contrast to the complete disarray of the two bourgeois blocs, Venizelism and Antivenizelism, and their major parties, the Liberal and People's parties, respectively, the KKE was in 1936 already implementing its new and extremely promising strategy of the "Popular Front" and was at last prepared to seize the historic moment. Apart from its unprecedented overture to the refugees as an undifferentiated group irrespective of class, the party also gave concrete form to the alliance of peasants and workers under the hegemony of the working class—a vision that had eluded the KKE since its inception. This form was the ostensible dissolution of the party's rural organizations for the benefit of the "Unified" Agrarian Party, followed by the constituting of an organic "Popular Front" between the two parties in July 1936. Amidst the mounting crisis of bourgeois hegemony, the wavering hitherto Venizelist masses of refu-

---

5. *Stillborn Republic*, 48–51, 80–81. See also N. P. Ephstratiou, *Laikon Komma* (People's Party) (Athens: Platon, 1948).

gees and other new smallholders who had benefited from the interwar land reform, as well as betrayed Republicans in general, would furnish the troops and allies that would turn the Popular Front into a formidable force five years later.[6] In complete agreement with Elephantis,[7] I also regard the Metaxas dictatorship as the outcome of an "organic crisis" in Gramscian terms. In more pedestrian terms, it was a lid placed on a boiling pot. The irony is that a German boot was required to kick the lid away.

The Situation Unfrozen in 1941

The Axis occupation, paradoxically, had a liberating effect, especially insofar as it entailed the departure of the king and his government. Georgios A. Vlahos had been manifestly wrong when he argued in 1935 that not even a "crowned cork" could cap the bottle of Greek politics. That cork had indeed worked, but the moment it was removed the bottle exploded. Stopped by the imposition of the dictatorship of the Fourth of August 1936, the political clock began to tick again in April 1941. When it did so, the protagonists were as prepared—or as unprepared—as they had been six years earlier.

In studies of the occupation and the resistance, it is a common and major misconception to regard the traditional bourgeois parties as somehow congenitally incapable of mass mobilization, supposedly because of their exclusively parliamentary organization and experience.[8] At best, this is a limited and partial view. After all, the remarkable organization of EDES in some areas (and even the embryonic organization of EKKA) did not require Communist-trained cadres. It is also a curiously ahistorical view. In the days of the National Schism, these same parties and their leaders had been capable of formidable mass mobilization and organization under analogous conditions of extraparliamentary struggle, war,

6. *Stillborn Republic,* 178, 222, 337. The backbone and only real party organizations of EAM were to be precisely the KKE and the Agrarian Party (AKE), the latter infiltrated by the former ever since 1936.

7. Angelos G. Elephantis, *E Epangelia tis Adynatis Epanastasis* (The promise of the impossible revolution) (Athens: Olkos, 1976), 160–61, 195–96.

8. See, for example, John A. Petropulos, "The Traditional Political Parties of Greece During the Axis Occupation," in *Greece in the 1940s,* ed. John O. Iatrides (Hanover, N.H.: University Press of New England, 1981), 27–28.

foreign intervention, and occupation. Their last demonstration of this capacity was in March 1935, when the Venizelist coup and its repression involved a reenactment of the territorial split of 1916.[9]

The key to the role (or lack thereof) of the traditional parties during the occupation should instead be sought in the diagnosis of their deadlock, exhaustion, and even bankruptcy already by 1936. During the intervening years of the dictatorship, the emerging broad consensus on the regime issue (monarchy vs. republic) actually made matters worse: such consensus was purely a reaction to the vagaries of the association between king and dictator. Moreover, it was confined to an isolated elite, without ever being put to the test of elections or even broad intraparty debate. Increasingly in agreement over the regime issue, the wrecks of the traditional parties were incapable of addressing other matters. I am even tempted to coin the term "political aphasia" to define their condition. No further evidence of this should be needed beyond the letter written by Sophoulis to Gonatas on 31 August 1941 and casually published in the latter's memoirs. It speaks of "the coming elections," the subsequent transfer of the party leadership to Gonatas, and their joint preparation of the Liberal Party's electoral tickets. There is not one word on, or even an allusion to, the wartime situation and enemy occupation—if only as a potential impediment to "the coming elections"![10] One is reminded of the acid irony of Kaphandaris in his characterization of Sophoulis in 1925 as someone perfectly ignorant of the country's real problems and for whom "everything is in a state of blissful monotony."[11] And yet, Sophoulis was the most respected of traditional party leaders during the 1940s, whose consent was usually regarded as essential for any agreement to stick. It was precisely the political vacuum exemplified and even personified by Sophoulis that was fully exploited and largely filled by the KKE.

My interpretation of EAM as the delayed expression of the radicalized Republicanism born of the March 1935 coup and its aftermath—when Venizelists and Communists were persecuted indiscriminately and joined forces against the threat of the restoration of the monarchy—may perhaps be disputed on the basis of EAM's initial agnosticism on the regime

9. *Stillborn Republic,* 290–91.

10. Stylianos Gonatas, *Apomnemonevmata Stylianou Gonata, 1897–1957* (Memoirs of Stylianos Gonatas, 1897–1957) (Athens: n.p., 1958), 400–401.

11. *Stillborn Republic,* 112.

issue. Yet there are ample indications of striking continuities in this respect on both the elite and the mass levels. And it is a pity that no study so far has endeavored to trace them in systematic fashion, possibly because they are taken for granted. Moreover, the regime issue, as the lowest common denominator defining political alignments and alliances, perforce became paramount—and, eventually, the catalyst that plunged the country into civil war.[12]

Despite its impressive wartime achievements, the KKE was no doubt also a captive of its past. It is perhaps no accident that these achievements coincided with a unique period of grace for the party, accidentally created by the combined absence of Nikos Zahariadis and the lack of effective communication with Moscow. Would it be too much to infer that the party was thereby forced to react creatively to novel situations thrust upon it? I can think of several eloquent examples of personal and local initiatives, especially in the early days of the resistance. Then and later, rigidities inherited from the party's past undoubtedly had a crippling effect, with major and often unintended repercussions. Nevertheless, the return of Zahariadis in 1945 was a critical turning point in this respect. He was by then literally, even physically, a man of the past—a Rip Van Winkle who had spent almost ten years in captivity and isolation, including the years of the resistance. His rejection of the proposed change in the party's title (see below) reveals everything about his incomprehension of the changed circumstances of the party and of the country.

Finally, continuity is most obvious on the military side. One has only to think of Stephanos Saraphis, Euripides Bakirtzis, Napoleon Zervas, Dimitrios Psarros, Ioannis Tsigantes, and even the absent Nikolaos Plastiras in order to conclude that the Republican military elite of the interwar period, and in particular those cashiered in 1935, exerted a greater combined political weight (as opposed to a strictly military one) than the self-made warlords headed, if not led, by the Communist Aris Velouhiotis. Moreover, the veterans of interwar (and earlier) army politics were shaped by their past to an even greater extent than their civilian counterparts, perhaps as befits military men. It may even be said that during the occupation they were obsessively settling old scores, each in his own way. The most notorious case may be that of Saraphis, whereas the most noble

---

12. See my chapter "The 1946 Election and Plebiscite: Prelude to Civil War," in *Greece in the 1940s,* 181–94.

was no doubt that of Psarros, who wore to his undeserved death the selfsame tunic on which the Antivenizelist mob had spat in 1935. Again, it is a pity that there has been no in-depth study of the continuity and commonality in these military biographies. Nonetheless, quantitative estimates of the political and professional background of the officers in ELAS, EDES, and EKKA indicate that an overwhelming majority were interwar Republicans, albeit with interesting and telling nuances (exemplified by Zervas himself).[13] Even the collaborationist Security Battalions originated in a Republican scheme hatched by Theodoros Pangalos and, apparently, Gonatas.[14] Their actual composition, however, reflects continuities in the opposite direction on the mass level, as one would expect from the creatures of Ioannis Rallis, the Royalist leader and quisling prime minister. In effect, their social geography bears a striking similarity to that of the Reservists of 1916, particularly in the Peloponnesus.[15]

In conclusion, one simply cannot even begin to understand the 1940s, and especially the occupation, without referring to the preceding interwar period. I would even argue that one cannot understand the decade except as an extension of the interwar period in several crucial respects. Otherwise, one's view is bound to be limited and incomplete, if not superficial: Greek developments are seen as mere reactions to external stimuli, such as the Axis aggression and occupation or British and, later, American and Soviet involvement—or else the various organizations, especially EAM, are seen as entirely novel, if not miraculous, apparitions.

From this perspective, one may also understand better why the promise of political and social change after liberation came to be effectively monopolized by the EAM coalition. Thanks mainly to British policy, the opposite camp came to be entirely dominated and represented by the traditional political parties and leaders, whose utter exhaustion and lack of vision was already apparent as early as 1936.

On a deeper and more fundamental level, however, the decade also involved critical discontinuities, since it entailed the bloody resolution of what had been a protracted crisis of national integration.

13. André Gerolymatos, "The Role of the Greek Officer Corps in the Resistance," *Journal of the Hellenic Diaspora* 11 (Fall 1984): 69–79.

14. John Louis Hondros, *Occupation and Resistance* (New York: Pella Publishing, 1983), 81–85. See also André Gerolymatos, "The Security Battalions and the Civil War," *Journal of the Hellenic Diaspora* 12 (Spring 1985): 17–27.

15. See *Stillborn Republic*, 72, and my forthcoming book on the subject.

A Crisis of National Integration

The National Schism of 1915 did not simply become obsolete after the Asia Minor disaster of 1922, as was commonly assumed then and later. It was, instead, transformed and perpetuated as a crisis of national integration *within* the definitive borders of the Greek state, condensed in three major cleavages that were, in fact, extensions of those of the previous decade. First, the earlier disparity between People and Nation was transposed and resumed as a bitter ethnic conflict between natives and refugees—the latter constituting the formerly unredeemed part of the nation. Second, the cleavage produced by the Balkan Wars and the ensuing territorial expansion, between the Orthodox Greek majority and various national (but also ethnic and religious) minorities, was also perpetuated after 1922, despite the state's justly vaunted national homogeneity created by the exchange of populations. No less than five national minorities remained: Turks, Slavo-Macedonians, Sephardic Jews, Chams, and Armenians. All of them except the last were concentrated in highly sensitive regions, including border areas, thereby retaining a political weight quite incommensurate with their actual numbers. Finally, the territorial cleavage between "Old Greece" and the "New Lands," which was also born out of the Balkan Wars and briefly crystallized into two rival states in 1916, continued unabated as an overriding split largely reflecting and subsuming other interwar cleavages, with the additional intensity and salience of a clear-cut geographic division. The concentration of both the refugees and the four most sensitive minorities in northern Greece transformed locally the generalized conflict between refugees and natives into a deadly national struggle between *Greek* refugees and *alien* natives.[16]

If the National Schism was perpetuated after 1922, the same was true of the most relevant differences between its protagonists. Venizelism remained the most consistent and dynamic agent of national integration— henceforth within the boundaries of the state. It assumed unreservedly responsibility for the exchange of populations—a necessary precondition for the achievement of national homogeneity. It undertook and, to a decisive extent, realized the historic task of rehabilitating and integrating the refugees into the Greek state. It pursued systematically the assimilation or at least the neutralization of the alien minorities that rep-

16. On all these cleavages, see *Stillborn Republic*, 182–302.

resented a potential threat to the sovereignty and territorial integrity of the state. Finally, particularly through its economic policy, but also through the overall program it implemented during the interwar period, Venizelism continued to constitute the historic agent for the integration of the New Lands into the state. In contrast, Antivenizelism essentially concentrated and embodied the multifarious reactions and resistances to national integration and the modern nation-state. Above all, it embodied the rejection of the refugees by the natives. To the alien and other minorities, it promised protection against the Greek state and the Orthodox Greek majority, for electoral rather than ideological reasons. Finally, Antivenizelism continued to express the introverted patriotism of Old Greece and its romantic nostalgia for an already mythical past, when the borders of the Greek state coincided with its own (that is, before 1912).

For its part, the KKE was ideologically predisposed to defend national minorities since its inception, in which the predominantly Jewish *Federación* of Thessaloniki played an incommensurate part. Yet the KKE also proved congenitally incapable of grasping, appreciating, and incorporating, however critically and selectively, even the most elementary and concrete tenets of nationalism and, consequently, of the national interest. On the contrary, the fledgling party was forced to adopt, on the so-called National Question, a surreal policy, which was blatantly treasonous by any standard. A poisonous gift of its infantile dependency on Moscow, this fateful policy tore the party apart, provided the most compelling grounds for its suppression, and deprived it of its potential audience—especially among the refugees in northern Greece, to whom the policy casually and callously promised no less than a new uprooting. The most vociferous and virulent phase in this policy was actually inaugurated in 1931 by Zahariadis upon his appointment by the Communist International as KKE leader with precisely that mandate. In 1935, the Popular Front strategy imposed an essentially cosmetic change in KKE policy. Although commonly hailed, then and later, as a radical break with the past, it was nothing of the sort. Far from resolving the issue once and for all, it merely represented a tactical and halfhearted move, leaving the party to be plagued again by the National Question in the coming years.[17]

However extreme, the case of the KKE illustrates a more general conclusion: by the end of the interwar period, party policies and the relevant

17. Ibid., 219–20, 232–36.

cleavages had not been diluted with the passage of time. On the contrary, the disastrous Venizelist coup of March 1935 and the ensuing repression had revived and exacerbated the two nationwide cleavages (between natives and refugees, and between Old Greece and the New Lands) to a degree at least comparable to that of the early interwar period, as the electoral results of January 1936 indicate.[18] As for the national minorities, suffice it to note that tensions between Venizelism and the Sephardic Jewish community of Thessaloniki culminated in an actual pogrom in 1931, followed by an anti-Semitic local electoral campaign in 1933. For his part, Metaxas as dictator inaugurated the most systematic repression to date of the Slavo-Macedonians, who had, ironically, voted for him en masse as party leader a decade earlier.[19] On the eve of the war, therefore, the continuing crisis of national integration was still a long way from being resolved.

The Crisis Overcome

The storm of a new foreign war and of another civil war, and the upheaval of postwar reconstruction, would be required for the old schism to be overcome definitively as a crisis of national integration. The children and grandchildren of the refugees would not know the ethnic hatred that their parents had faced. Almost all the alien minorities except one were to disappear. Postwar economic and political realignments would eventually wipe out the gap between Old Greece and the New Lands, while the distinction itself was finally forgotten. Moreover, by changing its content, target, and agent, nationalism would become unrecognizable: it would become "national-mindedness" (*ethnikofrosyne*). How did all this come about? To answer this question properly, a global and thorough analysis would be required, one at least equivalent to the study of the origins and development of the crisis itself. Here, I can only sketch a broad picture, with the plainest brushwork.

Among preexisting cleavages, the one immediately activated by the Axis occupation involved, as one would expect, the alien minorities.

18. Ibid., 274–75, 291.
19. Ibid., 249–52 and 259–61 in particular.

Both the Chams and the Slavo-Macedonians grasped the long-awaited opportunity to realize their own irredentist dreams by being united to Albania and Bulgaria, respectively (the latter eventually supplanted by Yugoslavia). Even the Koutsovlachs, a hitherto passive ethnic group, appeared for a while to lend themselves to similar schemes concocted by Italy.[20] In contrast, the quiescence of the Turkish minority obviously reflected the neutrality of its mother country. On the other hand, the Sephardic Jews of northern Greece became an easy target of Nazi bestiality, significantly without benefiting from Christian sympathy and solidarity like their assimilated brethren in Old Greece.[21] Almost all the Jews of Greece were never to return. At the end of the occupation, the Chams were driven out of the country by Zervas. The Slavo-Macedonians were driven out by the government forces and expelled once again at the end of the civil war. Armenians practically vanished from Greek society after the resumption and swift completion of their emigration to Soviet Armenia. By 1950, of the five interwar national minorities, only one was left: the Turks.

During the occupation, their long-standing struggle against the native but largely non-Greek population acted as a catalyst for the course taken by the refugees in northern Greece. The widespread notion, common then but even more so later, that the refugees in general joined EAM and the KKE, is grossly misleading.[22] Inspired above all by the orientation of the urban refugee periphery of Athens, Piraeus, Thessaloniki, Volos, and other towns, this misperception obscures the fact that the most notorious nationalist and even collaborationist bands in Macedonia were also composed of and even led by refugees—Pontic refugees in particular. Among rural (as opposed to urban) refugees, the agonizing experiences and di-

20. On this lesser-known problem, see Evangelos A. Averof, *E Politiki Plevra tou Koutsovlahikou Zitimatos* (The political side of the Koutsovlach question) (Athens: n.p., 1948); and Dimitrios P. Anestis, *To Koutsovlahikon Zitima* (The Koutsovlach question) (Larisa: Toufexes, 1961).

21. On this neglected contrast, precious indications may be gleaned from several sources, such as Michael Molho, ed., *In Memoriam: Hommage aux victimes juives des Nazis en Grèce*, 2nd ed. (Thessaloniki: Communauté Israélite de Thessalonique, 1973); and Errikos Sevillias, *Athens—Auschwitz*, trans. and introduction by Nikos Stavroulakis (Athens: Lycabettus Press, 1983). See also the contrast between Sephardic Jews and Greek Jews in *Stillborn Republic*, 253–62, 268.

22. See, for example, R. V. Burks, *The Dynamics of Communism in Eastern Europe* (Princeton: Princeton University Press, 1961), 57–58, and my comments in *Stillborn Republic*, 223–25.

lemmas of the occupation produced an unprecedented fratricidal split between Left and Right, which determined henceforth their loyalties, both in the civil war and in postwar politics.[23] Precisely this split was tantamount to the long-deferred but definitive integration and assimilation of the refugees into Greek society, as they ceased to constitute a single, politically cohesive, and, hence, distinctive social group.

These lasting refugee realignments both signaled and entailed a broader analogous process affecting the areas concerned as a whole: the New Lands and especially their continental mass in northern Greece. This process has yet to be traced and documented through the successive phases of civil strife and destruction during the occupation and the ensuing civil war but also, during the period of economic and political reconstruction that followed, at the hands of the victors. The outcome, however, is unmistakable on the electoral level, where the structural gap between Old Greece and the New Lands practically vanishes.[24] In 1955, the accession of Constantine Karamanlis to the premiership constituted, in a very real sense, the last act in this process. He was, after all, not only the first Macedonian prime minister since the annexation of the area, but also an Antivenizelist who began his parliamentary career in the fraudulent and one-sided elections of 1935.

If the crisis of national integration, which had been festering since 1915, was effectively over by 1955, the question may be raised whether the new schism between victors and vanquished of the civil war did not constitute a similar crisis. The answer has to be negative, on at least two grounds. This new schism was primarily and primordially political and not the condensation of distinct social cleavages—even though it had widespread social consequences by forcing its persecuted victims into an artificial social ghetto. Moreover, this new schism did not involve national integration, insofar as nationalism itself was thereby transmogrified.

23. See especially Stathis Damianakos, Elias Nikolakopoulos, and Dimitris Psyhogios, "Vergina: Georgikos Eksynchronismos kai Koinonikos Metaschematismos s'ena Chorio tes Kentrikis Makedonias" (Vergina: Agricultural modernization and social change in a village of central Macedonia), *Greek Review of Social Research*, no. 33–34 (1978), 470–78.

24. Elias Nikolakopoulos, *Kommata kai Vouleftikes Ekloges sten Hellada, 1946–1964* (Parties and parliamentary elections in Greece, 1946–1964) (Athens: National Social Research Center, 1985), 86–88 in particular. A more refined analysis would undoubtedly show that the residual difference between Old Greece and the New Lands is due entirely to their insular component (especially Crete, the Dodecanese, and Lesbos).

From Nationalism to "National-Mindedness"

Greek irredentism was effectively buried in Asia Minor, and its historic carrier, Venizelism, never quite recovered from its loss—despite sustained efforts during the interwar years to define and develop a new kind of national vision and national consciousness.[25] The Cyprus crisis of 1931 dealt a further blow to the integrity of the Venizelist tradition, reverberating in the defection of the Athenian newspaper *Estia,* hitherto its most authoritative voice. Nonetheless, the Dodecanese, the last unredeemed area to be annexed (in 1947), was to prove true to form by providing the decimated Liberal Party with a solid new stronghold. The heritage of Venizelist nationalism may be traced in the policies of the postwar Center in general and even, as a distant and distorted echo, in those of its prodigal son, the Pan-Hellenic Socialist Movement (PASOK).[26] Still, in recent years its only genuine incarnations have been two epigones of the Liberal Party, both from the Dodecanese, Georgios Mavros and Ioannis Zigdis, whose marginality requires no comment.

Against the manifest and manifold disarray of Venizelism, during the occupation both Left and Right attempted to appropriate the banner of nationalism. It may even be said that the banner was literally thrust upon the KKE when EAM was founded. Despite many dark sides, the KKE carried the banner well throughout the occupation. Even the most savage and unpardonable extermination of actual or potential rivals seems to have been inspired, at least in part, by a genuine if also paranoid suspicion of collaboration with the enemy—a suspicion that often turned into a self-fulfilling prophecy. Soon, however, the specter of the interwar National Question began to haunt the party once again and eventually the past, personified by Zahariadis, gained the upper hand. Whereas the course followed by the KKE on this issue and its treasonous conclusion in January 1949 are well known, a less-known episode in 1945 may be regarded as premonitory, even prophetic. Addressing the Seventh KKE Congress, Zahariadis bluntly rejected a proposal to change the party name from Communist Party *of Greece* (an embarrassing legacy of the

25. Among many examples, see in particular the speeches of George Papandreou as Minister of Education in his *Politika Themata* (Political themes) (Athens: Aetos, 1941), 182–202.

26. On PASOK as the "prodigal son" of the Center Union in more than the obvious sense, see my *Rise of the Green Sun: The Greek Election of 1981* (London: Centre of Contemporary Greek Studies, King's College, 1983).

defunct Communist International) to *Greek* Communist Party. His only argument was truly amazing in the context of October 1945: the party could not be called "Greek" since it included not only Greeks but also Jews, Turks, and "Macedonians" living *in* Greece.[27] It was "his master's voice" speaking, both literally and metaphorically: it was not only the voice of the loyal appointee of the Comintern, but also—far worse— an old recording played again, as if the epic of the resistance and the annihilation of the Jewish community had never happened. Curiously, this incident seems to be ignored even today, despite its obvious bearing on the subsequent course and eventual split of the party in 1968. Nevertheless, it remains topical so long as the KKE, almost alone in Europe, sticks to the old Comintern formula.

For the Right, "national-mindedness" was of course a capital invention. Despite its nominal affinity with the original label of the People's Party (in 1915–20), this was a radically novel concept. Also in this respect the ground had been prepared in 1935, when Antivenizelism offered itself as the only guarantor and guardian of the existing social order against Venizelo-communism—first by parliamentary means and then by royal dictatorship. Nonetheless, national-mindedness was concocted during the occupation. And, despite the contribution of some noted Republicans, it was an essentially Antivenizelist ideological machine. It was drastically different in content from the conventional nationalism of the Liberals, since the preservation of the domestic status quo took absolute precedence and overrode all other considerations, national independence and sovereignty included.[28] Consequently, its target was also different: it was aimed at the domestic rather than the foreign enemy—indeed, the role of the latter could even be reversed to that of a welcome ally. Its agent and guardian was of course different as well: Antivenizelism transfigured itself into the postwar Right, thanks also to many new recruits.

This mongrel of inverted bourgeois nationalism was first put to use in order to legitimize wartime collaboration and, later, in the rehabilitation of the collaborators after the liberation. It also served to legitimize the

---

27. *To 7° Synedrio tou KKE* (The 7th KKE Congress) (Athens, 1945), 5:24.

28. For the Liberals, the exact reverse had been true: everything, including the conservation of the social order itself, was explicitly subordinated to the national interest. Suffice it to cite in this connection the famous speech of Venizelos on 19 March 1911, in which he promised to be the safest bulwark of the social order, adding that he wanted it to follow progress and adapt to changing circumstances "so that it can help this State accomplish its high mission" (that is, irredentism).

most slavish acceptance and even invitation of foreign intervention and interference, well beyond the objective requirements of the situation. This process was to culminate with NATO membership in 1951, a development that embodied and crystallized precisely that spirit. The ensuing vagaries of policy over Cyprus are known and need no elaboration here. An almost forgotten but even more revealing episode involved the Turkish minority. In 1954, the Papagos government suddenly decreed that all hitherto Muslim institutions in Greek Thrace (schools, communal organizations, etc.) would henceforth be officially designated and labeled "Turkish"! Moreover, a new high school was offered to the minority, named after the then president of the Turkish Republic, who presided in person over its inauguration beside King Paul, while the Turkish and Greek flags flew overhead.[29] However short-lived (since it was ironically reciprocated with the 1955 pogroms against the Greeks in Istanbul and Izmir), this extravagant celebration of the joint accession to NATO nullified in a single stroke thirty years of Greek national policy and, worse, undermined irreparably its subsequent resumption. In such matters, it is enough that the foreign flag be permitted to float even for a single day.

Against this background, a curious nemesis began to take shape in the late 1950s, propelled mainly (though not exclusively) by the national struggle over Cyprus. The vanquished and persecuted Left could turn the tables at last and present a convincing indictment of the insatiably vindictive Right as a truly antinational force. Eventually, the Colonels' coup of 1967 represented, above all, a desperate attempt to salvage a thoroughly discredited ideological machine and its lesser, self-serving servants. The dictatorship, however, only managed to offer the *reductio ad absurdum* of the system it had sought to preserve, by providing the final and irreparable proof that "national-mindedness" would, in the end, impel and legitimize outright treason. Without lapsing into strictly contemporary polemics, the question may be raised, nonetheless, whether the vacuum caused by the decline of liberal nationalism and the total bankruptcy of "national-mindedness" has been filled. Or is it, perhaps, already too late?

29. See K. G. Andreadis, *E Mousoulmaniki Meionotis tis Dytikis Thrakis* (The Muslim minority of western Thrace) (Thessaloniki: Institute for Balkan Studies, 1956), 9–10, 13–17, and the photographs on 107–8 and 110–11. To make the telling connection with earlier Antivenizelist policy, see *Stillborn Republic*, 244–46.

3

The National Liberation Front (EAM), 1941–1947

A Reassessment

Hagen Fleischer

In the spring of 1941, when the German armed forces occupied Greece, they eagerly exploited Greece's prewar "authoritarian regime in its pre-existing form, except for changing the personnel."[1] This reshuffling of officials was limited in scope, however, and did not seriously affect the middle and lower levels of government bureaucracy. After King George and several dozen prominent members of the dictatorship fled to Crete (soon moving on to Cairo and London), the suppressive mechanism remained basically intact. Members of the bureaucracy—with a few notable exceptions—were in position to resume the "protection of law and order" while serving under the command of their new German masters.

Government-fostered violence and political suppression were to continue and increase under the occupation. The Germans capitalized on the fact that most Greeks were by now accustomed to violations of their

I am indebted to my friends and colleagues Susan Muckenfuss Caldwell and Ole L. Smith for their helpful suggestions in preparing the final text of this chapter.

1. Theodor Parisius, quoted in Hagen Fleischer, *Im Kreuzschatten der Mächte: Griechenland, 1941–1944 (Okkupation—Resistance—Kollaboration)* (Frankfurt, 1986), 184 (hereafter cited as Fleischer, *Kreuzschatten*).

civil rights and felt ambivalent toward their "legitimate" government in exile. This government, while posing as the defender of freedom and democracy—had neither dissociated itself from the dictatorial regime of the recent past nor organized any nucleus of resistance to the occupiers. These and other factors caused a deep uncertainty, if not outright confusion, among Greeks about the wisdom of standing up to the hitherto invincible Nazi war machine, especially in view of the increasing starvation among the populace, which obviously called forth other priorities.

It is not surprising, therefore, that the first manifestations of anti-Axis feelings, while widespread, were of an unorganized and spontaneous character.[2] Young people (among them the famous *saltadori* who stole provisions from Wehrmacht trucks) in particular revealed a dynamism that later they would display so vigorously. Overcoming almost five years of political paralysis posed much greater difficulties for adults, however. There were at the time two basic categories of people capable of inspiring and activating the paralyzed majority and transforming the existing potential for action into a coherent resistance movement. The first group was composed of the nation's traditional leaders, the politicians and the military caste; the other consisted of revolutionary and subversive elements of diverse ideological orientations. It would prove tragic for Greece that only those in the second category would undertake to fulfill their patriotic obligations.

To this day, critics attribute the sweeping success of the National Liberation Front (EAM) to the "treachery and unscrupulousness" of the Communist Party of Greece (KKE) which, allegedly from the beginning, had at its disposal a proven underground mechanism that it insidiously concealed behind the patriotic facade of the movement. Although the KKE's underground *experience* was unmatched in the bourgeois camp, the argument that it had a "well-preserved illegal *apparatus*" is nothing but an excuse for former abstentionists or embittered amateurs whose own resistance aspirations were thwarted by more clever rivals. There is established proof of the infiltration of the Communist Party (although not of its extent) by agents of Constantine Maniadakis, Metaxas's Minister of Security, and of the resulting state of chaos, distrust, and doubt within the party in the spring of 1941. That the damage was repaired, or

2. Hagen Fleischer, "To xekinima tou antistasiakou agona stin katechomeni Ellada: Kataveoles kai stathmoi" (The beginnings of the resistance struggle in occupied Greece: Origins and Milestones), *Anti*, 4 January 1985.

at least papered over, much faster than during other schismatic periods in the party's history, was largely due to the agreement in principle among all factions that the foreign invaders constituted the main enemy until liberation. Communist resistance activities began *before* the German invasion of the Soviet Union (Operation Barbarossa),[3] although they certainly acquired more vigor and effectiveness after that "historical date which changed the character of the war."[4] A "new" Central Committee was elected from among those cadres who had managed to escape from the deportation islands or concentration camps set up by the Metaxas regime. As they represented the untainted historic leadership, including those still imprisoned, the newcomers encountered no serious challenge from the quarreling factions in Athens and even took advantage of their rivals' preliminary initiatives in organizing the resistance. For instance, the Friends of the People, a group of progressive officers, was absorbed by EAM and put into action, as was the National Salvation Front (MES),[5] which had been organized by the so-called Old Central Committee in cooperation with those leftist personalities (Ilias Tsirimokos, Euripides Bakirtzis, Costas Gavriilidis, and their entourage) who would rally later with EAM and the Political Committee of National Liberation (PEEA). In addition, men like Athanasios Klaras (Aris) came from the periphery of the so-called Provisionals (*Prosorini Dioikisi*).

This attempt to organize a common front, a union or modern-day *philiki etaireia*, behind popular appeals for "a new 1821" reveals the readiness of the Left (Communists, Socialists, and Agrarians) to combine the struggle for national liberation with an effort to revive the short-lived trade unionist, "popular," and "anti-Fascist" coalitions created after (and, in part, even before) Dimitrov's famous plea at the Seventh Congress of the Comintern for the setting up of popular fronts. With the explicit inclusion, if not prominence, of the KKE in this front, the Left intended to return to the point at which the Metaxas coup of August 1936 had interrupted the evolutionary development of the bourgeois state into a "people's democracy" and to continue from there without leaping over intermediate stages so as not to alienate potential partners.

3. Fleischer, *Kreuzschatten,* 83ff., 90ff., 590.

4. According to the Communist interpretation, the Second World War was simply an inter-capitalist conflict until the invasion of the Soviet Union. See, for example, *Kommounistiki Epitheoresi,* February 1943, 15, and September 1943, 22.

5. Yiannis D. Petsopoulos, *Ta pragmatika aitia tis diagraphis mou apo to KKE* (The real reasons for my expulsion from the KKE) (Athens, 1946), 146ff.; Ilias Tsirimokos, "Tou ypsous kai tou vathous" (High and low), *Anexartitos Typos,* 12 July 1960.

Consequently, the anemically worded declaration of the Sixth Plenum of the KKE Central Committee called upon "the Greek people, [and] all parties and organizations to form a National Liberation Front" for the expulsion of the German and Italian invaders and for the creation of a democratic government that would safeguard the "integrity and independence of Greece." Moreover, the National Liberation Front was to provide for "the daily assistance to and defense of the Soviet Union," which (possibly because of awkward wording) was named the foremost duty of the Greek Communists. This possible slip of the pen—the result either of rhetorical habit or of the reaction to the Nazi invasion of the Soviet Union—profoundly stunned Lefteris Apostolou, the KKE's chief negotiator with the other parties, who decided to ignore this "terrible" backsliding toward the prewar mentality in his negotiations.[6]

Two weeks later, in the middle of July 1941, the charter of the newly founded National Workers' Liberation Front (EEAM), avoiding such eclectic references, proposed instead *cooperation* with organized labor in *all* countries under fascist yoke or threat, from the Balkans to China and from the Soviet Union to the United States and England. But the wording of the charter left no doubt that EEAM's struggle was to be strictly confined to national issues and aimed at the survival and liberation of the Greek people. At the same time, it would aim for the unification of all leftist forces in a coalition that would strive—after the expulsion of the occupiers—to win majority support in order to take over the government.[7]

Despite these declared objectives, complaints about the "retardation" of EEAM's development were frequently expressed in subsequent KKE discussions, and it took two years to achieve agreement on a joint "program of action" that was less vague than the charter but that again evaded crucial issues. Proclaiming its "aspiration to be the most progressive and consistent force of EAM and the whole national liberation struggle," EEAM stated openly its dual goals of national liberation and "safeguarding the people's full sovereignty." Apparently, "full sovereignty" was still subject to limitations, because the signatory parties also declared that, after the realization of their program, they would "continue the struggle of the working class until its complete liberation from

---

6. Cf. KKE, *Episima Keimena, 1940–1945* (Official texts, 1940–1945), vol. 5 (Rome, 1973), 63; and Lefteris Apostolou, *To xekinima tou EAM: Anamniseis kai didagmata* (The beginnings of EAM: Memoirs and teachings) (Athens, 1982), 55ff.

7. *Avgi*, 13 November 1960.

any economic, political and cultural class yoke, until socialism prevails." This goal included the formation of a "united party representing the whole working class" to replace the previous "coalition" of leftist forces.[8]

Although this ambitious scheme was never to show any prospect of realization, the more modest conception of a united trade union movement had already materialized. Socialists (Dimitrios Stratis), reformists (Yiannis Kalomoiris), and Communists had come together, mainly because of compromises made by the KKE—the most powerful of these organizations, given the vast predominance of Communist cadres in medium- and lower-level EEAM cells—which contented itself with a minority share of seats in the Central Committee. The outcome was promising, and in spite of the repeated efforts of the collaborationist authorities to prevent it (using labor veterans like Manolis Manoleas and Nikos Kalyvas), the General Confederation of Greek Workers (GSEE) and EEAM became de facto identical. Significantly, the GSEE's newly acquired prestige was such that for more than a year after liberation nearly all factions—despite their often bitter feuds—respected the resurrected idea of institutionalized unity, even preferring inequitable minority positions to splitting the GSEE.

It is not possible to consider here whether the substantial concessions on the part of the Communists reflected patriotic motives or their confidence that they would, in the long run, outwit a heterogenous and less determined majority. In fact, the KKE's readiness to compromise or even abandon traditional ideological positions (such as the a priori primacy of the working class) "for the national cause" fluctuated during the occupation. The most spontaneous and convincing of all its conciliatory phases was, beyond a doubt, that of 1941, when the initiative rested with such moderate and open-minded men as Andreas Tzimas, Pantelis Simos-Karagitsis, and Apostolou, who chose to disregard the virtually nonexistent Party Secretary Andreas Tsipas. In addition, many KKE cadres shared the widespread belief that not only individual survival but also the very "existence of the Greek race" was endangered.

Consequently, parallel to the talks for the unification of trade unionism and "all leftist forces," the KKE inspired other initiatives which, like that of EEAM, proclaimed the goals of national survival and liberation but appealed to a much larger and (with the exception of traitors) diver-

8. Ibid.

sified public. The first initiative was the creation of National Solidarity (EA), the "Red Cross of the Resistance," which was founded almost four weeks before Operation Barbarossa and exhibited a remarkable degree of toleration and impartiality in its relief work.[9] The second was the creation of EAM itself.

At the outset, it was only natural for the KKE to approach (and, in part, to be approached by) the small consanguineous parties of the Left: the newly founded (in May 1941) Union of People's Democracy (ELD),[10] which, remarkably enough, would turn out to be the toughest among them, even though it was led by a young convert, Ilias Tsirimokos, who had started his political career in the Liberal Party; the Socialist Party of Greece (SKE); and the Agrarian Party of Greece (AKE). The SKE and the AKE had come into being as a result of repeated splits. (They would split twice again, before and after liberation.) Such divisions were usually caused by the clash of personal ambition, as well as by the problem of demarcating ideological boundaries. The Socialists (of the SKE as well as of ELD) had a considerable number of gifted leading cadres but, like the Agrarians of the AKE, only a very limited number of devoted follow-ers—a disastrous deficiency in an agrarian country like Greece with its thorny social problems.

Thus it is not surprising that the Socialists were reluctant to sacrifice their convictions on the altar of national unity. Characteristically, the youth organizations of the SKE and ELD proudly called themselves the Socialist Revolutionary Vanguard (SEPE) and the People's Revolutionary Youth (LEN), respectively. They maintained these programmatic names until February 1943, when they merged in the melting pot of the United Panhellenic Organization of Youth (EPON), which was sponsored by EAM. In the summer of 1941, the SKE insisted that the projected libera-

9. The Communist leader Costas Karayiorgis continued to be critical: "[EA] must deci-sively free itself from any 'altruistic' and 'Christian' aristocratic deviation which castrates its national revolutionary character within the framework of EAM" ("Tria chronia agones tou Kommounistikou Kommatos sti Thessalia" [Three years of struggle of the Communist Party in Thessaly], O Leninistis 9–10 [May–June 1944], 23). Thus Karayiorgis unintentionally but authoritatively refuted all suggestions from the opposite camp that EA was nothing but a tool of the KKE or its "Trojan Horse."

10. On ELD's program and its perception of "Laiki Dimokratia," see its party organ, Mahi, as well as its various leaflets and brochures. A self-promoting publication of ELD's information bureau, E.L.D., no. 1, was reissued at least four times during 1943 alone. More accessible, though not quite so authoritative, are Tsirimokos's postwar writings, including one with the characteristic title "Synodoiporoi" (Fellow travelers), Mahi, 5 September–19 December 1948.

tion front should explicitly include in its statutes a clause against the restoration of the monarchy and a demand for the "social transformation" of state and society. After much effort, the KKE finally convinced its partners that such a course would appeal to only a minority of the people, and that therefore the solution of constitutional and political issues should be deferred until after the war. Instead, priority was to be given to more acute problems, such as feeding the starving population and organizing an effective resistance front that would include all patriotic Greeks, "even the honest Royalist"!

At this point, the official founding of EAM was delayed again in the hope that larger and more "respectable" parties, especially from the broader Venizelist spectrum, would consent to join.[11] However, the politicians consulted were only prepared to support a republican movement against the return of George II; they considered the struggle against the invaders premature, if not hopeless, and even pernicious. Apostolou proposed to work out a sober strategy for EAM that would avoid all "adventurism" in order not to provoke "unnecessary" reprisals. The leaders of the traditional *politikos kosmos* insisted on their "strategy of patience," however, promising only to maintain contact or, at best—as in the case of the newcomer Panayiotis Kanellopoulos and his small Unity Party— to cooperate loosely with EAM.[12]

At last, in early September 1941, the Seventh Plenum of the KKE Central Committee determined that, in view of the prevailing "most favorable preconditions," it was "time to pass from philology to practical action."[13] Hence, on the night of 27–28 September, only the representatives of the KKE, the SKE, ELD, and the AKE signed the EAM charter. Its text was cautiously and moderately worded and stylistically colorless. It clearly placed patriotic duties ahead of political or ideological considerations. Historically important, its significance nonetheless derives from the events that followed its signing rather than from the document itself. The dual goals of EAM were proclaimed as "the liberation of our Nation from the present foreign yoke in order to obtain the full independence of our country; [and] the formation of a provisional Government by EAM, immediately after the expulsion of the foreign occupiers, with the only

11. On these negotiations, see Apostolou, *To xekinima tou EAM*, 30ff.
12. On Kanellopoulos's own plans for promoting resistance, see Fleischer, *Kreuzschatten*, 102–3.
13. KKE, *Episima Keimena* (1973 ed.), 5:78.

aim to proclaim elections (by proportional representation) for a National Assembly, so that the sovereign People will decide on the form of its government." The pledge that this right would be defended "by all means of EAM . . . against any reactionary attempt" constitutes its only combative clause concerning future developments in domestic politics.[14] The fact that the document was written in formal "puristic" Greek (*katharevousa*), and included a promise "not to examine the past" or question the particular ideological and practical political orientation of any organization prepared to join EAM, suggests a strong desire to keep the field open for the widest possible cooperation.

Although responses from the autonomous political groups to whom this appeal was directed were slow in coming (a few tiny splinter parties earned for themselves places of unexpected prominence by joining), the concept and ideals of EAM met with quick approval from ordinary people. They were probably not responding to the still relatively unknown charter, however, which in any case had been diplomatically worded for the benefit of the non-Left political forces. As George Siantos soberly observed later (at the Eleventh Plenum of the KKE Central Committee), "the masses will never be mobilized by political issues. EAM . . . gained strength by starting the struggle for soup-kitchens and the other economic issues."[15]

Indeed, many of the miniature leaflets dating from the first phase of EAM's existence simply contained slogans decrying famine and misery or highlighting popular demands (for example, "Double rations!"). Similarly, the German occupiers were given repeated assurances that strike activity was solely economic in character and had no political undertones. However, EAM's first "manifesto," dated 10 October 1941 (and written in a moderate version of demotic Greek),[16] and the almost simultaneous appearance of a programmatic article by Simos-Karagitsis,[17] left no doubt that the starvation of the Greek people and the consequent threat to the survival of the Greek race were caused by the "foreign ty-

---

14. *Ethniki Antistasi* 1 (April 1962), 3–4.

15. KKE, *Episima Keimena, 1940–1945* (Athens, 1981), 5:429. This KKE publication should be distinguished from the edition produced by the Communist Party of the Interior in 1973 (note 6 above).

16. *Ethniki Antistasi* 1 (April 1962), 5–6; see also "To drama tis laikis diatrophis" (The drama of the people's sustenance), as well as the "appeal" to the Greek people, in ibid.

17. In the first issue (October 1941) of the KKE's theoretical organ, *Laiki Epitheorisi* (which later became *Kommounistiki Epitheorisi*). Karagitsis signed the article with the initials O. B., which stood for his wartime pseudonym, Orpheas Vlachopoulos.

rants' looting." Therefore, the tackling of practical problems—fighting for rice, pulse, soap, and other necessities, and particularly for an increase in bread rations from thirty to two hundred drams—qualified as acts of resistance against the occupiers and collaborators. In order to support all these "requisite activities," historical internal divisions had to be "pushed toward the margins of history." Both these and many other texts suggested discreetly that national liberation should be followed by the establishment of a democratic rule in accordance with the people's wishes. The term "people" included all social classes. This is nowhere more clearly exemplified than in EAM's manifesto, which specifically enumerates (in order) the Greek bourgeoisie, officers, noncommissioned officers, reservists, soldiers and invalids, officers and men of the police and gendarmerie, priests, youth of both sexes, women, and peasants. The groups that constituted EAM's potential stronghold—the petite bourgeoisie, craftsmen, workers, public and private clerks, and intellectuals—were listed together only in the last paragraph. In the manifesto's conclusion, all of these groups are addressed as "patriots." Dimitris Glinos was not simply engaging in wishful thinking when, in the summer of 1942, he postulated that the term "national" could no longer be usurped to camouflage the interests of an oligarchy: "Today *national* means *popular* [*pallaikos*]; today, thanks to the ever-growing self-awareness of all layers of the people, *nation* and *people* tend to coincide and must do so."[18]

In September 1942, Glinos made a strong contribution to the development of this popular movement under EAM's aegis with the anonymous publication of his guide to the character and aims of EAM, which was particularly effective in its appeal to youth and, after some delay, even to people in remote parts of the country. This well-crafted guide (which has often been mistaken for the statutes of EAM) demanded unity of purpose, organization, and guidance; in short, EAM must be the main authority in the field of resistance, in accordance with the popular wisdom that too many cooks spoil the broth or, as the Greeks would say, "Dawn is delayed when many roosters are crowing"! Glinos argued forcefully that liberty, once achieved, must be stabilized and safeguarded: "This is not possible if the people will not exercise their sovereign rights without limitation . . . in time of peace." This meant free elections, organized

18. *Kommounistiki Epitheorisi,* June 1942 (reprint ed., Athens, 1946), 45 (hereafter cited as *KOMEP*).

by a provisional government formed by the "leadership of the people's resistance struggle," that is, by EAM, resulting in a national assembly that would "compose the *laocratic* constitution in accordance with the sovereign will of the people."[19]

Apart from these few passages, Glinos's guide deals exclusively with the resistance period, outlining the required slogans and organizations and describing the many facets of the struggle and the means for its systematic escalation. Evoking three thousand years of tradition and continuity in Greek history, he depicts the fighters of EAM, ELAS, and the other suborganizations as the heirs of Greeks who fought at Marathon, at Salamis, in the War of Independence of 1821,[20] and in the Albanian war. In short, EAM's voice was to be identified with the voices of Rigas Pheraios and of the Philiki Etaireia.

Glinos's reference to the Albanian epic of 1940–41, and to the necessity of completing it,[21] struck an especially responsive chord among Greeks, given the widespread belief that, although Greece had been betrayed, it had not been defeated. And it was certainly true, Greeks rightly believed, that they had not been beaten by the Italians, who were so provocatively posing as the victors. The pioneering triumphs of the guerrilla movement (*andartiko*), in fact, had been accomplished against detachments of the *Armata Gloriosa* in the autumn and winter of 1942, in accordance with a deliberate strategy of escalation with respect to the targets of armed struggle. Following the directives of Siantos himself, ELAS activities had begun with attacks against isolated groups of gendarmes, "legionaries," and collaborators. But the resistance earned its spurs against the Italians, gathering arms and experience for the "climax": the fight against the Germans.[22]

Although the economic struggle and guerrilla warfare were complementary activities, the question of which should have priority was a source of disagreement in leading circles of the KKE and EAM, particularly dur-

19. *Ti einai kai ti thelei to Ethniko Apelevtherotiko Metopo* (What is and what is desired by EAM) (Athens, September 1942), 14, 16, 25–26.

20. The link to the fighters of 1821 was emphasized by the choice of pseudonyms among those in ELAS.

21. This reference to the victorious struggle in Albania included one of the few slogans that was a failure for EAM. In EAM's first manifesto, the "heroic *tsarouchi* (the evzone's pointed shoe)" had been declared a symbol of the new struggle. This metaphor for the gallant fighters of the Albanian front elicited no response, however, and was quietly dropped, long before it was expropriated by the collaborationist *Germanotsoliades*.

22. Fleischer, *Kreuzschatten*, 182.

ing the first half of the occupation period. Siantos's apothegm "The people do not eat bread with a pistol [*koumboura*]" points up this division. Postwar charges, mostly from among the New Left, that guerrilla warfare was neglected, were exaggerated, however, and often unjust.[23]

The history of ELAS as a resistance army has been well documented. Whatever uncertainties remain regarding its development cannot be considered in this chapter, which is restricted to a review of the repercussions of ELAS's activities on the mother organization. Numerically, ELAS never represented more than the twentieth part of EAM. Although EAM experienced a steady overall increase in its following, it went through numerous ups and downs, most of them related to the more spectacular activities of its armed branch.

In the occupied cities the first rumors about the presence of *andartes* in the "free mountains" caused thrills of excitement: here was a potential place of refuge from misery and persecution. Local villagers were initially more skeptical, but their attitude changed when they realized that the *andartes* were willing and able to impose a state of harsh but effective discipline and order in the mountains, thereby reducing violent criminality to an unprecedentedly low level. On the eve of liberation, even critical observers admitted "that the EAM has brought order into the mountains; that life and property are safe within its jurisdiction; and that there has been relatively little shooting of Greek citizens."[24] The merciless liquidation of "collaborators," as well as of unrepentant "brigands" was in general also greeted with public approval, provided the charges against them seemed to be true. ELAS's prestige was further enhanced after a number of successful engagements against the occupiers, although it suffered when enemy reprisals were unusually extensive and cruel.[25] In general, however, retaliatory executions by the occupation authorities—except in a few instances, as in the appalling case of Kalavryta—produced only locally limited aftereffects of intimidation. In contrast, countrywide

23. Petsopoulos, *Ta pragmatika aitia*, 37, 149–50. Cf. Fleischer, *Kreuzschatten*, 131, 610, and particularly idem, "Pos evlepe to KKE tin antistasi" (How the KKE viewed the resistance), *Anti*, 3 May 1975.

24. U.S. National Archives (hereafter cited as NARS), OSS RG 226:100116, Report 11098, 13 October 1944.

25. EAM and its related organizations repeatedly promised that the first postwar government would not only compensate people for all their material losses but also "care for and give pensions to all victims of the occupiers' brutality" (*Laokratia*, 22 June 1943, as quoted in KKE, *Episima Keimena* [1973 ed.], 5:399).

jubilation followed the news of the success of the Gorgopotamos, Siatista, and Sarantaporos operations; the victorious encounters under Operation Animals; the Italian capitulation; and even such a hoax as the doctored reports on the destruction of the Asopos viaduct.[26]

On the other hand, civil strife had a deflating and discouraging effect. Such was the case with the capture and supposed murder of Gen. Stephanos Saraphis—which, however, was more than counterbalanced by his later assumption of the military command of ELAS. The initial disarming of EKKA's (the republican resistance organization, National and Social Liberation) 5/42 Regiment, which was under the leadership of Dimitrios Psarros, had a similar effect at first. But such feelings were forgotten after the much-celebrated establishment of joint general headquarters for the three major guerrilla organizations, which brought together ELAS and its rivals, EDES (National Republican Greek League) and EKKA.

Public disillusionment and frustration reached new heights after the outbreak of open civil war between rival resistance bands in October 1943, when evidence of hypocrisy and ulterior political motives stained the shining shield of the *andartiko* movement.[27] Nevertheless, only a minority of the population crossed over into either active or passive collaboration with the occupiers. Those who remained loyal to the cause experienced a new sense of excitement as a result of the signing of the Plaka Agreement, ending civil war between ELAS and EDES, and of the two-phase constitution of PEEA, only to be deflated once more by news of the murder of Psarros at the hands of ELAS. The disastrous Psarros incident did not become widely known in that part of the country already controlled by EAM, however, and was in any case soon overshadowed by news of events in the Middle East, especially the mutiny of the "Free Greek" troops there. From the spring of 1944, until liberation in October

26. Because of ELAS's understandable reluctance to take part, the Asopos viaduct was blown up by British saboteurs acting alone. Nevertheless, the success was expropriated and celebrated by various newspapers of the EAM camp (see, for example, *Rizospastis,* 10 July 1943; *Epimeliteia,* 24 July 1943). On the other hand, the destruction of the Kournovo tunnel, an outstanding military achievement of ELAS, resulted in the heavy loss of life due to German reprisals. Therefore, in a special issue published on 18 June 1943, *Rizospastis* denied any responsibility for the operation, calling the sabotage a camouflaged "fascist crime" and comparing it to the murders of Katyn!

27. Fleischer, *Kreuzschatten,* 361. This decline in the guerrillas' prestige in the winter of 1943–44 was noted not only by Greek and British sources but also—with understandable satisfaction—by the Germans, who nevertheless missed their last chance to reduce the *andartiko* to a few scattered bands in the remote mountain areas.

of that year, EAM's relations with the traditional Greek political forces active in the Middle East were the determining factor for public opinion and morale within Greece itself.

Although the prestige of the government in exile was not particularly high, EAM's rank and file, like most Greeks, wanted a consensus to exist between EAM and the state's official representatives abroad, especially since the latter were clearly backed by the nation's traditional ally, Great Britain. In consequence, the signing of the Lebanon Agreement and EAM's participation in the government of "national unity" were greeted with enthusiasm by the majority of Greeks.[28] This had also been the case earlier with the signing of the National Bands Agreement and the concomitant recognition of the resistance organization by General Headquarters Middle East.[29]

EAM's call for national unity reflected not only a patriotic stand but also sound tactics. Such appeals were popular, attracting large numbers of new sympathizers. This steady growth of support enabled EAM to argue that it represented "the incarnation of the people's desires" as well as "every good, honest and progressive element of the country"[30]—a claim that gradually appeared to gain validity as EAM grew. It made good sense, therefore, for the EAM Central Committee to declare in its report on its first two years that the Atlantic Charter and the "will of the people" were the pillars of its policy. Together they promised to underpin a "laocratic solution" for Greece's internal affairs after liberation[31] since, in the absence of foreign intervention (promised by the Atlantic Charter), EAM and the nation would be synonymous.

Not surprisingly, the anti-EAM factions, although scattered and divided, were horrified by this vision of the future. They postulated that it would be necessary "to sacrifice EAM for Greece, if we do not want someday to have Greece sacrificed for EAM."[32] Although the large fol-

28. Fleischer, *Kreuzschatten,* 502, 722.

29. I strongly disagree with the current "New Left" view that the National Bands Agreement was the first link in a chain of capitulations (followed by the Plaka, Lebanon, Caserta, and Varkiza accords). I agree with C. M. Woodhouse, who viewed the final version of the agreement as a triumph for EAM/ELAS (as noted in his diary, 18 June 1943). See Fleischer, *Kreuzschatten,* 221.

30. Yiannis Zevgos, *KOMEP,* no. 17 (September 1943), 10.

31. *I dichroni drasi tou EAM yia tin ethniki apelevtherosi kai ti laokratiki lysi tou esoterikou zitimatos tis choras mas* (The two-year activities of EAM for national liberation and for people's power as a solution to the domestic problem of our country) (Athens, 29 August 1943), 8.

32. Ellinikon Aima, *To EAM apenanti tou Ethnous* (EAM facing the nation) (Athens, July 1943), 3 and passim.

lowing of EAM could not be disputed, anti-EAM pamphlets asserted that the people (the "worthy elements") had been cajoled, tricked, or even forced into a deceptive appearance of unity; EAM was blamed for "monopolizing" the resistance.

This last charge is a subject that deserves a separate study. Here I will only point out that it would have been rather strange if EAM/ELAS, which was by far the largest and most powerful resistance force, had behaved more "liberally" and "generously" than its minor rivals in the limited areas controlled by them.[33] Thus, despite repeated and often lengthy intervals of goodwill and cooperation,[34] ELAS ultimately tried to rid itself of actual or potential antagonists through voluntary or coerced absorption or annihilation. This explanation does not of course settle the still-lively disputes over who initiated the actions that triggered various conflicts; the fact remains that the web of cause and effect is unusually complex in civil confrontations.

Nonetheless, EAM always refuted the charge that it sought to dominate the resistance. Unfortunately, its oblique arguments tended to lend credence to the accusation. Its defenders, then and since, Communist or not, have tried to refocus the accusation of monopolization exclusively upon the KKE, rather than upon EAM as a whole. And since, they claim, the KKE, like EAM, was always eager to secure the cooperation and incorporation of new partners from the entire political spectrum, "never had an accusation been more slanderous."[35] However, EAM's continuous efforts to persuade other parties and organizations to take joint action *within* its framework, or at least in cooperation *with* it,[36] demonstrate a

33. See, for example, the melancholy comment by the Liberal newspaper *Phloga,* 6 September 1944: "All of them—small and large organizations alike—endeavored to monopolize the National Struggle."

34. Andreas Tzimas, the first "commissar" in ELAS's general headquarters, sincerely promoted such a policy, at least until his return from the abortive Cairo mission in September 1943. Consequently, his remarkable speech at the Kastania Conference in July 1943 extolling tolerance had no demagogic or deceptive undercurrents (*Yia ti levteria, tin laokratia* [For liberty, for people power], Elevtheri Ellada [1943], 3–4).

35. See Lefteris Apostolou, *Ti ekame to EAM yia tin Ellada* (What EAM did for Greece) (Athens, 1945), 34ff.; and Petros Roussos, *I megali tetraetia* (The great four-year period) (1966), 32–33.

36. EAM withdrew from its previous hard-line position—probably because of changes in the internal and external situation—demonstrating that it was content to pursue concerted action. In its note of 14 December 1943, it urged the political parties to agree on the constitution of a unity government: "By this declaration, EAM once more radically disproves the slander that it intends to monopolize the National struggle" (KKE, *Episima Keimena* [1973 ed.], 5:408). At least three events were related to the timing of this appeal: the stalemate in its armed conflict with EDES; the news that Tito had set up his government-like Liberation Committee;

definite hostility toward those who remained outside the organization. On the other hand, EAM's undeniable efforts to include other political groups suggest that these groups wasted an opportunity to bring about a scenario that might have reduced considerably the possibility of any one camp monopolizing the resistance.

EAM's desire to win over the bourgeois parties and integrate them within its structure was a perpetual, if oscillating, phenomenon of the period under review, the swings away being largely the result of KKE tactics. The advances EAM made toward these parties in December 1942—given their generous terms—represent perhaps the most important, albeit least well known, of its goodwill offensives. It offered the bourgeois parties six of a total of eight seats on a new central committee, with the KKE and the minor founding parties sharing the remaining two. On the eve of liberation, a provisional government would be formed on the same numerical basis. With the Communists holding a single seat, any fear of EAM's "monopolization by the KKE" could finally be laid to rest.[37] Themistocles Sophoulis, the leader of the Liberal Party and dean of the *politikos kosmos,* pondered this proposal for some fateful weeks. Here was an opportunity to unite the bulk of the democratic groups against all proponents, domestic or foreign, of undemocratic solutions. The Liberals and moderate conservatives were presented with the chance to abandon their self-imposed abstentionism by assuming a major role in a restructured EAM and, even more important, in the leadership of the resistance movement, as members of comparable political groups had done in other countries, such as France and Denmark.[38] Under such an arrangement, the fatal identification of national resistance with "antinational" communism, which was destined to have tremendous postwar repercussions, would have been largely avoided.

In the end, an agreement failed to materialize. It is still not possible to pinpoint the deeper causes of this failure or to distinguish them from the pretexts offered by those involved. But among these were certainly the issue of national claims and the constitutional question with regard to

---

and circulation of George II's compromising letter concerning his postwar return to Greece, which reportedly impressed the leaders of the *politikos kosmos* (Public Record Office [PRO], FO 371/43678: R 2263; Fleischer, *Kreuzschatten,* 354–55, 384).

37. Apostolou, *Ti ekame to EAM,* 34–35; and the author's interview with Andreas Tzimas. See also Themistocles Tsatsos, *O Dekemvrios 1944* (December 1944) (Athens, 1945), 19–20.

38. For a recent critical survey of this subject, see Hans Kirchhoff, *Kamp eller tilpasning: Politikerne og modstanden 1940–1945* (Copenhagen, 1987). See also Kirchhoff's excellent

the monarchy. There was also the fear that ELAS, whose numbers were increasing, would initiate a class struggle. This fear was sparked by the news that Aris had executed Nikos Maratheas, a big landowner accused of collaboration.[39] The rift was successfully widened by Yiannis Tsigantes, the controversial emissary of the government in exile, who was extremely busy in Athens at the time. The decisive factor, however, was most likely that the Greek bourgeoisie lacked the leadership of a powerful personality of the caliber of Charles de Gaulle, Jean Moulin, or J. Christmas Møller. George Kartalis, John Sophianopoulos, and George Papandreou were wavering and, in any event, had little influence; Panayiotis Kanellopoulos, who was uncertain of his own possibilities, had left the country. The most respected leaders—Sophoulis, who was old, and George Kaphandaris, who was ill—hesitated. Most of the rest were either mediocre or staunchly royalist (some were both); some inhabited the twilight zone between passivity and collaboration.

It was mainly this lack of political leadership that decided the issue; this became obvious when similar opportunities developed in the spring and summer of 1943. At this point, Sophoulis decided not to honor a draft agreement with KKE/EAM that he had initialed. Soon thereafter, the possibility of integrating even the government in exile into the EAM-sponsored consensus emerged in Cairo. The obstructionist tactics of King George II and the objections of Prime Minister Churchill notwithstanding, it is clear that the established Greek politicians, while disagreeing among themselves about the distribution of power, were united in their determination to block the rise of any others who might want to reshuffle the cards of the social system for a "new deal." In their view, the mere existence of EAM constituted a deadly threat, especially since its following had swelled at the expense of the old parties, which lost a significant portion of their traditional clientele and supporters.

The growth of EAM had been accelerated by the lack of cohesiveness and stability within the Greek middle class. Hidden cracks in the heterogenous structure of this stratum became visible under the impact of the devastating starvation of the apocalyptic winter of 1941–42. Under the blows of a famine of epidemic proportions, large segments of the prewar

---

three-volume work, *Augustoprøret 1943: Samarbejdspolitikkens fald. En studie i kollaboration og modstand* (Copenhagen, 1979).

39. This "outrage" alarmed not only Liberals like Kaphandaris but even such prominent EAMites as Tsirimokos and Glinos (Fleischer, *Kreuzschatten*, 135).

petite bourgeoisie crumbled and were reduced to the level of the proletariat. This process of proletarianization also affected the poor of the prewar era. The refugees from Asia Minor, for example, had been packed for two decades into miserable barrack colonies often located only a few minutes away from the better neighborhoods. They had always taken a firm anticonservative (antiroyalist) stand, but only a minority of them had supported the KKE or the broader Left. Due to their "historical linkage" to Eleftherios Venizelos, the majority of these refugees had represented one of the strongest electoral bastions of the Liberals, voting much further to the right than their socioeconomic circumstances justified. Violations of civil liberties by the Metaxas regime and, even more, open repression by the Axis occupiers, combined with economic hardships and epidemic starvation to render them more "class conscious," pushing them to the left.

The agrarian population also developed a new political consciousness. This was particularly true of those who lived in the mountains, people who had been ignored by governments in Athens almost continuously from the establishment of the modern Greek state and who were remembered by politicians only during electoral campaigns. The creation of PEEA in March 1944 formalized a development that had been under way since 1941–42, thanks to the lack of interest displayed by the Italian occupation authorities toward the poverty-stricken inhabitants of the remote Pindus mountain range. Here, since no consistent EAM policy had yet developed, the first stages of self-administration can be traced back to various spontaneous initiatives. Nearly all of the enterprising individuals (such as Georgoulas Beikos) or groups who undertook these initiatives already were—or were soon to become—KKE (or EAM) members. However, certain innovative or even "revolutionary" schemes and codes, such as Code Poseidon,[40] were bogged down as a result of misgivings on the part of both the bourgeois and the "orthodox" Communist quarters within EAM. At that time, EAM's leadership had decided, pending the founding of a broader-based "political committee" with governmental functions (PEEA), to approach again the *politikos kosmos,* along with the rival guerrilla organizations, EDES and EKKA.

---

40. In December 1942, Beikos, along with two other EAM cadres, drafted a series of regulations for "self-government and people's justice" for their home villages in the mountainous district of Evrytania, which was virtually under the control of EAM/ELAS. This "first people's law," which soon spread and provided the basis for the innovative administration of the

Although these approaches failed to produce any immediate results, PEEA, once founded by EAM and various "independent personalities," always tried to keep the door open. Accordingly, the committee's extensive legislative work in running the administration of the liberated areas[41] was consciously cautious in its content and wording, in order not to aggravate the non-EAM "democratic forces." In particular, PEEA did not challenge the notion of a broadly defined national unity; nor did it go beyond the ideological limits of a strongly progressive liberalism, even postulating that the prewar civil and criminal laws had to remain in force.[42] Moreover, despite repeated protests by leftist intellectuals, the methods of self-administration it introduced, and the justice handed down by its people's courts, apparently corresponded to popular sentiment.

On the results of EAM's initiatives and the "state" apparatus it created with the help of PEEA, the testimony of C. M. Woodhouse, an astute observer who was ideologically and practically opposed to the movement, carries particular weight:

> Having acquired control of almost the whole country, except the principal communications used by the Germans, they had given it things that it had never known before. Communications in the mountains, by wireless, courier and telephone, have never been so good before or since; even motor roads were mended and used by EAM/ELAS. . . . The benefits of civilization and culture trickled into the mountains for the first time. Schools, local government, law-courts and public utilities, which the war had ended, worked again. Theatres, factories, parliamentary assemblies began for the first time. Communal life was organised in place of the traditional individualism of the Greek peasant. . . . EAM/

guerrilla-held regions of Evrytania and western Thessaly, became popularly known as Code Poseidon (Fleischer, *Kreuzschatten*, 399–400).

41. The *Deltio Praxeon kai Apophaseon* (Bulletin of acts and decisions), regularly issued by PEEA, directed "self-government and people's justice," as well as virtually all aspects of everyday life, in Free Greece. For the first time in Greek history, regulations with legislative power were written in demotic Greek.

42. *Deltio Praxeon kai Apophaseon*, 15 April 1944. Subsequently, Ilias Tsirimokos, the "Secretary of Justice," was sharply criticized, and a partial revision of this "reactionary" position was made. Thereafter, at least in the lower courts, the guiding principle for all decisions was to be "whatever is commonly considered right and just" (*Deltio Praxeon kai Apophaseon*, 20 July 1944). The practical consequences of this revision remained limited.

ELAS set the pace in the creation of something that Governments of Greece had neglected: an organised state in the Greek mountains. All the virtues and vices of such an experiment could be seen; for when the people whom no one has ever helped started helping themselves, their methods are vigorous and not always nice.[43]

There is no doubt that EAM gave those previously slighted regions a new "quality of life." This process was helped considerably by the exuberant participation of the young (both locals and outsiders) and by the mass exodus from the occupied cities. Writers and other intellectuals, many organized in the ranks of EAM, supported the traditionally leftist local teachers in their educational duties, as well as in their indoctrination efforts, and gave instruction for the first time in Greek history to many adult illiterates. Hippocrates' science was practiced in hamlets where doctors had never been seen before; according to EA records, 163 "people's hospitals," 670 small "clinics," and 1,253 "people's dispensaries" were established.[44] Despite these achievements, the "spirit" and morale of the general public would not have changed if EAM had not managed to activate the most conservative and backward element of a backward population hitherto submerged in stupor and submissiveness: the women.

Unfortunately, not a single scholarly study exists on this subject, and even a partial elucidation is beyond the scope of this chapter. However, it may be useful to present some official data pertaining to female participation in the movement. In Thessaly, one of EAM's strongest bastions, 86,026 women and girls were registered in EAM in May 1944, amounting to 35.4 percent of its entire membership. The percentages of female members varied from region to region (ranging from 42.3 percent in the nomós of Larissa to 24 percent in the nomós of Karditsa) and between towns and the countryside. This probably reflects, at least in part, local differences in recruiting tactics and proselytizing zeal. In the functional suborganizations, the highest percentages were reached in EA (52 percent) and EPON (43 percent). The women's share in the Workers'

43. C. M. Woodhouse, Apple of Discord (London: Hutchinson, 1948), 146–47.
44. Ethniki Allileggyi, Mia prospatheia ki enas athlos: To ergo tis Ethnikis Allileggyis Elladas (One effort and one feat: The work of National Greek Solidarity) (Athens, 1945), 89.

EAM was only 16 percent. The lowest figure known is that for the ELAS reservist army (10 percent);[45] female representation in the active ELAS was much less, notwithstanding the rather deceptive picture offered by many postwar publications, which carried illustrations of handsome and heroic-looking women in uniform.

Admittedly, the utilization of female enthusiasm and devotion to the movement remained largely within the framework of traditional sex roles. For example, 54,750,000 pieces of underwear were laundered by EA women for ELAS and recorded by them with indefatigable accuracy.[46] However, only a handful of women were elected to the National Assembly, the parliamentary body established in Free Greece in the spring of 1944, virtually all of them leading cadres or wives of prominent leftist leaders (Chrysa Hadzivasiliou-Roussou, Katie Zevgou, Maria Svolou). Although the gains of women may appear to have been modest in retrospect, they must be measured against the position of women in society before the war. Under the enemy occupation many women fought a twofold struggle, "striving," as one woman put it, "for liberation from the occupiers and from their husbands as well."[47] Women who fought, in whatever way, the foreign invaders, or who saw other women fight in the war, could no longer be easily intimidated by a masculine supremacy imposed by notions of "divine" or "natural law." The effects of EAM's emancipatory achievements were felt even after 1945, although some gains were lost.

It may be useful here to consider a synoptic balance sheet of EAM's work and role in Free Greece. First among these is the creation of ELAS, whose existence and activities were a *conditio sine qua non* for the shaping of the new state. Undoubtedly, matters were made easier at the outset by the occupiers' limited interest in the more remote and barren areas of the country and later by their shortage of available troops for large-scale sweeps. But these factors do not diminish the credit due to ELAS for the fact that by 1944 the bulk of the country was no longer under the effective control of the occupation forces as required under Article 42 of the Hague Convention. Although the Wehrmacht was able to attack almost

45. Karayiorgis, "Tria chronia agones," 14–15, 17.
46. Ethniki Allileggyi, *Mia prospatheia,* 60.
47. Phoivos Grigoriadis, *To Andartiko* (The guerrilla movement) (Athens, 1964), 3:108; author's interview with Louisa Tzimas.

any location at almost any time (e.g., the destruction of the ELAS strong-hold of Karpenisi in August 1944), it could not carry out such operations repeatedly because of the strain on its limited resources. Moreover, such actions were usually hastily conceived vindictive strikes against selected targets, made without the intention or the possibility of permanent occupation.

Second, within this emergent state, EAM/ELAS promoted the emancipation of the peasant population in general, often resorting to drastic methods. The effects of its efforts could be seen most clearly among the young, who were the most receptive to change, and among women, previously the most backward.

Third, the new state did not oust any other Greek authority. The government in exile had never exerted any control over the homeland, while the collaborationist regime in Athens, impotent from the beginning, had become defunct (although it continued to have a shadowy existence in such ghettos of German puissance as the bourgeois quarters of Athens).

Fourth, for the first time in modern Greek history, the centers of decision-making were to be found in the countryside, and indeed in its previously most neglected regions. In the aftermath of the Lebanon Conference, when he was trying to create a government of national unity, the Greek Prime Minister in Cairo had to wait for a reaction "from the mountains"! In terms of political importance, the capital was degenerating into the "periphery"; in geostrategic terms, it was an enclave under seige, connected with the new centers of Greece almost entirely by EAM/ELAS channels.

Despite its successes, EAM/ELAS also had its dark side. As Woodhouse points out, most of its "vices" were typical of such movements. The administration of Free Greece was largely entrusted to men who had only recently escaped from protracted detention and whose principal virtue was toughness: they had endured jail, thrashings, and even torture without betraying their cause. Embittered, suspicious, and barely aware of the historical significance of the moment, they assumed leading roles in the greatest political movement Greece had ever experienced. In these positions they often resorted to a rigid activism characterized by coerced recruiting, the suppression of independent opinion, and worst of all, a near-hysterical paranoia that at times led to unnecessary bloodshed. Frequently, a victim's only crime was his refusal to join EAM. Sometimes even loyal cadres of EAM (and of the KKE, such as Pantelis Damasko-poulos) were executed as alleged "agents" and "traitors." (It is important to note that the Germans did attempt to infiltrate Free Greece[48] and that, therefore, the fear of agents and traitors was not unfounded.) Nevertheless, it should be stressed that the achievements of this powerful movement far outweighed its aberrations.

It is futile to attempt to determine, even approximately, the number of EAM's "members"[49] and sympathizers for either the occupied or the liberated areas of the country.[50] EAM sources do not agree as to whether their organization attracted the "overwhelming majority" or only a "very large portion" of the nation.[51] However, some light is shed on this issue by a remarkably fair and astute observation made by a member of the anti-EAM camp. On the eve of the "second round" of the civil war (the *Dekemvriana*), one of EDES's leaders, Iraklis Petimezas, commented on EAM's amazing success:

> EAM always was, and still is, a minority in the country, but carries the greatest proportion of sacrifice and of activity. Thus, let us say, in a certain town with 1,000 citizens, of these 200 are EAM and 800 of other views. The 200 of EAM act consistently, with system and unity, while of the other 800 only 100 take action, and they are split into ten political groups. This is true throughout the country. . . . EAM holds an absolute majority only among young people. . . . EAM has shown that, although a minority, it had deep roots in the country.[52]

48. See my introduction to "Imerologio [Diary of] Phaidona Maidoni, 24.6–10.9, 1944," *Mnimon* 9 (1984): 45ff.

49. Lars Baerentzen, in the sole scholarly study on this subject, could only conclude that EAM members were "many and active" ("I laiki ypostirixi tou EAM sto telos tis katochis" [The popular support of EAM at the end of the occupation], ibid., 173).

50. In Free Greece, it was undoubtedly safer to be in EAM than to remain outside. Interesting and even humorous details about abuses in recruiting practices, which depended largely on the local "responsible" organizer (*ypevthinos*), can be found in Karayiorgis, "Tria chronia agones," 19ff. See also Fleischer, *Kreuzschatten*, 405–6.

51. See, for example, Baerentzen, "I laiki ypostirixi"; and ELD Central Committee, *Theseis yia ta Dekemvriana* (Positions regarding the Dekemvriana) (Athens, 1945), 28. Compare this with Ioannidis's remarkable concession, made after the dissolution of the Comintern, that the liberation movement "must acquire an all-national character and not a narrow EAMite one as is the case today" (KKE Central Committee, *I dialysi tis Kom. Diethnous kai i pali yia ti levteri kai laokratoumeni Ellada* [The dissolution of the Comintern and the struggle for a free Greece ruled by the people] [Athens, June 1943], 14).

52. PRO, FO 371/43738: R 21462. Subsequently, Petimezas's opinion became even more favorable, although he never joined the Left. See *Neoi Thesmoi* 8 (July 1946): 4; *Rizospastis*, 28 September 1947.

Although the proportion he gives for EAM seems too low—and was in fact subsequently revised by Petimezas himself—Petimezas's analysis supports EAM's claims that it represented a large majority of the "working" and "fighting people." His model is interesting because it can also be used to describe with some degree of accuracy the relationship between the KKE and the others *within* EAM.

We are now ready to examine the controversial question of whether there really was any substantial difference between the KKE and EAM, or whether the *politikos kosmos* was justified in its refusal to negotiate with EAM, which it perceived as a cover, insisting instead on direct talks with the KKE. Their doyen, Sophoulis, summarized those convictions in the apothegm that EAM was "nothing but the KKE and little Tsirimokos."[53] This mistrust was not eased by EAM's loud denunciations of such charges as "reactionary calumnies";[54] it was increased by the attempts of even prominent Communists to conceal their affiliation with KKE,[55] as well as by the formation of "independent" resistance organizations, obviously set up by KKE cadres, that subsequently applied for participation in EAM.[56]

The non-Communist components of EAM (mainly ELD) realized from the outset the risk of being absorbed or outweighed in the movement. They had scant followings, and their members and even their cadres possessed limited organizational skills and little underground experience. Those of centrist (Liberal) origin were not used to rigid party discipline or compulsory adherence to a program. Their desire to preserve their freedom of action often led toward divergence and division. Apostolou tried to quiet their fears with the argument that the KKE welcomed the participation of smaller associates, whose independent existence was necessary to ensure EAM's lasting success. Admittedly, the idea of work-

---

53. "To Tsirimokaki" (Grigoriadis, *Andartiko*, 1:206).

54. See *Levteria* (Euboea), 21 October 1943; and Arthur Edmonds, "With Greek Guerrillas" (unpublished manuscript), 68, 80. (Unless noted otherwise, all unpublished materials cited are in the author's possession.) See also Siantos's interview in the *Daily Herald*, 2 November 1944, as quoted in KKE, *Episima Keimena* (1973 ed.), 5:273.

55. See Woodhouse on his talks with the leadership of the KKE and EAM in Athens in early 1943 (*Akropolis*, 21 and 22 April 1965 and elsewhere). See also Thanasis Mitsopoulos, *Sta makedonika vouna: To 30. Syntagma tou ELAS* (In the mountains of Macedonia: The 30th regiment of ELAS) (Geneva, 1971), 95–96, 124.

56. The most important example of this was Iphikrates Hadziemmanuel's "independent" group: Democrats.

ing in harmony with non-Communist groups was not unanimously accepted within the KKE; the opposition included Thanasis Hadzis, Apostolou's successor as General Secretary, who represented the faction that did view EAM as merely a facade for the promotion of party goals.[57]

For different reasons, the adherents of both strategies within the KKE saw cooperation with the Socialists as essential. This situation represented a unique opportunity for the Socialists, provided they took a common stand, at least on the major issues. Whenever they did, the term "fellow travelers" took on a new meaning, and the tail appeared to wag the dog. However, when the Socialists were not united, the KKE was able to capitalize on the situation, isolating its more stubborn partners or, as a last resort, even excluding them from EAM as "splitters," without damage to the facade of overall unity. A brief recapitulation of several instances of dissension within EAM will illustrate the point.

The KKE's success in pushing for a national platform for EAM that eschewed socialist ideological ballast has already been mentioned. But when Hadzis soon thereafter attempted to attract royalist groups by offering them further ideological concessions, his efforts were blocked by the joint opposition of ELD, the SKE, and the AKE. This unity could not be transformed into a common platform denouncing the monarchy—a revision of the EAM program by which they still hoped to win over the Liberals. Their conflicting proposals, however, were easily defeated by the KKE.[58] In the beginning of 1942, a new crisis arose when Hadzis tried to impose a Communist successor to Stavros Veopoulos (SKE), the recently imprisoned Secretary of the EAM City Committee, but the majority would not yield and elected the Agrarian Dionysios Benetatos. In the aftermath of this defeat, the KKE forced an enlargement and rearrangement of EAM's Central Committee by causing representatives of EEAM, EA, and the other functional suborganizations to be added to it. Later, the KKE succeeded in having added as well the political officers (*ypevthinoi*) of the larger regional committees, who were mostly Communists.[59]

57. Apostolou, *To xekinima tou EAM,* 43–45, 59; Petsopoulos, *Ta pragmatika aitia,* 18, 96ff.

58. Dionysios Benetatos, *To chroniko tis katochis, 1941–1944* (The chronicle of the occupation) (Athens, 1963), 74ff.

59. Ibid., 118ff. Indications of this dissension are in *Embros,* 13 January 1942. Concerning the Central Committee, see L. S. Stavrianos, "The Greek National Liberation Front (EAM): A Study in Resistance Organization and Administration," *Journal of Modern History* 24 (March 1952): 46, the earliest and still one of the best essays on EAM.

Consequently, relations between the Communists and their more independent-minded partners in the EAM Central Committee worsened. Their disagreements rarely centered on fundamental ideological differences, however. In fact, the KKE was willing to compromise to put a stop to any "revolutionary" adventures in isolated regions of the countryside.[60] Therefore, the various interpretations of what a postwar "People's Democracy" might look like seemed largely compatible. Its actual implementation, however, would be based on practical considerations—guidance of the extremely influential press, disposition of revenues, control of recruiting, and similar organizational functions—and here the Hadzis wing of the KKE opposed any compromise on the "a priori preponderance of the working class and its party." The rift between the Communists and the others was widened by additional factors, some of them external. At the close of 1942, both the AKE and the SKE broke up into two sections, with Apostolos Voyiadzis (as a locum tenens for the imprisoned Gavriilidis) and Dimitrios Stratis leading the majority factions that remained within EAM. The dissenters, who in the beginning were numerically almost equal to those factions remaining in EAM, soon faded away, rallying around Benetatos and Christos Homenidis, respectively. Both were able and respected men. Benetatos founded the Agrarian Social Democratic Party, which, assisted by a few splinter groups, tried in vain to establish a more moderate liberation front, although it did produce some of the most impressive underground periodicals of the era. Homenidis attempted to keep the name SKE for his splinter group but was totally ignored by the public. He finally rejoined EAM, only to be captured in action and hanged by the Security Battalions recruited by the Germans.

Even though the Communists prevailed in these instances, they could not afford to jeopardize EAM's character by forcing a large-scale reduction of its constituent parties. Consequently, the KKE was obliged to yield at least twice to its minor partners (although by this time the AKE had become little more than a substitute for the KKE).[61] In the first in-

60. The "Red Major" at Kalambaka, and other quixotic "revolutionaries" who operated primarily in Thessaly, considered the EAM program to be too "soft" and "out of date." These mavericks were prone to declaring "red dictatorships" and to composing slogans that were embarrassing to the leadership of the KKE (Karayiorgis, "Tria chronia agones," 20–21; author's interview with Lazaros Arseniou, Athens, 1983).

61. This process accelerated after the Italian capitulation, when Gavriilidis managed to escape from prison and again took over leadership of the AKE.

stance, the KKE yielded on the issue of national claims, which it had always considered a chauvinistic anathema. It had previously supported only the relatively uncomplicated aspirations for Cyprus and the Dodecanese, held by Britain and Italy, respectively, for whom the KKE had no sympathy. By degrees, over the course of more than a year, a consensus tantamount to a complete reversal of previous KKE positions was achieved. This dramatic change became manifest in November 1943 when the EAM Central Committee put forth claims not only for Northern Epirus but also for "strategic corrections of the Northern frontiers."[62] Thus, for the sake of EAM unity, the KKE risked angering the Albanian and Bulgarian Communist parties and the resistance fronts dominated by them.

The second instance, which was even more important, concerned the settling of the protracted crisis following the Lebanon Conference. In explaining the eventual volte-face of the leftist leadership in the mountains in July-August 1944, most writers are preoccupied with the foreign factor, that is, with the intervention of the British, who insisted on Papandreou, and the arrival of the Soviet mission under Popov with its putative "directives from Stalin." There can be no question that the flagrant intervention of the British, as well as the demonstrative nonintervention of the Soviets, disconcerted the Communist leadership. However, it was the unexpectedly stiff opposition from Alexander Svolos, the non-Communist President of PEEA, and his associates in PEEA and EAM, probably reflecting the wishes of the majority of the people, that tipped the scale.[63]

Their independent course during the critical months of the summer of 1944 sparked an adverse reaction in the KKE, particularly among middle- and lower-level cadres. The members of the ELD Central Committee later recalled with considerable bitterness being treated with growing suspicion and intolerance by the Communists, who applied increasingly hostile labels to them, progressing from "non-Communist" and "conservative" to "reactionary" and "traitor."[64] Relations were better at higher party levels. Siantos and other members of the politburo

---

62. EAM Central Committee, *Tipota krypho ap' ton Elliniko lao* (No secrets from the Greek people) (Athens, 17 November 1943), 3, 8; Fleischer, *Kreuzschatten*, 269ff., 695.

63. For details, see Fleischer, *Kreuzschatten*, 489–504; and *Archeio tis Politikis Epitropis Ethnikis Apelevtherosis (P.E.E.A.), Praktika Synedriaseon* (Archive of the Political Committee for National Liberation, minutes of meetings) (Athens, 1990), 140ff.

64. ELD Central Committee, *Theseis*, 45, 47ff.

repeatedly assured Svolos that they felt bound to preserve the democratic coalition and that the KKE had no plans to seize power by force. This is not the place to consider the issue of EAM's (or the KKE's) short-term and long-term objectives. Any such discussion would necessarily remain highly speculative because it is impossible to determine whether the remarkable moderation of EAM/ELAS during the fall of 1944 was due to a miscalculation (i.e., an overestimation of the Allied forces that had landed in Greece at the time of liberation) or whether it is evidence disproving British suspicions that EAM's primary goal had always been to gain control of the country during and following the war, resistance having been a secondary consideration "only for purposes subservient to the primary object of winning political power."[65]

Although the main chain of events before and during the German evacuation seemed to justify the assurances given to Svolos and, more generally, the most optimistic hopes for a peaceful evolution to a democratic postwar Greece, the atmosphere was soon poisoned once again by clumsy tactics, mutual distrust, and lack of composure. In November 1944, both the British and the KKE expected a clash, and when Churchill decided "We must not shrink from it, provided the ground is well chosen," the KKE, for its part, was ready "to take up the challenge."[66] Since there did not remain much room for the moderates in either camp, ELD and the SKE considered dissociating themselves from EAM or demanding its restructuring in accordance with the new situation. In the Central Committee's session of 1 December 1944, however, both parties reluctantly agreed that the united Left should insist on the full demobilization of all "volunteer forces." Of all the parties involved, the Socialists were the most surprised by the events of "Bloody Sunday" (3 December) and its even gorier aftermath. Overcoming their initial shock, they urged a quick reconciliation without concealing their disapproval of civil war. Nevertheless, they deferred all plans for the reorganization of EAM and likewise resisted all pressures and enticements from the government camp and its British protectors to denounce "KKE aggression," declaring that they were not prepared to stab their partners in the back, not even by remaining neutral, a position that, in fact, would

---

65. Woodhouse, *Apple of Discord*, 141; PRO, FO 371/37207: R 11673.
66. Churchill quotation: PRO, FO 371/43697: R 19672; KKE response: Siantos, 28 November 1944, as quoted in John O. Iatrides, *Revolt in Athens* (Princeton: Princeton University Press, 1972), 179; and KKE, *Episima Keimena* (1973 ed.), 5:485.

have amounted to desertion.[67] On the other hand, they were deeply irritated by the KKE's high-handed tactics, including the activities of the Central Committee of ELAS, whose resurrection had taken them entirely by surprise, and the repeated press announcements about peace initiatives and negotiations of "the Central Committee of EAM," about which they had not been consulted. Stratis demanded that General Secretary Dimitris (Mitsos) Partsalidis convene the Central Committee at once to allow the other parties in EAM to take part in the decision-making process for which, in any event, they shared responsibility.

Thus, on 13 and 14 December, the EAM Central Committee discussed the Socialists' demand for an "immediate conciliatory solution" based on their view that any persistence in the confrontation would inevitably be defeated, with unpredictable risks for the nation in general and for the leftist movement in particular. During the heated dispute, Partsalidis refused to yield, and even deleted from the written record certain critical comments and conclusions presented by the opposing faction. Consequently, EAM's resulting public appeal of 15 December, while moderately worded, did not reflect many of the Socialist positions.

The delivery of Gen. Ronald Scobie's conditions for ending the hostilities caused additional rounds of fierce debate, which grew even more impassioned when the KKE publicly announced its determination to fight on "until victory" in face of the great British counteroffensive that had already begun and would finally prove decisive. There is a paucity of reliable information on these debates, but some of the arguments presented in the session of 20 December are offered here for the first time. At the outset, Svolos, President of the defunct PEEA, once again strongly advocated accepting Scobie's terms, because they represented a matter of prestige for Great Britain but were not considered "harmful to our camp." He was opposed by Yiannis Zevgos, who belittled the strength of the available British forces, asserting: "We need not be frightened by the military conflict, nor be deterred by sacrifices; . . . through unwavering perseverance we can succeed and Scobie will give in." Zevgos hoped that public opinion in Great Britain and the United States would prevent the use of British troops against former allies. Karagitsis of EA and Hadziemmanuel of the Democratic Party seconded their comrade, as did Gavriilidis of the AKE, who advocated the formation of an antigovernment. Only two speakers sided with Svolos; the rest vacillated between irrecon-

67. See, for example, ELD Central Committee, *Theseis*, 35, 38–39.

cilable positions, mostly leaning toward that of the ELAS Central Committee.[68]

During Churchill's famous Christmas visit to Athens, the organizers of the first conference between the enemy camps purposely ignored EAM and invited the KKE alone to participate, a move that, considering the divergence of opinion within EAM, may have pleased the KKE, especially since its delegation included Partsalidis, who was then also secretary of the EAM Central Committee. The minor parties in EAM were understandably irritated at receiving their first information about the meeting from the newspaper extras, and demanded to take part in the second conference. The EAM Central Committee agreed to a delegation consisting of Partsalidis, Svolos, Gavriilidis, and Georgios Georgalas, but the last three were not able to attend in the end because of unexplained "technical difficulties." Thus one more opportunity for broader cooperation was lost.

The more moderate regional committees of ELD, the SKE, and the AKE in Macedonia publicly denounced "the irreconcilable policy of the KKE,"[69] while there and in other EAM-dominated areas the members of these parties were often treated as "second-rate citizens."[70] Although this resulted in a further shaking of mutual confidence, most leading "fellow travelers" followed ELAS and the KKE in their evacuation of Athens, partly from fear of rightist revenge but also from a sense of solidarity. The same feeling induced the Socialists to participate in EAM's delegation and share responsibility at the Varkiza Conference as well.

At the same time, the question of whether EAM could be preserved in any form was already under discussion. ELD and the SKE maintained that common goals and interests rendered cooperation not only feasible but necessary. However, they insisted on a structure guaranteeing full organizational autonomy and freedom of opinion. They were unwilling to have their views suppressed by dubious "majority votes," as had been the case during the occupation period when they had constantly faced the dilemma of submitting to "discipline" and "unity," or otherwise being held responsible for "splitting the struggle for liberation."

68. The information on the *Dekemvriana* is largely based on scattered unpublished evidence, such as unofficial and fragmentary minutes of sessions of the EAM Central Committee, in the author's possession.

69. Declaration of 13 January 1945, in *Documents Regarding the Situation in Greece, January 1945* (London: His Majesty's Stationery Office, 1945), 14.

70. ELD Central Committee, *Theseis,* 50. See also Georg Eckert, "Beobachtungen aus dem Winter 1944/45" (unpublished report, Archiv für Soziale Demokratie, Bonn).

One might certainly ask why the KKE was not prepared at the time to accept this arrangement, since the later reorganization of EAM was almost identical with these initial ELD proposals.[71] The Socialists had in the meantime virtually decided on their immediate withdrawal from EAM and were advancing more radical demands: that the postwar EAM be rebuilt as a democratic mass organization independent of all parties; that it not be entitled to interfere in their internal affairs; and that its activities be restricted to the *political* struggle.[72] Three days later, on 5 April 1945, a few independent Socialists, including Svolos, agreed with the SKE and ELD on a platform for their immediate merger into a united party. The Socialists were obviously unwilling to give the KKE more time to consider their demands, fearing that any further indecisiveness or lack of autonomy on their part would be detrimental to their own ends.[73]

For its part, it was essential to the KKE to develop quickly a successor or substitute for the movement, especially since it had the name EAM at its disposal. In his report to the Eleventh Plenum, Siantos urged his audience to protect EAM as the "apple of their eye." Moreover, he recognized the need to give it new substance and a new structure, turning it into a looser coalition. Although the resulting resolution was discreetly worded, on the day it was published (24 April 1945), the rump Central Committee of EAM decided that with the country's liberation the time had come for a "political and organizational readaptation of its alliance" as a precondition for the realization of the "remaining" programmatic ends and, in particular, for the "final consolidation of people's sovereignty" and the "eradication of Fascism from all aspects of our political life" in accordance with the principles of the Yalta and Varkiza accords.[74] These aims, which included the moral and practical justification of the wartime resistance movement and the safeguarding of "national independence,"[75] were to be secured by the coordinated action of "a purely political coalition of parties." The revised EAM would no longer include suborganizations. Some of them were dissolved or merged; oth-

---

71. Takis Kyrkos, personal communication with the author, Athens, 1987.

72. Unpublished letter from Tsirimokos to Partsalidis, 2 April 1945.

73. For the outcome of this attempt to form a united party, see Hagen Fleischer, "The 'Third Factor': The Struggle for an Independent Socialist Policy During the Greek Civil War," in *Studies in the History of the Greek Civil War, 1945–1949*, ed. Lars Baerentzen, John O. Iatrides, and Ole L. Smith (Copenhagen: Museum Tusculanum, 1987), 189–212.

74. KKE, *Episima Keimena* (1981 ed.), 5:428ff.

75. This slogan, which was not in widespread use during the occupation, gained new force prior to the *Dekemvriana* and was employed in an excessive and sterile way in the course of the civil war. See *Phyllo tou Laou*, 27 January 1947.

ers, like EPON, continued their existence but ostensibly functioned as separate entities. The constituent parties could preserve their "absolute political and organizational independence and full equality" and were entitled to promote their own interests outside the coalition. Minorities could not be outvoted because decisions had to be unanimous and only these, together with the common program, were to be obligatory.[76]

During the next few weeks, several parties declared their intention (or ratified previous decisions) to join this coalition. They included the AKE, the Democratic Union (headed by Stavros Kritikas and Eleftherios Proimakis), the Independent Agrarians (Apostolos Voyiadzis), and two new amalgamations: the Democratic Radical Party (led by Mihalis Kyrkos and Alkiviadis Loulis), which contained Hadziemmanuel's Democratic Party, a Communist cover organization; and the SKE, which had absorbed various splinter groups in order to counterbalance and, if possible, to demolish its inimical sister party outside EAM, Stratis's rival SKE, which in the meantime had merged with ELD. The Left Liberals, a tiny group led by Neokosmos Grigoriadis and Stamatis Hadzibeis, did not enter EAM but cooperated with it on a permanent basis. This arrangement was particularly valuable because it allowed EAM to make pompous press announcements referring to "the common position held by EAM and the Left Liberals" on various subjects.

The absence of any noteworthy non-Communist component in this reconstituted EAM ("Now not even the Tsirimokaki!") was noted by many, and not only by conservatives. In the meetings of the SK-ELD Central Committee, KKE and EAM were generally used as synonyms, the former being preferred. Moreover, SK-ELD publicly claimed to represent the Socialist "view" of the former resistance movement, thereby challenging the other "view" and provoking EAM's indignation.[77]

Such well-informed individuals as the Communist maverick Yiannis Petsopoulos accused the KKE of having "lent" not only cadres to its "partners" in EAM but even their entire "small popular following."[78] Indeed, Gavriilidis' AKE, which since early 1944 had been a cover organization for the Communists, developed into the KKE's official alias in rural areas. This was effectively a renewal of the stillborn United Agrarian Party, which had been jointly promoted by the KKE (Sixth Congress

76. *Elevtheri Ellada,* 25 April 1945.
77. Compare, for example, *Elevtheria,* 7 August 1945, and *Elevtheri Ellada,* 8 August 1945.
78. *Phyllo tou Laou,* 27 January 1947. See also Petsopoulos, *Ta pragmatika aitia,* 157.

and Second Plenum) and the Agrarian leader Sophianopoulos, who reached agreement in July 1936 on the eve of the Metaxas dictatorship.[79] This became official policy once more in June 1945 with the Twelfth Plenum decision to dissolve all KKE rural organizations and transfer them to the AKE, which represented "the political unity of the democratic forces in the village."[80] Thus, with a stroke of the pen, the peasants who had been proselytized during the war were brought under Communist influence without "debasing" the supposedly proletarian and ideologically monolithic character of the KKE. Similarly, although to a lesser degree, the Democratic Radical Party ended up with Communists in leading positions after absorbing the "Democrats" of Hadziemmanuel, who doubtless was the KKE's appointed watchdog for the rather enterprising Kyrkos.[81] In any event, the overwhelming strength of the KKE, compared with all of its partners in the new EAM, can hardly be disputed. In internal reports from cadre meetings in Crete, the proportion of Communists to all others is given as 9 to 1, 19 to 5, and even 69 to 1![82]

A survey of the leftist newspapers with countrywide circulation, as well as the more important local newspapers, is even more revealing of KKE influence. In January 1946, on the eve of the civil war, EAM published directly 42 newspapers (among them 17 dailies) and controlled 16 "independent" publications (including one daily that officially embraced the "principles of people's democracy" without listing further political identification. Of the 35 newspapers openly professing a party affiliation, 20 (among them 2 dailies) were issued by the KKE, 12 by the AKE, and only 3 by all the other parties in EAM. To these should be added 43 organs of consanguineous organizations also advocating a "people's democracy": 20 were edited by trade unionist and professional branch associations; among the others, 8 were organs of EPON and 6 of EA; the rest expressed the views of organizations of women, veterans, invalids, reservists, tuberculars, and the like.[83]

After the war, the even stronger tendency among the leftist leadership to consider EAM as a supplement to the KKE (or vice versa) was re-

79. *Saranda chronia tou KKE, 1918–1958* (Forty years of the KKE, 1918–1958) (Politikes kai Logotechnikes Ekdoseis, 1958), 425–26, 432, 442ff.

80. Ibid., 533.

81. Takis Kyrkos, personal communication.

82. EAM, Nomarchiaki Epitropi Irakliou, "Vdomadiatiko Deltio Douleias" (unpublished weekly bulletin), 11–17 June 1945.

83. I plan to publish a more detailed survey of this issue.

flected in the decision to change EAM's central organ, *Elevtheri Ellada,* into an afternoon newspaper. Until then, the "movement" had been represented nationwide by two morning publications, *Elevtheri Ellada* and the Communist *Rizospastis.*[84] Likewise, a close comparison of official KKE declarations and those issued subsequently by EAM reveals striking similarities between them.[85] The occasional presence of apparent differences can be explained to some degree by the desire of the Communists and the others in EAM to camouflage the KKE's overwhelming role. Special attention was paid to organizational questions. The fact that more than two-thirds of the members of EAM were attracted by its general principles, and not by the tenets of any one of its constituent parties, was a particular source of concern.[86]

Soon after the restructuring of the coalition, the idea arose that minor parties, which were virtually unrepresented at the lower levels of EAM, might draw from the movement's abundant human pool: unaffiliated members and cadres should join the most "contiguous" party.[87] However, this issue remained a challenge for the organizers. EAM's following had always been much larger than the sum of its member parties' adherents; indeed, this was one of the main reasons for its remarkable success. Yet, after Varkiza, EAM had been reshaped as a party coalition, which was hardly compatible with the persistent predominance in its ranks of members without any party affiliation. Referring to this paradox, the KKE showed understanding when it concluded that in these circumstances EAM itself had become the substitute for the missing party affiliation.[88] Actually, after the increase in its membership during the occupation, the KKE was more than content with its numbers and thereafter tried to reduce quantity in favor of "monolithic" quality. This was clearly demonstrated by the above-mentioned mass transfer of rural organizations from the KKE to the AKE. By contrast, the Communists' minor

84. See *Elevtheri Ellada,* 29 June and 9 July 1945.

85. Compare the program of *Laiki Dimokratia* in *Rizospastis,* 17 June 1945, and in *Elevtheri Ellada,* 23 and 30 July 1945. Compare also the published materials of the Eleventh and Twelfth Plenums, the Seventh Congress, and the Sixth Conference of the Kommounistiki Organosis Athinas (KOA).

86. KOA, *I ekti syndiaskepsi tis Kommounistikis Organosis Athinas, 28–29 Septemvri 1945* (The Sixth Conference of the Communist Organization of Athens, 28–29 September 1945) (Athens, 1945), 42ff.

87. EAM Central Committee, instruction to the Cretan Regional Committee of EAM, 8 March 1945 (unpublished).

88. KOA, *I ekti syndiaskepsi,* 42ff.

associates in EAM had totally different concerns. They therefore urged "loose" or "scattered" (*skorpia*) EAMites to enter the nearest party harbor.[89] Nonetheless, for the reasons given above, no such obligation was ever imposed.

The principle of equal representation of all the parties (but only of the parties) was assured by the appointment of their representatives at all levels of leadership except the lowest one. The committees of the grassroots (*vasis*) groups alone were democratically chosen—the deputies often being elected from among nonaligned members—and they alone represented EAM as a whole. When experience showed that enthusiasm and efficiency were at their peak at the *vasis* level, the electoral system was for a time applied optionally to the next higher level (*tomeas*) as well.[90] In the summer of 1946, EAM's Second Panhellenic Conference decided that, henceforth, councils (*symvoulia*) parallel to the existing committees of party deputies were to be elected democratically at all hierarchical levels and "naturally will represent mainly the mass of EAM members and cadres who are outside of the parties."[91]

These developments indicate that EAM continued to attract large numbers of democratic supporters. EAM's influence was especially evident in 1945 and 1946 when it was able to mobilize its membership for large demonstrations and other mass gatherings for such events as its own anniversary celebrations and the preelection and plebiscite campaigns. But the controversy over Communist control and camouflage would not die, particularly since the KKE (and the AKE in the countryside) persisted in its efforts to dominate EAM's adherents.

In refounding EAM, the KKE had faced a dilemma. In order to attract a wider response than simply from the Communist Party itself, EAM had to be more than a facade. Yet in order to prevent rapid disintegration, the desire for autonomy and the range of opinion within the movement had to be "guided" or, if necessary, restrained. Concerning the first point, it was hoped that the organization's inherited prestige and the handful of old or new "independent" personalities who had joined would attract people to EAM. As for the second consideration, the KKE had at its command an effective mechanism of control up to and including the

89. See, for example, the resolution concerning organizational issues in *Elevtheri Ellada,* 7 November 1945.

90. Ibid. See also EAM, Nomarchiaki Epitropi Irakliou, "Enkyklios," 27 March 1945 (unpublished).

91. *Elevtheri Ellada,* 11 July 1946.

highest level. Partsalidis remained General Secretary of EAM, and the Athens City Committee was steered by a Communist (Antonis Roussos), as were most of the more important local committees. As a concession to moderate circles, Mihalis Kyrkos, a respected politician with a bourgeois background, was appointed publisher of *Elevtheri Ellada;* but Vasilis Ephraimidis, who was on the newspaper's editorial staff, kept a watchful eye on him, as did Hadziemmanuel. This Communist supervision must have caused problems. Men like Kyrkos were not likely to have acquiesced in being treated like puppets. Unfortunately, nearly all of EAM's records that could have shed light on this question were either destroyed or are inaccessible. Needless to say, internal dissension was hardly ever made public.[92]

On most propaganda topics promoted throughout the period after the refounding of EAM, its positions coincide closely with those of the KKE. The first confidential directive issued by high-level EAM committees[93] conceded that "reactionary calumnies about alleged crimes by EAMites" during the *Dekemvriana* had done "much harm to us." It was therefore necessary to remind Greeks of the achievements of EAM/ELAS in the resistance and about the brutalities committed by the occupiers and their Greek collaborators. The directive stressed that "those are our best weapons." In looking to the future, EAM was determined to take the initiative in fostering domestic peace and democracy along the lines of the Yalta and Varkiza accords by creating an "All-Democratic Front" embracing all shades of republicanism and aimed "against the restoration of monarcho-fascism." Accordingly, after the end of the Second World War, Kyrkos indicated the beginning of a new era for EAM by changing its motto and that of *Elevtheri Ellada* from "Death to Fascism" to the much broader "For Democracy and Social Reform [*anaplasi*]." EAM began to act as a political pressure group. Among other things, it continued to exploit for its own ends (as it had done during the occupation) the economic misery of the Greek people. Demands for "fair elec-

92. Our knowledge of this issue would benefit greatly from a systematic comparison of EAM periodicals, especially of those originating outside Athens, where the mechanism of control was not always as efficient as within the city. In this study, however, I must confine myself to a brief examination of instances in which divergences (actual or attempted) between EAM strategy and KKE positions may be detected.

93. See, for example, EAM, Nomarchiaki Epitropi Irakliou, "Syntomes odigies yia tous organotes" (Brief instructions for the organizers), 7 February 1945; and EAM Central Committee, "Yia oles tis epitropes periochon tou EAM" (For all the district committees of EAM), no. 157, 7 March 1945 (both unpublished).

tions" and a "general amnesty," and protests against the right-wing terror, were issued along with demands for stable prices for oil, raisins, and other necessities.

In contrast, the KKE and EAM diverged on the question of national claims and on the concept of the nation generally. EAM claimed that it represented "the healthy and truly nationalist [ethnikophron] incarnation of democracy and·of the Left" and worked hard for the realization of these claims, despite the slander directed against it. With remarkable zeal, EAM defended Greece's "inalienable right" to Northern Epirus, and to the other regions in question, and supported frontier changes that would have come at the expense of Bulgaria. It also raised, and vigorously supported, a claim to Eastern Thrace.[94] The Communist leadership initially supported such territorial aspirations rather cautiously (later it would be accused of "social chauvinism") and then gradually distanced itself from them, although it continued to tolerate the occasional nationalist outbursts in the EAM media. The reason for this was obvious: the demands were not only popular, but EAM's positions could be offered as proof of the existence of non-Communist components in the organization, without causing serious harm to the KKE's aims. Furthermore, given the persistence of its Socialist allies on this question, a clash over the issue of national claims would have put EAM's cohesiveness to the test.

On other crucial points, one has to search for the nuances in the KKE and EAM positions. The frequent appeals to prevent "new anomalies" or even open civil war, for example, seemed more urgent and passionate in EAM's Elevtheri Ellada than in Rizospastis; and when Kyrkos emphasized the "people's detestation" for any foreign intervention, he expressly named the Russians along with the Germans and the British.[95] There were few noticeable signs of the serious dissension on the issue of abstention (apochi) from the elections of March 1946, which, since its non-Communist parties had pleaded for participation, imperiled EAM's very existence.[96] In this instance, the KKE—or, more precisely, its Zahariadis wing—with the support of "external" republicans ranging from Kaphandaris to SK-ELD, was able to impose its line upon the others.

94. See, for example, Elevtheri Ellada, 27 and 29 May, 1–3 June, 28 September 1945, and 1 August 1946.

95. Elevtheri Ellada, 22 May 1946.

96. Personal communications from Takis Kyrkos, Achilleas Gregoroyiannis, Aristovoulos Manesis, and others.

The progressive deterioration of the political situation alarmed the Socialist faction in EAM. As guerrilla activity intensified and, in particular, when the headquarters of the Democratic Army was established, EAM reacted more quickly than the KKE and denied more vigorously any responsibility for recruiting or providing guidance to the guerrillas.[97] Furthermore, the Socialists repeatedly took the initiative, most dramatically in March and July 1947, in making conciliatory approaches toward Dimitrios Maximos, Sophoulis, Emmanuel Tsouderos, and others. They were frustrated in these attempts by opposition from both extremes of the political spectrum but mainly, according to Kyrkos, from the Tsaldaris camp, which was encouraged in its opposition by certain American advisers.[98]

Despite its consent, however tentative, to Kyrkos's feelers, the KKE contributed heavily to the escalation of the crisis. Miltiades Porphyroyenis's famous declaration at the French Communist Party's congress on 27 June 1947 in Strasbourg of the necessity of creating a separate "free" state in northern Greece resulted in a storm of rumor and accusation that affected the Socialists, as well as the KKE, and impaired the cohesiveness of EAM much more than the subsequent mass arrests in July. The breaking point was finally reached after the Third Plenum (September 1947), when the KKE tried, in exhausting sessions, to persuade its allies in EAM to join in the projected government in the mountains. After their stubborn refusal to do so—which, however, did not take the form of an open denunciation of the proposals—the KKE proceeded alone to constitute the Provisional Democratic Government under the guerrilla leader Markos Vaphiadis.

After this point, EAM faded away as a political entity. By October 1947, the banning of the leftist press had deprived EAM of its public media and the KKE made no serious attempt to supply it with the means for an effective underground newspaper network. The Communist leadership, having lost its prominent independent supporters, resolved to pursue a "dynamic" strategy, and in so doing wrote off the unity model embodied in EAM. This, rather than government oppression, was the

97. See *Elevtheri Ellada*, 15 and 30 October 1946, and *Rizospastis*, 31 October 1946. It should be noted, however, that immediately after Aris Velouhiotis's death, *Elevtheri Ellada*—again, in contrast to the official KKE attitude—paid him and his "epic" resistance an impressive tribute ("Aris Velouhiotis: I andartiki epopoiia tou ethnous" [Aris Velouhiotis: The guerrilla epic of the nation], 22 June–9 August 1945).

98. Mihalis Kyrkos, diary excerpts, *Avgi*, 20/22 January 1980.

main reason for EAM's collapse. At first, the official outlawing of EAM caused sympathetic agitation abroad, but without support and inspiration from the Greeks themselves foreign interest in EAM soon withered away. In 1948, there was still sporadic mention of EAM, but at the Fourth Plenum of its Central Committee in July the KKE noted that its only remaining partner in this "alliance" was the AKE.[99] The Fifth Plenum in January 1949 "forgot" EAM entirely, referring only to the AKE (and to the wartime ELAS, but in a rather deprecatory manner); at the time of the reshuffling of the Provisional Democratic Government in April 1949, the KKE did not consider it worthwhile to specify whether the new "Prime Minister," Mitsos Partsalidis, still functioned as General Secretary of EAM.[100]

In the end, the non-Communist politicians who had risked their reputations, their careers, and even their lives by cooperating with the KKE within the framework of EAM had their hopes dashed, since their efforts ultimately met with failure. It is idle to speculate whether or when they missed chances for a better outcome. It would be unjust to denounce the Socialists in EAM simply as Communist fellow travelers, and they certainly did not constitute a distinct strain within the broader socialist movement. Whether Socialists joined EAM, or remained outside, was usually a matter of accident. Their decisions were based on their personal affiliations and aversions, and influenced by their political ambitions. Differences could crop up suddenly, engendering confrontation where there had been cooperation. Developments on the national and international scenes also came into play. But ideological incompatibility, including the dilemma of "to sin or not to sin" by collaborating with the KKE, was of secondary importance—as evidenced by their frequent crossing of the line. Kyrkos, for example, participated in the preliminaries of merging ELD and the SKE. Passalidis belonged to the first Central Committee of this union before he went over to the rival SKE and, thereby, to EAM. For some time, the spokesman for this Socialist party within EAM was the lawyer Georgios Oikonomou, who had been one

99. *Exormisi*, 1 August 1948, quoted in *Saranda chronia tou KKE*, 565. In November 1948, Markos Vaphiadis did not include EAM among the "political mass organizations" (KKE, *Episima Keimena, 1945–1949* [Athens, 1987], 6:472).

100. At almost the same time, in what sounded like echoes of a better past, the KKE Central Committee accused Minister of Public Order Constantine Rendis of a treacherous ("blood-dripping") attempt to *split* EAM (KKE, *Episima Keimena* [1987 ed.], 6:367).

of the outstanding cadres of EAM in 1941–42. He split from the SKE and left EAM during the occupation, returning to EAM after Varkiza, only to leave it once again after the *apochi*. He then helped to establish the Independent Socialist Group (ASO), where he was reunited with old companions from EAM, including Georgios Laskaris and Benetatos. Similarly, Voyiadzis, the leader of the tiny Independent Agrarian Party, which had been briefly a partner of the KKE prior to the Metaxas dictatorship, signed the charter of the "new" EAM, thus revalidating his signature on the original EAM document of September 1941. He was immediately ridiculed by SK-ELD as a "party of one" (*"Kapetan Enas"*). Some months later he approached SK-ELD, to be derided, in turn, by *Elevtheri Ellada*.

Relations between EAM (including the KKE) and SK-ELD alternated continuously between tension and cooperation. The day after the EAM media accused its former allies of "desertion," of "opportunism," and of "compromising," an EAM audience applauded (admittedly with interspersed shouts for unity) a speech by SK-ELD Secretary Tsirimokos in the packed Panathinaikos Stadium.[101] It should be added that the Socialists outside the post-Varkiza EAM were often more "radical" and more pro-KKE than those inside. Early in 1946, for example, SK-ELD advocated abstention from the upcoming national elections and may in fact have precipitated the KKE's eventual decision to abstain. Moreover, in the autumn of the following year, several top cadres of SK-ELD (Tsirimokos and Stavros Kanellopoulos at least) made it obvious that they were willing to join the Provisional Democratic Government, although in the end they did not do so.[102]

After liberation and the *Dekemvriana,* however, Socialists in and out of EAM were faced with the same dilemma: of having to choose "between illegality and sectarianism." The only other course open to them (which Kalomoiris pleaded for), desertion to the government camp, was unpalatable.[103] In the end, they procrastinated until others had decided the issue for them. Not until the KKE established close relations with the

101. Cf. *Elevtheri Ellada,* 22 and 24 December 1945.

102. Fleischer, "Third Factor," 197, 205, 208, and references therein to the unpublished protocols of the SK-ELD Central Committee sessions.

103. Yiannis Kalomoiris, Memorandum, Sosialergatiki Syndikalistiki Parataxi, 21 August 1946; and *Vivlio praktikon tis eklegeisis apo to ogdoo synedrio dioikisis tis GSEE* (Minutes of the GSEE Executive elected by the eighth conference), protocol of the session of 23 August 1946 (both unpublished).

separatist Slavo-Macedonian National Liberation Front (NOF) did both groups of Socialists distance themselves from the Communists, who appeared by their action to have returned to their bankrupt prewar positions on the delicate Macedonian question.

Following the civil war of 1946–49, and again after the fall of the military junta in 1974, leftist writers debated such subjects as "How and Why the People's Liberation Struggle of Greece Met with Defeat" or, with a touch of drama, "Why the 'Victorious Revolution' and 'EAM's Popular Sovereignty' Were Lost (or Betrayed)."[104] They indulged themselves in explaining how the lost paradise on earth might have been saved, often engaging in excessive speculation in the process. Almost all of these writers had one thing in common: they were Communist cadres and therefore evaluated developments from a more or less narrow party perspective. Those who denounced the KKE's undeniable vacillations during the occupation between the opposing strategies personified by Tito and Togliatti, for example, displayed a clear preference for the former. Yet such a strategy would have conflicted fundamentally with the original program of EAM; the adoption of Tito's concept would have reduced EAM's whole existence to stage dressing. Given the benefit of hindsight, we might consider here the alternative strategies open to EAM, and their chances of success at the time, but such a discussion would take us far beyond the scope of this study, which deals with the extent of EAM's autonomy and authenticity in theory and in practice, and with KKE strategy only within this framework.

Suffice it to say that the Yugoslav strategy, particularly if it had been pursued in the fall of 1944 on the eve of the German withdrawal, would almost certainly have been successful. On the other hand, a consistent application of the opposing strategy (that of national unity as expressed in EAM's charter), also held promise for EAM, as well as for the peaceful

---

104. See, for example, Dimos Thesprotos, *Avtokritiki: Yiati chathike i laiki exousia tou EAM, 1940–1945* (Self-criticism: Why EAM lost its popular sovereignty, 1940–1945) (Athens, 1977); Thanasis Hadzis, *I nikiphora epanastasi pou chathike, 1941–1945* (The victorious revolution that was lost, 1941–1945), 3 vols. (Athens, 1977–79); Dimitris Vlandas, *I prodomeni epanastasi, 1941–1944: Politiki istoria tou KKE* (The betrayed revolution, 1941–1944: The political history of the KKE) (Athens, 1977); Themis Moschatos, *I Ethniki mas Antistasi i prodomeni* (Our betrayed national resistance) (Athens, 1980). For Tito's view, see the vehement attack on the KKE written by his main representative in Macedonia, Svetozar Vukmanović-Tempo, *How and Why the People's Liberation Struggle of Greece Met with Defeat* (London, 1950). This was published—after the Yugoslav rupture with the Cominform—in many languages (all based on the [shorter] original version that appeared in *Borba*, 29 August–1 September 1949).

evolution of the country as a whole. Instead, EAM vacillated between the two, pursuing a reactive strategy that answered the "needs" of the moment. This was not only shortsighted but also foreclosed the possibility of either strategy succeeding.

For evidence supporting the view that either strategy, consistently applied, might have worked, one could look at developments in several peripheral regions of Greece, where indigenous resistance movements sprang into existence under the banner of EAM but remained "virtually independent"[105] for a long time. In such places, the vacillations of the central leadership had no effect: one or the other of the two concepts was applied spontaneously and pretty much consistently. The "Tito strategy" was applied in the Evros region, for example,[106] and the "unity strategy" was attempted on various islands, and both secured an undisputed predominance for the local variants of EAM. However, under the much less favorable conditions that prevailed after Varkiza, both strategies held only limited prospects for even partial success.

It is clear that the outcome of the 1947 crisis, and the resulting violence, prevented EAM from completing its intended course. These events enabled its adversaries on the Right to consider EAM almost entirely in the context of the second (post-liberation) period, and to charge it with responsibility for the civil war. In this view, EAM's (i.e., the KKE's) activities and achievements during the occupation period were seen as nothing more than camouflage for its real aim: gaining civil power. Each failed attempt to achieve this end had simply resulted in a new "round" of civil war. On the other hand, most leftist evaluations of EAM (unfortunately there are few non-Communist studies) ignore the second period, focusing instead on the "epic" of the resistance. These different outlooks, combined with ideological hostility and a desire for individual vindication on the part of the commentators, have resulted in a body of literature that rarely rises above the level of vilification or idealization and that is both sterile and dangerous.

105. British observers on the island of Lesbos commented on this, for instance, while also stressing the local EAM's preparedness to cooperate (PRO, FO 371/43674: R 225). The same was even more the case on several small islands.
106. Angeliki Laiou, "Andartes and symmachikes apostoles ston Germanokratoumeno Evro: I martyria tou Alekou Georgiadi" (Guerrillas and allied missions in German-occupied Evros: The testimony of Alekos Georgiadis), in *I Ellada, 1936–1944: Diktatoria—Katochi—Antistasi* (Greece, 1936–1944: Dictatorship—occupation—resistance), ed. H. Fleischer and Nikos Svoronos (Athens, 1989), 302ff.

History has shown that dogmatic disputes are hardly ever settled by sober discussion. It is therefore important to strip away the remaining axiomatic and Manichaean elements in the civil war "schism" and in its historiography. The reestablishment of democracy in 1974, as well as the long overdue legal recognition of all wartime resistance organizations— including EAM/ELAS, which was by far the largest and most effective— have corrected the scale of values and opened the way for a fair dialogue. In the summer of 1989, the Greek state took another step in this direction by abolishing all remaining decrees and laws still in force that had perpetuated the animosities, as well as the practical consequences, of the civil war for forty years after the end of the actual fighting. This initiative was made possible by a "historic compromise": the unprecedented parliamentary cooperation between the Communists (as the major component of the Left alliance) and the conservatives. Legislation by itself cannot end an era of hate and mistrust; it cannot guarantee that a fair dialogue will take place; it cannot prevent the development of a new revanchism or attempts by the holders of ideological "truths" (of whatever color) to monopolize the discussion. Yet, there is a well-founded hope for the gradual weakening of the prejudices that cloud the atmosphere, thanks to a more frank and honest approach, for which the terrain is now clear at least in theory.

4

Communist Perceptions, Strategy, and Tactics, 1945–1949

Ole L. Smith

The perceptions, strategy, and tactics of the Greek Communist Party (KKE) changed—sometimes almost imperceptibly, sometimes dramatically—during the course of the Greek civil war. This chapter illustrates those changes and explains the motives behind them.

Any historian of the KKE of this period faces difficulties that are well known and need only be alluded to here. The scarcity of contemporary sources; the post–civil war disputes within the party itself; the diverse and conflicting opinions of later historians, who had access to much less evidence than we have at our disposal today; and the secretive tendencies of those who hold important source material not yet released to scholars mean that the historian has to rely too much on guesswork and speculation. Accordingly, what is presented here should be viewed as no more than one possible interpretation of some of the more significant historical facts, as we can piece them together at this time.

Our information regarding certain parts of the period in question is far more complete than that for other parts, and a number of issues have been discussed so extensively that much of what we would like to know is now established. (In particular, for the time up to 1948, we are fortunate to have the highly illuminating series of articles by Philippos Iliou[1]). This fact explains the unevenness of the present analysis: because of the problem of sources, some issues are much easier to discuss than others. In addition, it must be said at the outset that much of what has been written about the KKE in this period is based on questionable information and simplistic views, often of a distinct cold war vintage. There are exceptions, of course, and this chapter owes much to the scholarly work of such historians as Matthias Esche and Philippos Iliou, who unfortunately are very seldom quoted in the literature on the subject—the former because he wrote in German,[2] the latter because his fine analysis goes too much against the conventional wisdom and, moreover, because his work appeared in a Greek newspaper, an unlikely source of serious scholarship.[3]

Because the period covered by Iliou did not extend beyond the autumn and early winter 1947, it is impossible to know whether his views on the civil war as a whole coincide with the interpretation presented here. Nevertheless, it should be plain that there are basic agreements so far as the period 1945–47 is concerned. I have argued elsewhere that the policy of the KKE until at least the Third Plenum of the Central Committee in September 1947 can be seen as an attempt to avert civil war.[4] Here I will extend my analysis along these lines in order to show a different appreciation of the basic problems. It is my hope that the views set out below may be radical enough to provoke discussion of certain theories that have been accepted simply because many commentators on the period harbor preconceived notions about the KKE.

1. "O emfilios polemos stin Ellada" (The civil war in Greece), *Avgi*, 2 December 1979–23 January 1980. Unfortunately, there are at present no indications that the series, which stops at the end of 1947, will be continued.

2. Matthias Esche, *Die kommunistische Partei Griechenlands, 1941–1949*, vol. 27 of *Studien zur modernen Geschichte* (Munich: R. Oldenbourg, 1982).

3. Other newspaper series of DSE (Democratic Army of Greece) and KKE (Communist Party of Greece) documents are not nearly as well researched and leave much to be desired. See, for example, *Eleftherotipia*, December 1978–January 1979, January–June 1986.

4. "Self-Defence and Communist Policy, 1945–1947," in *Studies in the History of the Greek Civil War, 1945–1949*, ed. Lars Baerentzen, John O. Iatrides, and Ole L. Smith (Copenhagen: Museum Tusculanum, 1987), 159–77.

From Varkiza to the Formation of the Democratic Army

Because I have discussed this earlier period in detail elsewhere, I will offer only a brief summary here. Throughout this period, the KKE tried to influence and develop its mass political base in order to promote a peaceful development in the country. The discussions at the Central Committee's Twelfth Plenum and the party's Seventh Congress in 1945 were dominated by attempts to formulate realistic and viable prospects for democratic development, for the reconstruction of Greek society and the Greek economy, and for a peaceful solution to the political conflicts inherited from the period of the Metaxas dictatorship and the war.[5] More specifically, the KKE's vision for postwar Greece can be found in the draft party program discussed at the congress. The KKE regarded cooperation within the EAM coalition as decisive for the establishment of a bourgeois-democratic society and declared that the party was ready to make compromises in order to preserve unity within EAM. The "people's democracy" envisaged by the KKE amounted to a radical democratization of Greek society, pointing toward a socialist transformation. The program emphasized that the right to private property would not be affected, that private initiative in the economic sector would not be regulated by considerations other than the public welfare, and that, within the framework of national economic planning, private investment would be encouraged. The program further promised simplified state institutions and a national legislature subject to direct popular control, as well as popular self-government and administration of justice. A new constitution would guarantee freedom of speech and other basic democratic liberties, religious freedom, and absolute freedom in scientific research and criticism. Further, the full equality of the sexes was to be recognized. Ethnic minorities were promised full equality and the right to self-determination.

In order to achieve these goals, economic reconstruction as a means to national independence and self-sufficiency was to be given high priority. Nikos Zahariadis' report to the Seventh Congress emphasized in particular the need to develop heavy industry based on national resources. The party's economic program also called for the cancellation of the foreign

5. The Twelfth Plenum and Seventh Congress documents are printed in volume 6 of *To KKE: Episima Keimena* (The KKE: Official texts) (Athens: Sinhroni Epohi, 1987). Hereafter cited as *E.K.6.*

debt and the abolition of foreign controls over the Greek economy. Foreign corporations were to be nationalized, together with big monopolies, and no preferential treatment was to be given to foreign companies. Banks and insurance companies, transportation, and key industries were also to be taken over by the state and, finally, a strong system of progressive taxation was to be introduced.

Internationally, Greece was to aim at cooperation with the Soviet Union and the neighboring people's democracies. As a Mediterranean country in need of foreign loans for reconstruction, Greece would also seek to maintain close cooperation and understanding with Britain, provided Greek independence was respected.

Although this program remained in draft form, never coming close to being ratified, it must be regarded as a fairly precise indication of what the KKE viewed as politically feasible and acceptable to the forces in the EAM coalition in 1945. In retrospect, one may doubt whether—given the extreme polarization—such a political program would have had much of a future at the time. Nevertheless, the moderate demands contained in the draft and the absence of explicit partisan Communist views suggest that the KKE was prepared to go very far in order to secure a broad consensus for immediate reforms, restore normal democratic life, and develop postwar Greece within familiar terms of reference. The KKE's strategic goal was to create a representative government with EAM's participation, a government that would be able to bridge the gulf created by the war and to safeguard gains toward a fully democratic Greece.[6] The KKE believed that this solution to the Greek crisis would sooner or later be adopted by the majority of the population as the only possible solution, and that one of the main obstacles, if not *the* main obstacle, to this outcome was the British military presence, which violated not only the independence of the Greek nation, but also the popular will.[7]

It can hardly be doubted that, in the KKE's view, Britain was willing to support all governmental combinations except one that included the participation of EAM. Accordingly, the Communists were convinced

---

6. See "Political Decision of the Seventh Congress," ibid., 80–81.

7. See the cautious wording of the Twelfth Plenum (ibid., 34) and the open stand at the Seventh Congress (ibid., 81). In his report to the Twelfth Plenum, Zahariadis was much more outspoken against the British (see Central Committee of the KKE, *Deka Chronia Agones, 1935–1945* [Ten years of struggle, 1935–1945] [1945], 279), and he was even more so in his first speech (293ff.), where he spoke of the "continuation of the Occupation."

that unless the British authorities could be persuaded to abandon their opposition to the Left, either through the impossibility of bringing about political stability without EAM, or through pressure from the KKE and abroad, a solution to the country's problems would not be possible until the British were compelled to remove their troops from Greece and withdraw their political and economic backing of the Right.[8] There is little evidence that at this stage either the United States or Soviet Russia was regarded as an active force on the Greek scene, or as a factor to be reckoned with at all, except for the remote possibility that they might exert pressure on the British government. The KKE was still uncertain about how much the United States was going to involve itself in postwar Europe and, until March 1946, it had no clear idea of Soviet views and intentions.[9] The Greek Communist Party was probably unaware of the way in which the Greek situation was used by Stalin to secure his influence in Eastern Europe.[10] It is possible that the KKE had doubts about Moscow's support, but this was never expressed openly. Significantly, direct contact with the Soviet government was not established until much later. In fact, one can make a good case for the view that direct communication on a permanent basis between the Greek Communists and Moscow was never established during the civil war period. This situation should be taken into account whenever it is argued that the KKE played a central role in Soviet diplomatic strategy: had that been the case, Moscow would have required much more control over the Greek party.

Until early 1946, the KKE confined its efforts to generating lawful parliamentary and political support among the population, although it is clear that the possibility of resorting to force was discussed at least unofficially and its prospects increased, beginning with the development of mass self-defense tactics, in the fall of 1945. But mass self-defense was not perceived as anything but a forceful defensive measure; it was not designed as an offensive weapon.

A change in policy can be seen in January-February 1946. Growing

8. The slogan "The British Must Go" was officially launched in the politburo decision of 6 September 1946 (E.K.6, 60–61).

9. It is often assumed that the Greek Communists acted in close collaboration with the Communist Party of the Soviet Union. That this was not the case is demonstrated by the fact that in January 1946 the CPSU told Partsalidis that the KKE should keep all options open, whereupon the KKE ignored the advice and decided not to take part in the national elections of March 1946.

10. There is a definite connection between Soviet reaction to the British presence in Greece and the establishment of Soviet control over postwar Romania. See Peter Stavrakis' chapter in this volume.

impatient with Britain's interference in Greek domestic politics and with its determination to keep the Left out of the nation's political life, and facing the violence of a white terror as well as the fear of a monarchist coup, the KKE looked for more effective means of putting pressure on the government. At this time, the KKE's plans centered around two possibilities: a long-term armed defense against the rightist terror, which could be intensified according to local conditions and political developments, and a short-term defense against a monarchist putsch. Even for KKE officials these two lines of possible action were difficult to distinguish from each other. As a result, subsequent efforts to determine the initial phases of the civil war have been blurred. However, existing information on these issues cannot be construed any other way.[11]

After the Second Plenum of the Central Committee in February 1946, things began to move faster. The KKE had now decided to employ self-defense tactics in a much more forceful way to press for political change.[12] In reaching this decision, the party was supported not only by the Yugoslavs but apparently also by the Soviet authorities, although it is not absolutely clear at which level. Persistent speculation about a meeting between Zahariadis and Stalin at the beginning of April 1946 cannot be dismissed. However, the important point is that Zahariadis saw Soviet representatives (if not Stalin himself) at the Czech Communist Party congress *after* the KKE had decided to pursue a more offensive line of action simultaneously with lawful activity. Still, the goal was not a military solution but a parliamentary one. The ultimate goal even at this time was free elections and a representative government.[13]

That the KKE did not wish to rush things can also be seen from the

11. For my analysis of KKE policy during 1946, see "The Problems of the Second Plenum of the Central Committee of the KKE, 1946," *Journal of the Hellenic Diaspora* 12 (1985), 43–62.

12. I assume this to be the contents of paragraph 4 in the decision of the Second Plenum. The famous ellipsis at paragraph 4 in the published text of the decision is reproduced in *E.K.6*, 178, with the explanation that it has not been possible to verify the reason for the omission and that the text therefore has been reprinted exactly as it appeared in *Rizospastis*, 17 February 1946. In his recent autobiography, Vasilis Bartziotas prints what he purports to be the text of paragraph 4 (*Exinta Chronia Kommounistis* [Sixty years a Communist] [Athens: Sihroni Epohi, 1986], 236). In fact, what he gives as the text is taken from Zahariadis' speech at the Sixth Plenum of October 1959 and cannot be regarded as an exact quotation of the omitted passage. Bartziotas also claims that he took this text from copies of the decision found in the KKE archives. One can only speculate about why he changed the account given previously in *O Agonas tou D.S.E.* (The struggle of the DSE) (Athens: Sihroni Epohi, 1981), which for many reasons is much more convincing. Bartziotas repeats his earlier version a few pages later (240).

13. For Zahariadis' contacts with foreign Communist leaders at this time, see Smith, "Problems of the Second Plenum," 56ff.

fact that although Zahariadis met Tito and other top leaders of the Yugoslav Communist Party (CPY) in March–April 1946 and enlisted their support, Markos was not sent to the mountains to organize military activity until September of that year. On the other hand, it must be stressed that as yet we have no precise information as to what agreements were reached between Zahariadis and the CPY leadership.[14] Nevertheless, what triggered developments were not initiatives of the KKE but the measures taken by the Greek government during the summer, including the emergency laws, as well as the escalation of rightist violence in the wake of the parliamentary elections of March 1946. Indeed, the KKE seems to have moved very cautiously, and there is evidence that opinion was divided as to how fast the party-sponsored armed groups should be built up. Although Zahariadis must have discussed the proposed strength of the armed groups with the Yugoslavs (since they were to supply weapons) and with Markos, the sources available to us are unclear on this point. Yiannis Ioannidis, who was in Belgrade as head of the KKE politburo group there and who was in much closer contact with the CPY, sought to keep mobilization limited, while Zahariadis initially gave Markos and other former ELAS officers considerably more ambitious orders.[15]

The documents released by the KKE (Interior) in 1979 and published by Iliou include several telegrams from this period between Ioannidis in Belgrade and Zahariadis in Athens, but the strength of the armed groups and the promised support from the CPY are never mentioned in concrete terms.[16] One can only speculate whether this gap is accidental, or

14. On the agreements with the Yugoslavs, we have only the enigmatic statements by Zahariadis at the Seventh Plenum in 1957 about the agreements with the Yugoslavs (Panos Dimitriou, ed., *Diaspasi tou KKE* [The breakup of the KKE], vol. 1 [Athens: Politika Provlimata, 1975]); see Ole L. Smith, "A Turning Point in the Greek Civil War, 1945–1949: The Meeting Between Zahariadis and Markos in July 1946," *Scandinavian Studies in Modern Greek* 3 (1978): 40. See also R. Kirjazovski, *Narodno Osloboditelniot Front i Drugite Organizacii na Makedoncite od Egejska Makedonija, 1945–1949* (Skopje: Kultura, 1985), 156ff.

15. See Smith, "A Turning Point in the Greek Civil War," 35ff.; and idem, "Problems of the Second Plenum," 59ff.

16. The report on the situation in Greece dated 12 September 1946, which was sent to the fraternal parties in the Soviet Union, Yugoslavia, and Bulgaria, states that the immediate goal is preparing an army of 15,000–20,000 men, for which the KKE requests assistance (*Avgi*, 6 December 1979). The wording does not suggest that such assistance had already been discussed and agreed upon. On 21 September 1946, Ioannidis telegraphed Zahariadis that Markos had been sent to his post and that the first steps had been taken. What these were is not stated (*Avgi*, 4 December 1979). According to Iliou, this goal of arming 20,000 in the immediate future was not implemented or discussed again.

whether the documents were selected in such a way that the role of the Yugoslavs would be obscured. Whatever the case, I do not believe that the selection was Iliou's responsibility. Similarly, one also looks for Soviet reactions in these documents, but very few can be found, although there must have been at least unofficial indications of Soviet views on the topics discussed. At present, it is impossible to say when and by whom these documents were purged, but one can hardly doubt that some pieces in the puzzle are missing. Moreover, based on the points where important information seems to be missing, one gets the impression that both Soviet and Yugoslav interests have been protected.[17]

At any rate, the Yugoslavs later tried to cultivate the impression that they had decided to support the KKE when Markos was sent to the mountains in October 1946 to establish the headquarters of the Democratic Army of Greece (DSE) and that their support was motivated by international solidarity.[18] I do not question that such motives were also involved, but the suggested timetable is not convincing. Perhaps the support was agreed upon much earlier but was not implemented before the KKE decided to establish DSE Headquarters. Or, alternatively, the Yugoslav aid took four months to materialize, with the result that the formation of a partisan army had by then become impossible.

On the other hand, political initiatives for a peaceful solution to the crisis were still undertaken by the Greek Communists. At this time, the KKE tried to create support for a neutral Greece, guaranteed by the Great Powers, as a way out of the impending civil war. For unknown reasons, this proposal did not find favor with the Soviet government and was tacitly dropped.[19] Furthermore, the plebiscite on the monarchy in November 1946 elicited parliamentary and political initiatives from the

---

17. The character of the collection is very mysterious, to say the least, perhaps because it was "stolen" from the KKE archives during the party's split in 1968. In his introductory statement (*Avgi*, 2 December 1979), Iliou writes that "with the split in 1968, the archives were also divided." It is therefore impossible to determine whether the gaps in question exist in the original ante-1968 KKE archives or only in the present KKE Interior archives. That the archives of the KKE Central Committee contain relevant material not seen by Iliou is evident from *E.K.*6.

18. See Elisabeth Barker, "The Yugoslavs and the Greek Civil War, 1946–1949," in *Studies in the History of the Greek Civil War*, 301–2, which is based on Yugoslav sources exclusively.

19. The published telegrams (*Avgi*, 2 December 1979) suggest that Zahariadis asked Dimitrov's opinion regarding neutrality for Greece in a message on 30 August 1946. On 10 November 1946, Ioannidis informed Zahariadis that Dimitrov agreed with the idea, but he also asked whether Zahariadis had received a reply from Moscow through other channels. Zahariadis responded on 20 November that Moscow's reaction was negative, and Ioannidis now asked Dimitrov whether he had knowledge of Moscow's views. We have no information about Zaha-

KKE that had no meaning if a military solution was envisaged as the only way out of the crisis. We do not know with any certainty whether in its actions the KKE was hampered by serious doubts about Soviet views. However, there is nothing to indicate that the mobilization of the Democratic Army was restricted or stopped until Georgi Dimitrov, the Bulgarian Communist leader, was in a position to tell the KKE leadership in December 1946 that the international situation and the approaching winter did not favor the escalation of the military conflict. Similarly, we do not know whether this message was to be regarded as a brake on the numerical development of the DSE.[20]

After 1945, it was also clear that the British were facing serious difficulties. The KKE leaders could not have failed to appreciate that the British were going to withdraw their forces from Greece in the near future. Troop reductions began in September 1946. The change of perspective in February 1947, which will be discussed below, may well have had something to do with such expectations on the part of the Greek Communists. There is nothing to show that the KKE was aware of London's attempts to get Washington to take over Britain's role in Greece. At the very least, the Greek Communists could not have envisaged in early 1947 that American involvement in the Greek crisis would take the form of the Truman Doctrine. Nor is there evidence that the KKE considered realistically the international repercussions of a British retreat under circumstances in which the more active defensive activity of the persecuted Left was widely interpreted as instigated by Greece's northern neighbors and, therefore, as a Soviet bid for a Mediterranean outlet and a takeover of the entire Balkans. If the KKE took account of such views, there appears to be no mention of them in party documents. Vague references to international complications are too unspecific to show whether the KKE leaders had, on their own, weighed the possible impact of foreign factors and of international balance-of-power considerations on the Greek con-

---

riadis' direct contact with Moscow at that time, although apparently Ioannidis assumed that Zahariadis could communicate with the CPSU independently of Dimitrov. It is clear that nothing came of Zahariadis' courageous initiative, although the Soviet position is not directly known, and neither is the Yugoslav position on this issue.

20. The text of Dimitrov's telegram is printed in *Avgi*, 2 December 1979. Dimitrov's reply expressly spoke for the Soviet government as well. Again, the Yugoslav position is not known. The KKE had given as its immediate goal a partisan army of 15,000–20,000, but nothing in Dimitrov's reply indicates whether this was thought to represent an excessive escalation of the armed conflict.

flict, or had such perspectives presented to them in a persuasive way. The KKE seems to have been remarkably blind to other possibilities beyond a short-lived local conflict or, at the most, a protracted struggle ending with EAM's entry into a Greek government.[21] Dimitrov's message may have delayed for a few months such developments as were planned by the Greek Communists in February 1947.

From the Formation of the DSE to the Third Plenum

In February 1947, there was a change in the outlook of the KKE, although we are as yet unable to say exactly what happened to cause a distinct shift in the dual strategy followed previously. Whatever the reasons, at a politburo meeting in February 1947, it was concluded that armed conflict was now to be regarded as the more likely outcome of the crisis and, accordingly, measures were taken to give priority to the preparation for a military solution. As already suggested, this decision may have been motivated by rumors about a British withdrawal from Greece, but we do not know for certain what prompted this step. The source for the politburo decision is a single reference in a later document.[22] However, there is clear and unmistakable evidence that initiatives were taken after February that can be viewed as resulting from a decision to step up military preparations, without at the same time abandoning the precarious legal standing of the KKE. In April 1947, a directive to this effect was sent to Markos, and there were meetings with Tito and Stalin in April and May.[23] We also know that Yugoslav assistance was increased at the same time, with explicit Soviet approval.[24] It becomes

21. Dimitrov's reply of November 1946 alludes to "the international situation," but Ioannidis' telegram to Zahariadis 10 November 1946 (*Avgi*, 2 December 1979) does not indicate what Dimitrov (or the Soviets) had in mind. It must be stressed that, even after March 1947, the KKE did not take much account of international repercussions of the conflict.

22. In a memorandum to Stalin dated 13 May 1947 (*Avgi*, 14 December 1979), Zahariadis wrote: "The Politburo of the Central Committee of the KKE, at its meeting in the middle of February 1947, after having examined the situation, concluded that while continuing to exploit in full all legal possibilities, the democratic movement should regard the armed struggle as becoming more important, and a series of practical measures were taken." There is nothing in Iliou's collection of documents about such a meeting and decision, and nothing can be found in the most recent volume of KKE official documents.

23. For the meeting with Tito, see Iliou in *Avgi*, 9 December 1979; on the meeting with Stalin in Moscow, see *Avgi*, 12 December 1979.

24. Barker, "Yugoslavs and the Greek Civil War," 303–4.

evident from available documents that KKE strategy now centered on establishing a liberated Greece in the northern provinces, and that the occupation of Thessaloniki, assisted by the local Communist organizations, was seriously contemplated—and all this must have been discussed by Zahariadis in his meetings with Tito and Stalin. From Belgrade, Ioannidis was able to promise substantial Yugoslav supplies to Markos, who was given orders to make arrangements along these lines.[25] Similarly, Vasilis Bartziotas in Thessaloniki was ordered to get armed self-defense groups ready for action.[26]

Unfortunately, we are unable to determine what was behind these developments because we do not have the necessary information about the KKE's inner deliberations during this period. The important point is that, so far as we can see, these decisions were made by the KKE *before* the talks with Stalin and Tito. Their reactions could not have been such as to make the KKE pause or change its plans. One hopes that the relevant politburo documents will become available some day; to judge from what we know already, the February 1947 decision may be much more important for our understanding of KKE policy than the much-debated resolution of the Second Plenum of February 1946.

Perhaps the main reason for the change in the Communists' tactics was a mistaken perception of the Truman administration's determination to risk a full-scale conflict over Greece and Turkey. The KKE and its allies, including the Soviet government, must have regarded the expected British withdrawal from Greece as an indication of Western disengagement, since no one could have foreseen the extremely hurried American decision to step in after March 1947.[27] It is perhaps understandable that the Greek Communists were under the fatal illusion that the way to power was now open to them. It is more difficult to explain how the Soviet government could have overlooked the growing U.S. interest in the eastern Mediterranean and the Middle East and underestimated the

25. See *Avgi*, 9 December 1979 (telegram from 2 April 1946); and Ioannidis' telegram to Markos on the Moscow talks, *Avgi*, 12 December 1979. On the other hand, in his memoirs, Gerasimos Maltezos claims that in January 1947 he prepared a DSE general staff plan along the same lines, acting on his own and unaware of the political line of the KKE (*Dimokratikos Stratos Elladas* [Democratic Army of Greece] [Athens: n.p., 1984], 85, 90).

26. See Smith, "Self-Defence and Communist Policy," 175. Sometime after the Third Plenum, Bartziotas was in fact ordered to support an attack on Thessaloniki itself; he refused, viewing the plan as unrealistic (*Exinta Chronia Kommounistis*, 267–68).

27. This depends on whether the KKE was aware of the change in British policy. On the decision-making in Washington, see Lawrence S. Wittner, *American Intervention in Greece, 1943–1949* (New York: Columbia University Press, 1982), 66ff.

Truman administration's dogged persistence in overcoming opposition in Congress to costly European ventures.[28] However, the facts as we have them seem to indicate that both the KKE and its allies found the time ripe for bolder action and did not think that great risks were involved. They may have believed that nothing short of a direct American military invasion could save Greece from a DSE victory, and that economic assistance to the Athens regime would be insufficient—economic assistance to Greece had thus far been singularly ineffective—but also that such help would not be felt until it was too late to make a difference. As we shall see, there are certain indications that the Greek Communists took the Truman Doctrine more seriously into account a few months later. By then, however, the KKE had made its final moves and was faced with a growing inability to implement its grandiose goals.

Whatever the reasons for the change of policy, the sequence of ensuing events is reasonably clear and significant. On 6 April, after months of hesitation and pressure from Ioannidis in Belgrade (who, it must be assumed, acted in line with Yugoslav and Soviet fears for Zahariadis' personal safety in Athens), the Secretary General of the KKE arrived in Belgrade incognito.[29] The Greek authorities seem not to have been aware that Zahariadis had left the country.[30] On 17 April, Zahariadis and Ioannidis sent a long telegram to Markos, stating in detail the new strategy and tactics of the KKE and the DSE and promising to secure the necessary material aid. It was pointed out to Markos that the primary object now was the liberation of a large territory in the north and the development of the DSE into a regular army.[31] On 21 April, Zahariadis had a meeting with Tito, and on the following day sent him an extensive memo

28. If nothing else, the handling of the 1946 Iranian crisis showed U.S. concern over developments in the Middle East.

29. A telegram to the CPY, signed by Mikhail Sergeiev, a Soviet representative in Belgrade, and dated 4 October 1946, states that Zahariadis should leave Greece (*Avgi*, 8 December 1979). For a variety of reasons, Zahariadis did not leave the country until much later (see Iliou in *Avgi*, 8 December 1979). A recently published Zahariadis letter (dated 18 September 1947) to the politburo group in Athens suggests that the presence of Zahariadis in Athens was intimately connected with the policy priorities of the KKE. So long as he remained there, the party's legal activity was considered the most important. In his letter, Zahariadis expressly refers to the doubts and hesitations experienced in March 1947 (*E.K.6*, 444).

30. In order to explain his absence from Greece, *Rizospastis* falsely reported that Zahariadis was taking part in the French Communist Party's congress in Strasbourg. His presence in Belgrade was known only to a very small group (*Avgi*, 9 December 1979).

31. The directive to Markos is reprinted in *Avgi*, 11 December 1979. It should be noted that transforming the DSE into a regular army was the idea of the DSE's headquarters staff (see note 25), rather than the brainchild of Zahariadis.

on the Greek situation, the positions of the KKE, and the outline of plans for a Free Greece with Thessaloniki at its center. In this connection, Zahariadis mentioned as an immediate goal the increase of the DSE's numerical strength to 50,000 men within a short time.[32] Although we have no evidence of the Yugoslav reaction, the tenor of Zahariadis' memo suggests that Tito could not have had substantial objections—which is important, considering that the planned increase depended almost exclusively on the willingness of the Yugoslavs to supply the necessary weapons. Zahariadis must have been convinced that Tito was able to help the KKE along the lines suggested and that the CPY agreed with the proposed plans. Otherwise, Zahariadis' memo makes no sense. The KKE leader also asked Tito to help him travel to Moscow in order to discuss matters with the Soviet authorities.[33] In May 1947 we find Zahariadis in Moscow, where he asked for meetings with Soviet officials—a topic not covered by the available documents, but we have the report Zahariadis gave to the leadership of the Communist Party of the Soviet Union (CPSU), in which he analyzed developments in Greece since the Varkiza Agreement of February 1945.[34] It is from this document that we know about the KKE's February 1947 decision to regard the armed struggle as its most important activity. In his report, Zahariadis also set forth plans for the creation of a regular army of 50,000 men, but for some unknown reason he did not mention the ulterior goal of establishing a liberated territory. Zahariadis wrote that the reconstructed and strengthened DSE would be able to deliver decisive blows against the enemy and achieve the broader goals of the democratic movement. What these were is not mentioned in the report, but it is inconceivable that they were not discussed in detail at Zahariadis' meetings with Soviet officials.

Thus, there cannot be any doubt that Stalin and Tito allowed Zahariadis to go ahead with his plans with promises of increased assistance. The reports to the Yugoslavs and to Stalin are emphatic on the point that the DSE could not develop the necessary strength without substantial supplies of aid from outside sources. And as the next KKE initiatives demonstrate, Zahariadis had no reason to doubt that the aid would be forthcoming. Unfortunately, however, he had no control over the timetable.

It is useful at this point to consider briefly the situation in which the

---

32. *Avgi*, 9 December 1979.
33. See Iliou in *Avgi*, 12 December 1979.
34. Reprinted in *Avgi*, 12–14 December 1979. This document deserves to be studied in greater detail than is possible here.

KKE found itself. For a long time it has been argued that Zahariadis, in close collaboration with a small group of "henchmen" in the party leadership, secretly pursued his own course and that from the moment of his return to Greece in May 1945 he had been dedicated to the idea of a "model revolution." This is generally the accepted interpretation in many studies, including Esche's book on the KKE.[35] However, until the Third Plenum in September 1947, there is no indication in the available documents that Zahariadis' plans met with any serious opposition. Although it is true that he was apparently unwilling to let George Siantos, the former Secretary of the Central Committee and wartime leader of the KKE, remain in Athens while he himself traveled outside Greece, we do not know the reason; moreover, Siantos was fully aware of the military preparations under way.[36] So far as we can see, during the second half of 1946 the problem for the KKE was not divided counsels in the leadership, as had been the case earlier. Rather, it was the difficulties inherent in seeking to maintain a delicate balance between organizing a partisan force in the mountains and simultaneously carrying on legal political work in the urban centers at a time when the extreme Right was doing everything possible to force party members and sympathizers to resort to desperate counterattacks.[37] This dual strategy was extremely difficult to present and make intelligible to KKE members, who needed guidance if the party machinery was to function properly. Under the circumstances, the party objectives could not be stated in categorical terms. A communications gulf was thus created between the party in Athens and in the provinces, and matters did not improve as decisions increasingly came to be made in Belgrade, where Zahariadis and Ioannidis lost direct contact with Athens. The two were very soon unable to appreciate how conditions in Greece were changing or to understand the difficulties faced by the party's legal movement, which was exposed to police repression and subject to parliamentary illusions through its associates in EAM and among the Socialists, whose cooperation the KKE continued to value greatly.[38]

35. Esche, *Die kommunistische Partei Griechenlands,* 214ff., especially 221ff.

36. This has been overlooked by Esche (see ibid., p. 244, n. 8; Smith, "Problems of the Second Plenum," p. 50, n. 31). On Zahariadis' distrust of Siantos, see Iliou in *Avgi,* 15 December 1979.

37. The so-called split between Communist leaders in the mountains and the cities has often been misconstrued. See Smith, "Self-Defence and Communist Policy," 173ff.

38. On the relations between the KKE and the various socialist parties and groups, see Hagen Fleischer, "The 'Third Factor': The Struggle for an Independent Socialist Policy During the Greek Civil War," in *Studies in the History of the Greek Civil War,* 189ff. The rumors about

We now come to the final phase before the eruption of open civil war. In June 1947, the KKE made its last official proposal for compromise and a political solution. At the French Communist Party congress in Strasbourg, Miltiades Porphyroyenis declared openly that if the Greek government persisted in its negative attitude toward the Left, the democratic forces would have no choice but to create a Free Greece. The KKE, he said, was still willing to negotiate a settlement under certain conditions. The terms offered by the KKE included free democratic elections as the absolute minimum; it would now be up to the government to decide whether it wanted a peaceful settlement based on compromise. If not, the democratic forces had already created the preconditions necessary for the establishment of a separate Free Greece with its own government and state institutions.[39] The Athens government reacted with mass arrests between 8 and 9 July, a development that the KKE regarded as the end of the political process. From this point on, a peaceful settlement and national reconciliation were seen as possible through military strength only. The door to negotiations had been slammed shut.[40]

It is interesting to observe how much the American authorities in Athens misjudged the situation. From Lawrence Wittner's careful analysis, it appears that even well-informed embassy officials believed the KKE was split between top cadres lobbying for government posts (this was the Americans' interpretation of the demand for a representative government) and lower-ranking members fighting in the mountains. Porphyroyenis' Strasbourg appeal was also seen as an indication of division within the party, since attempts to achieve compromise appeared to be made simultaneously with the waging of partisan war.[41] However, the Greek Liberals were not mistaken in their assessment. At this late hour—although probably nobody in Athens understood how late it was—The-

Tsirimokos leading a "mountain government" are well founded (see ibid., 204–5). See also Anastasiadis' report on the reactions to the KKE's Strasbourg declaration (Avgi, 22 December 1979).

39. Key passages of Porphyroyenis' speech are in E.K.6, 440–43, especially 442–43. He apparently had contacts with the CPSU after leaving Athens for Strasbourg. A telegram from Zahariadis to Baranov in Moscow reports: "Porfyrogenis is now here [in Belgrade] with a visa and will come to you next week" (Avgi, 15 December 1979). It follows that the KKE's announcement at the Strasbourg congress of a "Free Greece" had been planned several weeks in advance.

40. For KKE reactions to the arrests, see the telegrams from Anastasiadis in Athens to Ioannidis (Avgi, 23 December 1979).

41. Wittner, American Intervention in Greece, 107ff.

mistocles Sophoulis appeared to take an initiative that might have averted catastrophe if his efforts had not been cut short by the king, with support by the United States, and by the government's program of mass arrests, which removed from the scene the chief KKE spokesman, Mitsos Partsalidis.[42]

Prompted by Mihalis Kyrkos, who was well aware of the KKE's views, Sophoulis had a meeting with Prime Minister Dimitrios Maximos and later with King Paul. According to U.S. Ambassador Lincoln MacVeagh, the king reacted by calling Sophoulis a "second Kerensky," while according to Kyrkos (who saw Sophoulis immediately after the meeting with the king), the latter expressed the view that it was too late: the American authorities would never accept a compromise that they would regard as a defeat for themselves. Whatever the truth behind these conflicting accounts, they suggest that there was still reason to hope. The political reaction in Athens to the Strasbourg declaration makes it clear that there was still room for maneuver. However, after the arrests of Communists all hope was gone. Thus, the KKE leaders and their associates may well have decided that they had no other options and had reached the end of the road.[43]

A week later, on 17 July, Petros Roussos wrote a long exposé for the Soviet government in which he described the situation as seen by the KKE. In his analysis, he stated categorically that through the mass arrests monarcho-fascism had closed the door to further negotiations and that the popular movement had no other choice but to resort to armed struggle. He regarded the initiatives taken by the forces of the political Center as window dressing, if not deliberate fraud. The Athens government, having signed the treaty of 20 June for the implementation of the Truman Doctrine, was now wholly dependent on the United States; this agreement made Greece a spearhead of American imperialism against the Soviet Union. Roussos's characterization of the Sophoulis and Kyrkos initiatives is plain and leaves little doubt as to what the KKE

42. As Iliou observes (*Avgi*, 23 December 1979), the arrest of Partsalidis was considered a heavy loss to the party, and preparations for his escape from imprisonment at Ikaria were begun immediately.

43. Wittner, *American Intervention in Greece*, 108; *Avgi*, 22 January 1980. See also *Avgi*, 22 and 23 December 1979. Telegrams from Anastasiadis and Partsalidis (8 July 1947) suggest that EAM had contacts with Sophoulis, Tsouderos, and the Socialist leader Stratis Someritis—which came to nothing, however, because of the arrests of Communist leaders. See also Fleischer, "The 'Third Factor,'" 202ff.

thought of them. Nevertheless, one can only speculate as to what might have happened if the mass arrests had not broken off contacts between the country's political factions.[44]

Roussos devoted a large section of his memorandum to a description of the military situation, stressing the need for material support. The DSE lacked food and weapons; it also needed more experienced cadres. Still, the overall tenor of his message was optimistic, and nothing suggests that Roussos was expecting anything from the Soviet authorities but wholehearted agreement with the proposed tactics and strategy of the DSE.

In early August, in a secret directive from Ioannidis, Markos was instructed to speed up the process of building up the DSE. The KKE leadership, which no longer regarded the permanent control of specific territory as an absolute requirement for the achievement of the party's objectives, now believed that the time had come to go ahead with the creation of a Free Greece. Furthermore, Markos was told that equipment for a 100 percent increase in the DSE's manpower was now at his disposal; the only problem was how to distribute the supplies.[45] It is a pity that we do not know what changes in the situation were reflected in these views of the KKE leaders or the exact nature of the distribution problems. In a letter to Tito a few days later, Ioannidis appears to suggest that the distribution problem was how to get the supplies to Thessaloniki and central Greece; on the other hand, Ioannidis' phrase "You cannot take it over" suggests that the question was how to get the materiel into Greece in the first place.[46] In any case, the conditions for an open bid for power were now fulfilled. The stage was set for the official presentation and adoption of the new strategy at the Third Plenum of the Central Committee of the KKE.

From the Third Plenum to Defeat

There had been no meeting of the KKE Central Committee for eighteen months. It was therefore necessary, in view of the important changes in

44. *Avgi,* 16 and 18 December 1979.
45. Telegrams of 5 and 7 August 1947 to Markos, in *Avgi,* 25 December 1979.
46. Letter of 12 August 1947 and telegram of 7 August 1947, in *Avgi,* 25 December 1979.

policy during the summer of 1947, to call a plenum of the committee, even if it would not be possible to convene it in the prescribed fashion: some members were in Athens and in other cities, while others were in the mountains or in Belgrade.[47] Although the Third Plenum has been characterized as a coup by Zahariadis,[48] there are no indications that this was the case. Its irregular composition (only six members were present) was not the result of a deliberate attempt by Zahariadis to impose his views on a small minority; the idiosyncratic nature of this meeting was entirely due to circumstances beyond anyone's control. Moreover, there was still no open opposition to the leadership in Belgrade. On the other hand, there were certain divergences between Belgrade and Athens in the appreciation of the political situation prevailing in Greece.[49] Although these differences were noticed by the leadership in Belgrade before the meeting, nothing in the available record suggests that Zahariadis called the plenum in order to get the new policy adopted without having

47. Nikos Zahariadis, Leonidas Stringos, Petros Roussos, Yiannis Ioannidis, Giorgis Erythriadis, and Markos (who had come to Yugoslavia for the purpose) were in Belgrade. Stergios Anastasiadis, Dimitris Vlandas, Chrysa Hadzivasiliou, Panayiotis Mavromatis, Giorgis Blanas, Sotiris Soukaras, and Costas Karayiorgis took part in the Athens section of the Third Plenum. Of the remaining members, Vasilis Bartziotas was in Thessaloniki; Costas Koliyiannis, Zisis Zographos, Mihalis Tsantis, Giorgis Gousias, Mitsos Vatousianos, and Miltiades Porphyroyenis were in the mountains and did not take part in the deliberations. Dimitris Partsalidis, Nikos Ambatzis, Panos Dimitriou, Mitsos Paparigas, and Theodoros Makridis had been arrested, while George Siantos, Nikos Zagourtzis, and Yiannis Zevgos were dead. Vasilis Markezinis and Nikos Ploumbidis were in Athens but did not take part in the meeting. I have not been able to verify the whereabouts at the time of the remaining members of the Central Committee.

48. Most recently by Esche, *Die kommunistische Partei Griechenlands*, 284. Although Esche appears to have had access to archival material, his account of the Third Plenum is incorrect on several points. The meeting took place in Yugoslavia, presumably in Belgrade, not in the Greek mountains, and Koliyiannis and Porphyroyenis were not present; see the documents printed in *Avgi*, 1 and 9 January 1980 (proceedings and telegram of 15 September 1947), and the telegram of 15 August 1947 (*Avgi*, 29 December 1979) from Ioannidis to Markos in which Markos is asked to come to a meeting not later than the end of August. It appears that Markos had been informed of this before 15 August 1947. On 27 August 1947, Ioannidis told Anastasiadis that the participants had gathered "here" (presumably Belgrade) (*Avgi*, 28 December 1979). Remarkably, the account in *E.K.6* (p. 245) also reports that the Third Plenum took place in the mountains (*sto vouno*). In fact, the Third Plenum took place on 11–12 September 1947, not 12–15 September, although the official announcement reprinted in *E.K.6* is dated 15 September 1947.

49. For the situation in Athens, see the report of 23 June 1947 in *Avgi*, 28 December 1979. For the agreement within the KKE leadership at the time, see Iliou in *Avgi*, 3 January 1980. As he correctly observes, the only difference between the group in Belgrade and the group in Athens concerned the members of the KKE who had been exiled.

to contend with protests from committee members in Athens. The documents produced by the meeting were to be sent to Athens to be discussed there.[50]

In Athens, however, even after the mass arrests in July, the politburo group led by Stergios Anastasiadis and Chrysa Hadzivasiliou continued to regard legal political work as the most important aspect of party activity. A resolution along these lines printed in *Rizospastis* at the end of July elicited severe criticism from Ioannidis in Belgrade, who understandably found that the statement offered no practical guidance to party members. Instead, the resolution spoke vaguely of "defense" and "victory for the popular unity and reconciliation," as if the Strasbourg declaration had never been issued. Ioannidis demanded to know who was responsible for this gaffe, and although the reply from Athens is not known, the resolution was probably written by Hadzivasiliou. Such lack of understanding between party leaders in Athens and in Belgrade was going to become even more of a problem after the Third Plenum.[51]

The Third Plenum and the formal resolution it produced signified the end of legality for the party. Although the KKE was not formally outlawed until December because of fears of international reaction, its press was closed down because of *Rizospastis*' publication of what amounted to a call to arms. In a secret decision, the plenum and the military conference, which was held at the same meeting, adopted the plans already prepared for a speedy increase in the DSE's strength and for the formation of a Free Greece. In his report to the plenum, Markos specified that the planned increase was to be from 25,000 to 50,000 men, a realistic goal at that time and a necessary precondition for the implementation of the larger strategic objectives. This increase was to be completed in the spring of 1948. In addition, the DSE was to be reconstructed along the lines of a conventional army.[52] It is not useful here to deal with the

50. Ioannidis telegram, 27 August 1947 (*Avgi*, 28 December 1979).
51. Text in *E.K.6*, 242–44. Ioannidis' criticism is in a telegram dated 8 August 1947 (*Avgi*, 28 December 1979).
52. The Third Plenum documents available to date are (a) the official resolution, printed in *Rizospastis*, 8 October 1947 (*E.K.6*, 245–47); (b) the text of the political decision released to party members only and now known from a Russian translation (retranslated in *Avgi*, 6 January 1980); (c) the summary proceedings, also known only from a Russian translation (retranslated in *Avgi*, 1 January 1980); and (d) the plan for Operation Limnes, adopted by the plenum (*Avgi*, 6 January 1980). The editors of *E.K.6* note that the text of the political decision has not been located (p. 245). The retranslation from the Russian text in *Avgi* is not precise, as a comparison of passages from the original Greek text in the 1948 decision about Markos shows (*E.K.6*,

controversy over whether Markos did in fact, as he was later accused of doing, "deceive" the Central Committee by presenting inflated figures of the DSE forces. The available documents give no clear answer, while the number 24,000 is mentioned in several places as the DSE strength at that time. What Markos may have said during these discussions is not known.[53] The decisions made represented the official adoption of deliberations and planning since February and, as throughout this period the party leadership had no reason to doubt that its allies were willing and able to support the DSE to the extent required, the plenum's decisions did not appear as unrealistic as they would to later observers and critics.[54]

In September 1947, the perceptions, tactics, and strategy of the KKE leadership were based largely on realistic considerations. The problems did not appear insoluble, but in retrospect, after reading the party's decisions and detailed military plans, one can only conclude that U.S. involvement in Greece, as well as the problems of recruitment for the DSE, was either overlooked or at least treated superficially. In fact, the only reference to the American factor at this time is in a letter to Andrei Zhdanov, Stalin's close collaborator, written ten days before the plenum, in which Zahariadis asserts that the democratic movement in Greece would oppose any further U.S. interference no matter what form it took.[55] Obviously, Zahariadis and the other KKE leaders had not yet understood that the American involvement in Greece was to be different from the lukewarm British effort. What is not clear is whether the Soviet government was operating under a similar illusion.

To judge from the available documents, the most serious problem re-

---

309, 320). For Markos's report to the Third Plenum, see the summary proceedings printed in *Avgi.*

53. The politburo decision of 15 November 1948 gives no numbers but states that Markos "misled the Third Plenum because he presented nonexistent figures." In *O Agonas tou D.S.E.,* Vasilis Bartziotas writes that Markos gave 35,000 as the actual strength of the DSE, although in fact it was only 18,000 (p. 40). He also refers to an episode during the 2 December 1947 conference in which these numbers were conceded by Markos (p. 41). Besides being mentioned in Markos's report, the number 22,000–24,000 also appears as the Democratic Army's strength in the plan for Operation Limnes.

54. In his introduction to Zahariadis' letter to Zhdanov (*Avgi,* 30 December 1979), Iliou points out that Zahariadis' optimistic remarks must have been based on previous talks with allies of the KKE. Since 1956, most KKE officials and historians have regarded the Third Plenum decisions as having been out of touch with reality. See, for example, Bartziotas, *O Agonas tou D.S.E.,* 41 (echoing Markos's platform [*E.K.*6, 485]).

55. *Avgi,* 30 December 1979.

flected in the Third Plenum decisions was the state of affairs in the party organizations. It was this point that had brought into the open the differences in perceptions between Athens and Belgrade. The sharp criticism from Belgrade contained in the published document[56] produced a rebuttal from Athens that showed a fundamental and disastrous lack of communication between the two sections of the politburo. The Athens section rejected criticism of those who "preferred to go into jail instead of going to the mountains."[57] As Anastasiadis explained, "We did not tell these people what they should do."[58] It is hard to believe that the leaders in Belgrade would criticize as having deserted the struggle party followers who had been sent to jail instead of joining the DSE, considering that the KKE still, as it had certainly done earlier, advised former ELAS officers to remain legal instead of joining the partisans. Precisely when party organizations changed policy on this question we cannot say. If a change had not in fact occurred, the statements in the Third Plenum resolution would be grossly insulting and unacceptable. The only reasonable conclusion is that the party leaders in Belgrade thought that the choice of going to the mountains had been presented to party members and sympathizers, while the Athens group believed that Communists had still not been clearly told what to do, and that they certainly were not being encouraged to join the DSE.[59]

In later years, the decisions of the Third Plenum became the focus of extended and bitter discussions within the KKE. The most serious of these party debates will be discussed further below. Here it is important to stress that the available documents from the Third Plenum and from the period immediately prior to the meeting reveal no dissension concerning the major features of strategic and tactical planning. Immediately following the Third Plenum, however, we find the first indications that something is wrong, although the paucity of sources does not permit us to discover the truth behind the recriminations. On 12 August, before

56. In its published resolution, the politburo criticized the "doubts and hesitation shown by isolated Communists" and emphasized that the "work of the Communists in the cities . . . lagged behind" (*E.K.6*, 246).

57. In the secret decision, a lengthy paragraph 3 criticized the "pathetic" reaction of KKE members to government repression.

58. Letter to Ioannidis [?], 13 October 1947, in *Avgi*, 10 January 1980.

59. Much probably depended on the local party leaders. Bartziotas writes that in June 1946 he ordered officers to go to the mountains to avoid arrest (*Exinta Chronia Kommounistis*, 246). The opposite happened in Athens, where top officers, such as Stephanos Saraphis and Theodoros Makridis, were arrested and exiled.

the plenum, Zahariadis, in a letter to Tito, asked for a meeting between Tito, Markos, and himself.[60] But the published KKE documents make no mention of such a meeting, nor does a letter to the CPY Central Committee, sent after the Third Plenum, refer to or ask for a meeting.[61] From statements made much later by Markos, we know that there was in fact a meeting among the three after the Third Plenum and that, for unexplained reasons, Markos kept it a secret until 1983 that he had been present.[62] At this meeting, Tito is reported to have emphasized that the DSE should operate as a lightly armed partisan force, which was the exact opposite not only of what had been decided at the plenum but also of what had been presented several times in discussions with the CPY during 1947. Markos claims that after the meeting he asked Zahariadis what had become of the Yugoslav promises to support an army of 50,000 and suggests that Zahariadis had deceived the KKE Central Committee on this issue.[63] Because Markos was regarded as responsible for the unrealistic decisions at the Third Plenum, it is obvious that in his 1983 account he is trying to put the blame back on Zahariadis. Since we have no reliable information about the meeting in question, and do not even know whether it ever took place, we cannot go further. The fact remains, however, that Zahariadis requested a meeting, and in the letter to the CPY Central Committee the appeals for aid are repeated in such a way that it is hard to see how Ioannidis and Zahariadis could have truthfully claimed a few weeks earlier that the necessary quantities of aid had already been secured.[64]

In the same letter to the Yugoslavs, Zahariadis mentioned two other problems facing the KKE. First, he openly admitted that a serious intraparty controversy existed between the semilegal party organizations in Athens and the leadership in the mountains. He criticized the Athens-based Communists for harboring parliamentary illusions and for not having understood the new strategy involving the use of force: in short, they had underestimated the role of the armed struggle and continued to

60. *Avgi*, 26 December 1979.

61. *Avgi*, 11 January 1980.

62. See Markos's interview in *Avgi*, 29 March 1983, in which he refers to a meeting with Tito and Zahariadis immediately after the Third Plenum. In 1978, he denied ever having met Tito (D. Gousidis, *Markos Vaphiadis: Martiries* [Markos Vaphiadis: Testimony] [Athens: Epikairotita, 1983], 20).

63. *Avgi*, 29 March 1983.

64. One must agree with Iliou that "the needs were still gigantic" (*Avgi*, 11 January 1980).

think that the party's political efforts had top priority. As a result, Zahariadis admitted that the KKE was endeavoring to keep both options open, and he was well aware of the difficulties resulting from this ambiguity. Nevertheless, he blamed the legally functioning party organizations in a manner suggesting that he considered them to be a major obstacle to the further development of the long-term objectives of the KKE.[65]

The second problem Zahariadis mentioned was the lack of open international solidarity with the DSE. He asked whether it would be possible to have it officially emphasized that European democratic opinion recognized the existence of a Greece other than the Athens regime. Clearly, the KKE believed that European Communists could do more on this score and found their silence inexplicable. This problem was to become more acute after the formation of the provisional government in late December 1947. Probably the reason it was raised by Zahariadis in his letter to the Yugoslavs is that the KKE had begun to feel the impact of the American support to the Greek government and needed to counterbalance the propaganda that the Truman administration was helping Greece "preserve its freedom and independence."

It is difficult to gauge the effect of the news about the establishment of the Cominform, which reached the KKE at the beginning of October 1947.[66] The Greek Communist leadership had not been informed about the important organizational meeting in Poland. In a letter to the CPSU dated 6 October, Zahariadis asked whether it would be possible for the KKE to join the Cominform. The Soviet reply is not known.[67] The way, however, in which the request was expressed suggests that the KKE did not know what the Cominform was intended to be, and must have re-

65. *Avgi*, 11 January 1980. It is not clear on what evidence Zahariadis based his view of the situation in Athens, unless it was on Anastasiadis' [?] report of June 1947 (*Avgi*, 28 December 1979). When Zahariadis wrote to Tito, the Third Plenum in Athens had not yet taken place (it met on 27 September 1947), and the few available telegrams to and from Athens shed no light on this matter. On 15 September 1947, Ioannidis gave the number of cadres to be sent to the Democratic Army, and on 19 September he ordered Vlandas, among others, to report for duty immediately (*Avgi*, 9 January 1980), possibly suggesting some impatience with the party leadership in Athens. In a letter to the politburo in Athens dated 18 September 1947, Zahariadis apparently emphasized that he himself, as everyone else, had to go to the DSE (*E.K.6*, 444). Writing in *Avgi* (9 January 1980), Iliou surmises the existence of such a letter, which had not been located at the time.

66. The first reaction was Ioannidis' request to Anastasiadis that the news about the Cominform be given broad publicity (telegram, 5 October 1947, in *Avgi*, 9 January 1980).

67. *Avgi*, 12 January 1980.

garded it as a parallel organization to the defunct Comintern. That the KKE was not invited, while the other two Western parties of significance—the French and the Italian—were, shows that the Soviet Union was not prepared to give the KKE the kind of official support that Zahariadis had asked not only of Tito but also of Zhdanov.[68] In this connection, it is important to point out that Andrei Zhdanov was the main Soviet representative at the October meeting and that, according to Italian and Yugoslav sources, apparently the Soviet government did not wish the Cominform to deal with the Greek question. Although the KKE was unaware of this, its leadership must have been greatly disappointed that it had not been invited to the meeting or even told about what was to happen there. Further reactions to the KKE's exclusion from the Cominform are not known, and thus we cannot say whether the affair had any impact on KKE perceptions of the developing situation. One can speculate, however, that it did not, for the campaign to have the provisional government recognized suggests that the KKE was laboring under illusions as to the risks its allies were prepared to take in order to give official expression of their solidarity with their Greek comrades.

The final go-ahead for the formation of a free Greek state, with its own government and institutions, which had been in preparation for some time, was given at a KKE politburo meeting on 2 December 1947.[69] Three weeks later, on 24 December, Radio Free Greece officially announced the news, which met with very mixed reactions. In the meantime, there had been hectic activity in Athens, where Anastasiadis had tried to recruit representatives of EAM and SK-ELD to join the new government in the mountains. The telegrams exchanged between the Democratic Army's headquarters and party officials in Athens suggest that at least two high-ranking cadres of SK-ELD were willing to do so, and the

68. Letter to Zhdanov (*Avgi*, 30 December 1979). According to Zhdanov's report at the Cominform meeting, Greece lay within the area dominated by the United States, while the armed struggle in China and Greece was barely mentioned in passing. For a criticism of Stalin's conceptions of the Cominform, see F. Claudin, *The Communist Movement* (Harmondsworth: Penguin, 1975), 46ff.; and Paolo Spriano, *I communisti europei e Stalin* (Turin: Einaudi, 1983), 280ff.

69. This was the first meeting of DSE Headquarters in which Zahariadis took part. For the decisions of the meeting, see *E.K.6*, 249–51; for the politburo decision about Markos, see ibid., 310–11. According to Bartziotas (*Exinta Chronia Kommounistis*, 278), Markos was heavily criticized for having given inflated figures of DSE strength at the Third Plenum (see note 53 above). On the meeting, see also Iliou in *Avgi*, 15 January 1980; and on the detailed plans for mobilization decided on 7 December 1947, see *Avgi*, 17 January 1980. See also the politburo letter of 9 December 1947 (*E.K.6*, 252–54).

name of the highly respected intellectual, Rosa Imvrioti, is also mentioned. Although Anastasiadis made it clear that it would be very difficult to get them out of Athens, this could hardly be the only reason that in the end they did not join the "antigovernment." The two members of the Socialist Party are mentioned only by their pseudonyms, and one can only speculate about their identities.[70] Thus, the government whose formation was officially announced on Christmas Eve, and was headed by Markos, was composed exclusively of KKE members and well-known party sympathizers. One may conclude that by this move the KKE had isolated itself from the forces that still had influence within the traditional Center. As has been persuasively argued, from this point on, SK-ELD drifted toward a vocal anticommunism.[71] We cannot say with any certainty whether there had been prior soundings in the Eastern European capitals as to the chances for securing official recognition of the Provisional Democratic Government (PDG). However, it is highly likely that such soundings did in fact take place. It is reasonable to assume that the KKE had more reliable information concerning the stand of its allies than the mere fact that previous declarations of its intention to set up a government in the mountains had met with no opposition from the Communist authorities abroad. In any event, in the absence of information on this issue, writers have been free to speculate about blackmail tactics by Zahariadis. Moreover, it is probably not accidental that nothing relevant can be found in the documents published by Iliou. The Yugoslavs at least must have made their views known in writing, since both Zahariadis and Ioannidis were by then back in Greece.[72]

As is well known, no foreign government recognized the PDG, and for

70. For an excellent analysis of the Socialists' reaction, see Fleischer, "The 'Third Factor,'" 209–10. For international repercussions, see Wittner, *American Intervention in Greece,* 260–61. Anastasiadis' telegram of 19 December 1947 was published in *Avgi,* 19 January 1980. Iliou does not speculate about the identity of the person from among ELD's leadership called Agathon, but he suggests Tsirimokos as a possible candidate in the case of the pseudonym Hitros. According to Fleischer, Tsirimokos at one point considered the post of Prime Minister in an antigovernment coalition (see note 38 above), and Stavros Kanellopoulos favored aligning SK-ELD with the KKE.

71. Fleischer, "The 'Third Factor,'" 211.

72. On British and American perceptions of Yugoslav attitudes toward a Markos government, see Elisabeth Barker, "Yugoslav Policy Towards Greece 1947–1949," in *Studies in the History of the Greek Civil War,* 268ff. It is significant that, in May 1947, Yugoslav Vice Foreign Minister Aleš Bebler answered with a definite negative when asked by the British ambassador in Belgrade, Charles Peake, whether the Yugoslav government was prepared to recognize "some supposed authority" in Greece other than the present Greek government (ibid., 269).

anyone tempted to do so the American warning against such action carried great weight. Nevertheless, for a time, the question persisted whether the Markos government would be recognized. When it became clear that this would not happen, a top-level conference of the DSE and the KKE on 15 January 1948 reviewed the situation. It had been decided in December that the Third Plenum decisions should be followed up by a meeting in February,[73] and one suspects that the conference of 15 January was necessitated by the critical situation created as a result of the failure of the provisional government to win recognition, as well as by the defeat of the DSE in the battle for the town of Konitsa.

Unfortunately, the series of documents published by Iliou stops here, following the establishment of the PDG, and we are left with only a few official KKE statements and a multitude of conflicting, mostly subsequently written, reports. For the ensuing events, therefore, one can provide only a general overview of the principal developments, insofar as the available evidence allows useful conclusions to be drawn at all. It is possible that one may be misled by the lack of sources. However, the historian cannot fail to note a growing tendency in the decisions of the KKE leadership after December 1947 to refrain from adjusting its policy to the realities of the situation.

The little information we have on the January conference suggests that the party's real problems were not discussed.[74] In later years, Markos tried to convey the impression that he had seriously criticized the decisions of the Third Plenum, and writers have used their imagination to give us dramatic descriptions of the conference and of an alleged controversy between Zahariadis and Markos.[75] By now, it is almost certain that nothing so serious actually happened, and that it was finally agreed to attribute the prevailing difficulties to the failure to implement properly

73. Politburo decision of 2 December 1947 (*E.K.6*, 251).

74. The basic sources are Zahariadis' speeches, which appear in edited form in the 1948 pamphlet "Oli st'armata, ola gia ti niki" (All to arms, all for victory), now most easily accessible in the reprint of N. Zahariadis, *Epilogi ergon* (Selected works) (Athens: Protoporos, n.d.), 23–85. Firsthand reports of the meeting may be found in Bartziotas, *O Agonas tou D.S.E.,* 41; Bartziotas, *Exinta Chronia Kommounistis,* 282; and Markos's speech from the Seventh Plenum (1957), published in *Neos Kosmos* 3–4 (1957): 60. See also Markos's 1948 "platform" (*E.K.6*, 485). A long passage from Ioannidis' unpublished diary on the meeting appears in G. Gousias, *I eties gia tis ittes, ti diaspasi tou KKE kai tis Ellinikis aristeras* (The causes of the defeats, the split in the KKE and the Greek left), vol. 1 (Athens: Na iperetoume to lao, n.d.), 292–94.

75. Dominique Eudes, *The Kapetanios: Partisans and Civil War in Greece, 1943–1949* (London: NLB, 1972), 309. The account in Ioannidis' diary is free of hindsight and seems to put the matter in proper perspective.

the party's decisions—decisions that were thus still regarded as realistic. The goal of liberating large parts of northern Greece in order to gain a solid foothold for the PDG, and of holding on to the areas thus freed with static defense, was upheld. In the rest of the country and behind enemy lines, partisan warfare was to continue.

There is no evidence that the party leadership at this time and during the following months seriously considered adjusting KKE policy to the changing realities. The prospects for the liberation of Greek Macedonia depended on whether the necessary reserves of the Democratic Army could be built up. The plans laid at the Third Plenum and again at the December conference could not be implemented, especially since there was little progress in recruitment. In December 1947, and again in March 1948, KKE members were told that staying away from the struggle that now raged in the mountains amounted to treason.[76] Nevertheless, the very detailed plans for recruitment in various parts of the country, and the appeals to party members in the cities to join the Democratic Army, led nowhere: the Athens government resorted to the effective tactic of moving the population out of partisan-infested rural areas into the towns,[77] and the new security measures were particularly harsh. In fact, it took months to organize the safe exodus to the mountains of a few party officials who were able to get away from the ever-tightening grip of the police. The DSE had some success in making the rural areas completely unsafe for the Athens regime and was able to re-group its forces following attacks and mopping-up operations by government troops, with the result that the morale of the army and of the politicians became extremely low. However, the expected breakthrough never came. On the contrary, in the spring of 1948 the strongholds in Roumeli were temporarily purged of partisans by government forces in Operation Dawn (Haravgi).

In May 1948, Radio Free Greece broadcast an appeal for a peaceful settlement of the conflict, which was naturally regarded in Athens as a sign of the insurgents' weakness following the relative success of the government forces in Roumeli.[78] This development deserves to be men-

76. Politburo decision of 2 December 1947, in E.K.6, 250, and "Open Letter to Party Members in Athens," quoted in part in E.K.6, 291. It is not known why E.K.6 did not include this text in full. See Esche, Die kommunistische Partei Griechenlands, 295.

77. Angeliki E. Laiou, "Population Movements in the Greek Countryside During the Civil War," in Studies in the History of the Greek Civil War, 64ff.

78. See Wittner, American Intervention in Greece, 264–65; Esche, Die kommunistische Partei Griechenlands, 299–300.

tioned because in the following months there were rumors about a Soviet initiative for negotiations, and there was also a canard concerning an alleged initiative from Deputy Prime Minister Constantine Tsaldaris in July 1948 to open direct negotiations with the KKE, which was reportedly rejected outright by Zahariadis. The Soviet feeler to the Greek government was not regarded as sincere by British and American authorities, while the story about a Tsaldaris emissary to Markos can now be shown to have been based on misunderstandings, although it still turns up from time to time in polemical discourse in Greece.[79] There is no evidence that the American or the Greek government seriously contemplated anything but a total military victory, however elusive it may have appeared in the summer of 1948, nor is there anything to prove that the KKE refused to negotiate an end to the civil war.

In late summer 1948, the partial defeat of the government forces on Mount Grammos nearly caused the government to fall. Nevertheless, the KKE was facing grave difficulties at the same time. Tito's expulsion from the Cominform on 28 June must have come as a shock to the KKE leaders, who probably had no clear idea of what was afoot.[80] However, the split between Tito and Stalin had no immediate effect on the Greek situation, since Yugoslav aid to the Democratic Army seems to have continued uninterrupted.[81] Initially, the KKE took no official stand on the Yugoslav-Soviet crisis. Nevertheless, the split had repercussions within the Greek Communist leadership, although there is considerable debate as to their timing and extent.

The news about Tito's expulsion from the Cominform and the open Yugoslav-Soviet rift came during the bloody battles on Mount Grammos. Yugoslav sources claim that within two days of the Cominform resolution, that development, together with Zahariadis' siding with Stalin against the advice of Markos, was broadcast to the political com-

79. See Wittner, *American Intervention in Greece*, 264; B. Kontis, *I Angloamerikaniki politiki kai to elliniko provlima, 1945–1949* (Anglo-American policy and the Greek problem, 1945–1949) (Thessaloniki: Paratiritis, 1984). See also Ole Smith, "The Tsaldaris Offers for Negotiations, 1948: A Lost Opportunity or a Canard?" *Epsilon—Modern Greek and Balkan Studies* 1 (1987): 83ff.

80. Because of the friction between the CPY and the CPSU, we have no information about measures the KKE took. But see Barker, "Yugoslav Policy Towards Greece," 275–76, and Ioannidis' diary published in *Eleftherotipia*, 5 February 1980. The Greek Communists must have observed the withdrawal of Soviet advisers and military mission from Yugoslavia in March 1948.

81. However, in the fall of 1948 a decrease in Yugoslav aid was reported to the United Nations (Barker, "Yugoslavs and the Greek Civil War," 304).

missars of the DSE. For several reasons this cannot be true, even though Vladimir Dedijer, Tito's biographer, says that the KKE stand "astounded us."[82] According to official KKE documents, the party's decision to side with the Cominform and against Tito was not taken until the Fourth Plenum of the KKE Central Committee, which took place one month later, and even then the decision was kept secret.[83] This suggests that Zahariadis—even if he instinctively would have followed Stalin, as most other Communist leaders would have done, and did—had to handle the matter very carefully, and he would not have publicly and casually proclaimed his stand against Tito two days after the Cominform resolution.[84] Perhaps Dedijer is mistaken here and may be thinking of the decision of the Fourth Plenum on 29 July, which was in fact communicated to the political commissars of the DSE a few days later.[85]

The reason for raising this issue here—apart from the fact that the Cominform crisis had important consequences for the civil war later on—is that, according to some accounts, the split triggered dissension within the KKE. From his account, it is clear that Dedijer regarded Markos as Tito's man—a view shared by less well informed observers then and now—and that he attributed the showdown between Markos and Zahariadis to their different appreciations of the Cominform conflict. Dedijer asserts that Markos was against breaking with Tito and that Yugoslav support to the Democratic Army dwindled when Markos

82. Vladimir Dedijer, *Novi Prilozi za Biografiju Josipa Broza Tita,* vol. 3 (Belgrade: Rad, 1984), 268, as quoted in Barker, "Yugoslavs and the Greek Civil War," 304.

83. *E.K.6,* 274–75.

84. In an interview printed in *Politika,* 14 and 15 June 1982, Markos gave a strange account of events: In the spring of 1948, Stalin sent a letter to Markos and Zahariadis about Moscow's problems with the CPY, whereupon Zahariadis went to Belgrade and told the Yugoslavs that the KKE had to side with Stalin, but not formally. Zahariadis had also planned to go to Moscow, but he returned to the Greek mountains and called a Central Committee meeting on 28 June 1948 (Barker, "Yugoslav Policy Towards Greece," 275ff.). Although Milovan Djilas confirms (*Vlast* [London: Naša Reč, 1983], 201, as cited in Barker, "Yugoslav Policy Towards Greece," 276) that Zahariadis met him and Ranković in Belgrade after the Cominform meeting, the date of the KKE Central Committee meeting given by Markos is almost certainly wrong. There was no Central Committee meeting on 28 June, but the Fourth Plenum took place on 28 July. Gousias writes that he and other DSE officers were briefed on 2 July about the Cominform decision (*I eties gia tis ittes,* 376). Kirjazovski, relying on Yugoslav sources, writes that Zahariadis was in Belgrade on 10–12 June and in Moscow on 13–15 June and that there was a politburo meeting on 30 June, and he quotes a telegram of the same date to the DSE political commissars (*Narodno osloboditelniot front,* 240–41, 243ff.).

85. According to Maltezos, the staff at DSE Headquarters was not told anything before they were briefed about the Fourth Plenum decision on 31 July or 1 August 1948 (*Dimokratikos Stratos Elladas,* 252).

was removed from his post. This view coincides with the Yugoslav party's claim that it came to the assistance of the KKE when Markos was sent to the mountains to head the insurgency.[86] However, there is no evidence that at the Fourth Plenum Markos opposed siding with Stalin, and as far as we know, in his many subsequent statements he never indicated that he had a special sympathy for Tito at the time. He was, of course, branded as a Titoist and may have deliberately avoided saying anything that might be used to prove that he was. The evidence for his "Titoism" would seem to amount to no more than his preference for Yugoslav-style partisan tactics when it was obvious that the DSE had nothing to gain from positional warfare. Thus, we cannot make too much of what has been said about his reaction to the decisions of the Fourth Plenum— especially in view of the fact that, at the very least, he did not vote against them.[87] In any event, there does not seem to have been any serious discussion of KKE policy at the Fourth Plenum: earlier decisions were still upheld, although their lack of realism must have begun to dawn on those present at the meeting.

In September 1948, Zahariadis was in Moscow for consultations with the Soviet leadership. Our only source for Zahariadis' appeals for material aid and for the results of these meetings is not especially trustworthy: according to Giorgis Gousias, the DSE was promised the necessary light weapons and heavy artillery, and even aircraft, that would make possible the supply of its isolated forces in central Greece and the Peloponnesus.[88] The accuracy of this account is quite questionable, and in any case material aid of this kind was never delivered. Perhaps Zahariadis once again mistook promises for facts—or his close collaborators, including Gousias, were fooled. The most reasonable explanation may be that the KKE's trusted partners were motivated by other priorities and goals, while the Greek Communists had no control over international developments. Moreover, the KKE leaders did not appear to take into consideration the changed situation. It is also unclear how transportation and distribution problems affected the flow of supplies.

Removed from his post as commander of the DSE at the end of August

86. See Barker, "Yugoslavs and the Greek Civil War," 304.

87. Maltezos writes of Markos's reactions after the briefing at DSE Headquarters and appears to be certain that Markos sided with Tito. As is obvious from his account, Maltezos and Markos were not on good terms (*Dimokratikos Stratos Elladas*, 252ff.).

88. Gousias, *I eties gia tis ittes*, 440, partly corroborated by Mihalis Tsantis' account in *Avgi*, 10 February 1980. Early in 1948, the DSE had begun to enlist individuals who had served in the air force.

1948, when, according to some sources, he suffered a nervous break-down (although political considerations may also have been involved), Markos returned from Moscow to take part in the politburo meeting of 15 November, where the document later known as Markos's "platform" was discussed.[89] In this statement, he tried to offer a general assessment of developments and to set out a future course of action in light of the Democratic Army's experience. It is worth recalling that this document originally formed part of Markos's report to the Communist Party of the Soviet Union and thus, to a certain extent, constituted his apologia.[90] Contrary to the oft-repeated myth that a Markos-Zahariadis feud had existed almost from the start of the war, this was the first time that Markos expressed in so many words a radically different view of the situation. Now Markos found fault with the whole development of the armed struggle, starting with the Second Plenum. As for the decisions of the Third Plenum, he now viewed them as wishful thinking and far re-moved from reality. He advocated instead a return to partisan tactics, a change that the professional staff officers at DSE Headquarters regarded as tantamount to suicide.[91] Unfortunately, the many sound observations contained in Markos's platform represented the wisdom of hindsight and came much too late, while his radical criticism of measures for which he was no less responsible than the other politburo members made further meaningful discussion impossible. In fact, his views were curtly dis-missed as being antiparty.[92] Zahariadis and the majority of the politburo members still believed, or professed to believe, that military victory was within reach after all.

In retrospect, it is clear that this was the KKE's last opportunity to change its perspective on the armed struggle. Despite some spectacular military successes in early 1949,[93] in essence the war had been lost. But there was no willingness to face harsh realities, not even when the Soviet Union, sometime during early 1949, advised the Greek Communists to stop fighting and withdraw, possibly because this admonition was

89. On the meeting, see Gousias, *I eties gia tis ittes,* 451ff. This account, however, must be treated with caution until it is corroborated by other sources.

90. Bartziotas, *O Agonas tou D.S.E.,* 42.

91. Maltezos is particularly critical of Markos's partisan tactics (*Dimokratikos Stratos Ella-das,* 287–88, 317, 324–25).

92. See the politburo decision of 15 November 1948 on the "opportunistic platform of Markos Vaphiadis" (*E.K.6,* 299–316).

93. The most impressive operation was Florakis' and Diamantis' attacks on Karpenisi in January–February 1949, when the town was held by DSE forces for two weeks.

changed again very soon.[94] Nor had Tito's closing of the Yugoslav border any appreciable effect, although the move resulted in the added problem of how to treat the very large Slavo-Macedonian minority in the Democratic Army and led to the KKE's most unfortunate flirtation with the idea of Macedonian autonomy.[95]

In hindsight, one may conclude that the war's outcome was decided in the summer of 1947 when the KKE opted for a course of action that now can be seen to have led nowhere. Of course, whether the KKE should have realized this at the time is another question. Perhaps it could not. For the historian and for the present analysis, the main point is that the KKE decided to launch a struggle in which the party became totally dependent on foreign factors over which it had no control. This is true not only with regard to the material support from outside sources— which was not in its timing or volume adequate for the needs of the DSE—and to the international situation over which the Greek Communists had even less control, but also with regard to the help the United States gave the Greek government, which enabled the Athens regime to employ even the most unsavory means in its efforts to defeat the insurgents.

On the basis of available evidence, one must conclude that throughout the long and bitter conflict the KKE remained curiously blind to changes in the political situation in Greece, in Europe, and in the United States. Why this was so could perhaps be better understood if we had access to Yugoslav and Soviet documents. It was from their allies that the KKE leaders got the impression that the Greek Communists could venture out on the tightrope. They obviously never looked down to see what lay beneath them.

94. According to Gousias, Zahariadis, who was in Moscow in April 1949, was told that the Albanians and the Bulgarians were to close their frontiers on 1 May 1949 for fear of giving the United States an excuse to invade Albania. At the beginning of May, however, Zahariadis told DSE Headquarters that plans for withdrawal should be given up and military activity should be increased (*I eties gia tis ittes,* 500–501, 507).

95. See the essay by Evangelos Kofos in this volume.

5

The Changing Structure of the Right, 1945–1950

David H. Close

The forces of the Right in the period 1945–50 have received remarkably little attention from scholars. This chapter, in an introductory way, describes those forces and shows how power was distributed among them. In view of the fact that they were fighting for their survival, their lack of cohesion is striking. Because the Right depended heavily on violence to maintain itself in these years, its repressive forces—chiefly the army officer corps, but also the police, militia, and illegal paramilitary bands—were politicized and influential. The Right's inclination toward authoritarianism, however, was restrained by a realization that the British and the Americans opposed the establishment of a dictatorship. It fell to parliamentary politicians, therefore, to provide leadership for the varied components of the Right. They performed this role poorly, not only because they were hampered by historical divisions within the Right, but even more because they lacked a leader with sufficient personal authority to impose unity.

The Right After Liberation

The rightist parties that took shape before the general elections of March 1946 were defined by their support for the monarchy and were made up largely of those who had belonged to the Antivenizelist camp before the suppression of political activity by the Metaxas dictatorship in August 1936. Of these parties, the most important was the Populist Party. The Populists had been divided since 1935, but they managed to reunite in 1945, in response to the incentive created by the Varkiza Agreement that signaled the end of the Communist-led uprising in Athens (the *Dekemvriana*) in December 1944. This incentive was the prospect of an imminent plebiscite on the question of restoring the monarchy, to be followed closely by general elections. The Right had an excellent opportunity to win both the plebiscite and the elections by exploiting its dominance of the security forces and the public reaction against the resistance movement, EAM, in the aftermath of the *Dekemvriana*. But the Populist Party remained separated from two other segments of the old Right. The first of these, the participants in Metaxas's dictatorial government, included some talented individuals—eight of whom were to secure prominent public positions in the 1950s—but at the time they were disqualified from power by the resentment that politicians of all other parties felt at having been persecuted under the dictatorship. Few Metaxists secured reelection as deputies in 1946, and they were rejected as electoral allies by the Populists. Even more discredited were those who had participated in the wartime quisling governments, among whom there was only one politician of any importance (Ioannis Rallis), but among whom there were some experienced army officers.

The ranks of the Right were swollen by politicians who since 1942 had converted to monarchism in response to the threat of the leftist EAM. These converts believed that the monarchy would form a more effective barrier against the ambitions of the Communist Party (KKE) than a republican form of government, which would be vulnerable to subversion by the Communists, given the KKE's proven capacity for mass organization and conspiracy. By late 1944, an increasing number of centrists were coming to sympathize with this view, as were many people who had been persecuted or frightened by EAM. Those opposed to EAM were numerous in all regions, and in some areas—for example, in the rural Peloponnesus, the Cyclades, and the Ionian islands—they constituted an overwhelming majority. The conversion of centrists to monarchism continued after liberation and was evident even in their traditional strongholds of Thrace and Crete.[1] Factions led by Stylianos Gonatas and Apostolos Alexandris allied themselves with the Populist Party in the United National Camp (EPE). Another group, led by the wartime resistance leader Napoleon Zervas, took an extreme anticommunist stance but remained independent of the Populists. There were also important converts to the Right in the army: two of the most influential officers after the Varkiza Agreement, Constantine Ventiris (Deputy Chief of the General Staff) and Solon Gikas (for a time head of the conspiratorial organization IDEA) were former Venizelists.

The rightist politicians were the most powerful exponents of views that were to a large extent shared by many politicians of the Center, a factor that led to the formation of the Center-Right National Political Union, which remained neutral on the issue of the monarchy. The National Political Union comprised the parties of Sophocles Venizelos, Panayiotis Kanellopoulos, and George Papandreou, a trio whose differences of principle with the Right seem to have been confined mainly to the issue of the monarchy, which ceased to divide the parties of the Center and the Right after the monarchy's restoration in September 1946. The Liberal Party (the main component of the Center) broke ranks with the Right in 1945 both in opposing the restoration of the monarchy and in adopting a more conciliatory approach toward the Left. But between 1947 and 1949, when the issue of the monarchy had been laid to rest and conciliation with the Left had become impractical, the Liberals also lost much of their ideological distinctiveness. Thus, what might be termed the national camp during the civil war had vague boundaries and extended well beyond the confines of the Right as conventionally defined.

The rightist politicians were especially influential within this camp because their key views (support for the monarchy and a willingness to take tough measures against the Left) were shared by the dominant factions in the army and the police, as well as by the illegal anticommunist bands

---

1. U.S. National Archives, Washington, D.C. (hereafter cited as NARS), 868.00/4-1845, L. J. Cromie, "Western Greece: A Regional Survey"; 868.00/6-1345, Weekly Report, 19 March–4 April 1945; 868.00/6-2045, Weekly Report, 6–9 June. Divisions among Liberals are described in G. Daphnes, *Sophocles Venizelos* (Athens: Ikaros, 1970), 348–53. NARS, RG 226, OSS, L55815; Records of the British Foreign Office, Public Record Office (hereafter cited as FO), 286/1166, J. Smith-Hughes, re Crete, 11 May–6 June 1945; F. Smothers, W. H. McNeill, and E. McNeill, *Report on the Greeks* (New York: Twentieth Century Fund, 1948), 177–84.

that flourished in the anarchic conditions of 1945. Centrist army officers, of whom a number were appointed by the governments of 1945, lacked the determination and cohesion of their rightist colleagues, and although centrist politicians deplored the rightist bias of the security forces, they no doubt felt dependent upon them for protection against the leftist-populist EAM.

The primary desire of the Right was to restore an oligarchical political system, with the king as a source of patronage and head of the armed forces. Most rightist politicians preferred, out of habit and conviction, to work through parliamentary institutions, although they had limited respect for the rights of their opponents. Certainly the Populist leader, Constantine Tsaldaris, emphasized his belief in parliamentary government after his party gained power in the elections of 1946.[2] If there were any rightist politicians who disliked parliamentarianism, they were forced, by British and later by American influence, to pretend otherwise. But it is likely that most rightist officers of the army and the police would have preferred a dictatorship and looked with some nostalgia upon what they saw as the capable leadership, efficient administration, and suppression of Communist organizations that had characterized the Metaxas regime.

In any event, the restoration of the monarchy was seen by the Right as essential to the maintenance of traditional values and practices, which in 1945 were being challenged by the leftist forces in EAM. The challenge became sharper and more specific when, in August, EAM published its official electoral program, accompanied by a condensed and illustrated version for popular consumption. EAM—which advocated impersonal loyalty to a movement and mass participation in the political process by a wide range of regional and social groups, including the underprivileged, who had been held in submission under the traditional order through deference, patronage, and official pressure—took particular aim at the dispensation of power and office through patron-client relationships, a form of political organization based on personal, family, and regional loyalties. The top reaches of political power were generally confined to those of wealth who had family connections and cultivated manners, while authority locally was vested in socially prominent personalities. The oligarchical nature of the Populist Party, for example, is

2. *Akropolis*, 14 September 1947.

illustrated by the fact that after liberation it held no conference that was open to local cadres and former deputies until December 1950 (and that was only a regional conference).[3]

The Right subscribed to a political system characterized by a politicized and centralized state bureaucracy, which maintained control over local governments and extensive influence over the population. The parliamentary Right believed that deputies should mediate between this administrative machine and the public, and that politicians should intercede with it on behalf of their clients. Recruitment to the civil service, and to many professions, should continue to be conducted through an archaic educational system, which taught its graduates a form of the language (*katharevousa*) barely intelligible to most people. This was the language of politics, administration, journalism, and the law. The Right favored the continuation of a system that historically had been biased in favor of the interests of proprietors and private entrepreneurs, and under which employees had few legal protections, taxes were highly regressive, and little was spent on social welfare. EAM promised to institute radical reforms in these areas, reforms that would have undoubtedly been very popular. It also promised to nationalize major parts of the economy, a promise that stimulated the other parties to emphasize the virtues of private enterprise.

The challenge from EAM strengthened another element of the rightist dogma: militant nationalism. Before the war, the Right had no special claim to this sentiment. After the war, the Right benefited from the Greek Communists' association with Greece's northern neighbors, who were the objects of strong public resentment and fear. Although encouraged by the rightist press, such feelings were largely spontaneous, and they were especially strong in the frontier provinces, where during the war Greeks had suffered under the Bulgarian occupation and from harassment by ethnic minorities armed by the Axis powers. The Greek inhabitants of western Macedonia, for example, were worried by the heightened ethnic consciousness that was evident among the region's Slavophone population. This consciousness was seen to be a source of danger because it was being exploited by the leaders of the new confederal state of Communist Yugoslavia, with its autonomous republic of Macedonia.

3. Ekdoseis Laikou Kommatos (Populist Party publication) 1; *Synedrion Thessalonikes* (Thessaloniki conference), preface, 128.

A further stimulus to nationalism was the belief on the part of most of the public that Greece, having emerged from the war on the winning side, was entitled to territorial rewards at the expense of neighboring states that had supported the Axis; this was an expectation to which all political parties had to appeal. By an illogical but natural process, this belief was combined with fear of attack by those states now that they were becoming Soviet satellites.[4]

Another part of the rightist dogma that was stimulated by the challenge from EAM was the defense of Orthodox Christianity. Like its counterparts in Italy and Spain, the Greek Right was keen to associate the national church with the power structure. Later, for example, a different patron saint would be adopted for each branch of the armed forces and the police. Defense of the church gave the Right a sense of purpose and was associated both with patriotism and with traditional moral values, such as patriarchal authority in the family. But religion had little impact on the 1946 elections, probably because the KKE did not appear to present an out-and-out threat to the church. Generally speaking, the church leadership inclined toward the Right. The regent, Archbishop Damaskinos, privately favored the Right because of his anxiety about the KKE's intentions toward the church.[5] The two bishops who had supported EAM during the occupation were suspended. But the Holy Synod resisted the pressure from the Right to involve itself directly in politics, and not until mid-1947 did it formally condemn the Communist rebellion.[6]

Rightist political groups received large grants from the nervous wealthy. Those who had profited from economic collaboration with the Germans or from speculating in scarce commodities—thousands of entrepreneurs large and small—now constituted an important social group. The targets of widespread public anger, they were frightened by the prospect of an EAM government, or even of another such government as that led by Petros Voulgaris in 1945, which had tried to tax

4. NARS, RG 84, Confidential File 1945, W. H. McNeill, "The Political Embroglio" (c. August 1945); C. F. Edson to MacVeagh, 19 April 1945; Confidential File 1946, G. M. Widney to U.S. Embassy, 6 November 1946; Confidential File 1949, R. B. Memminger to O. S. Crosby, 7 December 1949. NARS, 868.00/7-2045, Weekly Progress Report no. 37; U.S. Department of State, *Foreign Relations of the United States* (hereafter cited as *FRUS*), 1946, 7:141.

5. *FRUS*, 1945, 8:177; Smothers et al., *Report on the Greeks*, 143–44.

6. NARS, RG 84, Confidential File 1947, MacVeagh to Secretary of State, 27 June 1947.

them and control prices. Right-wing politicians appealed to this group by opposing such forms of state intervention.[7] Rightist groups also received significant support from Greeks living in Egypt who wanted to be able to transfer their wealth to a secure political environment in Greece. Some extremists, like George Grivas, head of the monarchist wartime organization "X," raised considerable sums from such people (in part, it seems, by extortion). But in the long run, people of higher status, like the Populist politician Petros Mavromihalis, were more successful in fundraising, presumably because the Populists enjoyed an especially close association with big business.[8]

The end result of these currents—monarchist, oligarchical, nationalist, religious, and laissez-faire—was an emotionally intense but intellectually crude ideology that linked nearly all army and police officers, Populist politicians of good family, and political roughnecks (insofar as the last had any ideas). The ideology became roughly synonymous with that officially known as *ethnikofrosene* (national-mindedness), which inspired vigorous organizing activity in most parts of the country.

The rightist revival of 1945–46 therefore clearly owed much to ideological zeal and public support, but it also owed much to intimidation. After the Varkiza Agreement, the repressive forces of the Right performed the vital function of breaking the authority of EAM, which still prevailed in most of the country, except in the main cities and on many of the islands.

At the time of the Varkiza Agreement in February 1945, the strongest of these armed organizations was the National Guard, a militia commanded by army officers. At the end of the *Dekemvriana,* it had 19,000 members. By the end of May 1945, National Guard units were established in all provinces, and it reached its peak enlistment of 60,000 soon afterward. At first the National Guard consisted largely of zealous anticommunist volunteers, including members of the terrorist organization

7. G. M. Alexander, *The Prelude to the Truman Doctrine: British Policy in Greece, 1944–1947* (Oxford: Clarendon Press, 1982), 123–24; Lawrence S. Wittner, *American Intervention in Greece, 1943–1949* (New York: Columbia University Press, 1982), 115–16; Christos Hadziiossif, "Economic Stabilization and Political Unrest: Greece, 1944–1947," in *Studies in the History of the Greek Civil War, 1945–1949,* ed. Lars Baerentzen, John O. Iatrides, and Ole L. Smith (Copenhagen: Museum Tusculanum, 1987), 26–37; Kostas Vergopoulos, "The Emergence of the New Bourgeoisie, 1944–1952," in *Greece in the 1940s,* ed. John O. Iatrides (Hanover, N.H.: University of New England Press, 1981), 302.

8. NARS, RG 226, XL 11220, XL 55168; U.S. Embassy report on "X," *Journal of the Hellenic Diaspora* 12 (Spring 1985): 42.

"X" and former members of the collaborationist Security Battalions. After the *Dekemvriana,* it was increasingly made up of civilian conscripts who were called up as army reservists. The army and police officers who organized the conscription worked to ensure that zealous nationalists were selected and left-wingers were excluded. Hastily recruited and generally ill-disciplined, many battalions behaved with such riotous and indiscriminate brutality toward suspected leftists that, beginning in July 1945, the government began to reduce the force and divert resources to the police.[9]

The police (the gendarmerie in most of the country, and the city police in Athens, Piraeus, Patras, and Corfu), after the Varkiza Agreement, were the most exclusively and zealously anticommunist of the security forces. Historically, the police organizations had been in the forefront of the official fight against communism, and consequently their members became the prime targets of Communist reprisals, which had been severe during the fighting in December 1944. Until late in the civil war, leftist guerrillas commonly executed captured police officers; for their part, the police behaved with a savagery that sometimes shocked even the army.[10] Their discipline in 1945 was poor because their numbers had been hastily expanded so as to enable them to keep order during the expected plebiscite, which was eventually held in September 1946. Within about twelve months of the Varkiza Agreement, the two forces mushroomed from 13,000 or less to over 29,000 (compared with a prewar level of about 20,000). Many incompetent officers (including some who had been appointed by the quisling governments) were kept, and the training of recruits was rushed. The combination of political bias and poor discipline explains why the police customarily mistreated left-wingers, often in cooperation with the National Guard or right-wing rowdies.[11] Their behavior was not seriously modified by the British police training mission, which operated from July 1945, or by the series of centrist or

9. NARS, RG 3l9, U.S. Military Attaché to War Department, 11 March 1947; RG 84, Confidential File 1945, W. H. McNeill, "The Political Embroglio" (c. August 1945); 868.00/4-1745, Military Liaison Weekly Report No. 25; 868.00/4-2445, Weekly Report No. 26; 868.00/5-1545, "Political Developments in Greece, May 1–15."

10. FO 371/67080/16, R16213; NARS, RG 319, Salonika Consul to War Department, 24 May 1947; Military Attaché to War Department, 7 November 1948.

11. FO 371/58754/25; 371/58758/52, 54, British Police Mission Progress Reports, January and May 1946; 371/48372/4, Consul General Thessaloniki to D. W. Lascelles, 27 October 1945. It is impossible to be sure of police strength before the Varkiza Agreement because much of the force was scattered or seconded to the National Guard.

Liberal governments that held office until the national elections of March 1946. Themselves biased against the Left, the British and the Greek governments of this period did little except (in the Greek government's case) exhort the police to restrain themselves or (in the British case) occasionally order the transfer of a few offending police officers.[12]

The National Guard and the police were commonly helped in hunting and persecuting left-wingers by the right-wing extremists in "X" or in the irregular bands, which were especially numerous in Epirus, Thessaly, western Macedonia, and the southern Peloponnesus. In many areas these outnumbered the official forces even as late as the end of 1946. The official forces (including the army) usually welcomed their help and—despite strong British disapproval—distributed arms (such as those found in captured EAM caches) to them in vast quantities (15,000 weapons by August 1946, according to British intelligence).[13] Members of the extremist organizations penetrated the official forces to a considerable extent in 1945. National Guard recruits in Epirus, for example, were largely recruited from among members of EDES, the wartime anti-communist resistance organization. Many members of the National Guard in Thessaloniki and Arcadia reportedly belonged to "X," as did five hundred gendarmes in Thessaloniki alone. American intelligence officers suspected that "X" coordinated the persecution of the Left, which was zealous and systematic by the police and the National Guard.[14]

The army at the time of the Varkiza Agreement numbered 8,800 men and consisted of the Mountain (or Third, or Rimini) Brigade and the Sacred Battalion. These formed the nucleus of a force that by the end of the year had been expanded to 75,000, mostly partially trained, troops. As a result of purges of the Mountain Brigade and the Sacred Battalion by the British in 1944 when the Greek troops were still in the Middle East, both were solidly right-wing. The later expansion of the army was supervised by a British military mission, which favored the right-wing

12. NARS, 868.00/5-1545, "Political Developments in Greece, May 1–15, 1945: Internal Politics"; 868.00/6-1345, Weekly Report No. 33; FO 371/58753/185-7, R2318; 371/48372/10; FO 286/1169, Capt. C. W. Fassnidge, 21 June 1945; 286/1175, Lt.-Col. M. Bayley, 11 May 1946; Smothers et al., *Report on the Greeks*, 166.

13. NARS, 868.00/10-1446, L. MacVeagh to Secretary of State; 868.00/10-2546, L. Mac-Veagh to Secretary of State; FO 288/1181, Patras Consul to Norton, 17 November 1946.

14. NARS, RG 84, Confidential File 1945, C. F. Edson to MacVeagh, 19 April 1945; 868.00/6-1345, Weekly Report for 27 May–2 June; RG 226, Research and Analysis, L58008, Source "Z" ("Pericles"), 5 July 1945; U.S. Embassy report on "X," *Journal of the Hellenic Diaspora* 12 (Spring 1985): 41.

officers who had worked with the British army in 1944.[15] The officers themselves were dominated by two conspiratorial leagues, SAN (League of Young Officers) and IDEA (Sacred League of Greek Officers). The first, under the leadership of Gen. Constantine Ventiris, formed "the inner cabal of the Greek General Staff," according to American diplomatic sources,[16] and effectively controlled appointments and promotions. The second was politically more fanatical and included what was probably a large minority of the officer corps up to the rank of major.[17] In 1944, many officers and officer cadets belonged to "X" (five hundred, according to "X" itself). It seems that fewer did so in 1945, but Ventiris and his associates exercised considerable influence over "X," while many other officers sympathized with its aims.[18]

The reports of British and American observers suggest that most officers would have backed a coup during 1945 to restore the monarchy, had they not been prevented from doing so by the British, who maintained control over military supplies, as well as a military presence in Greece in numbers superior to the Greek army.[19] Nevertheless, on several occasions during the year after the Varkiza Agreement, a coup by officers and "X"-ites seemed imminent. Ventiris dissuaded the hotheads of "X" from attempting a coup in October 1945. In November, however, officers and "X"-ites were aroused once again by the formation of a Liberal government, which transferred Ventiris to a provincial command and ordered the release of many leftist prisoners from civilian jails. The latter move led indirectly to defiance of the government by uniformed "X"-ites

---

15. T. Tsakalotos, *Saranda Chronia Stratiotis tes Elladas* (Forty years soldier of Greece), vol. 2 (Athens: Akropolis, 1960), 26–27. According to a report by an American diplomat, the British mission, far from being consciously political as claimed by the Greek Left, "thinks of little besides boating parties, amateur horse races, billets, rations, demobilization and getting home" (NARS, 868.00/7-1646, Gwynn to Secretary of State). Nevertheless, it was anticommunist, and this was another reason why it was not inclined to seek out and suppress right-wing terrorism.

16. Memorandum, 26 October 1945, in *Journal of the Hellenic Diaspora* 12 (Spring 1985): 46–50.

17. The estimate of IDEA's size quoted above was "about 2,000." This seems too high, because Alexander Papagos claimed in 1952 that the total number of those who had ever belonged to IDEA was 2,500, while an official American estimate of 1948 was 700–750 (NARS, 868.00/11-1948, Grady to Secretary of State; see also N. A. Stavrou, *Allied Politics and Military Interventions* [Athens: Papazeses, 1974], 110, 134).

18. NARS, 868.00/4-3045, OSS report forwarded by L. C. Honck; W. Byford-Jones, *Grivas and the Story of EOKA* (London: Hale, 1959), 28; W. H. McNeill, *The Greek Dilemma* (London: Gollancz, 1947), 179–80.

19. NARS, 868.00/1-1946, W. H. McNeill memo.

in Kalamata, who overwhelmed the police (many of whom were in any case sympathetic to the "X"-ites' cause), released their friends from jail, and withdrew with about eighty hostages. Under orders from the government and the British authorities, a Greek army unit established martial law, removed twenty-one local police officers, and arrested numerous rightists, including (thanks to a British police officer) the local "X"-ite leader, Manganas.[20] This determined action against extremists of the Right, the result of combined British and Liberal pressure, was not to be repeated in the years 1946–49.

Outside Athens, voluntary nationalist organizations appeared and multiplied after the security forces suppressed EAM. As the American assistant military attaché, W. H. McNeill, observed, the progress through the provinces of the National Guard during the four months after Varkiza was followed locally by "a sort of miniature counterrevolution. The rightists of each village and town came into the open, and proceeded to do all in their power to turn the tables and silence their opponents. A rash of self-styled Nationalist organizations grew up within a matter of weeks."[21] Adopting grandiose titles (such as the Patriotic Organization of National Regeneration in Thessaloniki, or the League of Nationalist Youth in Veroia), such organizations seem to have appeared in every town. They tried to counter EAM's activities on every front—terrorism, propaganda, youth organization. An OSS observer claimed that in Epirus (as in the northern Peloponnesus and central Greece, where he had also traveled) they controlled the life of the community, including appointments to local government and the UNRRA (United Nations Relief and Rehabilitation Administration) committees.[22]

Many of them sought links with "X," whose officials as early as April 1945 toured the provinces to assist affiliation. Consequently, by December, "X" had branches in every region of the country except Epirus, which remained under the domination of EDES, and Crete, where republican bodies remained supreme. Considering the vigor of rightist organizing activity, the claim by "X" in October 1945 to having increased its membership to 200,000 seems plausible, although no doubt much of this membership was nominal.

20. FO 371/78416/-, R4111; 371/58850/40, Norton to F.O., 21 February 1946; 371/58755/ 17-18, R4008.
21. McNeill, *Greek Dilemma,* 165.
22. NARS, RG 226, Source Z, 8 July 1945; Military Liaison Weekly Report, 868.00/4-2445, 868.00/7-2045, 868.00/5-2845.

At about this time, in order to facilitate its fundraising efforts, "X" formed an association with its chief rivals, Zervas's EDES and PE (Panhellenic Union), led by the veteran monarchist conspirator retired Air Marshal George Reppas.[23] But this federation, like "X" itself, was flimsy and ephemeral. EDES, with the regional base it had established in Epirus during the occupation, was the only part of the federation to emerge from the general elections as a political force. "X" got hardly any votes, and the Populist government maintained the ban recently imposed by its Liberal predecessor on its national organization. "X" survived only as local groups of vigilantes who helped the army and the police in their witch hunts against leftists.[24]

The Populist politicians who were to be the eventual beneficiaries of this wave of zeal and terrorism were, like many of the old *politikos kosmos,* reemerging into public view after their long seclusion during the years of dictatorship and occupation. There were no nationally famous figures among them. Their advantage was that their old rallying cry—the monarchy—was now popular, thanks to the public reaction against EAM. Restoration of the monarchy implied power for the professional politicians of the Populist Party. Preoccupied with the issue of restoration, the Populists, as well as some Liberals, were reluctant to face the main problems of the country—the need for economic reconstruction and social welfare—which were in any case insoluble without foreign aid. In 1947, the American authors of *Report on the Greeks* noted that the evasiveness of rightist politicians on such matters contrasted with the thoughtful interest of Communist leaders.[25]

Not surprisingly, the rightist and centrist politicians had difficulty in appealing to youth. This is attested by the Populist Spyros Theotokis and by Anastasios Pepones, a student of liberal rather than leftist sympathies who remarked that, in contrast to EAM, the centrist parties had weak youth organizations while the Populists apparently had none.[26] It appears that the rightist politicians failed to exploit the grass-roots enthusi-

23. U.S. Embassy Report, *Journal of the Hellenic Diaspora* 12 (Spring 1985): 40; RG 226, OSS XL21682, 41498. The label "X" was later applied loosely in some localities to various bands or home-guard units.

24. C. M. Woodhouse, *Apple of Discord* (London: Hutchinson, 1948), 266–67; FO 371/ 72201/-, R6734.

25. Smothers et al., *Report on the Greeks,* 204–7; Woodhouse, *Apple of Discord,* 115; *FRUS, 1945,* 8:167.

26. A. Pepones, *Prosopike Martiria* (Personal testimony) (Athens: Kedros, 1970), 42, 150; S. Theotokis, *Politikai Anamnesis* (Political recollections) (Athens: n.p., 1985), 100–101, 132.

asm for the nationalist cause that manifested itself after Varkiza. The alienation of youth was also reflected in the political leadership. The average age of prime ministers in the years 1945–55 was about seventy, while half of the deputies elected in 1946 had been deputies in 1936 or earlier. The general shortage of young talent seems to have been especially marked on the Right, as indicated by the composition of the group of deputies first elected in 1946; except for Spyros Markezinis, most of those who later achieved distinction entered parliament as members of the relatively small center groups.[27]

The Populist Party, the main parliamentary organization on the Right, was historically a coalition of locally based and financially semi-independent factions. It had been divided since 1935 and leaderless since the death of Panayiotis Tsaldaris in 1936. After the factions reunited in 1945, the party was managed by a committee made up of Constantine Tsaldaris, Petros Mavromihalis, John Theotokis, and Stephanos Stephanopoulos—all of whom had been ministers before 1936—each representing one of the factions.[28] Tsaldaris, who became Prime Minister and party leader after the March 1946 general elections, was the nephew of Panayiotis Tsaldaris. Although respected within his party for his personal decency and his loyalty to the monarchy during the occupation, he was considered even by friendly observers to lack ability and strength of character. He conducted himself with little distinction either as party leader or as Prime Minister. He seems to have made little impression on the public, and soon earned the contempt of the British and American governments for his inept advocacy of Greece's territorial claims.[29]

King George II, the focus of right-wing attention, was incapable of inspiring affection and politically ineffectual. After returning to Athens in September 1946, he was seldom seen in public, and he included the Populists in the contempt he felt for politicians in general. The Populists

27. I. Nikolakopoulos, *Kommata ke Voulevtikes Ekloyes sten Ellada, 1946–1964* (Parties and parliamentary elections in Greece, 1946–1964) (Athens: Ethniko Kentro Kinonikon Erevnon, 1985), 146; G. Daphnes, *Ta Ellinika Politika Kommata, 1821–1961* (Greek political parties, 1821–1961), (Athens: n.p., 1961), 153.

28. Alexander, *Prelude to the Truman Doctrine,* 86–87, 103; NARS, 868.00/10-1345, Mac-Veagh to Secretary of State; 868.00/7-949, O. S. Crosby's memo of conversation with P. Mavromihalis on 5 July 1949.

29. McNeill, *Greek Dilemma,* 195; G. I. Pesmazoglou, *My Public Life* (Athens: Diogenes, 1982), 182–83; Alexander, *Prelude to the Truman Doctrine,* 205, 227, 235; NARS, RG 84, box 163, R. A. Gibson to Secretary of State, 21 April 1947.

reciprocated his coolness.[30] The American Ambassador, Lincoln Mac-Veagh, found him "the same old muddled, indecisive figure that he always was. Nobody loves him, trusts him, or believes in him."[31]

The Populists' strategy in 1945 was to press the British, and the Greek governments, which the British virtually nominated, to hold the plebiscite on the monarchy as early as possible. When the British decided that the general elections should come first, the Populists decided to give the elections the character of a constitutional plebiscite. Soon after the Varkiza Agreement was signed, they began to venture into the provinces to rebuild their networks of electoral influence, able to promise patronage because of their good prospects of coming to power. While they, like all rightist politicians in the late 1940s, assured the British and the Americans of their devotion to democracy and their desire for fair elections,[32] they were nonetheless content to benefit from the unconstitutional influence exerted on their behalf by the repressive forces of the Right and by the state bureaucracy. Intimidation was commonly directed against the supporters of the Liberal candidates. Although rightists did not enter government before the general elections, they benefited from the anti-communism of the postwar centrist and Liberal administrations. Thus the officials appointed by the Voulgaris government of April-October 1945 biased voter registration heavily in favor of the Right and discriminated generally against the Left in the distribution of UNRRA relief.[33] The Liberal government of Themistocles Sophoulis (November-April) evidently could not counter this bias, or do much to restrain rightist intimidation. The repressive forces that were the agents of this intimidation seem to have been linked closely with rightist politicians. Thus, the Populists worked quite closely with "X." Mavromihalis, the most powerful figure in the party after Tsaldaris, was said to be the treasurer of "X" in October 1945.[34] As for the army officers, the Populists were probably friendly with many, but do not seem to have had any authority over them.

30. C. L. Sulzberger, *A Long Row of Candles: Memoirs and Diaries, 1934–1954* (New York: Macmillan, 1969), 301; Smothers et al., *Report on the Greeks*, 147.

31. John O. Iatrides, ed., *Ambassador MacVeagh Reports: Greece, 1933–1947* (Princeton: Princeton University Press, 1980), 704.

32. NARS, 868.00/10-1345, MacVeagh to Secretary of State.

33. NARS, RG 226, OSS L57824; U.S. Embassy memo, in *Journal of the Hellenic Diaspora* 12 (Spring 1985): 35.

34. Ibid., 42.

By January 1946, it was apparent to Populist politicians that they had overreached themselves. Their supporters' violence had provoked a hostile public reaction and caused the date of the elections to be deferred.[35] EAM was successfully exploiting economic scarcity, which could be blamed in part on profiteers backing the Right. By a series of mass demonstrations, EAM showed that it was still the best-organized party. As the American diplomat Karl Rankin noted in February 1946, EAM "is a unified, dynamic movement that knows what it wants. . . . In contrast the right and center parties present a picture of leaderless disunity and muddled incompetence." W. H. McNeill later added that the extreme Right never elicited the same degree of public enthusiasm as EAM had done in 1944.[36] By refusing to form a coalition government with the Liberals, the Populists lost their chance to influence the choice of an electoral system for Greece. Sophoulis' government chose proportional representation, under which the Populists were unsure of winning a majority.[37] They were saved, however, by the unexpected decision of the KKE, EAM, and some centrist politicians to abstain from participating in the elections in protest against rightist intimidation.

The Right in Power

The rightist groups were able to win 236 out of the 354 parliamentary seats in the elections of March 1946. Twenty of the 236 were won by Zervas's followers, and 9 were won by a small group consisting mainly of former Metaxists. Nearly all the rest went to the United Nationalist Camp (EPE), consisting mainly of the Populist Party with 156 deputies, Stylianos Gonatas's group with 34, and Apostolos Alexandris' group with 5.[38] The Populists accordingly formed the new government. Gonatas and Alexandris were given ministries, and the Populist backbenchers henceforth exerted strong influence on the government in matters of pa-

35. Alexander, *Prelude to the Truman Doctrine*, 138, 150–51; FO 286/1166, report on Crete, 6–12 November 1945.

36. NARS, 868.00/2-1446; McNeill, *Greek Dilemma*, 165.

37. NARS, 868.00/10-945, Weekly Progress Report; 868.00/1-2746, MacVeagh to Secretary of State.

38. See Nikolakopoulos, *Kommata ke Voulevtikes Ekloyes*, 132; NARS, 868.00/7-2647, memo of conversation with Tsaldaris.

tronage and internal security. This influence was applied through two large committees that were formed in order to represent, respectively, the senior members of the party and the backbenchers. The backbenchers' committee communicated with ministers and local party organizations.[39]

The Right's lack of administrative talent and experience in governing soon became apparent. Tsaldaris' government exasperated foreign officials with its combination of partisanship and incompetence. As Minister of the Army and (temporarily) of the Navy and Air Force, Mavromihalis (whom King George described as "stupid") promptly wrecked the Air Ministry with his appointments and thereafter disgusted the British and the Americans with his support for rightist bandits. One Minister of Supply was described by a British official as "a clogging influence." A Minister of Health, who claimed that he would prefer malaria to go untreated rather than let one Communist remain in public employment, was characterized by an UNRRA official as "a fool and a rogue." The British were appalled by his successor, a wartime collaborator who obstructed the course of justice on behalf of other collaborators.[40] Perhaps the most disastrous appointment came in February 1947, at the hands of Tsaldaris' successor, Dimitrios Maximos. As Minister of Public Order, Napoleon Zervas converted much of the gendarmerie into inefficient military formations and ordered ill-prepared mass arrests. Both the British and the Americans opposed his appointment, suspecting him of wartime collaboration and of harboring dictatorial ambitions. They succeeded in ousting him in August 1947, when the American chief of the U.S. economic mission, Dwight Griswold, said, "I feel he is making more Communists than he is eliminating."[41]

The deficiencies of Tsaldaris' government were severe handicaps in its fight against communism. Consequently, it was pressed hard by the British and the Americans, from about October 1946, to drop extremists and to include opposition leaders. The great difficulty (after the plebi-

39. NARS, 868/5-1949, H. B. Minor to Secretary of State.

40. Alexander, *Prelude to the Truman Doctrine*, 220; FO 371/58850/146-7; 286/1174, N. M. Goodman to J. W. Nicholls, 19 September 1946; 286/1174, D. Balfour, 5 November 1946; *FRUS, 1946*, 7:234.

41. NARS, 868.00/8-1447, Griswold to McGhee, 14 August 1947; 868.00/7-1747, 7-2347, 7-2447, U.S. Embassy to Secretary of State; RG 84, Confidential File 1947, notes of meeting of 3 September 1947; RG 319, American Embassy to Secretary of State, 25 February 1947, 4 March 1947; FO 371/67143/-, R7902; 371/87131/-, police mission report for March 1947, p. 1; 286/1174, Zervas to Norton, 7 November 1946, with minutes; Wittner, *American Intervention*, 110.

scite was out of the way) was that the opposition leaders—that is, the centrists Panayiotis Kanellopoulos, George Papandreou, and Sophocles Venizelos, and the Liberal Themistocles Sophoulis—demanded that Tsaldaris step down and that they be accorded senior posts corresponding to their status as former Prime Ministers (a position that had been held by none in Tsaldaris' government). Tsaldaris, because of pressure from his own party, could not at first comply. He was forced to do so in 1947, however, by a combination of pressure from the United States and the recognition by a growing number of rightists of the need for a coalition government in order to rally public support against the Left.[42] His government gave way in January 1947 to a coalition headed by the neutral Maximos, which included the centrists but not the Sophoulist Liberals.

This government, however, was no more moderate in its security policies than its immediate predecessors. Although, at first, Maximos tried to give an impression of moderation by offering an amnesty to outlaws, by releasing certain categories of deportees, and by ordering the dissolution of unofficial right-wing organizations, these measures had little effect and were soon outweighed by Zervas's activities.[43] Zervas had in 1946 become the hero of the right-wing critics of the government—both inside and outside the Populist Party—who had been exerting strong parliamentary pressure for greater militancy against the Left. Such was his reputation as a fighter of Communists that his appointment was at first supported even by the centrist ministers, who in general became defenders of right-wing security policy against attacks by Sophoulist Liberals and against the weight of foreign opinion.

After capturing power, the Populist Party purged all branches of the state bureaucracy. The purge was thorough, even by traditional Greek standards, because the prevailing economic hardship presumably intensified the demand for political patronage. In terms of the Populists' ability to govern, however, the purge was damaging because they had inadequate reserves of talent to draw upon. This was especially true with respect to the nomarchs, most of whom were replaced—even in the Venizelist strongholds of Crete and Thrace—because they in turn appointed

42. Alexander, *Prelude to the Truman Doctrine,* 189–91, 232–33; Iatrides, *Ambassador MacVeagh Reports,* 709–10, 714–15.
43. FO 371/67143/-, R7902.

the vital relief committees and filled vacancies on municipal councils, most of which came to be controlled by the Right.[44] The government, allegedly acting to expel Communists, conducted extensive purges of the civil service, the teaching profession, trade unions, and the powerful Agricultural Bank.[45] It easily secured the assent of the British authorities to replacement of the generally elderly and ineffective republicans appointed by previous governments to senior positions in the police and army. Generals with strong political credentials—Panayiotis Spiliotopoulos and, later, Constantine Ventiris—were appointed to head the General Staff.[46]

The rightist government that came to power in 1946 sympathized fully with the persecution of the Left by the police and the army, and instead of trying to restrain them, as preceding governments had done, it pushed them to take even more drastic measures and granted them wider powers. British misgivings over the wisdom of this course soon developed into outright opposition. However, the new government's support by a large parliamentary majority gave it considerable independence from British influence.[47] In May 1946, the government restored the prewar security commissions, which deported to internal exile, without trial— and usually, it seems, without much question—those singled out by local police officers. The total number of people thus deported to islands during the civil war is uncertain, but it is in the tens of thousands.[48] For some time, these deportations were ineffective, as well as indiscriminate, because police intelligence was often poor. Moreover, at least some of the arrests were made on narrowly partisan grounds. The extent to which the gendarmerie was used for partisan purposes was revealed in the plebiscite of September 1946, when it terrorized leftists and centrists. After

44. NARS, 868.00/6-1748, record of conversation between Griswold, Venizelos, Rendis; 868.00/7-1448, Griswold to Secretary of State; 868.00/5-2549, H. B. Minor; 868.00/8-849, idem, RG 84, Confidential File 1949, B. Y. Berry to Chief AMAG, 7 January 1949; FO 371/72318/-, Vice Consul Kavalla to Consul General Thessaloniki, 15 November 1948; 371/47104/25, R2219.

45. NARS, 868.00/1-3149; 781.00/7-1050; RG 84, Confidential File 1949, R. B. Memminger to O. S. Crosby, 7 December 1949; N. C. Alivizatos, *Les institutions politiques de la Grèce à travers les crises, 1922–1974* (Paris: R. Pichon and R. Durand-Auzias, 1979), 372.

46. Alexander, *Prelude to the Truman Doctrine*, 196; FO 371/58757/141, R8293; 371/67029/-, R2711.

47. FO 371/67076/131-3, R105; 371/58941/16, R17739; 371/58758/-, Police Mission Report, May 1946, p. 4.

48. See, for example, the U.S. figure of 18,000 on 1 September 1947 (*FRUS*, 1948, 4:82).

the plebiscite, the gendarmerie censored even the centrist press in the provinces.[49]

It was largely the gendarmerie on which the government relied to fight the guerrillas for more than a year after the March 1946 elections. The army was untrained for guerrilla warfare and was partly incapacitated by the recruitment of left-wing national servicemen. Thus, as late as April 1947, the gendarmerie was mainly responsible for military operations in the Peloponnesus and central Greece and had an important role farther north as well.[50] Zervas, with strong support from rightist deputies, took the process of militarizing the gendarmerie to extremes. He increased the gendarmerie from 28,000 to 31,000 by recruiting army reservists without police training, organizing much of this force into twenty-three battalions (plus other units equivalent to five more battalions), which he led in unsuccessful operations in the southern Peloponnesus.[51]

The anticommunist bandits were gradually given official status. Army officers saw them as a useful means of combating leftist bands, and they even helped to organize new bands. Some bandits (such as Anton Tsaous in Macedonia) were granted military rank, while others, such as Katsareas and Zaras, enjoyed semiofficial status as former officers of the army or the gendarmerie.[52] Most of the rightist bands on the mainland were gradually absorbed into the locally recruited and financed militias that were organized by the army and the government, known initially as MAY (Rural Security Units), a static type, and MAD (National Defense Units), a more mobile type. This process was begun in October 1946 by army officers under the direction of Mavromihalis as Minister of the Army.[53] The strength of these units, many of which behaved in a lawless and vindictive manner, increased to nearly 41,000 by May 1948, despite categorical American opposition to their existence. One State Department official, A. L. Moffat, thought that they were in some instances "almost

49. NARS, 868.00/4-1047, MacVeagh to Secretary of State.

50. FO 371/67030/-, Zervas to National Defence Council, 21 June 1947; 371/67052/113, R7270; 371/58759/116.

51. NARS, RG 84, Confidential File 1947, note of meeting of 3 September 1947; RG 319, U.S. Embassy to Secretary of State, 26 April 1947; FO 371/37131/1; 371/67131/1.

52. NARS, RG 319, Army Staff, intelligence report from office of Military Attaché W. R. Cory, 10 March 1947; FO 371/78389/-, monthly intelligence review no. 12, 5 May 1949; 371/72327/-, Patras Consul, 17 May 1948; 286/1181, Patras Consul, 17 November 1946.

53. FO 371/58759/-, R16396; D. Zapheiropoulos, O *Antisimmoriakos Agon, 1945–1949* (The antibandit struggle, 1945–1949), vol. 1 (Athens: n.p., 1956), 101.

as great a scourge as the guerrillas themselves."[54] During 1947, some of these units were little more than the private armies of politicians, and one, in the Chania nome, was actually led by a parliamentary deputy, Colonel Gyparis. Several such units in the southern Peloponnesus were patronized by Mavromihalis, others by the Populist politician Theodoros Tourkovasillis. In the spring of 1947, these units came into conflict with Zervas's auxiliary gendarmes, who were themselves recruited in part from local thugs. All of these groups terrorized civilians, thus increasing the popularity of leftist bands.[55] Nonetheless, the civil war that unfolded in 1946 and 1947 was fought on the government's side to a large extent by these miscellaneous (and usually ineffective) organizations directed by rightist politicians.

It is true that Tsaldaris' government quickly gave the army vast powers over civilians, from Epirus and Thessaly northward, by subjecting the police to its control for operational purposes and by establishing courts-martial to try those suspected of supporting the guerrillas. The courts-martial tried 37,000 people during the civil war and convicted 17,300.[56] In other ways, however, rightist politicians retained considerable influence over the army almost up to the time Gen. Alexander Papagos became commander in chief in January 1949. Senior appointments were repeatedly reshuffled for political reasons, while the geographical distribution of military units seems in practice to have been determined more by political considerations than by military ones, because of the demand by deputies (who sometimes threatened to withdraw their support from the government)[57] that military units be deployed to protect their constituents from guerrilla attacks. The politicians thus played into the guerrillas' hands by scattering the army in static defense duties.

There is no doubt that the civil war was greatly intensified by the security policies pursued by the Populist-dominated governments of April 1946 to August 1947.[58] Leftist civilians were driven to guerrilla activity by fear of persecution or by denial of relief supplies, while the Commu-

54. NARS, RG 334, JUSMAPG, Greece General Decimal File 1947–48, entry 146, box 49; RG 319, JUSMAPG, Plans & Ops., Greek General Staff Table, May 1948; 868.00/7-148, Griswold to Secretary of State; 868.00/1-849, R. A. Gibson to Secretary of State.
55. NARS, RG 84, Confidential File 1948, O. M. Marcy to K. L. Rankin, 21 March 1948; RG 319, U.S. Embassy to Secretary of State, 26 April 1947; 868.00/8-1247, F. Ayer Jr., memo; FO 371/67030/-, Norton-Foreign Office, 26 April 1947.
56. NARS, 868.00/8-1849, Minor to Secretary of State.
57. FO 371/72328/-, R13201.
58. As demonstrated at the time by Smothers et al., *Report on the Greeks*, 153.

nist leaders resorted to increasingly drastic retaliatory measures against which the government failed to act effectively. For a time, rightist politicians benefited from these trends. The anticommunist population was forced to submit to the repressive forces out of fear of the leftists, while the Communists discredited themselves with their escalating response to the actions directed against them. The British, and the Americans in turn, were forced to lend their support to the government, as rightist politicians had calculated that they would.[59] In the long run, however, the policies of the Right were self-destructive, and they were particularly damaging to the Populist Party.

The Populists in Retreat

A serious blow befell the Populists in September 1947 when, to strengthen the government, they were compelled by American officials to form a coalition with their main rivals, Sophoulis' Liberals, who had been preaching moderation toward the Left. Sophoulis himself became Prime Minister, while ten ministries went to his followers, including two vital to security policy: Christos Ladas became Minister of Justice, and Constantine Rendis became Minister of Public Order. Thereafter, Tsaldaris repeatedly explored the possibility of a return to a purely rightist government, only to find this avenue blocked by the Americans, who were supported by the British and the king.[60] Indeed, the need for a coalition government was increasingly accepted by leading Populists, some of whom, including Stephanopoulos and Dimitrios Helmis, forced Tsaldaris to make further concessions to Sophoulis in November 1948,[61] when the Populists lost control of the Ministry of the Army. In January 1949, the Populists retreated further by admitting into the government Panayiotis Kanellopoulos and the maverick rightist Spyros Markezinis (who was soon to advocate legalizing the Communist Party). The Populists lost the Ministry of the Interior and were left with only 11 ministries (the other rightists holding 3) out of 28; all of the rightist groups together held only 2 posts in the inner cabinet of 5. This reshuffle was accompa-

59. Iatrides, *Ambassador MacVeagh Reports*, 704.
60. NARS, 868.00/12-1147, Keeley to Secretary of State; 868.00/11-2648, Rankin to Secretary of State.
61. NARS, 868.00/12-1147; 868.00/11-2648.

nied by the appointment to the new post of Commander in Chief of the Armed Forces of Alexander Papagos, a move long advocated by the king, as well as by Sophoulis, who perhaps saw it as a means of denying rightist politicians influence over military appointments and operations.[62] In April 1949, the Markezinis group of three was replaced by Liberals. In September, the Populists lost a long battle to obstruct a scheme (backed by the Americans) to replace the nomarchs with officials with increased powers to be appointed on merit rather than on partisan grounds. Populists and Liberals were about equally represented among the new nomarchs.[63]

As the Populists lost their control over patronage, their parliamentary position weakened. This process seems to have been started by the restoration of the monarchy, a goal that had produced a stimulus to unity. Thus, in February 1947, Markezinis attracted some Populists to his New Party, which had nineteen deputies. The Populists' concessions to the Liberals also provoked frequent discontent from their backbenchers and put increasing strains on party unity.[64] In October 1948, Polyzois Oikonomidis caused twelve deputies to secede, reducing the party strength to 131 seats. Between May 1949 and the general elections of March 1950, revolts and secessions continued. By May, Dimitrios Londos, a leading member of the party, was organizing a movement of revolt—the so-called Populist Rally—against Tsaldaris, and by July Mavromihalis had also lost faith in Tsaldaris. He would soon desert the party and participate in the elections in alliance with former Metaxists. Of the four factions that had formed the Populist Party in 1946, only those of Tsaldaris and Stephanopoulos remained in the party in 1950.[65]

After the formation of the Sophoulis coalition, the Populists also lost influence over their allies. The Gonatas group (twenty-four deputies) and the Zervas group (twenty-one deputies) henceforth acted more independently, apparently in order to make themselves available as coalition partners with Sophoulis. Eventually, either during or after the 1950 elec-

62. NARS, 868.00/12-1147; 868.00/11-2648; S. Hourmouzios, *No Ordinary Crown: A Biography of King Paul of the Hellenes* (London: Weidenfeld & Nicolson, 1972), 198.

63. NARS, 868.00/5-2549 and 868.00/9-2649, both Minor to Secretary of State; 781.00/12–253, Thessaloniki Consul to State Department.

64. 868.00/11-2648, Rankin to Secretary of State; 868.00/6-348, Embassy to Secretary of State.

65. NARS, 868.00/11-2648, Rankin to Secretary of State; 868.00/7-949, O. S. Crosby, memo of conversation with Mavromihalis on 5 July; 868.00/5-1949, Minor to Secretary of State; Nikolakopoulos, *Kommata ke Voulevtikes Ekloyes*, 159–60; FO 371/78389/-, R7777.

tions, they rejoined the Liberals. Before doing so, they were considered to be to the right of the Populists, and so—like the Metaxist group of ten deputies led by Tourkovasillis—they were excluded by American veto from being serious candidates for office.[66] Meanwhile, the Venizelist and Sophoulist Liberals, who had reunited in November 1947, had a total of eighty-three deputies.

Sophoulis and his Liberal colleagues wished to combat communism in a more humane and discriminating manner than their predecessors had done. Sophoulis began his term of office in September 1947 with the most determined amnesty for outlaws applied so far, and Rendis, as Minister of Public Order, repeatedly exhorted the police to show moderation. They probably succeeded in restraining persecution of Liberals. But they associated themselves with the essential features of rightist policy, i.e., the attributes of an ideologically homogeneous state, based on the concept of *ethnikofrosene* and on arbitrary powers of arrest and detention by the security forces. This policy was actually given stronger expression by Public Law 509 of December 1947, for which the Liberal Ladas was responsible as Minister of Justice. This law broadened the category of offenses punishable by the police and the security commissions.[67] Shortly afterward, Ladas revived the prewar requirement that applicants for all public employment and a wide range of other positions sign a certificate of loyalty issued by the police. Meanwhile, under Rendis, mass arrests and deportations continued, and there is no evidence that he reduced their scale.[68] Whatever reformist intentions the Liberals may have had were largely frustrated by rightist domination of parliament and the bureaucracy. Liberal ministers were subject to continual pressure by right-wing deputies to persecute leftists and spare rightist lawbreakers. Such pressure was responsible, for example, for the draconian antistrike law of December 1947 (which Sophoulis willingly rescinded when told to do so by his American advisers); for the confirmation of death sentences handed out between February and May 1948 to more than two hundred leftist prisoners, most of them convicted for acts committed during the *Dekemvriana;* and for the moves late in 1949 to grant amnesty to right-

66. NARS, 868.00/12-247, Keeley to Secretary of State; 868.00/11-2648, Rankin to Secretary of State; Nikolakopoulos, *Kommata ke Voulevtikes Ekloyes,* 159–60.

67. Alivizatos, *Les institutions politiques,* 403–4.

68. NARS, 868.00/1-848 and 868.00/1-2048, 868.00/8-2749, all Rankin to Secretary of State.

wing bandits.[69] The Liberal ministers were also constrained by the polarization of the country. By late 1947, the civil war had escalated to such an extent that they had little option but to comply with the requirements of the security forces.

Meanwhile, Rendis and his associates in the Ministry of Public Order tried to build up a personal following within the police through numerous transfers and promotions. But it is clear that they did not change the attitudes of the bulk of the gendarmerie toward the leftist guerrillas and rightist bandits. Nor did they manage to break up the local connections that many officers had formed with rightist organizations.[70] They were constrained by, among other things, the fact that the Ministry of the Interior and the nomarchies remained in rightist hands until 1949. The attitude of the security forces was, as all could have foreseen, a crippling handicap to the success of Sophoulis' amnesty. When a deputy who was Sophoulis' nephew tried to negotiate the surrender of a left-wing guerrilla band in Samos, for example, the local MAY contingent sabotaged his efforts and was defended in parliament by Populist deputies.[71]

The army's composition and its policies toward the Left were essentially unaffected by Liberal ministers. Sophoulis was forced by the Americans to give up his initial idea of transferring to active status Venizelist generals from among the reservists on List B, which had been created by Nikolaos Plastiras's government early in 1945. Thereafter, he even found it difficult to prevent the Populist Minister of the Army from making blatantly partisan appointments of his own from List B.[72] The Liberal ministers had little effect on the activities of the special courts-martial, which came under the authority of regional military commanders and—insofar as they could be controlled at all by civilian ministers—that of the Minister of the Army. Shortly after the Populists relinquished control of the Ministry of the Army in November 1948, many of its functions were taken over by Papagos as Commander in Chief. In De-

69. NARS, 868.00/12-2947, memo of conversation involving Sophoulis, Rendis, Griswold, and C. Golden dated 23 December 1947; 868.00/19-849, Minor to Secretary of State; FO 371/72353/-, R5614.

70. NARS, 881.501/5-2250, R. B. Memminger to Secretary of State.

71. NARS, RG 84, Confidential File 1947, memo by G. Mylonas, 18 December 1947; 868.00/12-1847, U.S. Embassy to Secretary of State.

72. NARS, 868.00/9-647, MacVeagh to Secretary of State; 868.00/12-2947, memo of conversation involving Griswold, Sophoulis, and Rendis, 23 December 1947.

cember 1947, Sophoulis had to ask the Minister of the Army to direct the Athens court-martial to drop what were clearly vindictive proceedings against editors of four leading Liberal newspapers.[73] However, a Liberal Minister of Justice, George Melas, managed to introduce a limited provision for appeal from court-martial sentences to a Council of Pardons made up of senior civilian judges.[74]

As the army acquired increasing responsibility for internal security, it encroached on the powers of rightist politicians. In July 1947, the Supreme National Defense Council and High Military Command, responding to American pressure, prepared to transfer to the army the military responsibilities of the police. In October, orders were given to disband the auxiliary gendarmes, and with them the gendarmerie battalions. By the end of the year, the army had become responsible for internal security throughout the mainland. Thereafter, those gendarmes still engaged in combat (who still numbered several thousand in mid-1948) were under military command.[75] After 1947, the militia also slipped out of the control of political patrons and came increasingly under the supervision of regional military commanders. It was not until after the civil war, however, that military authorities imposed effective discipline on the militia.[76]

Meanwhile, the special courts-martial were extended to new areas (including Athens, in October 1947). Although they were attentive to charges brought by "X"-ite groups, military commanders showed an increasing tendency to defy the government. Apart from the case of the Liberal newspaper editors, there was the rearrest, on the orders of Gen. Thomas Pentzopoulos, in May 1948 of the two people who had appealed successfully to the Council of Pardons.[77] While the right-wing press in Athens applauded such acts of defiance, right-wing politicians viewed them with misgiving. Both Mavromihalis and Markezinis pri-

73. NARS, 868.00/9-647; 868.00/12-2947.
74. This reviewed death sentences imposed by a 3 to 2 majority (FO 371/722202/-, R13872). See also, NARS, RG 319, U.S. Embassy to Secretary of State, 27 May 1948; RG 84, Confidential File 1948, memo of 2 July 1947 conversation between R. G. Miner and G. Melas.
75. NARS, RG 319, Plans & Ops., 091.7TS, W. G. Livesay, 28 July 1947; FO 371/67131/1; A. Daskalakis, *Istoria tes Ellinikes Chorofilakes* (History of the Greek gendarmerie), vol. 2 (Athens: Tsiveriotis, 1973), 671, 683.
76. NARS, 868.00/6-1748, record of conversation of C. Rendis, S. Venizelos and D. P. Griswold on 4 June 1948; 868.00/11-548; FO 371/72327/-, R7039; 371/78386/-, R6231; 371/87771/-, RG 1642/4.
77. NARS, RG 319, U.S. Embassy to Secretary of State, 27 May 1948, 5 November 1948.

vately deprecated Pentzopoulos's action as an example of the tendency on the part of powerful officers to defy the government.[78] On the other hand, rightist politicians were ready to extend the army's powers to arrest summarily those suspected of supporting guerrillas. In October 1948, Minister of the Army Georgios Stratos induced Sophoulis to agree to the imposition of martial law throughout the country, which made Liberal newspapers and politicians apprehensive but did not evoke serious opposition from them.[79] The special courts-martial were extended to nearly all nomarchies, and the regional military commanders were given sweeping powers of censorship and the authority to restrict civilians' movements and make mass arrests. The last were conducted by the police on the basis of information they provided; the military authorities subsequently participated with the police in screening deportees for release.[80] While the civil war lasted, the military was also largely responsible for organizing and aiding the process of resettling refugee villagers.[81]

Thus, until the lifting of martial law, (between December 1949 and February 1950) security policy, including responsibility for granting amnesties, passed mainly into the hands of the regional military commanders. These commanders were responsible to Papagos, who wielded complete control over senior appointments and promotions in the army, and considerable control over military operations, although even at this date the disposition of troops was strongly influenced by political considerations.[82] In important ways, however, Papagos was impervious to political influence, as was revealed after the end of large-scale fighting, when for some months he resisted pressure by Populist as well as Liberal politicians to lift martial law.[83]

After the 1946 elections, most army officers naturally favored the Populist Party because of its uncompromising opposition to the Left, and

78. Ibid., 27 May 1948.

79. NARS, RG 319, U.S. Embassy to Secretary of State, 5 November 1948, 31 December 1948, 4 January 1949; 868.00/11-448, U.S. Embassy to Secretary of State; FO 371/71492/-, R2859.

80. FO 371/78385/-, R2563, R3086; 371/78387/-, R8872; 371/78414/-, R3929, 4698, 8819; NARS, RG 319, U.S. Embassy to Secretary of State, 30 December 1948; 868.00/5-2549, Grady to Secretary of State; Alivizatos, *Les institutions politiques,* 369–70.

81. FO 371/78385/-, R4927; 371/78386/-, R4982; NARS, 868.00/10-349, survey by Thessaloniki Consul; 868.00/7-1149, dispatch no. 90 by Thessaloniki Consul.

82. FO 371/78394/-, R943; NARS, 868.00/5-1349 and 781.00/3-551, U.S. Embassy to Secretary of State.

83. NARS, RG 84, Confidential File 1949, Minor to Secretary of State, 16 December 1949; FO 371/78340/-, R11327.

distrusted Liberals for their advocacy of what they saw as appeasement.[84] Members of IDEA were placed by the Populist-dominated governments of 1946–47 in positions where they could obstruct the careers of those with liberal opinions and advance the careers of extreme rightists, including former members of the Security Battalions.[85] When the Populists lost their dominance in the ministerial crisis of August 1947, Ventiris and a corps commander virtually ordered the king, on behalf of the army, to solve the crisis, which the king did by reappointing Tsaldaris as Prime Minister. The Americans then intervened and forced Tsaldaris' resignation in favor of Sophoulis.[86]

Thus, the Americans, who by now exercised extensive control over the army, drove a wedge between the high command and its political allies. For some time under the Sophoulis coalition, friendly relations continued between politically active officers and the Populist leaders, and the Populist retention of the Ministry of the Army must have facilitated this relationship.[87] During 1948, however, politically conscious officers became increasingly disdainful and self-confident in their attitude toward politicians in general. IDEA began to press its opinions on politicians and to maintain that it represented the whole officer corps, which was far from the truth. Its political interventions were fumbling. The boldest of them during the civil war was probably a circular that it sent in November 1948 to leading politicians of all parties hinting at "bad results" unless a "government above parties" was formed. The recipients ignored the demand as inconsequential, and the army had little or no influence during the ministerial crisis that occurred that month.[88] It appears that the brewing political discontent among the officer corps was relieved by Papagos's subsequent appointment as Commander in Chief.[89] Thereafter, the army stood out as the most ideologically cohesive, as well as the most powerful, body on the Right.

84. NARS, 868.00/12-2347, "Summary of Miscellaneous Conversations of Governor Griswold"; 868.00/12-3047; RG 319, Plans & Ops., 091.713 (1949), vol. 1, a biographical note on Gen. Solon Ghikas.

85. Stavrou, *Allied Politics,* 112–16.

86. Iatrides, *Ambassador MacVeagh Reports,* 724.

87. Stavrou speculates that IDEA cooperated with Stratos at the end of 1947 in an attempt to influence appointments to the high command (*Allied Politics,* 127). This seems possible. Rendis told Griswold on 28 December that Tsaldaris was flirting with a powerful clique of officers who hoped for a military dictatorship but that Mavromihalis had recently rebuffed them, saying he still believed in parliamentary government (NARS, 868.00/12-2347/12-3947).

88. NARS, 781.00/10-2751, R. Memminger to Secretary of State; 868.00/11-1948, Grady to Secretary of State; 868.00/11-2648, K. L. Rankin memo.

89. NARS, 781.00/10-2751, R. Memminger to Secretary of State.

During 1948, the Populists' influence was threatened by the monarchy, as well as by the army. King George, like his younger brother and successor, Paul (who became king in April 1947), had no incentive to favor the Right because Liberal and centrist politicians had accepted without question the results of the plebiscite of 1946. Instead, during the years 1946–49, the two monarchs supported British and American efforts to construct and preserve coalition governments.[90] Paul aspired to be something more than a British-American agent, however. He and Queen Frederica began in early 1947 to win nonpartisan support by their provincial tours and by Frederica's social work—activities in which they seem to have been more assiduous, or at least more successful, than any rightist politician. Frederica also showed skill in influencing American representatives.[91] The royal pair thus acquired political confidence.

Paul's first major initiative, early in 1948, was to advocate the appointment of his palace official Papagos as Commander in Chief, a position the general had held in the Albanian war of 1940–41. The fact that, even with Sophoulis' support, it took him about a year to achieve this aim was due in part to British and American doubt about the need for the new post.[92] In November 1948, the king went further and proposed to the British and American ambassadors, during a long ministerial crisis, that Papagos become head of a nonparty government in partnership with Markezinis, who was then Paul's trusted adviser. During the next ministerial crisis in January, Paul had to be restrained by the British and the Americans from installing such a government. But by threatening to do so he forced the rightist and centrist politicians to settle their differences and form a government.[93] This included Markezinis and two followers: all three were political novices who, although talented, owed their ministerial status to Paul's backing. In April 1949, Tsaldaris exploited Markezinis' apparent implication in a financial scandal to oust him from the government, a move that Paul and Papagos took as a personal affront. Again, Paul had to be restrained by the Americans from impetuous inter-

90. Alexander, *Prelude to the Truman Doctrine*, 210, 219, 237; Wittner, *American Intervention*, 112.

91. Wittner, *American Intervention*, 247; NARS, RG 84, Confidential File 1949, R. Memminger to O. S. Crosby, 7 December 1949; Th. Grigoropoulos, *Apo ten Korife tou Lofou* (From the top of the hill) (Athens: n.p., 1966), 358–59. Grigoropoulos refers admiringly to frequent visits by the royal pair to war zones.

92. *FRUS*, 1948, 4:201; NARS, 868.00/11-2648, Rankin to Secretary of State; 868.00/10-1748, G. C. Marshall, memo of conversation with king; FO 371/72258/-, R 2676.

93. *FRUS*, 1949, 6:234, 241; Hourmouzios, *No Ordinary Crown*, 206; NARS, 868.00/11-2648, Rankin to Secretary of State.

vention, this time aimed at ousting Tsaldaris from the government.[94] For the rest of the year, Populists and Liberals were stimulated to cooperate by fear of royal intervention, while Tsaldaris maneuvered in devious and ineffectual ways to curb the king's influence.[95]

During the second half of 1949, it seemed probable that Papagos would enter politics so as to participate in the next election. Papagos and the king (who still assumed that he guided Papagos's actions) considered the move, but in December decided independently against it.[96] Meanwhile, Markezinis fueled speculation in the press by proposing a government of himself and Papagos that would carry out urgent reforms while the elections were postponed. The latter step would have been illegal and was firmly opposed by the British and the Americans. But the likelihood of Papagos's entry into politics struck politicians with dismay, because they anticipated that he would steal most of the Right's and many of the Center's votes.[97]

The Collapse of the Populists

The nervousness of politicians about competition from Papagos can be explained by the public discredit into which they had fallen. Reports from many British and American observers in the provinces indicated that those members of the nationalist public who showed any interest in politics viewed politicians with disgust and despair, while the rest—apparently the great majority—appeared to be indifferent, a result of the politicians' failure either to project their personalities or to do anything to improve people's living conditions.[98]

What politicians most conspicuously failed to provide was leadership, whether in expounding the nationalist cause or in organizing relief work. Many (perhaps a majority) lived in the security of Athens and did little

94. *FRUS,* 1949, 6:295–96, 309–10, 314; NARS, 868.00/5-1349, Minor to Secretary of State.

95. NARS, 868.00/11-249, O. S. Crosby to R. Memminger.

96. NARS, RG 84, Confidential File 1949, Grady to Secretary of State, 7 December 1949; *FRUS,* 1949, 6:466.

97. See note 95 above; NARS, 868.00/11-249, O. S. Crosby to R. Memminger.

98. See, for example, NARS, RG 84, Confidential File 1948, O. M. Marcy to K. L. Rankin, 21 March 1948; R. Memminger to O. S. Crosby, 7 December 1949; 868.00/7-1149, Thessaloniki Consul, dispatch 90; FO 371/72328/-, R12880, J. G. Minnies, September 1948.

to raise public morale by undertaking provincial tours or visiting their constituencies.[99] To those in the provinces suffering from the civil war, politicians seemed to do little except bicker continually over the spoils of office. With some exceptions, regional and local officials did little or nothing to promote economic reconstruction or provide relief to refugees.[100] Thus, by 1949, it was natural for the nationalist public, including Populist supporters, to focus its hopes for peace and prosperity on the army and on Papagos, rather than on politicians.[101]

In retrospect, the malaise of the postwar Greek political system can be attributed largely to the fact that, having been paralyzed between 1936 and 1946, it was then subjected to the strains of economic collapse and civil war. These strains intensified the long-standing defects in the system: the excessive centralization of decision-making, the individualism of politicians, partisan manipulation of the state bureaucracy, and the excessively low level of integrity and efficiency among civil servants.[102] In these circumstances, politicians could hardly hope to enhance their reputations. But Populist politicians suffered especially because of their low caliber, and because they dominated the state. Inefficient officials were nearly all Populist appointees, and absentee deputies were often Populist supporters. The Populist Party became deeply implicated in official corruption. A damaging case (involving a former Minister of Transport) became public just before the 1950 elections.[103] The party also suffered from the failure to fulfill its election promises in 1946 to restore the economy, improve public order, and (except for the addition of the Dodecanese) increase national territory.[104] It is clear, moreover, that the party suffered from a public reaction against the excesses perpetrated by its armed supporters in the right-wing bands, the militia, and the police.[105]

99. NARS, 868.00/6-848 and 868.00/7-1449, both Rankin to Secretary of State; 868.00/9-3049, R. A. Gibson to Secretary of State.

100. FO 371/72328/-, R12506.

101. FO 371/78385/-, R1614; S. Linardatos, *Apo ton Emfilio stin Hounta* (From the civil war to the junta), vol. 1 (Athens: Papazeses, 1977), 60–62.

102. NARS, 868.00/19-146, W. H. McNeill memo; FO 286/1169, C. M. Woodhouse memo, 11 August 1945; 371/78394/-, R9431.

103. Linardatos, *Apo ton Emfilio stin Hounta*, 34–36.

104. NARS, RG 84, Confidential File 1949, Memminger to Crosby, 7 December 1949; RG 319, Thessaloniki Consul to War Department, 7 June 1947.

105. NARS, 868.00/1-2949, Rankin to Secretary of State; RG 84, Confidential File 1949, Crosby, 9 May 1949.

The Populists' electoral weakness was increased by their disunity and loss of patronage.[106] The electoral prospects of the Populists, and of the Right generally, were further diminished by the thorough measures that Stylianos Maniadakis, the Minister of Public Order in Theotokis' caretaker government, took in early 1950 to ensure at least the appearance of conditions for free and open general elections. To this end, Maniadakis traveled throughout the country lecturing the police on their duties. His government also secured the submission to police authority of the remaining right-wing bandits by offering them amnesty. The result was that there was considerably less intimidation in the general elections of 1950 than in those of 1946, especially in places open to government control, such as the larger cities, within the army, and even in the Makronissos prison camp.[107]

The outcome of the elections was partly determined by the prior realignment of candidates, which was in itself a recognition of the changed balance of power.[108] Apart from the disunity of the Populists, and the desertion to the Center of Gonatas and Zervas, the main change was the participation in the elections of a large proportion of the groups that had abstained in 1946. These (represented by the centrist National Progressive Center Union [EPEK] and the leftist Democratic Camp [DP]), secured 26.1 percent of the vote. The elections resulted in an immense drop in the rightists' support, from 64.7 percent of the vote in 1946 to 37.2 percent in 1950. The Populists did worse: whereas in 1946 they dominated the National Political Union (EPE), which got 55.1 percent of the vote, in 1950 they secured only 18.8 percent of the vote. They were left with only 62 deputies (other rightist groups ended up with 24 deputies) in a parliament of 250.

The Right After the Elections of 1950

There was now a sharp contrast between the weakness of the Right in parliament and its continuing control of other state institutions, includ-

106. NARS, 868.00/11-249, Crosby to Memminger; 868.00/8-1749 and 868.00/8-849, both Minor to Secretary of State.

107. NARS, 781.00/3-250 and 781.00/3-1350, both U.S. Embassy to Secretary of State; 781.00/3-2750, Crosby to Memminger; FO 371/87771/-, RG 1642/4; 371/78414/-, R10389; Nikolakopoulos, *Kommata ke Voulevtikes Ekloyes*, 166–67; Pepones, *Prosopike Martiria*, 174.

108. Nikolakopoulos, *Kommata ke Voulevtikes Ekloyes*, 162–71, 394–95.

ing the courts and education, the army and the police, and its influence over the monarchy and the American embassy. These institutions retained great influence over government policy, especially over policy with respect to left-wing subversion. For example, in order to fight the Left, the army and the police continued to rely on the emergency provisions of the civil war: administrative deportation and special courts-martial. These were potent political weapons, which were used to intimidate supporters of the Socialists in the 1950 elections. Another surviving wartime institution was the militia (now known as the National Defense Battalions [TEA]), which gave the army a means of organizing the nationalist elements of the rural population and which, at Papagos's insistence, remained mobilized during the 1950 elections.[109] Villagers were also supervised—thoroughly and rigorously—by a police force still obsessed by fear of Communist subversion. In the towns, trade unions had been rendered incapable of defending the interests of employees by repeated government interventions since 1946 against leftists in their ranks. The practices of these state institutions controlled by the Right were tolerated by powerful politicians of the Center,[110] who shared the Right's obsession with national security at a time when Greece seemed to be on the front line of the cold war. Greece's political and social structures therefore continued to be dominated by the values of the Right or, more accurately, by the values of the nationalist camp, of which the Right was the main part. The release of political detainees proceeded at a faster pace, probably, than most of the Right thought safe. This, and the continued instability of governments in the years 1950–52, were causes for anxiety. However, the monarchy and the American embassy acted as restraints on excessive leniency to the Left, and intervened repeatedly, in different ways, to secure conservative and stable government.

The chief weakness of the Right after the elections of 1950 was its continued lack of a political nucleus. The period between the 1950 elections and those of September 1951 witnessed the decline of the Populist Party and the rise of Papagos's Greek Rally as the dominant conservative political movement. The Populists, with their feeble leadership, shortage of political talent, and numerical weakness in parliament could no longer command respect from the other forces of the Right. Consequently, these forces, which lacked cohesion, fought among themselves.

109. FO 371/87683/-, RG 10134/1,3; 371/95121/-, RG 10106/26.
110. Daphnes, *Ta Ellinika Politika*, 454–64.

The king contributed to the disaffection by his poor political judgment and his changing personal dislikes. After the 1950 elections, he tried to prevent Nikolaos Plastiras from becoming Prime Minister by stalling, but he was forced to desist in this course by the American ambassador, Henry Grady, whom he snubbed in retaliation for this humiliation. By the time Papagos finally entered politics, in July 1951, the king had fallen out with him, opposing him openly and intriguing against him privately.[111]

The army and the police apparently remained generally unsympathetic to parliamentary democracy, because of its tendency to produce unstable governments and give power to politicians perceived as lenient toward the Left. Most army and police officers seemed to prefer a dictatorial government headed by Papagos, who was unwilling, however, to play the role of dictator. When, in May 1951, Papagos resigned as Commander in Chief, IDEA officers made a characteristically half-baked attempt at a coup on his behalf, which was quashed by Papagos himself.[112]

Meanwhile, the fortunes of the Populist Party continued to decline. As an aftereffect of its dominance during the civil war, it suffered from revelations of corruption. In November 1950, another scandal (this time concerning the administration of the port of Piraeus) provoked the secession of Stephanopoulos and twenty-six other deputies.[113] Papagos's entry into politics in July 1951 was—as many observers expected—the coup de grâce for the Populist Party. With his promises of inspiring leadership, stable and cohesive government, and honest and efficient administration, Papagos mobilized the power of the Right that was latent in the electoral system. As a result, his Greek Rally immediately gained the support of many Populist politicians; in the elections of 1951 it emerged as the main party of the new Right and gained ground at the expense of the Center. These trends continued in 1952, when the Greek Rally attracted nearly all sections of the traditional Right and many centrists who were ideologically close to it. In the elections that year, the Greek Rally won a large

111. G. I. Pesmazoglou, *My Public Life* (Athens: Diogenes, 1982), 193–94; FO 371/9510/-, RG 1011/1; 371/87663/-, RG 10111/9; NARS, 781.00/4-460, Memminger to Secretary of State; *The Declassified Documents Retrospective Collection*, 489F.

112. P. Kanellopoulos, *Istorika Dokimia* (Historical essays) (Athens: n.p., 1979), 25–26. FO 371/87651/-, RG 1018/40; NARS, 781.00/2-1751, Yost to Secretary of State; 781.00(W)/4-750, military attaché; NARS, 781.00(W)6-151.

113. FO 371/95118/-, Norton to Foreign Office, 22 August 1951; 371/95117/-, RG 10114; FO 371/95106/-, 5–6, Norton's review of the year 1950.

majority and achieved its goal of single-party government.[114] Thus, Papagos gave cohesion not only to the old Right but to the entire nationalist camp.

Some causes of the Populists' collapse were largely beyond their control. First, public resentment over the hardships of the civil war was directed at the Populists because they dominated the machinery of state while the war was in progress. Second, they were subjected to continual American pressure during the civil war to cede offices to centrist politicians so as to bring greater competence and public support to the government. Third, the increasing power of the army gave Papagos a level of prestige that overshadowed that of the rightist politicians. Other causes of the Populists' collapse were arguably avoidable. First among these was the escalation of the civil war in 1946–47, which was due primarily to the "white terror" with which the Populists associated themselves. The terror produced masses of recruits to the Democratic Army, which the Populist-dominated governments of 1946–47 proved incapable of weakening. Populist politicians failed thereafter to raise public morale, which they might have done by giving speeches and making visits to war zones. The fact that they became junior partners in the coalition governments of 1947–49, and that their party continued to decline after the civil war, is a reflection of their political inadequacies. Contemporary observers expressed poor opinions of the leadership qualities of Tsaldaris and other Populist leaders. Of the four leading Populists in 1945, only Stephanos Stephanopoulos held ministerial office after 1950.

Why were the Populists such incompetent political leaders during the civil war? Their shortcomings—especially their ruthlessness in pursuing party and personal interests at the expense of the public interest—were shared by some politicians of the Center and might therefore be ascribed to the old political culture in general. After 1946, nothing other than partisan animosities appear to have divided Populists from some centrists, but this had the inevitable result of dividing the nationalist camp. The fact that the Populists could not find more capable allies, or recruits, could also be attributed to developments between 1936 and 1944. The Metaxas dictatorship of 1936–41 and the quisling governments of 1941–44 were rightist in complexion, and those politicians who had participated in them were effectively disqualified from office in the later

114. Nikolakopoulos, *Kommata ke Voulevtikes Ekloyes*, 201–4.

1940s. Because the regimes of 1936–44 were so unpopular, they pushed the young toward the Left and the Center, which helps to explain the Right's shortage of young talent.

In 1945, the limited and obsolescent Populist Party found, in its old rallying cry, the monarchy—given fresh relevance by the public reaction against EAM—the path to power. But the return to power of the Populist politicians after the country's liberation was due not so much to their own talents as to the blunders of others: those of EAM in perpetrating terrorism after liberation and in abstaining from the 1946 elections; those of the British in tolerating the white terror and then insisting that an election be held under its influence. After 1951 the Right would turn away from the Populists' old guard to follow a new and more dynamic leadership.

6

The Executive in the Post-Liberation Period, 1944–1949

Nicos C. Alivizatos

For the constitutional developments of postwar Greece, the Lebanon, Caserta, and Varkiza agreements were documents of the utmost importance: not only did they prescribe in detail the process of the return to political normalcy,[1] they also outlined the main principles of the coun-

1. From a constitutional point of view, chapter 5 of the Lebanon Charter of 20 May 1944 was extremely significant. The Government of National Unity, headed by George Papandreou, pledged to establish, after the country's liberation, "the respect of order and freedom, that [would] enable the people to decide in a sovereign way, without psychological and material pressure, the political and social regime, as well as the government of its choice." Moreover, Papandreou specified that the people's choice had to be made as soon as possible and that, with regard to the regime question, all political leaders who had joined the Government of National Unity were understood to adhere to the views they had already expressed on this matter—in other words, that the king should refrain from returning to Greece before a free referendum had been held to determine whether the country was to have a crowned or republican form of democracy. Under the Caserta Agreement of 26 September 1944, Stephanos Saraphis and Napoleon Zervas had placed ELAS and EDES forces under the authority of the Government of National Unity, which in turn had placed them under the command of Gen. Ronald Scobie, the British officer appointed by the supreme allied commander to command the allied forces in Greece. Finally, the Varkiza Agreement, signed on 12 February 1945, reflected the divisions that emerged after the December 1944 crisis. Far more detailed than the Lebanon and Caserta agreements, it provided for the demobilization of ELAS and, as a counterpart, for the restora-

try's future constitution.[2] Representing a "preconstitution"—to use a term invented by Maurice Duverger[3]—these three documents were supposed to regulate the transition to democracy, almost ten years after its demise, and to control the action of provisional governments until a constitutional assembly had been called through free elections. Their validity rested on the fact that all of the political forces that had taken part in the national resistance movement during the enemy occupation had unreservedly adhered to them.[4] Thus, these documents should have become the starting point of the political process following the country's liberation.

It is not within the scope of this chapter to examine why these preconstitutional agreements did not fulfill their purpose. Nor is this the proper place to affix blame or to single out the factors that contributed to the disregard of the main provisions of the agreements almost as soon as they were concluded, with the result that the constitutional order that had existed before the Metaxas dictatorship of 4 August 1936 was unex-

---

tion of civil liberties, the lifting of martial law, amnesty for political crimes committed during the Athens revolt, the formation of a national army, and the purging from civil and security services of wartime collaborators and other undesirables. Article IX stipulated that a referendum on the "regime issue" was to take place "at the earliest possible date, and in any case within the current year," and that thereafter general elections to a constituent assembly were to be held "as quickly as possible." For the texts of the Lebanon and Caserta agreements in the original Greek, see George Papandreou, *I Apelevtherosis tis Ellados* (The liberation of Greece), 3rd ed. (Athens: Elliniki Ekdotiki, 1948), 73–81, 159–63. For the text of the Varkiza Agreement, see *Government Gazette,* section A'/23 March 1945, 235–37. For an English translation (which contains inaccuracies), see C. M. Woodhouse, *Apple of Discord* (London: Hutchinson, n.d.), 305–10.

2. This was mainly true of article I (Liberties) and article V (National Army) of the Varkiza Agreement. However, the persistent use of the term "government" (*kyvernesis*) in all three "preconstitutional" agreements was significant in many respects, inasmuch as it heralded the establishment of a parliamentary regime with executive authority in the hands of a cabinet made up of elected officials. (This is elaborated on in the text below.)

3. To qualify the legal nature of the French constitutional law of 2 November 1945, which was approved by referendum and provided not only for the exercise of political power until a new constitution was voted but also for the main lines of the latter, see M. Duverger, *Institutions politiques et droit constitutionnel,* 10th ed. (Paris: PUF, 1968), 465–67.

4. At the same time, they secured the support of the Allies, namely the British. In fact, formal British endorsement appeared only on the Caserta Agreement, which bore the signatures of Gen. Henry Maitland Wilson, the Supreme Allied Commander, Mediterranean Theatre, and Harold Macmillan, the British Resident Minister. Nevertheless, the British had followed the Lebanon and Varkiza conferences very closely and may have previously approved the contents of the two agreements. See Reginald Leeper, *When Greek Meets Greek* (London: Chatto & Windus, 1950), 50–52, 143–46.

pectedly revived.[5] Unlike the "regime issue"—which was supposed to remain on hold until determined by a referendum[6]—the three documents were quite clear with regard to the form of government post-liberation Greece was to have: any division of authority at the highest levels of the state was to be abolished; Greece was to be a parliamentary democracy—crowned or republican—and real power was to be concentrated in the hands of a cabinet responsible to a freely elected national assembly. Therefore, regardless of the details of the system to be adopted, *executive authority would no longer be shared by the king* (should the latter's return be approved by the people), *but would be in the hands of a cabinet, whose power would derive from and reflect the people's sovereign will.*[7]

Surprisingly, this important constitutional choice, which corresponded with Greek parliamentary tradition of the late nineteenth century,[8] was never openly challenged in the political discourse after 1944, by either the Right or the Left. Nevertheless, disagreement over this key issue obviously existed, which raises doubts about the sincerity of the promise of both sides to respect the arrangement.

Although throughout the 1940s the cabinet was substantially strengthened on the institutional level, it never became the undisputed seat of political power. This was because the cabinet's authority was undermined or usurped by such political actors as the Allies, the army, and the crown.

This chapter describes the evolution of these competing centers of po-

5. This resulted from the convening in 1946 of a revisionary assembly, rather than a constitutional assembly, and from the revival (with the assistance of the courts) of the constitution of 1911, as amended in 1935.

6. See the statement made by George Papandreou on 12 June 1944 on the occasion of the first meeting—although without the participation of EAM ministers—of the Government of National Unity. Papandreou's eloquent remarks were another in a series of efforts undertaken since 1943 to persuade the king to declare that he would not to return to Greece before the referendum on the regime issue was held.

7. In my view, there was also unanimous agreement on the closely linked and extremely delicate question of the system to be applied for the election of the constitutional assembly: all parties agreed to revive the 1936 system of proportional representation in order to ensure that all major political groupings were represented in parliament.

8. This tradition was strongly influenced by (although it is not a mere copy of) the "Westminster" majoritarian parliamentary system, which had traditionally been considered as appropriate for Greece. For an excellent review of the characteristics of this tradition, see Nicholas Kaltchas, *Introduction to the Constitutional History of Modern Greece* (New York: Columbia University Press, 1940).

litical authority, which were to survive the civil war and to continue to play a significant role in Greek public life in the 1950s and 1960s, up to the fall of the Colonels' junta in 1974.

The Institutional Reinforcement of the Cabinet and the Concept of Impermeability

The concentration of exclusive legislative authority in the cabinet developed in two distinct historical phases. The first began with the country's liberation in October 1944 and lasted until the general elections of 31 March 1946. The second phase extended from the appointment of the Tsaldaris cabinet in April 1946 to the dissolution of the fourth revisionary parliament on 7 January 1950.

During the first phase, six provisional cabinets that, from a legal standpoint, had almost unrestricted powers were formed. They represented the concentration of both constitutional and legislative power, and the only legal barrier to their actions was the preconstitution contained in the Lebanon and Caserta agreements that preceded the December 1944 uprising in Athens and in the Varkiza Agreement of February 1945.[9] Since no elections were held, the legitimacy of the cabinets was closely linked to their political representativeness. The first, the Papandreou cabinet, which remained in office until 2 December 1944, consisted of representatives of the entire spectrum of the national resistance movement.[10] Of the remaining five, the Plastiras cabinet was of Center-Left orientation, and the Sophoulis cabinet genuinely represented the Center, while the Voulgaris cabinet and the short-lived cabinets of Archbishop Damaskinos and Panayiotis Kanellopoulos of October and November 1945 leaned to the Center-Right.[11]

9. The Varkiza Agreement was ratified by Constitutional Act 23 of 23 March 1945, under the Plastiras government. Constitutional Act 21 of 24 February 1945, under the same government, regulated in detail the exercise of constitutional and legislative powers by the regent and the cabinet "until the holding of general elections."

10. The EAM ministers resigned from the Government of National Unity over the issue of demobilization, which was directly related to the enforcement of the Caserta "preconstitutional" agreement (mainly of articles 3 and 6).

11. For a detailed account of government and ministerial changes in the immediate postliberation period, see Alkiviadis Provatas, *Politiki istoria tis Ellados, 1821–1980: Nomothetika kai Ektelestika somata* (Political history of Greece, 1821–1980: Legislative and executive bodies) (Athens: Organismos Ekdoseos Didactikon Vivlion, 1980), 560–98. For statistics on the subsequent period up to 1952, see Keith Legg, "Musical Chairs in Athens: Analyzing Political

These five cabinets issued a total of 116 constitutional acts covering a wide range of issues, such as the punishment of collaborators, the approval and enforcement of the Varkiza Agreement, the reinstatement of civil servants dismissed by the Metaxas dictatorship and by the collaborators, the institution of disciplinary measures against civil servants who had participated in the December 1944 uprising, and the amnesty issue. They undertook a review of the quisling government's legislation,[12] and they issued more than 1,100 "necessity laws," i.e., executive acts, covering an equally wide range of issues. All constitutional acts and necessity laws contained a provision that they would be subject to ratification by the future national assembly. However, with few exceptions, review by the national assembly did not take place until April 1952.[13]

No substantive changes took place after the election of the first postwar parliament in March 1946. In theory, both constitutional and legislative powers rested with the national assembly and were supposed to be exercised through the adoption of constitutional resolutions and parliamentary laws, respectively, by simple majority.[14] Nevertheless, the national assembly—incorrectly called "revisionary," although it had in fact almost unlimited constitutional powers[15]—was in practice replaced in these functions by the cabinets that succeeded each other through the end of 1949. On the one hand, the cabinets issued constitutional resolutions and legislative decrees on the basis of a series of extremely broad and vague authorizations approved by a national assembly very eager to transfer to the cabinet its own responsibilities. These legislative acts were issued either with or without the approval of a special fifty-member par-

Instability, 1946–1952," in *Studies in the History of the Greek Civil War, 1945–1949*, ed. Lars Baerentzen, John O. Iatrides, and Ole L. Smith (Copenhagen: Museum Tusculanum, 1987), 9–24.

12. Regarding the legal nature and actions of the post-Varkiza governments, see Nicos C. Alivizatos, *Les institutions politiques de la Grèce à travers les crises, 1922–1974* (Paris: Librairie Générale de Droit et de Jurisprudence, 1979), 110ff., 121ff.

13. At that time, the parliament elected on 9 September 1951, which was predominantly centrist, ratified by constitutional resolution all legislative acts that had been enacted in an irregular way since the country's liberation, including all "emergency" measures of the civil war years. On the peculiarities of the constitutional resolution, see Alivizatos, *Les institutions politiques,* 424ff.

14. Constitutional resolution A, 12 June 1946.

15. The denomination "revisionary" was used for the first time in the royal decree of 19 January 1946, by which the nation was invited to elect the first post-liberation parliament. As noted above (note 5), this wording had important political implications because a revisionary assembly was not authorized to undertake radical constitutional changes.

liamentary committee, known as the Delegation Committee.[16] On the other hand, the cabinets unilaterally enacted necessity laws and issued executive decrees without any authorization from the national assembly, claiming that, under the extraordinary circumstances prevailing in the country, urgent measures needed to be taken—if need be, in violation of standing constitutional rules.[17]

Thus, of 1,500 legislative acts adopted from 1946 to 1949, only 300 had been voted on by parliament prior to their enforcement.[18] It is worth noting in this respect that only a small number of the measures adopted by the executive during that period were justified by the need to deal with the rebellion, since for the most part they referred to routine or secondary issues that had nothing to do with the civil war.[19] In addition, only a very small portion of the measures enacted unilaterally by the executive were submitted, many months after their enactment, to the national assembly for ratification. Each of the ten cabinets of the civil war period, irrespective of political orientation, followed these improper practices, despite the fact that the national assembly elected in 1946 was dominated by a strong majority of the Center and extreme Right.

This concentration of legislative functions in the hands of the executive and, consequently, the decline of the parliament's constitutional role, resulted in the emergence, for the first time in a lasting way, of "impermeable" or "out-of-bounds" areas, on which no parliamentary debate or public discussion was permitted. Although the prohibition of public scrutiny of the regulation of "sensitive" issues had occurred in the past during periods of crisis,[20] it had never been as extensive or persistent as would be the case with executive legislative action during the civil war. A precedent was thus created that, despite feeble attempts by some

16. The committee was eventually institutionalized by article 35 of the constitution of 1952.

17. For a detailed account of this practice and its wider implications, see the classic analysis of Aristovoulos Manessis, *Peri anagkastikon nomon* (On necessity laws) (Athens: Sakkoulas Publishers, 1953).

18. For more statistics, see Nikolaos Calodoucas, "To nomothetikon ergon, apo ton eklogon tis D' Anatheoritikis Voulis (33.3.1946) mehri ton eklogon tis 9 Septemvriou 1951" (Legislative work, from the elections of the fourth revisionary assembly [31 March 1946] to the elections of 9 September 1951), in *Codix Nomon* (1951), 1058ff.

19. For instance, necessity law 876 of 1949 provided for the creation of one position for a marble cutter at the School of Fine Arts of Athens.

20. Regular parliamentary procedures for the enactment of new legislation had previously been substantially bypassed during the Balkan Wars (1912–13) and in the course of the political crises between 1917 and 1920 and in 1935 and 1936.

courts to restrict its scope,[21] had a profound effect on the way in which laws were enacted in succeeding decades and to this day.[22]

A second practice, which led to greater impermeability within the executive branch itself in the 1940s, was the assignment of important tasks to small government committees on a permanent basis, rather than to the entire cabinet. The establishment of the Supreme Council of National Defense (ASEA) and the Currency Committee are cases in point.

ASEA was reinstated by the Sophoulis cabinet in December 1945 with considerably wider powers than its prewar predecessor. It had seven members, was chaired by the Prime Minister, and, in theory, had control over the three branches of the armed forces through the appointment and assignment of their commanding officers.[23] The five-member Currency Committee, created by the same cabinet in February 1946,[24] was in theory responsible for determining the monetary and credit policies of the country.

With those deliberately small committees, the decision-making process in crucial areas of government action was definitely speeded up. At the same time, however, impermeability was further reinforced, since even cabinet members were not aware of the issues under consideration by these bodies. Thus, the principle of collective ministerial responsibility was in fact violated and, at a higher political level, the cohesion of the post-1947 coalition cabinets was undermined.

A third development that affected the structure of the post-liberation executive authority was the creation of numerous new ministries. Although some of these reflected the needs of the moment (for example, the Ministry of Supply, the Reconstruction Ministry, and the "general administrations" of a number of agencies that were headed by cabinet members), some met more permanent organizational needs and therefore remained in place after the 1940s. This was the case with the Ministry of Coordination, established by the Sophoulis cabinet in December

21. The Council of State, the country's supreme administrative court, attempted to restrict these practices after liberation and during the civil war. See Alivizatos, *Les institutions politiques,* 112ff., 126ff.

22. The practice of "occult" legislation—to use an expression coined by Aristovoulos Manessis—survived even the restoration of democracy in 1974 as a means of avoiding "annoying" publicity in the regulation of "delicate" questions. Measures enacted through this procedure are in general ratified ex post facto by parliament and hence retroactively validated.

23. Necessity law 730, 15 December 1945.

24. Necessity law 1015, 27 February 1946.

1945, with Emmanuel Tsouderos as its first head, which proved to be the most important postwar innovation in the reorganization of the cabinet. This new ministry was entrusted with overall supervision and coordination of the work of all of the so-called productive ministries (the National Economy Ministry, later named the Commerce Ministry, and the Finance, Agriculture, Supply, Labor, Communications, Recovery, and Merchant Marine ministries), and its role was further strengthened in the years that followed.[25] This was also the case with the Ministry of Public Order, established with Gen. Pafsanias Katsotas at the helm by the Kanellopoulos cabinet in November 1945,[26] which took over from the Ministry of the Interior all matters relating to public order and security so as to achieve greater efficiency under conditions of increased impermeability. In 1947, under the direction of the politically uncontrollable Napoleon Zervas, the jurisdiction and authority of this ministry reached its peak.[27]

The Political Decline of the Cabinet

The institutional reinforcement of executive authority described above was not accompanied by an enhancement of the cabinet's political role. On the contrary, the cabinet was undermined by three political actors who claimed their own autonomous roles in the decision-making process during the civil war: the Western allies, the army, and the crown.

The role of Britain and—after May 1947—of the United States in Greek public life is well known, and there is no need to expound on it here. From an institutional point of view, however, one element deserves attention. On many occasions, Allied intervention in the Greek government's decision-making was open, official, and institutionalized, and therefore had lasting consequences. Several typical cases may be mentioned to illustrate the point.

According to the 1946 necessity law that reestablished ASEA, for example, the chiefs of the British army, navy, air, and police missions in

25. Necessity law 718, 11 December 1945.
26. Necessity law 638, 1 November 1945.
27. On the term of the former EDES leader as Minister of Public Order from 23 February to 29 August 1947, see the critical account of his predecessor, Spyros Mercouris, in *To Vima*, 23 September 1947.

Greece could be invited to participate in the deliberations of the seven-member council "whenever the council wishes them to be present as consultants, on any specific issue."[28] Under the same law, these British officers were full nonvoting members of the Greek Joint Chiefs of Staff.[29] In addition, the chief of the British army mission, as well as his American counterpart after 1948, were regular nonvoting members of the Supreme Military Council.[30] With respect to the latter, a 1948 necessity law provided in addition that the presence of the British and American members was required for a quorum, unless they themselves had given written notice of their inability to attend.[31]

A 1946 necessity law institutionalized the participation of a British representative and an American representative on the Currency Committee. The foreigners were voting members of the committee, and all decisions relating to the issuance of bank notes had to be unanimous. In this case, the law conformed with the provisions of the economic agreement of 24 January 1946 between Britain and Greece. In a letter from Foreign Minister Ernest Bevin to Tsouderos, which the Greek authorities accepted as binding, it had been stipulated that

> the Greek Government, as a further measure to establish confidence in the currency, will by Greek Law set up a Currency Committee, which will have statutory management of the note issue. The Committee will consist of the Greek Minister of Coordination as president, the Greek Minister of Finance, the Governor of the Bank of Greece, a member of U.K. nationality and a member of U.S.A. nationality, whom the Greek Government will invite to act as members of the Committee. *New issues of currency will only be made with the unanimous approval of the Committee.*[32]

Under the terms of an agreement between the United States and Greece, ratified by a necessity law enacted in 1948, an American citizen was to be appointed Governor of the Greek Social Security Administration (IKA). Among his other duties, the Governor was "to review and

28. Article 3, necessity law 730, 15 December 1945.
29. Article 5, necessity law 730, 15 December 1945.
30. Article 1, necessity law 731, 15 December 1945.
31. Article 1, section 2, necessity law 780, 14 September 1948.
32. Section 5(h) of the Anglo-Greek Agreement of 24 January 1946, ratified by necessity law 971, 20 February 1946 (emphasis added).

approve all actions related to [IKA personnel] career issues, including appointments, assignments, promotions, demotions, termination and disciplinary measures." His decisions on such matters were to be published in the *Government Gazette* without previous approval by the Greek authorities.[33]

Equally wide were the powers of the American Managing Director of the Department of Foreign Trade of the Ministry of National Economy, who even approved applications of private individuals and firms wishing to import or export products of any kind.[34]

Last, but not least in view of the ideological significance of the issue, the U.S.-Greece agreement of 12 April 1949 regarding the establishment of a radio station in Thessaloniki provided that the station would operate under the authority of a six-member committee composed of three Greek and three American citizens, and that decisions were to be made on all matters by the affirmative vote of at least four members, regardless of the number of those attending.[35]

The characterization of Greek policies during the civil war as "appendages of American policies"[36] is probably an exaggeration, inasmuch as it does not take sufficiently into consideration the weight of local factors, including the eagerness of the Athenian political elites to accept open foreign intervention on such a broad range of issues. What should be stressed, however, is that the instrument of foreign pressure was official and institutionalized. Article 9 of the U.S.-Greece agreement of 8 July 1947 concerning relief assistance to Greece clearly provided that the U.S. government could unilaterally "stop or alter its program of assistance whenever in its determination other circumstances warrant such action."[37]

33. Article 4, section 3, of the Greek-American Agreement of 25 October 1948, ratified by necessity law 852, 31 December 1948. A subsequent agreement, ratified by necessity law 1347 in 1949, specified that the American administrator of IKA had "the authority to establish the organization of IKA, by decisions of his own published in the *Government Gazette*" in order to form new services, divisions, and offices, and had the "power to change and supercede existing contrary IKA regulations."

34. Article 6, section B, legislative decree 480, 31 October 1947.

35. Memorandum prepared by Henry Grady, dated 12 April 1949, accepted by the Greek government and ratified by legislative decree, 17 October 1949 (no. 1191/49).

36. Michael Mark Amen, "American Institutional Penetration into Greek Military and Political Policymaking Structures: June 1947–October 1949," *Journal of the Hellenic Diaspora* 5 (Fall 1978): 113.

37. "Agreement Between the U.S.A. and the Kingdom of Greece Concerning Relief Assistance to the People of Greece," ratified by necessity law 764, 3 September 1946.

The wording of article 10 of the U.S.-Greece agreement of 20 June 1947 regarding aid to Greece was even more direct: "If the Government of Greece does not take reasonable steps to effectuate those measures proposed in its note of 15 June 1947, or subsequently agreed upon, which are essential to reconstruction and recovery of Greece," the agreement could be terminated unilaterally by the government of the United States.[38]

After the beginning of the civil war in March-April 1946, the role of the army rapidly increased in scope. The notorious Constitutional Resolution C of July 1946 permitted the establishment of courts-martial, initially in the northern districts and subsequently throughout Greece.[39] Following the declaration of martial law after the assassination of Minister of Justice Christos Ladas on 1 May 1948, all powers of civil authorities relating to public order and security matters were also formally transferred to the military.[40] The process of establishing the autonomy of the military reached its peak with the appointment of Gen. Alexander Papagos as Commander in Chief of the Greek armed forces in January 1949. Having insisted on the abolition of ASEA, Papagos assumed "almost dictatorial" powers, according to Gen. Dimitrios Zafeiropoulos, one of the most serious commentators on the period.[41] By necessity law 882 of 1949, Papagos was empowered to determine the army's composition, to decide on its operations, to create or dissolve units, and to recommission retired officers without consulting with the government or any other authority. To the contrary, his decisions were binding on the ministers nominally responsible for such matters.[42]

38. "Agreement on Aid to Greece," ratified by necessity law 763, 2 September 1947. For an excellent review of the various institutional forms of American influence in Greece during the first phase of the civil war, see A. A. Fatouros, "Building Formal Structures of Penetration: The United States in Greece, 1947–1948," in *Greece in the 1940s: A Nation in Crisis*, ed. John O. Iatrides (Hanover, N.H.: University Press of New England, 1981), 238–58.

39. Article 11, Constitutional Resolution C, 18 July 1946. For a list of the thirty-one "extraordinary" military courts established throughout the country during the civil war, see C. Oikonomopoulos, *Ektakta stratodikeia kai nomothesia aphorosa tin dimosian taxin kai asphaleian* (Extraordinary military courts and legislation on public order and security) (Athens, 1951), 5ff.

40. Under article 4 of law ΔΞΘ of 1912, reactivated (for the first time since February 1945) by royal decree on 1 May 1948, martial law was put into effect, first in the Athens area and subsequently all over Greece, and maintained in force until 11 February 1950.

41. D. Zafeiropoulos, *O antisimmoriakos agon, 1945–1949* (The antibandit struggle, 1945–1949) (Athens, 1956), 533, 535.

42. Necessity law 882, 20 January 1949, ratified by legislative decree 1090, 24 September 1949.

This institutional insulation of the armed forces from civilian executive authority reflected a tendency that had first appeared in 1935, after the purge of the Venizelist elements from the officer corps.[43] In 1945, as a result of the failure of the Plastiras cabinet to reinstate the Venizelist officers who had been dismissed in 1933 and once again in 1945, the officer corps retained the politically and ideologically monolithic character it had acquired under the Metaxas dictatorship and thereafter questioned more and more openly the capacity of the politicians to face the Communist challenge.[44] Anxious to preserve liberal appearances, the Americans disapproved of attempts by the secret officers' organization, IDEA, and other extremist groups within the army to establish an open dictatorship. They favored instead a solution that observed the forms of parliamentary government while entrusting the armed forces with the main responsibility for conducting the struggle against the Communist forces, which would inevitably extend the military's authority on matters normally falling under the jurisdiction of the civil authorities. This included military autonomy over the state-owned mass media,[45] growing military influence in the development and enforcement of internal security policies,[46] and the active participation of the military in almost all reconstruction programs.[47] Given the unquestioned prestige he enjoyed within the officer corps and the ties he maintained with the Western allies and with an important faction of politicians in Athens, General Papagos was the ideal person to establish and maintain the delicate balance between military and civilian authority in the years that followed, first as Commander in Chief and later as party leader and Prime Minister.

The role of the crown after liberation also changed. Although King George II lacked genuine popular support, the crown as an institution enjoyed unexpected legitimacy because, after the beginning of the civil

43. See N. C. Alivizatos, "The Greek Army in the Late Forties: Towards Institutional Autonomy," *Journal of the Hellenic Diaspora* 5 (Fall 1978): 35–45.

44. See the account of Panayiotis Kanellopoulos, *Istorika dokimia* (Historical essays) (Athens, 1975), 23–24.

45. Although in operation since the late 1940s, the armed forces radio and subsequent television service, which broadcast to the entire nation and not only to the military, was officially created by necessity law 1663 in 1951. It continued to function under the orders of the Joint Chiefs of Staff until 1982, when it was abolished.

46. Concerning the continued application, under the pressure of the military during the 1950s and 1960s, of the Metaxist necessity law 375 of 1936 on espionage, see Alivizatos, *Les institutions politiques*, 449ff.

47. Military participation was mainly through the Military Service for the Construction of Recovery Works (SYKEA), created in the late 1940s.

war, a significant number of its traditional Venizelist opponents, in their desire for security and law and order, increasingly viewed the monarchy as a stabilizing factor. Confirmed by the plebiscite of September 1946 that returned George to his throne, this newly acquired authority enabled an unpopular king to play once again an active role in Greek politics. Under the new circumstances, however, this role substantially diverged from the "interventionist" model he and his father, King Constantine, had employed during the period of the "National Schism" in the years between the world wars. The king was no longer to be the actual or symbolic leader of a single political party. Rather, he was to become the symbol of national unity and, at the same time, the arbiter of all bourgeois parties. Therefore, his main task would be to suppress rather than aggravate the old cleavages between the Liberals and the Antivenizelists.

It is therefore not surprising that, from the first moment of his return to Greece, George made it clear he would devote all his energy to building a better future for the nation and that the "harms of the past" (that is, from the period of the National Schism) should be allowed to fade into oblivion.[48] It is also significant that, according to Panayiotis Pipinelis, his devoted adviser and official biographer, the most important achievement of the king's third and short-lived reign (George II died on 1 April 1947) was that he managed to persuade Constantine Tsaldaris to endorse and eventually actively support a coalition cabinet that would better reflect the new spirit and the determination of all "national" forces to stand united in confronting the Communist revolt.[49] After George's death, King Paul was even more successful in this task. Despite his wife's highhanded political initiatives, he succeeded in further consolidating the anticommunist front through subtle maneuvering and ministerial manipulations, which continued until the end of the civil strife.[50]

Thus, in the handling of the major issues during the civil war, the crown's role was of a structural rather than a directly interventionist nature. It primarily expressed the views of the Western allies and reflected personal policy priorities only on such secondary issues as relief and so-

48. Message to the Greek people, 28 September 1946, *Government Gazette,* section A'1946: 1645.

49. P. Pipinelis, *Georgios B'* (George II) (Athens, 1951), 196, 199.

50. The king's task was further facilitated by the fact that no single political party enjoyed a majority in the 1946 revisionary assembly. See Legg's concept of "unstable equilibria" in "Musical Chairs," 17ff.

cial welfare activities, in which, by establishing a nationwide network of devoted agents, Queen Frederica excelled for years, free from any supervision or control by parliament and government authorities.[51]

In the aftermath of the Second World War, most Western European countries underwent constitutional revolutions. Greece did not. The political ideals and social values of the Greek resistance movement were not integrated into the nation's post-liberation institutions. On the contrary, they were rejected by the victors in the civil war, who, thanks to this upheaval, managed to do what they could not have imagined only a few years earlier: divest the *esprit de la résistance* of its reformist appeal in a society that was eager above all to live in peace. Thus, for Greece, unlike Italy and France, which had equally important wartime resistance movements, the issue after liberation was not how to reconcile—on the political and institutional levels—the pursuit of social justice with the rules of parliamentary government. Instead, the goal of the dominant forces was to maintain the appearance of constitutional legality in the eyes of the international community, which was unwilling to tolerate the revival of an open dictatorship so soon after the defeat of the Axis.

The conditions created by a devastating civil war, in a country that was emerging from a catastrophic foreign occupation, could certainly account for the deviations from the normal rules of parliamentary government. Under the circumstances existing in Greece in the mid-1940s, the scrupulous observance of constitutional legality would have clashed with the need for centralized authority and efficiency in the handling of public affairs so as to crush the enemy and make recovery possible. However, by being so blatant and institutionalized, these deviations from the rules of parliamentary government, described in this chapter, caused *a latent and lasting cleavage between a constitutional system that called itself a liberal democracy and a completely different reality insofar as the exercise of power was concerned.* This cleavage between the *état légal* and the *état réel* was the most important institutional consequence of the Greek civil war.

Although no open dictatorship was established by the victors, the antidemocratic institutional legacies of the civil war survived the Communist

51. These activities were carried out mainly through the Ethnikon Idrima (National Foundation), established by royal decree on 15 March 1947. Concerning this notorious institution and its activities in the decades that followed, see Jean Maynaud, *Oi politikes dinameis stin Ellada* (Political forces in Greece) (Athens: Spoudes Politikis Epistimis, 1966), 339–45.

defeat. It is not surprising, therefore, that throughout the 1950s and 1960s the governing process in Greece was characterized by dual legalities: the official *constitutional* legalities established under the constitution of 1952, and the unofficial *paraconstitutional* legalities, which were based on the measures enacted and the practices followed during the period of the civil war. The first set the rules of the official political forms, while the second aimed at maintaining the country's governing process within the unofficial but effective power bases and decision-making systems that had been established during the civil war. The latter included autonomous political roles for the army and for the Western allies, both of which were permitted to interfere in the government of the country, either directly or through the crown.

Under these circumstances, it soon became clear that the cabinet, which supposedly reflected the will of the Greek people as expressed through free national elections, was without real power. Although it had been reinforced under the constitution of 1952 and enjoyed, as a general rule throughout the 1950s and 1960s, comfortable and obedient parliamentary majorities, the cabinet was in reality accountable not only to the electorate but also to such paraconstitutional centers of power as the leadership of the armed forces and the representatives of the United States, whose consent, if not previous approval, was necessary for important decisions in a variety of areas, including foreign policy, national defense, and public order. Over the ensuing years, intervention in the governing process by these actors became less open and less institutionalized, but it continued nonetheless, now exercised through the crown. The importance of the monarchy increased significantly in the early 1960s, when political forces opposed to the perpetuation of this paraconstitutional order and advocating reform managed for the first time since the end of the civil war to win the general elections.

Ultimately, the *état légal* and the *état réel* came to coincide under the 1967 military dictatorship, which put an end to the peculiar Greek postwar parliamentary experience. Although this is not the place for a discussion of the causes of the Colonels' success in seizing and exercising power for more than seven years, it is clear from the above that the cabinet's lack of control over the military and the surrender of executive authority to the crown and the Western allies, combined with the other institutional legacies of the civil war, facilitated the junta's task. To the extent that it formalized these legacies, the Colonels' regime was not merely the product of the civil war but also its culmination. However, by seeking to enforce the same practices even against those, including the crown, who had tolerated their survival for almost two decades after the end of hostilities, the military accomplished something it could never have envisioned: it ended the civil war.

7

Stabilization, Development, and Government Economic Authority in the 1940s

Stavros B. Thomadakis

The systematic analysis of the "state of the economy" in Greece during the 1940s is hampered by the lack of historiographical groundwork on the economic mechanisms of the period. The lacuna is neither accidental nor a sign of flagging scholarly interest. On the contrary, scholarly perceptions of the decade's importance have steadily risen since the early 1970s, as has scholarly output. The influence of the political and military developments of the 1940s on subsequent developments has been recognized. Yet, a conceptual imbalance persists with respect to economic aspects of the period, which have not obtained similar recognition. Notably, most writers on postwar economic development in Greece choose the early 1950s as their point of departure and turn to the 1930s if long-term comparisons are required. This stance reveals an implicit but eloquent assumption: in terms of the economy, the 1940s was a period of

I would like to thank the participants in the Vilvorde Conference on the Greek Civil War, Copenhagen, June 1987, for their comments. Special thanks are also due to Yiorgos Chouliaras, John O. Iatrides, Angeliki Laiou, and George Stathakis for extensive and stimulating criticism on the ideas and interpretations offered in the earlier version of this essay.

interruption of the normal working of economic evolutionary forces, a period of shock and standstill during which long-term processes were held in abeyance.

We encounter at least two justifications for this assumption. One is the assertion that during the 1940s political and military factors dominated the historical process and relegated economic forces to minor status. This is implicit, for example, in the view that so long as the civil war lasted there was little that could be done about economic rehabilitation because the nation's energies were absorbed by the military conflict. Therefore, the thinking goes, historical analysis must be devoted to the political and military aspects of the period. The other justification is the assertion that even after liberation, and through the early 1950s, economic tasks were simple to conceive but difficult to implement. In other words, there were few problems of "strategy" but many problems of practice. The strategy was simply to repair the damage caused by war; the problems were mostly the lack of resources and governmental machinery necessary to accomplish this task. Therefore, this was a period of repairs, an abnormal interlude, during which the economy was managed on an emergency basis. Few, if any, meaningful generalizations could be extracted from the experience of those years relevant to the normal long-term forces that would shape Greek development in the postwar era.

Both these justifications are false. The civil war was not simply the outcome of a political-military rivalry between two contending political factions or leaderships. (Nor was it, for that matter, a more violent replay of the prewar schism between royalists and Venizelists.) It was a social crisis par excellence, with manifest features of class conflict. It was a clash that would ultimately be resolved by military force but that was not caused by military rivalry. Rather, its source was the conflicting visions with respect to the fundamental arrangement of Greece's postwar social order. The organization of the economy, the structure of economic power within the country, and which mechanisms would generate economic progress were important issues for each side. Thus, certainly at the level of ideological struggle, the economy was of central importance. Furthermore, the manifest class character of the conflict had profound implications on the way that each side came to perceive the feasibility, scope, and execution of the agenda of economic rehabilitation. Before any such national project could be undertaken, a minimum of social compliance was required of all social classes. The increasing polarization, which set in after the events of December 1944 and led eventually to the eruption of full-scale civil war in 1946, complicated and postponed the fulfillment of this condition. Thus, irrespective of which side won the civil war, the task of economic rehabilitation could not be conceived as simply a repair job. It would necessarily embody a much broader agenda, one that would embrace the formulation of terms of compliance in the function of the economic system on the part of various social classes. This is the sense in which we must assess the significance of the 1940s: as an era that left permanent marks on the postwar Greek economic order. In fact, the whole period from liberation to the end of the civil war could be seen as an era of "institutional formation" in which durable links were forged between the state and the economy. The search for such links under conditions of national polarization is an underlying theme of the problem of government economic authority in the early postwar period in Greece.

The basic tenet of this chapter is that it was not only the economy but also the economic authority of the government that was shattered during the years of German occupation. As a result, liberation presented Greece with a complex challenge: while the objective conditions of production had to be restored, the economic institutions of society also had to be rehabilitated—by being infused with new legitimacy. Each facet of the Greek problem was dependent on the other. Neither could be resolved without parallel resolution of the other. Polarization and civil strife hampered the process of recovery not simply by creating irregularities in the objective conditions of production but by eroding the grounds on which the legitimacy of economic institutions could be constructed. This was perhaps the more pernicious effect of the civil war on the economic order.

The 1940s is a period of Greek history for which the reading of aggregate indices of economic performance is of limited value. Both during the occupation and in the post-liberation period, there were significant rearrangements of economic roles and capabilities within society that largely escape aggregate indices: wealth distribution became very skewed, monetary values were obliterated by hyperinflation, the banking system was dismantled, the revenue-collection capability of the state shrank, and the internal market was dislocated, as was foreign trade. This nexus of economic problems signified that the national economic system had disintegrated and that recovery in Greece would necessarily entail the reintegration of fragmented functions into a refurbished national system. The degree to which this task was accomplished cannot be fully assessed by quantitative studies of levels of production or consumption, for example. In order to comprehend the process by which the national economic system was reconstituted as a coherent whole, more qualitative analysis is required. Such analysis underlines the centrality of the question of government economic authority.

Under the conditions prevailing in the 1940s, it was objectively only the government that could have undertaken the task of revival and reintegration of the various segments of the economy into a coherent national system. This was a task, however, that surpassed by far both the traditional capabilities and the fundamental outlook of the Greek state as they had evolved up to the immediate prewar period. In the mid-1940s, the state had to marshal and allocate resources on an unprecedented scale, one that mandated nothing less than national planning. The extension and reformulation of the machinery of the state to handle this task could have been accommodated either by radical internal transformation or by external actors. The response to this dilemma in fact marked one of the fundamental cleavages between the Right and the Left at the time. The latter outcome prevailed. In addition to military and economic resources, the British and, especially, the Americans supplied Greece with the administrative machinery that carried out state functions. It is well known, for example, that the American Mission for Aid to Greece wielded executive powers in a wide range of economic matters within the country. Thus, the problem of government economic authority was complicated by the additional distinction between "internal" and "external" authority. The relative weight and mutual effect of these two dimensions of authority are very important with respect to the analysis of the reconstitution of the national economic system. Did external economic authority foster internal authority, or did it diminish it even further? Would the state functions carried out by foreign powers eventually be transferred to the Greek state, or would they be abandoned later as the perceived emergency waned?

Problems of government authority in the economic sphere frequently translate into problems of data generation. This is certainly true of Greece in the 1940s. Contemporary reports and data are fragmented, unsystematic, and unreliable, which reinforces the tendency of economic historians to look at the period as a parenthetical decade. Again, it should be remembered that data collection and report-making are essential ingredients in the particular manifestation of economic power that we normally perceive as economic policy. Since the power to make policy, and the legitimacy of those who attempted to exercise it, were in deep crisis in the 1940s, the statistical trace left for the historian is blurred. The interjection of foreign economic authority, on the other hand, created an alternative source of information. A large number of both periodic and occasional reports were worked up by the agencies handling aid, and these inevitably constitute a major source of material for this and other studies. But aid suppliers were hardly detached observers. Both British and American authorities were committed to specific outcomes in the political clash that was shaking Greek society. Their staunch anti-communism was inconsistent with sensitivity toward the social issues that underpinned the Greek conflict. Their perspectives on the economy were more those of the engineer than the social-policy maker: how to maximize the desired effects of aid with a given volume of aid dollars was the overriding concern. As for the desired effects, they had to be succinct, measurable, and easily reportable to the higher authorities in Washington and London and to Congress or Parliament, as the case might be. Needless to say, they also had to be ideologically congruent with the broader policies of the respective foreign governments. These considerations had a definite effect on the analytical categories and magnitudes the foreign report makers were monitoring. For example, a casual reader of periodic American embassy reports on the economy can gather a great deal of information about Greece's foreign trade but precious little on unemployment. Was the former a more serious problem than the latter? It is very likely that it was not. But U.S. authorities placed high priority on foreign trade for two reasons. First, an improved trade balance would reduce the need for the supply of aid dollars. Second, the reestablishment of Greece's major prewar links with the West via foreign trade would strengthen its adherence to the capitalist camp.

One of the major features of economic policy in Greece during the post-liberation period was the choice of policy goals. The country was devastated by war and occupation, and pressing needs for relief, reconstruction, and development were pervasive. However, no national program for a comprehensive solution of these problems was worked out for several years. Instead, the foremost goal that appeared to absorb the attention of policymakers—both foreign and indigenous—was that of "stabilization." It is well worth asking what the content of "stabilization" policy was and what the implications of the high priority attached to this goal were. Informed practitioners then or now would understand stabilization to mean controlling inflation and government deficits. These were indeed valid requirements of the mid-1940s, when both inflation and public deficits were rampant. It is necessary, however, to go deeper than this if we are to understand the political economy of the period. The instabilities the policy sought to bring under control were symptoms of social conflict rather than merely the consequences of the physical destruction the economy had suffered during the war and occupation. It follows, and this is the major argument developed in this chapter, that what stabilization really entailed was the reconstitution of government authority in a political setting in which class antagonisms were increasingly polarized and in which the possibility of negotiated outcomes between the contending political camps was becoming more and more remote. It can be argued that within such a setting stabilization and reconstruction were incompatible alternatives. The mutual exclusivity of these goals was the fundamental reason the process of reconstruction did not really start in Greece until 1948, almost four years after liberation. This dismal condition amounted to a veritable reconstruction crisis. It was only with the flow of U.S. aid funds *and* the establishment of U.S. economic authority *within* Greece that a partial relaxation of the tension between stabilization and reconstruction became possible.

This chapter describes and assesses the forces that determined the economic outcomes of the turbulent decade of the 1940s in Greece. This task is complicated by the fact that politics and economics became highly intertwined in struggles and contradictions involving both Greek and foreign interests. It is therefore necessary to tackle the issues in a fashion that cuts across political, economic, and social perspectives. It should be clear, moreover, that both radical and conservative forces in Greece at the time were articulating their stances not only in programmatic pronouncements but also in specific social actions that would eventually culminate in military conflict and civil war. For that reason this analysis proceeds on several levels. It focuses on Greek social forces as much as possible, although incorporating foreign factors obviously cannot be avoided. It is the basic premise of this chapter that an examination of the factors inherent in Greek social formation is of paramount importance in comprehending the political-economic dynamics of the 1940s.

In the first section of the chapter, the focus is on the legacies of the German occupation, both in terms of the social meaning of the resistance movement and in terms of intellectual developments vis-à-vis economic change after liberation. The basic cleavage of social forces appeared in the economic field in the antagonistic functions of resistance institutions and the black market. At the level of state mechanisms, government economic authority was shattered under the pressure of permanent crisis and hyperinflation in the years of the occupation.

The next section of the chapter includes a critical exposition of the major developmental perspectives that emerged after liberation. This is accomplished through reference to documents and reports worked up by foreign organizations, the Greek government, and intellectuals of the Left. The basic assertion here is that, although virtually all proposals urged industrialization, there was significant divergence between the Right and the Left with respect to the means of achieving this goal and to its scope. Furthermore, as the decade drew to a close, ambitious plans were abandoned because the forces of the Left, which had been the most vocal proponents of industrialization, were defeated and because the forces of the Right, which had based their plans on continuous foreign assistance, saw their hopes dashed as aid programs were curtailed.

In the following section, it is argued that whereas reconstruction after liberation was contingent on effective public action emanating from a government with sound economic authority, the effectiveness of government and the credibility of economic institutions were not reestablished after liberation. The policy of exclusion toward the Left prevented the emergence of a new social compact and led to the social alienation of labor. As a result, reconstruction and development efforts became not feasible, and the objectives of government policy narrowed to the goal of stabilization. Given Greece's limited resources and the widening gap in social perceptions with respect to the organization of the economy, reconstruction and stabilization in fact became contradictory objectives.

In the final two sections, the focus is on stabilization policies. The potential for success of even this more narrow objective was dubious in the 1940s. The chief obstacle was the persistent speculative behavior of the local bourgeoisie, which was apparently unwilling to lend economic support to a government fighting a civil war for the preservation of the bourgeois social order. It is argued that the "unruly" behavior of the Greek bourgeoisie was not simply the outcome of fear or uncertainty. Rather, it was part of a rational strategy that presumed the institutionalization of foreign aid and sought the establishment of favorable positions in the new international order of open economies that was being hammered out under American hegemony in Western Europe. The institutional outcome of the conflict between stabilization goals and speculative behavior was the establishment of a pervasive system of regulation over the economic process. This system would survive in Greece for several decades after the end of the civil war.

The Legacies of Occupation

In the winter of 1941–42, the first winter under German occupation, tragedy and misfortune were visited upon the Greeks, especially the population of the cities.[1] Thousands died of famine, cold, and disease, and the problem of maintaining life and livelihood surfaced as the first priority of social existence and behavior. These conditions were due to a multiplicity of causes. Enemy appropriation of food and fuel, a drop in production, and paralysis in the transport system were basic factors. Loss of income and widespread unemployment accompanied the drop in production and trade. The disastrous shortages of subsistence goods that developed hit with particular force the poorer strata, mainly those who had no connecting links to the countryside. This was especially true, for example, of the refugees who had been settled at the edges of urban centers after their expulsion from Asia Minor in 1922. The same refugee settlements would soon become strongholds of EAM (National Liberation Front) and centers of resistance. The organization of resistance in precisely these quarters, and the intensity of its development among refugees, was a response to the life-threatening reality that enemy occupation represented for them.

Individual and collective resistance in the urban setting was strongly linked with the need to acquire some control over survival. This was the sphere in which political struggle and economic action met and merged into a powerful drive for the maintenance of the social conditions for preservation. The actions of "truck jumpers," who stole provisions from moving German convoys, were as much political as they were economic. The formation of neighborhood EAM committees in various urban sectors was as much economic as political activity. Mass resistance against

1. For a detailed view of the urban economy of Greece during the occupation, see Stavros B. Thomadakis, "Black Markets, Inflation, and Force in the Economy of Occupied Greece," in *Greece in the 1940s: A Nation in Crisis,* ed. John O. Iatrides (Hanover, N.H.: University of New England Press, 1981), 61–80.

labor requisition by the Axis, the struggles of labor for wage increases and payments in kind, the formation of consumer cooperatives in the workplace, and the effort to bolster and expand the rationing system were acts of resistance that lent political meaning to social action for economic preservation. This brand of politics, and its wide appeal among the population, was unprecedented in the Greek social experience. It was *anti-authoritarian* in the sense that it legitimized resistance against a government whose authority rested on the power of an occupying force. It was *self-reliant* in the sense that it fashioned its own means of action and reaped results without the mediation of traditional institutions. It was *egalitarian* in the sense that it defended the access of all to the basic means of livelihood. With respect to economic mechanisms, the resistance movement responded to the economic crisis by organizing mutual assistance, sabotaging the process of enemy economic appropriation, staging acts of reverse appropriation, and attempting to exercise a degree of control over production.

The elements of economic ideology that underpinned the resistance and its modes of economic intervention were prompted by an acute crisis, however, and offered a response to an emergency that threatened the survival of the population. Could these principles carry over in a more normal economic setting? Could they transcend their character as a defense of a rudimentary standard of living and become positive measures of economic management? Could they become the basis of a new national economic system? The answers to these questions must necessarily remain hypothetical because EAM never had the opportunity to pass from resistance to government, to apply the principles that grew out of the practice of resistance to the exercise of national economic policy. Yet, three points of historical relevance can be adduced. The first is that EAM's platform, and its wide political appeal, were rooted in a response to the accumulated deadlocks and contradictions of prewar society. It should be remembered that prewar Greece had undergone a tumultuous decade in the 1930s, during which time economic crisis, labor militancy, and the development of the Communist movement had posed serious challenges to the liberal social order. The Metaxas dictatorship, which was declared in 1936, had signaled the ultimate failure of the large parliamentary parties to come to terms with new social realities. By repressing the militancy of various sectors of society, the dictatorship managed to obtain a modicum of social tranquility that was, however, extremely tentative and fragile, given the lack of genuine popular support for the regime.[2] The shocks of war and occupation, and the conversion of the Metaxist state to a quisling government, unleashed social energies that had been previously kept at bay. EAM's spectacular growth can only be understood as an outcome of these energies; its agenda projected beyond the resistance to the social order that would prevail after liberation.[3] Thus, it can be plausibly argued that, as ideological constructs, the principles that enveloped economic practice did not lack historical perspective, nor were they conceived solely as emergency measures.

The second point is that by the end of the occupation EAM had become a major political organization with a grass-roots network and strong connections to labor unions, farmers' cooperatives, and intellectual circles. It had also been the basic force supporting the formation of the first government of the liberated zones, PEEA (Political Committee of National Liberation Struggle).[4] These facts suggest that EAM had the logistical structure and social basis for developing principles that were only embryonically manifested in the practice of resistance into wider precepts of national policy and to invest those precepts with political legitimacy. After all, the feasibility of democratic reforms in the economic sphere embodying the anti-authoritarian, self-reliant, and egalitarian traditions of the resistance could only be envisaged in the context of a social movement that espoused them and was organizationally capable of wielding state power. Thus, it does not make sense to judge the social goals in abstraction from their natural social bearers.

The third point has to do with the elaboration of principles in the sphere of ideas and public discussion. During the occupation, and especially as it neared its end, Greece witnessed considerable intellectual ferment. Dissatisfaction with the prewar condition of Greek society, and expectations of the new world economic order that would guarantee for all peoples "freedom from political oppression and economic want,"

2. For a good factual exposition of the Metaxas dictatorship, see Spyros Linardatos, *H Tetarti Avgoustou* (The fourth of August) (Athens, 1966).

3. This is clearly discerned in such classic texts as Dimitris Glinos, *Ti Einai kai Ti Thelei to EAM* (What EAM is and what it wants), as well as in the legislative output of PEEA, the provisional government of the liberated zones.

4. This government dissolved itself when the Government of National Unity, which included representatives of both EAM and the traditional political parties, was formed. During its tenure, PEEA published the "Code of Popular Justice" and the "Code of Local Self-Government," its most important institutional contributions.

were powerful stimuli to intellectuals of all persuasions to search for alternatives.[5] The ability of Greece to become economically viable, the reformulation of the role of the state in the direction of fostering economic development and social welfare, and the prospective international economic relations of Greece were central issues. Not only the intellectuals of the Left, but also those of conservative outlook, were now willing to discuss a new and more democratic economic arrangement of the social order.[6] This was undoubtedly an effect of the ideological influence of the resistance and the visibility of its principles. Furthermore, the intellectuals of the Left proceeded to elaborate an agenda for Greek economic development based on planning, industrialization, and worker participation. The crowning contribution of socialist thought was that of Dimitris Batsis in his now famous treatise, *Heavy Industry in Greece*.[7] Thus, the rudimentary principles that were embedded in the practices of the resistance had both a direct and an indirect impact on the conceptions of the Greek intelligentsia, on their formulation of priorities, and on their various proposals for the future.

One of the reasons for the widespread appeal of socialist ideas was that the economic crisis that enveloped Greece during the occupation defied class lines and social boundaries. During the years of German occupation, the poor were hardest hit, but they were not the only ones to be affected. The traditional middle strata of society also suffered privation and large-scale losses of previously acquired wealth. The two contributing mechanisms were inflation and the black market. Inflation was rampant throughout the occupation. Collaborationist governments, faced with the virtual collapse of tax revenues, were reduced to printing and placing in circulation ever larger amounts of paper money in order to pay for "occupation expenses," as well as the regular administrative expenditures of government. Conservative estimates of the currency in circulation in June 1944 place it at 6,000 times the prewar level. Over

5. For extensive documentation of views during the occupation and immediately after, see Christos Hadziiossif, "Apopseis Gyro Apo Tin Viosimotita tis Elladas kai to Rolo tis Viomichanias" (Views regarding Greece's viability and the role of industry), in *Afieroma sto Niko Svorono* (Festschrift for Nikos Svoronos), ed. Vasilis Kremydas, Chrysa Maltezou, and Nikolaos Panagiotakis (Rethymnon, 1986), 348–56.

6. The views expressed in the platforms of various traditional political formations are presented in Hadjiiossif, "Apopseis Gyro Apo Tin Viosimotita tis Elladas," especially 353–56.

7. Dimitris Batsis, *H Vareia Viomichania stin Ellada* (Heavy industry in Greece) (originally published in Athens in 1947; new edition, Athens, 1977).

the period from October 1941 to February 1944, a direct index of the price of staples showed an increase by a factor of almost 10,000.[8] This hyperinflation led to the annihilation of monetary savings (e.g., bank deposits or government bonds) and consequently deprived the middle strata of society of a portion of their economic reserves.

The black market was the other mechanism of impoverishment of the middle social strata. The tremendous shortages in everyday necessities were translated into violent price realignments whereby staple items commanded high "market value." Black markets quickly sprang up in response to this condition, and, in exchange for overpriced staples, people offered the tangible forms of wealth typically accumulated by the petite bourgeoisie: jewelry, household valuables, even real estate. As evidenced by brisk demand and price increases, the black market operated throughout the occupation, which meant deeper and deeper liquidation of petit bourgeois property. The end result was the impoverishment of a substantial section of the middle strata and the parallel enrichment of the black-marketers.

There are some important questions with respect to the social identity of the black-marketers. Who were they? How did they spring up? How did they use the wealth they accumulated? How did they renew their business? These questions merit serious research, but unfortunately little has been done to date. Recognizing the importance of this social group for the understanding of postwar developments, one author has boldly characterized them as "nouveaux riches" and has likened their enrichment during the occupation to a form of "primitive accumulation." He argues that they constituted the nucleus of a "new bourgeoisie" that, when it sought to assert itself within the postwar social order, found itself in conflict with the "old bourgeoisie."[9] This interpretation is only partially valid and can be misleading in some respects. The limited evidence available leads to modified conjectures that need only be summarized here.

The operation of the black market appears to have been wide in economic space and persistent in time. It probably went far beyond the short-lived and spontaneous initiatives of small opportunistic operators and rested on a more complex system of logistics and organization than

---

8. Thomadakis, "Black Markets," table 3.
9. Kostas Vergopoulos, "The Emergence of the New Bourgeoisie, 1944–1952," in *Greece in the 1940s*, 298–318.

is immediately apparent. The items that appeared on the black market included manufactured commodities, such as soap, alcohol, clothes, and medicine. This fact, in conjunction with evidence of factories working on their "own account" during the occupation, leads to the inference that black-market profits motivated some industrial production.[10] Linkages between production and distribution must have been in this case the basic mechanism of renewal and expansion of black-market activity. In this context, the operation of a successful black market would not have been based simply on entrepreneurial "animal spirits" and spontaneity, but on control of crucial forms of capital, such as factories, warehouses, and means of transport, as well as on such "intangibles" as access to the favors of occupation or collaborationist authorities. These inferences lead to several conclusions: First, that black-market profits were not a form of "primitive accumulation" but a means of revalorization of preexisting capital. Second, that black-marketers were, as a group, interconnected with preestablished merchants and industrialists. Third, that black markets were the visible tip of an underground economy that mobilized resources in a cycle of reproduction of capital. The monetary basis of this underground economy was gold, and concrete pieces of evidence suggest that the market for gold was an organic segment of the system. Fourth, what was really new about the social group of black-marketers and underground-economy operators was not so much its composition as its ability to "make markets" and secure accumulation without the interjection of state mechanisms. Fifth, that the chief antagonist of the type of economic function fostered by the development of black markets was the system buttressed by the resistance.[11]

Resistance and black markets were the two basic modes of social response to the crisis of war and occupation. Each mode led to the progressive articulation of a different economic system and inevitably sought to take control of increasing segments of social production. These two modes, and the economic systems they projected into, were the antithesis of each other. Resistance pushed for economic equality, black markets fostered inequality. Resistance pushed for collective solutions to the problem of distribution, black markets represented a private solution. Resistance needed to place the drive for control over collective livelihood in a political context in order to acquire social acceptance. Black-market

10. Thomadakis, "Black Markets," 67–70.
11. This is a summary and extension of the argument in Thomadakis, "Black Markets."

operators, on the other hand, had to take their actions out of political context in order to acquire social acceptance. The antithesis between the two modes was not simply ideological. It was real, and it led to direct conflict over the need to control supplies. EAM's constant effort to expose the identity of black-marketers and its attacks against their persons, property, and warehouses were tangible manifestations of the conflict, which grew to major dimensions during the last year of the occupation.

Despite their antithetical means and ends, the economic mechanisms of resistance and the black market had one thing in common: they both grew outside the field of state authority. Both were types of "underground" organizations, and each sought to fill the vacuum left by the paralysis or destruction of traditional institutions of state power. Their growth occurred in direct proportion to the decline of state authority. The progressive dissolution of state authority toward the end of the occupation stirred deep concerns among the representatives of traditional institutions. As the German domination of Greece was drawing to an end, the Advisory Council of the Bank of Greece—the main institution of economic control in prewar times—gave a vivid example of this concern by drawing up a report that was remarkable for its candor and foresight.[12] Written in October 1943, it deplored the uncontrollable inflation and warned that, in terms of "relations between classes" and civil order, the country was on the brink of social anarchy. It also proposed a plan for economic normalization that included the following measures: increased food imports to relieve the serious shortages; increased imports of gold to stabilize the currency; the imposition of taxes on items of consumption to revitalize public revenues; and the gathering of agricultural produce and its distribution under government auspices.

This cogent program was not primarily a plan for national economic salvation. It was more of a plan for the reconstitution of government authority in the economic field. The social anarchy it deplored was a manifestation of the growth of the resistance and the conflict between the alternative economic mechanisms that had developed underground. The two pillars upon which government authority was to be reconstituted were the control of food (the quintessential consumption good of that period) and of gold (the quintessential monetary good). The organization of agricultural production and distribution by the government repre-

12. See U.S. National Archives (hereafter cited as NARS), OSS Report 62289, as quoted in ibid., 78–79.

sented a form of rudimentary economic planning with respect to the provisioning of the urban population. But the authors envisaged the exercise of administrative authority by the state rather than the mobilization of popular initiatives around the plan. Here, the representatives of traditional state power revealed their ideological predilections by proposing to have the state supplant the black-marketers (they specifically mentioned the conversion of black-market profits into state revenues), but also by excluding from their field of vision alternative economic arrangements projected by the growth and vitality of the resistance and EAM. The main point, however, is that the problem was well defined and accurately identified: the occupation had spurred the growth of economic mechanisms that were beyond the control of government policy. The reinstitution of government authority was a primary objective, and it had to be founded on control over the means of subsistence, as well as over the means of payment. This early assessment of the problem of government economic authority and the means for its resolution accurately forecasted the policies that Greek governments would lay out after liberation, especially in the post–December 1944 period.

The Economic Challenges of Liberation: Long-Term Perspectives

Emerging from four years of German occupation, Greek society was burdened with many urgent needs. Supplying food, clothing, medicine, and shelter were undoubtedly tasks of first importance. These needs represented a requirement for the reestablishment of a minimum consumption standard for the population's survival, and they clearly warranted foreign assistance. During the latter part of occupation, the International Red Cross had filled a portion of these needs, especially in urban centers. After liberation, the British Military Liaison undertook the task of provisioning the population for several months and was succeeded by the United Nations Relief and Rehabilitation Administration (UNRRA) in the spring of 1945. The UNRRA program continued effectively until early 1947, at which point relief aid was subsumed under the U.S. aid program with the enunciation of the Truman Doctrine in March.[13] The

13. For a description of aid programs to Greece, see B. Sweet-Escott, *Greece: A Political and Economic Survey, 1939–1953* (London, 1954), chaps. 6, 7.

amount of relief aid offered through these channels was not negligible. The UNRRA program alone, for example, which accounted for the largest single aid component in the period 1945–49, furnished Greece with an estimated $415 million within roughly a one-and-a-half-year period.[14] In prewar terms, this amount represented almost 70 percent of Greece's 1939 national income.

The sheer magnitude of Greece's relief needs was an indication of the country's early dependence on foreign aid immediately after liberation. This early dependence, however, need not have become either permanent or systemic. Many other countries in Europe also required and received emergency assistance at this time. Yet, the course of their social and economic development was different from that of Greece after the early post-liberation years. Thus, it is at best a facile generalization to conclude that Greece's emergency needs predestined the country's postwar economic system to permanent dependence on outside aid and concomitant foreign intervention.

The factors that would ultimately determine the country's economic autonomy, or lack thereof, should therefore be sought not in the sphere of emergency consumption needs but rather in the sphere of production capabilities. The speed and terms under which Greek society could reorganize its productive arrangements would be the primary determinants of the country's future economic relations with the rest of the world. In fact, the degree to which Greece could succeed in reconstructing its productive system would limit the need for recourse to emergency outside relief. Conversely, the prolongation of dependence on such relief would be a sign of failure to reconstruct the national production system. It must be recalled in this respect that the production of items of basic necessity (e.g., grains, olive oil, textiles and leathers, and some building materials) was not outside the capacities of the Greek economy in the prewar period. A rapid redeployment of resources in these areas of production would probably have alleviated a large part of Greece's immediate needs. The obstacles to this redeployment were not simply technical obstacles, however. They were social as well, and they arose from fundamental choices and conflicts that would mar the entire process of national economic reconstruction once the country's urgent needs had been met.

14. Economic Cooperation Administration, *Greece: Country Study* (Washington, D.C., 1949), 11 (hereafter cited as *ECA Greece*).

The project of revamping the country's production system included three basic ingredients that corresponded to aspects of the production process itself. The first ingredient was the transformation of "wealth" into productive capital. The second was the transformation of "capacity to work" into productive labor. The third was the transformation of public funds into social capital through the formation of an adequate physical infrastructure to underpin the productive system. The task of securing all three ingredients had to be orchestrated through concurrent action on several fronts, through the timely use of limited resources, and through a clear conception of goals. Concurrent action was clearly required, because all three ingredients had to come together in time and space for the reconstitution of a workable system. Timely use of limited resources was also required if the transition period from economic chaos to productive order was to be as short as possible. Finally, clearly defined goals were necessary in order to instill purpose into economic decision-making and guide the commitment of resources. In short, the construction of the country's productive system had to be formulated on a national plan that embraced the mechanisms for harnessing and allocating resources on the basis of clear priorities, technical feasibility, and long-term perspective.

Times of crisis are also times of opportunity. As Greece emerged from war and occupation with a dismantled economic system, the opportunity to reconstitute the system on new foundations presented itself. This was enhanced by a general feeling in the international community that the postwar world order would be one of economic progress, peaceful cooperation, and improved welfare for all nations. The country's production capabilities did not have to remain within their prewar limits. They could be extended by turning to new products, improved techniques, and additional processing of domestically available raw materials. The route toward economic restructuring would have to be a drive toward industrialization. This much was obvious from an examination of the weaknesses of the prewar economy, in which the narrow industrial base impeded the modernization of agriculture, placed limits on the size of urban productive employment and the levels of consumption, and restricted the country's exports to a limited menu of agricultural commodities and minerals. Indeed, industrialization appeared as a common prescription in virtually all the comprehensive studies of the country's economic problems that appeared at the time. The single most important element signaling this orientation toward industrialization was the focus on the development of the country's electric energy system. Lacking commercially viable sources of oil or coal, Greece nonetheless had alternative domestic sources of energy, such as waterpower and lignite. Increased production of cheap electric power would affect productivity levels in both agriculture and industry, as well as allow a direct improvement in the standard of living of residential consumers.

One significant study of the energy sector was undertaken during the occupation under the aegis of the National Bank of Greece. Its conclusive recommendation was twofold. First, Greece should construct a unified national electric network with emphasis on long-distance transmission lines from major points of production to large agglomerations of users, that is, to the urban centers. Second, the network should be placed under public control, with state responsibility for investment in power stations and transmission facilities.[15] It is fair to say that while this plan reflected a correct assessment of the need for a unified system of power generation and transmission for rationalized operation and low-cost energy, it also reflected the special aspirations of the National Bank to become once again a privileged financial partner of the state. Perhaps the most significant point of the proposal was that electric power should become a nationalized industry, a goal that was eventually realized with the formation of the Public Power Corporation. This was clearly aimed at the prewar "Acheloos contract," entered into by the Metaxas regime and a group of American companies, which gave the latter exclusive rights for exploitation of the hydroelectric potential of the most promising waterway of the country. Under the National Bank scheme, such concessions of rights would have been precluded by nationalization.

Viewing problems from a different perspective, a United Nations FAO mission, which went to Greece in May 1946 to study the problems of Greek agriculture and fisheries, also recommended development of the energy and industrial sectors.[16] The rationale of the FAO report was that any serious improvement in agricultural production and income could be realized only if the methods of cultivation and product distribution were to undergo substantial change. This would require a degree of industrialization of the inputs used by farmers, the outputs produced, and

15. See Th. Raftopoulos, *To Ethniko Diktyo Ilektrismou tis Ellados* (The Greek national electricity network) (Athens, 1946); and Batsis, *H Vareia Viomichania,* part A.

16. United Nations, Food and Agriculture Organization, *Report of the FAO Mission for Greece,* March 1947.

even the tasks associated with village life. Flood control and irrigation projects were high on the agenda of the FAO mission, and they formed a natural complement to the development of hydroelectric power. The underlying notion of industrialization implicit in the mission's recommendations was a balanced-growth approach that would expand non-farm employment as productivity in agriculture improved, reduce the cost of industrial inputs to agriculture as productivity in manufacturing improved, and expand the purchasing power of the nonfarm population for the absorption of increased agricultural production as both the agricultural and the nonagricultural sectors developed. Although this was not its main concern, the report pointed to industries that could be fostered in tandem with its general recommendations, particularly those that would process primary agricultural commodities—food, footwear, textiles, and building materials. Such industries were also congruent with the FAO mission's pervasive emphasis on small-scale manufacturing in the form of either cottage industry or agricultural-cooperative ventures. One of the most intriguing aspects of the report was that despite its orientation toward labor-intensive industrial sectors, it estimated that Greece would still have surplus labor. As a result, it recommended both an expansion of services (with a significant emphasis on tourism) and a policy of encouraging emigration.[17]

The nexus of social actors who would carry forward the development drive recommended by the FAO mission was naturally an issue of great import. At the level of entrepreneurial initiatives, the mission's notions were rather vague, with one notable exception: its insistence on the elevation of cooperatives to self-determined vehicles of entrepreneurial activity that would be allowed to compete freely with private enterprise. The state and its subsidiary agencies (the Agricultural Bank, for example) would act more as facilitators than as agents issuing commands. In this spirit, the mission recommended that the government devote substantial energies to education, the dissemination of technical knowledge, and the provision of support services. The role of the international community was also clearly delineated. It was to act mainly as the provider of expert technical advice and development loans. The mission anticipated that whereas in the initial stages of implementation the development program would be financed through public agencies, this would gradually give way to private capital flows since, the report predicted, the program

17. Ibid.

would be able to service external loans.[18] Last but not least, and to the dismay of the British, who at the time had a large economic mission in place, the FAO team strongly recommended that the management of international activities in Greece be entrusted to a U.N. advisory mission, which would supplant national missions and coordinate all aspects of the aid effort for as long as Greece required international public assistance.

The social and ideological terms of reference of the FAO mission can be discerned if we consider the premises underlying its recommendations. The mission did not hesitate to declare its sympathy for the plight of the Greek farmer, nor did it refrain from stating in several instances whence it drew its inspirations. Being composed mostly of American agricultural experts, the mission's frame of reference was defined in terms of the experiences and social institutions that had mediated the transformation of American farming. Its advocacy of the transformation of Greek agriculture was ideologically framed as a brand of liberal populism. It urged the commercialization of agriculture without openly envisaging the formation of either large capitalist farming concerns or private commercial combines. Instead, it viewed cooperatives as a social institution that would maintain communal functions *internally* (e.g., the management of loans at the village level, the operation of communal agricultural machinery or means of transport), but operate *externally* as a type of collective capitalist, competing with private interests on an equal footing. This was congruent with the mission's strong recommendation that cooperatives remain insulated from politics and that their success or failure be judged by the outcome of a free-market test. Indeed, it projected the transformation of Greek agriculture as a market-mediated process. It rejected planned and command-type solutions and insisted that its proposed scheme could succeed better if farmers were allowed to respond to market opportunities without external compulsion. By projecting the market as a field of free choice, the mission ignored the long experience of the Greek peasant who, since the nineteenth century, had viewed the market (personified by the ubiquitous merchants) as the main source of compulsion in his economic existence.

In terms of intellectual antecedents, political frames of reference, and prescriptive orientation, the long study by Dimitris Batsis (*Heavy Industry in Greece*) was the antipodes of the FAO report. The Batsis study,

18. Ibid.

published in 1947, reflected the work of its author, as well as of other leftist intellectuals within the study group EP-AN, which was sponsored by EAM. Batsis himself was a Communist, and the major theses of his study found their way into the platform of the KKE.[19] The Batsis study shared with the FAO report the fundamental notion that industrialization was both feasible and desirable as the basis of a Greek development effort. However, it departed from the FAO report in almost every other respect. It proposed that the core of the industrialization program be the development of heavy industry, based initially on domestically available raw materials and proceeding to more sophisticated products as interindustry linkages matured. Under the time frame of the Batsis program, the first phase of industrial construction would encompass electric power, metallurgical industries (e.g., iron/steel, aluminum, magnesium), and chemical industries (e.g., nitrogenous products, paper, cement). In the second phase, construction would be expanded in the original industries and initiated in the machine industries, including in the production of agricultural machinery, means of transport, shipbuilding, and the like. The spatial organization of industrial construction was conceived in terms of integrated complexes that were to be set up near the sites of power production. As a result, the two major industrial poles would initially be located in western Roumeli and western Macedonia, clustered respectively around the major hydroelectric developments of the Acheloos and Aliakmon rivers. Additional complexes in Thessaly, eastern Roumeli, the Peloponnesus, and Crete would follow. It should be noted that an important dimension of the Batsis plan was the goal of peripheral development, which represented a change from the traditional concentration of economic activity in Athens and Thessaloniki.[20]

The starkest contrast between the Batsis program and all other contemporary proposals for development was in the sphere of development finance. Batsis elaborated a doctrine of "internal accumulation," arguing that the progressively expanding industrial economy would generate the means to finance its own growth. New industries would expand the circle of customers of preexisting industries, and growing industrial employment would safeguard the regenerative properties of the process. Internal accumulation had three requirements. The first was a national eco-

---

19. The Batsis theses are reflected in the speech of Secretary General Nikos Zahariadis to the Seventh Congress of the KKE.

20. Batsis, *H Vareia Viomichania*, 311–32, and especially table 43a.

nomic plan that would specify the timing and sectoral priorities of industrial investments. (Such a plan was elaborated in the study.) The second was the nationalization of critical sectors (e.g., power production) so that the productivity gains arising from the operation of these sectors could be transformed into investable resources for other sectors rather than realized as monopoly profits. The third was the strategic management of foreign borrowing so that loans could be obtained on the best possible terms and tied to productive uses that could support the loan service. As for the initial resources necessary to begin the process, Batsis calculated that a large part of them could come from within the country, even in 1947, provided current entrepreneurial profits were turned to investment, wealth accumulations obtained during the occupation and post-occupation periods through black markets and inflation were heavily taxed, and a domestic state loan was circulated. As a result of such strategies, Greece's dependence on external finance would be greatly reduced and foreign lenders would be relegated to a secondary role. The implementation of internal accumulation would maximize the country's economic autonomy and foster a neutral and truly multinational orientation in Greece's external economic policy.

The nexus of social actors who would carry out the development program in industry was to include public (i.e., nationalized) enterprises, worker-managed firms, and privately owned companies. This heterogeneous mix of economic agents would gain cohesion, Batsis believed, through implementation of the national economic plan, which would set up the priorities for investment decisions and the geographical dispersion of activities. A very important role in this process was to be assumed by the country's financial institutions, which would be integrated into a nationalized credit system and allocate financial resources in accordance with development priorities. It is significant that, instead of ruling out private enterprise, Batsis envisioned its role within a new economic reality created by the industrialization program. Contrary to its historic antecedents, the private firm in Greece would become primarily a productive agent, shedding its traditional character of speculative/merchant agent. However, Batsis did not propose to entrust the leadership of the industrialization task to private enterprise. Citing the failure of the Greek economic oligarchy to produce substantial economic development over the previous hundred years, as well as its extremely shortsighted and speculative posture since liberation, he stated in no uncertain terms that the development task should pass to other social agents, who should strive to serve not the class interests of a restricted oligarchy but the interests of workers, peasants, and the middle strata of society.

The intellectual terms of reference of the Batsis program were explicit in his work. The Soviet industrialization program was clearly a major source of inspiration, and references to it are interspersed throughout the study. At the same time, Batsis evaluated Greek potentialities and particularities in great detail and provided concrete numerical calculations.[21] His emphasis on the specificity of Greek problems was engendered by a critical reading of Greek economic history and a pervasive sense that not only Greece but the whole world would be charting new economic paths in the postwar era. Perhaps the most important element in Batsis' perspective was a strong undercurrent of confidence about the capabilities of the Greek social movement: the immense social energy that was harnessed by EAM and led to mass resistance during the occupation could be transformed after liberation into a force for development and economic construction. This fundamental conception implied that the economic program for industrialization would have to be implemented by a government that could indeed mobilize this social force. At a minimum, such a government would have to include the KKE and inspire confidence and wield authority across a broad social base. The main factor in determining the economic success of the program would be the ability of the government to wrest control of the process of construction from the economic oligarchy.

The Batsis program was never to be implemented. As social conflict and civil war loomed on Greece's political horizon, the possibility of a governmental role for the KKE dwindled. On the other side of the political divide, the various Greek governments failed to articulate a cogent development program until late 1948, four full years after liberation. The program that was finally worked up in 1948 was submitted to the Organization for European Economic Cooperation (OEEC) and formed part of the coordinated European Recovery Program of the U.S.-sponsored Economic Cooperation Administration (ECA).[22] The ECA mission in Greece (which had taken over the American Mission for Aid to Greece's economic responsibilities under the Marshall Plan) had a de-

---

21. Complete calculations of costs of industrial construction and costs of production were appended to the study for several critical sectors. They constituted a solid feasibility evaluation of income generation over time.

22. *ECA Greece,* chap. 2.

cisive influence on the direction and scope of the Greek program. In fact, it is fair to say that by combining administrative action within Greece and control over promised outside funds for reconstruction and development, the Americans should be credited for orchestrating the complex functions required for the formulation of a *credible* program. Their large role in this was inevitable, because they wielded a combination of competence and authority, which Greek governments perennially lacked.

The 1948 program was the most ambitious that any Greek government would formulate until the late 1950s.[23] It was mounted as a four-year package, and its total cost was put at $1.06 billion. In its report on Greece at the start of 1949, the ECA justified this very ambitious plan by stating that simple reconstruction of the prewar economy would not be an adequate objective and that a significant development effort should be undertaken.[24] As a result, the development of electric power and industry, the rehabilitation of agriculture, and the construction of infrastructure figured as the program's main targets. Once again, the expansion of the country's energy base was to be accomplished through the utilization of domestically available resources, e.g., lignite and hydroelectric generation. Hydroelectric production was to be combined with agricultural rehabilitation by permitting flood control, drainage, and irrigation, as the FAO mission had recommended. On the industrial side, the program envisioned the expansion of existing sectors, as well as the establishment of additional manufacturing capabilities in food processing, cement, chemicals (e.g., nitrogenous compounds, caustic soda), metallurgy (alumina and small-size steel production), and diesel engines. The output from these sectors was to be directed both to the domestic market and to the export market. On the agricultural side, land improvement, more efficient methods of cultivation (e.g., crop rotation), increased use of machinery and fertilizers, and some switching of crops (e.g., expansion of potato production as a substitute for grain) were specified. Finally, the construction of road and rail networks and the acquisition of means of transport were also high priorities under the program. On the whole, the government scheme sought to open up a path for Greek economic development that was closer to the FAO's balanced-growth approach than to Batsis' recommendation for a self-regenerating process of industrial expansion.

23. The program was supposed to cover the period 1949–52, which was the time frame of the European Recovery Program under the Marshall Plan.

24. *ECA Greece*, 28.

The 1948 development program was formulated on two basic premises. The first was the need to reorient the pattern of Greece's external trade. The second was the choice to develop industries that would utilize Greek resources that appeared to be in abundant supply. Greek external trade in the prewar period had involved mostly agricultural exports and industrial imports. Industrial development would therefore affect both sides of Greece's trade picture by fostering some industrial exports and replacing imports with local products. Surplus labor was viewed as Greece's most abundant resource, and as a result the program strongly encouraged labor-intensive industries. The prospect of creating capital-intensive heavy industry in Greece was rejected on the basis of that argument. Even the few metal-processing ventures that were included in the program (e.g., steel and alumina) were mentioned in the ECA country report as provisional proposals pending further study of their economic feasibility. Furthermore, the geographic orientation of Greek external trade would have to change from its prewar pattern. Thus, instead of the old reliance on Central European economies as Greece's main trading partners, the program aimed to increase trade with Western Europe and the United States.[25]

It is apparent that the broad premises of this development program flowed from the fundamental political and economic choices reflected in the Marshall Plan. Western Europe and the United States were looked upon as an economic bloc separate from Central and Eastern Europe and the Soviet "sphere of influence." Within the Western economic bloc, trade would be liberalized and each country would be inserted into the Western system of division of labor according to the doctrine of "comparative advantage." The political division of Europe and the emerging separation of economic blocs implied that Greece would be cut off from the overland trade routes crossing the Balkans. For all intents and purposes, it would function as an insular economy without a hinterland. Furthermore, its insertion into the Western economic bloc would also mean that this most backward country of Europe would have to discover and assert its "comparative advantage" in an economic landscape crowded with the most industrialized countries of the world. It is therefore not surprising that the focus of the development program was on Greece as a cheap-labor country and that industrialization was pointed toward light industry and modernized agriculture as the areas of Greece's specialization. Indeed, what does seem surprising is that the program

25. Ibid., 28, 37–41.

appeared more ambitious than internal and external conditions warranted at the time. For example, the program assumed that over half the estimated $1 billion needed for development investment would come from domestic resources. Given Greece's huge budget deficits and the unwillingness of private capital to undertake investments at that time, the assumption was unrealistic, as the ECA report clearly stated.[26] The program also tacitly assumed that the end of military operations against the Communists would automatically put an end to labor militancy, producing the necessary conditions for cheap labor. This, too, was unrealistic. Clearly, the authors of the program chose to err on the side of optimism because of political conditions. The government had to win a propaganda war, and the development program was a powerful tool against the Communists, who for years had been taunting right-wing governments for their inability to resolve the country's fundamental economic problems.[27]

One of the more interesting aspects of the 1948 development program was that although it made a broad presumption that private capital (Greek or foreign) would eventually play a role in the development process, actual control of the decision-making process and of allocations would in fact be vested in the U.S. mission. The two most critical areas of management of the development program were foreign-trade flows and investment-fund allocations. Through the instrumentalities of the American head of the foreign trade administration and veto power over the use of funds, the U.S. mission was able to exercise strict control over the implementation of the program and any adjustments that might be necessary in light of unpredicted conditions. Ironically, this fulfilled one of the fundamental conditions Batsis had specified in his own proposal. Economic development would not be entrusted to the Greek oligarchy except under the most stringent and sometimes openly suspicious management of American controllers.

As things turned out, this very ambitious development program was

26. "In submitting its original program . . . , the Greek Government assumed that private savings would be available in drachmae equivalent to 34 million dollars at current monetary values and that these Greek savings could be tapped to finance local reconstruction costs. This assumption *appears very dubious* at the present time" (ibid., 49, emphasis added).

27. On the occasion of the program's submission to the OEEC, both U.S. Ambassador Grady and Minister of Coordination Stephanopoulos delivered radio addresses in triumphant tones describing the rosy economic future promised by the new plan and U.S. assistance for its implementation. See U.S. National Archives, Department of State Records (hereafter cited as NARS, DSR), 868.00, Four Year Plan/11-2748.

doomed to slow death. Despite the fulfillment of one of its basic assumptions, namely that the civil war would end by mid-1949, the program was curtailed over the next three years and finally abandoned in 1952. The apparent reasons for this outcome were the progressive curtailment of U.S. developmental aid funds, the diversion of funds to meet immediate consumption and military needs, and the inability of the government to mobilize domestic resources for long-term investment. It is perhaps not unfair to say that the overly optimistic assumptions embedded in the formulation of the program had progressively undermined its actualization. According to at least one contemporary observer, it was the shift in U.S. priorities due to the outbreak of the Korean conflict that was the primary cause of the program's failure.[28] A more fundamental cause, however, was the dearth of domestic investment capital, public or private. This was clearly evoked in the last extensive study of the country's economic strategy: Kyriakos Varvaressos's *Report on Greece's Economic Problem*. This report was composed at the request of the Plastiras government in 1952. Varvaressos had held no public office in Greece since having resigned his last ministerial post in 1945. At the time he wrote this report, he had already held a high directorial post at the World Bank for several years.

The bulk of the Varvaressos report was concerned with reforms in the management of the public sector, the establishment of monetary control, and rectification of the country's balance-of-payments problem. The last part of the report was devoted to the longer perspective of economic development.[29] Citing the experience of many underdeveloped countries and the global perspective that he had acquired from his World Bank post, Varvaressos took a very critical stance vis-à-vis industrialization strategies. He supported this view with three general arguments. The first was that if every underdeveloped country sought to implement an ambitious program of industrialization, the developed countries' capacity to furnish capital goods would be surpassed by far, and consequently capital goods would be either unavailable or too expensive to make industrialization worthwhile. The second was that the primary allocation of resources to industrial investment would leave agriculture in a backward state in these countries. This would create food shortages among

28. Sweet-Escott, *Greece*, 111–13.

29. Kyriakos Varvaressos, *Ekthesis epi tou Oikonomikou Provlimatos tis Ellados* (Report on Greece's economic problems) (Athens, 1952), part E (hereafter cited as Varvaressos Report).

their nonagricultural populations and undermine their industrialization efforts. The third was that the problem of economic development was wrongly perceived as one of capital shortage. In reality, it was a problem of social backwardness where public administration, economic institutions, and private enterprise were inherently corrupt or inefficient and could not carry out the necessary and concentrated tasks of development. On the basis of his general arguments and his specific assessments of the situation, Varvaressos recommended that Greece abandon ambitious industrialization plans and instead strive for economic improvement by modernizing agriculture, revamping public administration, and bettering the standard of living of the "poorer classes." Relatively limited industrial initiatives should be connected mainly with the latter objective, linking small-industry capabilities with the production of commodities for mass consumption. Within this sphere of activities, the most promising area for industrial expansion was housing construction. A coordinated program in that sector would boost certain industrial activities (e.g., the production of building materials) and also serve to meet the tremendous need for shelter, which had been a pressing problem since the war. This strategy would allow Greece to develop within its means without undue dependence on foreign aid. It would also be consistent with much-desired monetary stability and a balance in external accounts.

The main feature of the Varvaressos proposal was its sanguine view of the country's capabilities on the basis of both the international situation and the experiences of domestic economic realities since liberation. Varvaressos's many critics characterized his proposal as a backward-looking scenario.[30] It would be fairer to say, however, that his advocacy of a limited development drive was rooted in an accurate diagnosis of prevailing social conditions. Embedded in all the other development proposals we have so far surveyed were two assumptions. One was that there were large capital resources available for investment. The other was that the social mechanisms necessary for the implementation of a development drive were in place. By 1952, both assumptions appeared to be discredited. The defeat of the Left had obliterated any possibility of radical re-

---

30. See Vergopoulos, "Emergence of the New Bourgeoisie," 306–8, for a recent critique. Contemporary critics ranged from Xenophon Zolotas, Governor of the Bank of Greece, to the Technical Chamber of Greece, who defended the need for Greece to embark on an industrialization drive.

structuring of economic power and the consequent promotion of the internal accumulation Batsis had envisioned. The curtailment of U.S. economic aid and the diversion of preassigned development assistance to consumption and military uses had proved both the futility of hoping for continuous long-term outside assistance and the inability of domestic socioeconomic structures to sustain an ambitious development effort. Against this background, the Varvaressos proposal sought feasible and moderate paths of economic improvement. Both in the 1952 report and in his earlier writings, Varvaressos was deeply pessimistic about the inclinations and the capabilities of the Greek "wealthy classes." He did not consider them capable either of mounting a development effort or of taking the necessary steps for bettering the lot of the masses of the poor. He therefore insisted that a purification of public administration and a large interventionist role for the state were necessary in order to bring about even the limited development he proposed. The promotion of small-scale industry, the government-sponsored expansion of housing construction, and the enhancement of agricultural production were initiatives that, based on new small entrepreneurial initiatives that could emerge from the lower social strata, could proceed outside the control of the economic oligarchy.

The Varvaressos report closed the circle of debate on industrialization strategies of the 1940s by being openly critical of "overblown expectations" concerning the development potential of Greece in the postwar world. From the perspective of 1952, neither the left-wing optimism of radical social change nor the right-wing optimism of unlimited outside aid seemed warranted. Varvaressos had personally never espoused either. His report to a centrist government was really a recommendation for "putting the house in order" and creating a modicum of social justice as a basis for national reconciliation and domestic stability. Varvaressos appeared oblivious to options that would later furnish new possibilities for more ambitious development, i.e., the attraction of foreign capital and the great expansion of "invisible receipts," such as tourist and shipping revenues, from abroad. And he did not envisage policies to encourage labor emigration, which were already being discussed in some quarters.[31] His perspective was instead geared to a scaled-down version of an economically autonomous path for the country, without the radical

---

31. An early paper on the U.S. mission's policy on manpower and emigration explicitly discussed the design and possible methods of fostering emigration. See NARS, DSR, 881.06/3-2450.

restructuring envisaged by Batsis, who was the other major proponent of autonomous development in the debates of the 1940s.

The orientation of the Varvaressos report toward small-scale industry and housing construction was strangely prescient of what would later develop, on a more or less haphazard basis, as the core of Greek economic growth in the following decades. The emergence and reproduction of small enterprise would prove to be a permanent feature of Greek social formation. Investment in housing construction would prove to be the predominant form of fixed-asset formation for many years, which would surpass by far the amount of industrial investment. As the final document in the debates on industrialization, the Varvaressos report coincided with two highly symbolic events that also took place in 1952. One was the definitive militarization of U.S. aid by the dissolution of the ECA and the transfer of aid responsibilities to the Mutual Security Agency. The other was the execution of Dimitris Batsis as a spy.

The abrupt shrinkage of development expectations urged in the Varvaressos report was primarily a reflection of the failure of the economic authorities to secure the basic ingredients required for a revamping of the country's productive system. In the seven years that had elapsed since liberation, domestic "wealth" had not been compelled to engage in productive investment, and domestic "capacity to work" had not been successfully converted to productive labor. The transformation of public funds into social capital in the form of physical infrastructure was seriously hampered by fiscal and monetary imbalances. Despite the formulation and public trumpeting of ambitious development plans, the energies of the various Greek governments and the foreign missions were mostly consumed in efforts aimed at "stabilization" and "current maintenance" of the economy. An accurate interpretation of the period must therefore focus on these failures and explain their recurrence.

The Issue of Government Economic Authority

Reconstituting the Greek economic system after liberation was predicated on fulfilling a long list of immediate requirements: relief for the starving population, repair of war damage to infrastructure, health care, shelter, resumption of basic production levels, monetary reform. None of these tasks could be entrusted to the "market." Extensive shortages,

lack of domestic purchasing power, explosive inflation, and extreme polarization between wealth and poverty precluded any possibility of
smoothly functioning markets. Furthermore, virtually the only agents of
"market forces" were the black-marketers of the occupation, who were
so profoundly stigmatized by their exploitation of popular misery as to
be completely bereft of social legitimacy. Clearly, therefore, the task of
reconstituting the country's economic system was to be primarily the responsibility of government. For this reason, the credibility and legitimacy
of the government became factors of immediate economic significance.

If government authority rather than market allocation was going to be
the primary mechanism for the reconstitution of the economic system,
that authority had to be asserted against the legacies of the occupation.
The practices of the quisling governments had destroyed the three basic
institutional underpinnings of traditional government economic authority: the power to tax, the power to issue money, and, subsidiary to the
latter, command over international reserves in the form of foreign exchange. The restoration of these functions to the government was necessary before the much more complex tasks of reconstruction and development planning could be contemplated. The destruction of the basic
institutional underpinnings of government economic authority did not
mean that these functions vanished from society. Rather, they had been
pushed underground and taken over in a fragmented fashion by the competing systems of resistance and the black market. EAM's amassing of
voluntary contributions or its expropriations of black-marketers' stocks
were embryonic forms of tax. The extraction of profits by black-
marketers could also be thought of as a form of tax inasmuch as it was
based on coercion rather than voluntary market transactions between
parties. The use of gold (and the appearance of barter arrangements)
showed up in the absence of a credible medium of circulation. The owners of gold controlled not only wealth per se but also the national and
international currency in the country.

The problem of reestablishing the *minimum* economic authority of
government was therefore a question of reabsorbing into the public sector the functions that had been pushed underground during the occupation. By the same token, the reconstitution of the national economic system could be seen as the integration of underground systems that had
developed as a result of the resistance and the occupation into a cohesive
national economic apparatus. The problem was that these underground
systems were not simply neutral fragments of an erstwhile functioning

economic entity. They were contradictory, with clashing principles and aspirations: the resistance and the black market projected economic modes of organization that were antithetical in both their means and their ends. This was a manifestation of class antagonism. Broadly speaking, the resistance projected the interests of the poorer classes that formed the mass of the population: workers and public employees, farmers, small merchants, and artisans. The black market, on the other hand, projected the interests and social actions of a merchant-industrial bourgeoisie that had discovered, in the wake of the dissolution of state authority, new opportunities for accumulation of wealth and the articulation of economic power.

There was therefore a deeper problem with government as a mechanism of social power, and this had to do with fundamental issues with respect to the legitimacy of the state. Traditional perceptions of the Greek state as a not-so-benevolent champion of popular interests had been vastly exacerbated by the Metaxas dictatorship and the collaborationist governments of the occupation, which had, not unexpectedly, included several personalities of the Metaxas regime. The extraordinary growth of EAM had held out the prospect of an alternative political authority closely entwined with popular interests and democratic participatory institutions through which the lower classes could exercise some degree of social control. By the time of liberation, in fact, EAM had become the bearer of public authority in most of the country. It had grass-roots organizations everywhere and a mass following. It was linked to labor unions and cooperatives. It controlled an army and a relief network. It sponsored (through PEEA) a system of courts, schools, and social services in the liberated zones. The reestablishment of government authority and the legitimation of the state would be heavily conditioned, therefore, on whether they proceeded with the participation of EAM or without it. As events turned out, after the collapse of the government of national unity in November 1944, those who were to direct government affairs would not only attempt to legitimize the state without EAM, but also seek to reestablish authority against EAM. The Varkiza Agreement of February 1945, which marked the end of the December armed confrontation between EAM and the British-sponsored Greek government, led to the disbanding of EAM's armed force, ELAS (National Popular Liberation Army). The course of events from that point until the eruption of full-scale civil war in the fall of 1946 could only be characterized as a relentless campaign on the part of the government and the British to dismantle every other facet of EAM's power base.[32] This strategy of polarization meant that the political and economic order would be constituted on an "exclusionist principle," since the Left would be allowed to play no role in the normal workings of that order. This fundamental choice had momentous implications for the reconstitution of the national economic system. It imposed enormous physical costs and interposed crippling impediments on the process of legitimizing new economic institutions. The foremost victim of the exclusionist principle followed by British-sponsored governments after liberation was the goal of economic reconstruction and development. As we have seen, a cogent program to attain that goal was not forthcoming until late in 1948, under American sponsorship. During the period of British intervention, which lasted until the beginning of 1947, such a goal appeared a distant utopia. It is not difficult to discern the reasons for this state of affairs. The government's collision course with the Left meant that pacification would occur not on the basis of political accommodation but on the basis of coercion. This mode of pacification had three direct implications in the economic sphere: it required large commitments of resources to the military, it delayed and distorted the effective administrative unification of the country under the authority of the government in Athens, and it subverted the grounds for social cooperation of labor in the reconstruction effort. Let us examine each of these implications in greater detail.

The formation of a large national army and other internal security units, and their maintenance on a permanent state of alert, was a clear and dominant priority after Varkiza. Their purpose was not to defend Greece against external threats but to establish what the government and its British allies perceived as "public order." The government's commitment to the military overrode its commitments to the civilian sphere. Although budget expenditures for the 1945–46 fiscal year are difficult to reconstruct, the priority placed on military expenditures is clear from the qualitative evidence.[33]

The government's emphasis on a military agenda only increased after

32. For a lucid and detailed exposition of political developments over this interval, see Heinz Richter, *British Intervention in Greece* (London: The Merlin Press, 1986), especially the chapter "Implementing the Varkiza Agreement—The White Terror," 125–76.

33. An important example arose in late summer 1946 when the Minister of War unilaterally granted large pay increases to officers. In the ensuing conflict with the Currency Committee over the need for budgetary restraint, the Minister of War apparently carried the day. See Gard-

the elections of March 1946, when the right-wing Tsaldaris government attempted to convert a doubtful electoral legitimacy (the Left having abstained from the elections) to unmitigated government authority. The first post-election budget, which was for the fiscal period 1946–47, reveals a clear picture of the government's priorities. Government expenditures were budgeted at 2,020 billion drachmae. Of these, 495 billion (24 percent) were earmarked for military and public security needs. In contrast, only an estimated 145 billion drachmae (7 percent) were budgeted for reconstruction. Total tax receipts and minor domestic public revenues were estimated at 803 billion, or about 40 percent of expenditures. The balance was to be covered by foreign aid. In addition, a sum of 700 billion drachmae was anticipated in the form of direct British military aid to the Greek armed forces. This brought the total estimated expenditures to 2,729 billion drachmae, of which 1,195 billion, or 44 percent, were slated for military needs.[34] Most probably, this was a minimum estimate, since some funds for civilian projects—public works, supplies for displaced populations, and the like—were indirect forms of military funding. Naturally, in ensuing budgets drawn up during the civil war, military expenditures would retain their prominence, but the 1946 budget is indicative of a trend that had set in before full-scale civil war had broken out.

Military expenditures were not only large in comparison to domestic state revenues or planned reconstruction expenditures, they were also beyond financial control within the fiscal allocation process. The British economic mission, in early 1947, criticized what must have been standard practice even before the civil war: the system of advances from the Ministry of Finance to the military ministries, whereby the latter had complete discretion over funds and no obligation of post audits.[35] This was a state of affairs that would not change materially in later years and that put the military/public-order establishment into an independent compartment of the fiscal activity of the state, with a sacrosanct budget beyond effective control. The relative autonomy of the military/public-order establishment meant that it could engage in bureaucratic self-

ner Patterson, "The Financial Experiences of Greece from Liberation to the Truman Doctrine" (Ph.D. diss., Harvard University, 1948), 386–91.

34. NARS, DSR, 868.50, Porter/4-2547, *Tentative Report of the American Economic Mission to Greece,* chap. 1, table 5, 33 (hereafter cited as Porter Report).

35. See *Final Report of the British Economic Mission to Greece,* 10 July 1947, NARS, Department of State File, 15–17 (hereafter cited as *Final British Mission Report*).

aggrandizement by pushing events toward military solutions and by defining crises in a self-serving manner, and that the measures it took in the course of its operations created tremendous economic burdens on the civilian sector of the economy. The military policy of population displacement during the civil war, which magnified the problem of the dislocation of production and the size of the relief rolls, is a case in point.[36] During the civil war, funds for reconstruction had to be repeatedly cut back as a result of overruns in military expenditures.[37] After the end of the civil war, the size of military expenditures would remain very high. On the basis of the 1951–52 budget, and noting that national income in 1951 was about the same as in 1938–39, Varvaressos estimated that public security expenditures in 1951–52 were 2.3 times what they had been in 1938–39.[38] This testified to the strength and continued relative autonomy of the military establishment after the civil war was over, which would become a permanent institutional feature of postwar public life and fiscal management.

The second impediment that the collision course between the government and the Left threw in the path of reconstruction and development was delay and distortion in the process of administrative unification of the country. At liberation, as well as during and after the December 1944 events, EAM's organizations were in control of most of the country. The central government was not in effective control of the provinces. The main focus of reconstruction and development efforts should, however, have been directed toward the provinces for several reasons. Most of the war damage had occurred there, and the rehabilitation of agriculture and the decentralization of industrial construction would have taken place mostly in the provinces. Large power-production projects, as well as the exploitation of mineral deposits, should logically have been aimed at the provinces.

Cooperation with, or at least accommodation of, EAM at an early stage would have facilitated both the planning and the implementation of reconstruction and the legitimation of development efforts through

36. See Angeliki E. Laiou, "Population Movements in the Greek Countryside During the Civil War," in *Studies in the History of the Greek Civil War, 1945–1949*, ed. Lars Baerentzen, John O. Iatrides, and Ole L. Smith (Copenhagen: Museum Tusculanum, 1987), 85–94.

37. See *ECA Greece*, 24–25, where it is noted that the use of counterpart funds for reconstruction purposes was constrained by budget overruns on the military expenditure side. See also Sweet-Escott, *Greece*, 111–16.

38. See Varvaressos Report, 26–27.

the mobilization of necessary participatory mechanisms at the provincial level. For it was no doubt inconceivable that any development program under which prewar structures would be changed could be launched without mechanisms for the articulation of local interests and objectives. Were the government to choose to confront EAM, this would mean that reconstruction and development efforts, insofar as they required a geographically decentralized plan of action, would be contingent on the demise of the EAM power base and the erection of an alternate mechanism of locally articulated state authority to drive the development initiatives. This "transition" from one authority regime to another would necessarily pose itself as an anterior requirement that would have to be fulfilled *before* any development plan could be formulated and executed. Indeed, this is what took place, and it took a traumatic form. In the aftermath of the Varkiza Agreement, the process of transition from one authority regime to another took the form of white terror. The persecution of EAM members by the gendarmerie, the National Guard, and the irregular bands of "X" was widespread in the Peloponnesus, central Greece, Thessaly, and Macedonia. No credible reconstruction effort could take place under circumstances in which either lawlessness or a one-sided view of public order was condoned by the representatives of the state. The white terror was also directed at the dismantling of grass-roots development initiatives, which since the occupation had been sponsored by EAM. As one recent critic has perceptively stated, "During the occupation, . . . EAM established schools and hospitals, repaired roads, created a communications network and even opened factories. These activities did not come to an end with liberation but were spontaneously extended to the regions previously under German control. Reconstruction began from the base upwards, without state instructions, under the organizing leadership of EAM. British intervention and the subsequent White Terror put an end to all this."[39] Needless to say, as the civil war assumed its full proportions, reconstruction and development necessarily became a lower priority, and the scope of such efforts narrowed to the repair and extension of infrastructure serving immediate military objectives. Thus, the more successful efforts focused on the rehabilitation of roads, rail lines, bridges, ports, and telecommunication facilities.[40]

---

39. Richter, *British Intervention*, 201.

40. See William H. McNeill, *Greece: American Aid in Action, 1947–1956* (New York, 1957), 47–65, for a description of priorities and problems of "rehabilitation."

The last, and perhaps most fundamental, impediment the collision course between the government and the Left presented to reconstruction and development was the social alienation of labor. This occurred on various levels. On the political level, EAM, in general, and the KKE, in particular, had arisen as mechanisms for the articulation of the interests of the working class and allied social strata (farmers, artisans, etc.). The strategy of post–December 1944 governments, which was built around the exclusionist principle, objectively implied the political disenfranchisement of these groups. It also implied an attempt to subsume the expression of class interests and objectives in the platforms of the traditional political parties (e.g., the Liberals, the Populists). With respect to the organized labor movement, this strategy required that leadership be wrested from the undisputably dominant force, EAM's labor organization ERGAS, and turned over to "loyal" labor unionists.

The sad history of state intervention in the labor movement begins with the visit of the British TUC delegation in January 1945, under the leadership of Sir Walter Citrine, and reaches its apogee in the Ninth Congress of the GSEE (General Confederation of Labor) in April 1948. At the Congress, "the factions competing for control of the leadership . . . consisted essentially of opportunists, right wingers, and those who had cooperated with the Metaxas regime and the Nazis."[41] These factions had little direct influence over the mass of workers and could offer no independent source of legitimacy to the government. On the contrary, they were attempting to build up a sort of legitimacy of their own by wielding the surrogate powers of the state. The renewed foundations of "state unionism," another institution of Greece's postwar economic order, were laid at this time and under these circumstances. The continued upheaval within the organized labor movement during the period from liberation to the end of the decade secured neither the acquiescence of labor in reconstruction designs nor the more limited objective of labor peace. Despite the intensification of antilabor police methods, and even the outright prohibition of strikes in the later years of the civil war, strike activity was extensive throughout the period, primarily because of workers' demands for wage adjustments against the ongoing inflation. One characteristic of the wage-adjustment process, evident from scattered sources throughout the period, was the government's attempts to con-

41. Adamantia Pollis, "U.S. Intervention in Greek Trade Unions, 1947–1950," in *Greece in the 1940s,* 271.

struct clientelist relations with special sections of labor—which only sowed instability, because special grants to one group immediately mobilized others in a quest for equal treatment.[42]

Finally, on the level of labor supply, the collision course created enormous problems since it eventually led to hundreds of thousands of men and women being unavailable to the labor market because of military activity, political internment, or forced displacement from their normal areas of residence and economic activity. No national reconstruction effort could succeed under such conditions. The absence of even rudimentary control over labor requirements and policy is revealed in the annual report of the U.S. embassy for 1949, which, in noting that a statistical service had at last been set up in the Ministry of Labor, observed that this was a much-needed step since "there are no accurate statistics on labor supply and manpower requirements, wages and earnings, average hours worked, productivity and work stoppages."[43] This was written one full year after the 1948 reconstruction and development plan had been dispatched to the OEEC for approval!

Taken together, these manifestations of the social alienation of labor meant that the possibility of a new social compact, which would ensure the cooperation of labor for the reconstitution of the national economic system, was shattered. Without a new social compact, reconstruction and development were in the last analysis not feasible, because they could not be achieved with forced labor, and because the planning required for such an effort could not be done in the midst of a worsening social conflict that was demanding inordinate military expenditures and producing conditions of lawlessness in the countryside. *The fundamental incompatibility of a reconstruction and development effort with the polarizing strategy of the exclusionist principle meant that the reconstitution of the economic system would have to be couched in terms of a much more narrow objective: economic stabilization.* In the articulation of economic policies from 1945 until the end of the decade, the goal of stabilization appears to have been continuously sought. It was the primary component of the policies of the governments that rotated in power in 1945. It was the predominant concern of the Greek-British London Agreement of January 1946 and of the British economic mission estab-

---

42. Examples are offered in Patterson, "Financial Experiences," in sections on wage policies.

43. NARS, DSR, 881.00/2-1750, *Annual Economic Report—Greece*, 43–47.

lished by that agreement. It was also a recurring and persistent theme in the policies followed by the U.S. economic mission from 1947 onward. The basic economic conditions against which the stabilization efforts were directed were inflation and the budget deficit. The essence of stabilization policies was the reconstitution of traditional mechanisms of government economic authority in the areas of taxation and money-issuance. Finally, the social objective of these policies was the legitimation of the state's economic powers among the merchant-industrial bourgeoisie and the formulation of a modus vivendi that would accommodate public-sector functions with the private interests of that class.

Perspectives on Stabilization

Although reconstruction and development required a relatively broad social compact that would ensure the compliance of all social classes, stabilization could be achieved primarily with the compliance of the bourgeoisie alone. The fact that stabilization was not fully attained in the 1940s is a reflection of the unwillingness of this class to comply with the economic goals of government policy, even though it endorsed the government's political-military goals.

Let us first consider the issue on the macroeconomic level in the areas of taxation and monetary power. With respect to taxing power, it is important to remember the historical context. First, the ability of the government to collect taxes had dissipated during the occupation. Second, the distribution of wealth and income had become extremely unequal during the war years. Third, even apart from the costs that arose as a result of post-liberation conflict, relief efforts and war-damage repairs required extraordinary expenditures that were beyond the ordinary allocations of the public budget. In such a context, the government would normally be expected to direct the tax burden to social groups that disposed of wealth and income. In this case, the only available tax base of any consequence was the wealth concentrated in the hands of the merchant-industrial bourgeoisie. (Batsis estimated this wealth in 1947 at a *minimum* of 30 billion prewar drachmae, about three times the amount of total tax receipts in 1938–39.)[44] This tax base could not be tapped,

44. Batsis, *H Vareia Viomichania*, 497–99.

Table 1. Tax Receipts in Current and Constant Prices (billion drachmae)

	1938–39	1946–47	1948–49	1950–51
Current Prices				
Direct taxes	2.625	171.1	501.3	958.0
Indirect taxes	11.217	535.1	2,237.8	3,417.0
Total	13.842	706.2	2,739.1	4,375.0
Direct/total (%)	19.0	24.2	18.3	21.9
Expenditure[a]	14.423	1,939.9	4,409.9	6,039.0
Taxes/expenditure (%)	96.0	36.4	62.1	72.4
1938–39 Prices				
Price index[b]	1	160	266	325
Total taxes	13.842	4.413	10.296	13.462
Expenditure	14.423	12.124	16.579	18.582
Adjusted Taxes				
Index of industrial production	100	59.5	80	118
Adjusted taxes[c]	13.842	7.417	12.870	11.408
Taxing power relative to 1938–39[d] (%)	100	53.6	93.0	82.4

SOURCES:

1946–47 budget figures: Gardner Patterson, "The Financial Experiences of Greece from Liberation to the Truman Doctrine" (Ph.D. diss., Harvard University, 1948), 395–96.

1948–49 budget figures: NARS, 881.00/2-1750, U.S. embassy (1950), 8–13.

1950–51 and 1938–39 budget figures: Kyriakos Varvaressos, *Ekthesis epi tou Oikonomikou Provlimatos tis Ellados* (Report on Greece's economic problem) (Athens, 1952), 36–39.

Price index and index of industrial production: Bank of Greece, Monthly Statistical Bulletins. (The source noted by the bank for index of industrial production is the Association of Greek Industrialists.)

Alternative Price Index per note *b*: Economic Cooperation Administration, *Greece: Country Study* (Washington, D.C., 1949), 27.

[a]Does not include direct foreign-aid expense for the military.
[b]This price index is taken from the calculations of the Bank of Greece. In 1948–49, the U.S. mission estimated a price index 25% higher than the one shown here.
[c]Total taxes in 1938–39 prices divided by (Index of Industrial Production 0.01).
[d]Adjusted taxes in each period divided by the 1938–39 level.

however, without officially discrediting the owners of this wealth. Proposals to tax profits resulting from wartime inflation were never seriously implemented. As in the prewar period, the bulk of tax collections would come from indirect rather than direct taxes.

In Table 1, we observe the evolution of tax receipts and offer some calculations for purposes of comparison. In the top panel of the table, we can note the composition of tax receipts and the continued very low percentage of direct taxes in the total. At the same time, we can see that postwar taxes were considerably lower than expenditures through the end of the decade. Thus, despite the major rearrangement of wealth that had occurred during the occupation, and despite the pressure from the expenditure side, the structure of the tax system remained much like the prewar system, in which the burden was placed on lower incomes disproportionately. The pressure from the expenditure side was alleviated in the post-liberation years by the flow of foreign aid. In the second panel of the table, we can see that in real terms (i.e., at 1938–39 prices) tax receipts did not reach prewar levels until 1950–51, whereas expenditures exceeded tax receipts after 1946–47. Thus, in aggregate terms, state revenues did not recover even to prewar levels by 1950–51. In the third panel, tentative calculations are offered with respect to adjusted tax receipts and relative levels of industrial production. On the basis of these calculations, taxing absorption in the 1940s appears inferior to that of 1938–39, and this is true even in 1950–51, when industrial production had exceeded the prewar level.

These indications clearly reflect a serious lag in the reconstitution of the state's taxing power in the late 1940s. Varvaressos's calculations corroborate an especially important aspect of this phenomenon. In his 1952 report, he pointed out that the tax burden placed on the merchant-industrial bourgeoisie in 1951–52 was about half what it had been before the war.[45]

With respect to the money-issuing power of the state, the main obstacle was the continuing inflation, which placed a serious constraint both on the government's ability to borrow domestically and on its ability to monetize its debts. In Table 2, we can observe the development of the price level in the post-liberation period. The price-level changes, which are shown semiannually, lead to three significant observations. The first is that 1945 saw an explosion of hyperinflation. This hyperinflation would dominate the thinking of policymakers in the remaining years of the decade as they faced the inherent instability of the monetary system. The second observation is that inflationary pressures continued to operate in 1946–50 but that price increases were of a much lower magnitude than in 1945. This was due to some degree to increased imports, but also to the institution of open-market transactions in gold at the start of 1946. These open-market operations in gold would continue during the remainder of the decade and beyond. (We shall return to the subject of

45. Varvaressos Report, 41–45.

Table 2. Semiannual Rates of Change in the Price Level (Base period: November 1944, Index = 1)

Period	Index	Average Rate of Semiannual Inflation (%)
June 1945	2.32	132
December 1945	38.52	1560
June 1946	33.11	−14
December 1946	36.30	10
July 1947	35.60	−2
December 1947	45.65	28
June 1948	51.59	13
December 1948	56.08	9
June 1949	62.44	11
December 1949	59.82	−4
June 1950	62.28	4
December 1950	68.52	10

SOURCE: Bank of Greece, Monthly Statistical Bulletins.

"gold policy" below.) The third observation is that the semiannual rates of inflation were positive and substantial throughout the period, with three curious exceptions of instances of negative rates. Reflections on the course of events during these curious intervals reveal that these interludes were clearly event-specific. The first half of 1946 saw the signing of the London Agreement, with its promises of renewed British aid and, more important, the inauguration of the "gold policy." The first half of 1947 saw the enunciation of the Truman Doctrine and the prospect of massive U.S. aid to Greece. Finally, the last half of 1949 witnessed the aftermath of the final defeat of the Democratic Army and the end of the civil war. The occurrence of deflationary interludes in these periods underscores the fact that inflation was basically a speculative phenomenon that exhibited great sensitivity to sudden shifts in expectations. During each of these deflationary episodes, speculative actions against the currency and the hoarding of commodities and gold declined temporarily. The main characteristic of the whole period of positive inflation, nonetheless, was the sustained action on the part of speculators, who continued to hoard and capitalize on shortages and need. Practically every economic commentator from 1945 until the early 1950s focused on this phenomenon of "psychological" inflation, which threatened to undermine the system at every turn.

Given the evidence, it is not extreme to posit that the stability of the economy in the post-liberation period was held hostage by speculators. The whole system of speculation was of course the direct descendant of the black markets of the occupation. With liberation, and the prospect of enormous amounts of supplies entering Greece for relief of its immediate needs, a huge new field opened up to speculative activity. It was in the earlier part of 1945, in fact, while relief was still being handled by the British Military Liaison, that the policy of routing relief supplies through private commercial channels was implemented.[46] This policy would essentially continue under UNRRA and U.S. aid schemes throughout the remainder of the decade. Yet, the various Greek governments and foreign economic missions continued to insist that controlling inflation was of primary importance for reestablishing the economic effectiveness of public policy. The problem was how to do it.

One option was to break the power of speculators with a concerted program of taxation on profits and wealth, price controls, and direct assumption of significant import transactions by the state. The closest that any post–December 1944 government came to such a program of stabilization was during the tenure of Varvaressos as Minister of Supply and Deputy Prime Minister in the summer of 1945. Varvaressos was sponsored by the British and propounded a stabilization program that was not inordinately dependent on external aid. Apparently, this was congruent with British goals because it would presumably normalize the Greek economy without a great burden on meager British resources. The Varvaressos program had three key elements. First, the imposition of a tax on merchants and industrialists. Second, price controls and wage controls. And third, control of essential imports, as well as of basic necessities produced domestically. The program did not include developmental goals. It was instead a state-sponsored austerity plan that sought a relatively even distribution of economic burdens. In the first two months of the Varvaressos tenure, the program appeared to work. Price inflation relented, and tax receipts were considerably boosted.[47] In the third month, the program collapsed and Varvaressos was forced to resign. The collapse was caused by a speculators' revolt that fomented fundamental political opposition to Varvaressos, who, in the end, stood alone without any support. Since the Left had been excluded from nor-

46. Angeliki Laiou-Thomadakis, "The Politics of Hunger: Economic Aid to Greece, 1943–45," *Journal of the Hellenic Diaspora* 7 (Summer 1980): 41–42.

47. Patterson, "Financial Experiences," 178–250.

mal political processes, the only remaining constituency with power to which the government could look as a political ally was the very merchant-industrial bourgeoisie that Varvaressos had sought to restrain.[48] Their victory against his program marked with great finality the abandonment of the antispeculative stabilization policy Varvaressos had propounded.

The power of private commercial interests to constrain government attempts at control also became apparent when UNRRA operations were drawing to an end in late 1946 and alternative arrangements were required to guarantee the flow of imports of necessary goods. Both the UNRRA services and the British economic mission recommended the creation of government agencies to procure commodities in short supply and surplus allied stores. Such organizations would control both the supply and the pricing of commodities for internal distribution. The government's response was less than vigorous, which was, as the British mission noted, "due to procrastination on the part of the government engendered . . . partly by its fear of the unfavorable reaction of Greek importers and partly to the dislike of some of the Ministers to abdicate their powers in favor of the agency."[49] This example offers a revealing view of the problem of government economic authority. The problem had two aspects. The government's fear of importers reveals the degree to which public authority was forced to channel policy in ways that suited private commercial interests. The reluctance of ministers to permit infringements on their turf was another aspect of the same problem. The politicians who rotated in ministerial posts sought to construct personalized bases of influence within the merchant-industrial bourgeoisie, and even to amass personal gain using their positions. This gave rise to ministerial squabbles over particular decisions or jurisdictions and was probably a major cause of the lack of effectiveness exhibited by the government and of the very harmful delays even in high-priority areas of distribution of supplies. Thus, the problem of government economic authority was not defined within a "government-versus-speculators" framework but was manifested within the very operations of government and in its laborious search for the boundaries between the private and public sectors.

48. An analysis of the Varvaressos program and its collapse is offered by Christos Hadziiossif, "Economic Stabilization and Political Unrest: Greece, 1944–1947," in *Studies in the History of the Greek Civil War,* 25–40.

49. *Interim Report of the British Economic Mission to Greece* (hereafter *Interim British Mission Report*), 31 January 1947 (in NARS, Department of State file), 26.

The institutional resolution of the problem of economic roles in the area of foreign trade was finally arranged in late 1947 by the U.S. mission, which was in a position to exercise its "external" authority for this purpose. A Foreign Trade Administration (FTA) was formed. Although this administration remained formally within the Greek government structure, it was headed by an American. The principal purpose of the FTA was to control the composition of imports in order to ensure that foreign exchange would not be wasted on luxury items and that basic necessities were imported in adequate quantities.[50] The FTA implemented this goal chiefly through a system of import licenses. Until mid-1948 at least, even this scheme encountered resistance from Greek importers, who apparently refused to apply for licenses to import commodities the FTA considered to be high-priority items.[51] The institutional arrangement represented by the FTA was typical in three respects. First, it did not eliminate private initiative but sought to regulate it. Second, the regulatory framework did not extend to all foreign trade, but only to a part of it. Thus, a parallel sphere of unregulated trade continued to exist side by side with the regulated one. Third, the regulatory impetus was really furnished by the U.S. mission, as manifested both by the mission's initiating action and by the placement of an American at the head of the regulatory machine. This institutional arrangement was not predicated on ideological choices. Rather, it was the outcome of practical necessity: without the regulatory intervention of the FTA, aid dollars would have ended up simply enriching merchant-speculators. If aid were to have some tangible effects on relief and basic reconstruction, which a vigilant U.S. Congress would expect, a degree of regulation was necessary. Yet, this regulation fell short of enforcing a complete antispeculative program like the one Varvaressos had earlier attempted to put in place. It created instead a "dual" structure that reflected a compromise between the aspirations of the local merchant-industrial bourgeoisie and the goals of the U.S. mission. It marked off certain areas for centralized control and left others to uninhibited "private initiative."

The prototypical institutional arrangement for this kind of regulation had already been set in place before the U.S. mission arrived in Greece. Not unexpectedly, it arose in the crucial area of monetary authority. This

---

50. See *ECA Greece*, 2–3.

51. NARS, DSR, 868.50/4-2348, *Embassy Comments on Economic Progress in Greece*, 23 April 1948, enclosure no. 5 (Trade and Commerce), 3–6.

was the famous Currency Committee, which originated with the London Agreement of January 1946 between the Greek and British governments. After the collapse of the Varvaressos program in September 1945, a new round of inflation had set in, and by the end of the year the whole economic situation was again out of control. The London Agreement was in response to this development, and its goal was to enforce a new stabilization policy. The creation of the Currency Committee was intended to provide a mechanism for "statutory management of the note issue," as the agreement explicitly required. The committee was made up of the Ministers for Coordination and Finance, the Governor of the Bank of Greece, and two foreign members (one British, one American).[52] Its decisions required unanimity.

The Currency Committee was only one aspect of the institutional arrangement that emanated from the London Agreement. The second was the enunciation of a policy of open-market sales of gold by the Bank of Greece to private individuals within the country for the purpose of stabilizing the value of the drachma. This amounted to an internal gold standard, which made the drachma convertible to specie. Although not explicitly provided for in the London Agreement, the implementation of this policy was approved by British authorities and was made possible by the provision of a currency stabilization credit of 10 million pounds sterling to Greece and the release of Bank of Greece reserves from prior restrictions by the Bank of England, both of which were stipulated by the London Agreement. The durability of these institutional arrangements was remarkable. The gold policy would remain in effect (with a few months' interruption in late 1947 at the insistence of the American mission) until the early 1960s. The Currency Committee would see its powers enlarged under American auspices and would remain in place until the early 1980s. Since these two aspects of the 1946 monetary stabilization package were to prove indispensable to Greek monetary management for a long time, it is worth examining the role of each, and their interconnections, in some detail.

The significance and implications of the gold policy must be seen in the social context of the early post-liberation period. Once the option of

---

52. The first American member of the committee was Gardner Patterson, who held the post until early 1947. He subsequently wrote the above-cited dissertation under the direction of Alvin Hansen at Harvard. As an insider's view of events from the standpoint of the Currency Committee, Patterson's work is an extremely valuable source.

breaking the power of speculators had been abandoned—as it was in 1945—the only remaining alternative was a policy of accommodation. The gold policy represented precisely that. The economic implications of the policy were twofold: First, gold sales acted as a mechanism for absorbing the excess supply of drachmae in circulation, thereby preventing the value of the drachma from tumbling, since it was de facto a convertible currency. Second, gold, as international specie, would normally make up the reserves of the national monetary system held by the central bank, but under the gold policy these reserves were converted from national to private stockpiles. The accumulation of private reserves of gold meant that while savings were diverted from productive investment, these same savings were readily exportable, since they represented international means of payment. The gold policy was clearly a trade-off. Stability in the value of the currency was to be achieved at the expense of a diversion of savings from productive investment and at the risk of capital export. Had stabilization of the currency been achieved within a brief interval, the trade-off might have been acceptable. Unfortunately, it was not attained for years, and the trade-off proved devastating. Reconstruction necessitated investment, but with the gold policy in place investment was not forthcoming, at least from domestic private sources. In 1946, which was the year with the most stable price level from December to December (see Table 2), the cost of this stability was a net sale of 2.2 million gold sovereigns by the Bank of Greece.[53]

At an average price of 140,000 drachmae to the sovereign, the total expenditure of resources amounted to 308 billion drachmae. Tax receipts for 1946–47 totaled 706 billion drachmae (see Table 1), and reconstruction expenditures were budgeted at 145 billion. The cost of the gold policy was therefore clearly enormous. Until the end of 1951, the Bank of Greece would offer net sales of gold amounting to a total of $60 million.[54] This represented as much as 12 percent of total U.S. nonmilitary aid to Greece up to the end of 1951. According to one estimate, 13 million gold coins were held privately in 1952.[55] At an average price of $12 per sovereign, this amounted to $156 million. Total bank deposits at the end of 1952 stood at about $90 million.[56]

53. Porter Report, chap. 2, table 4, p. 13.
54. Wray O. Candilis, *The Economy of Greece, 1944–1966* (New York, 1968), chart 3, p. 77.
55. Sweet-Escott, *Greece*, 156.
56. Bank of Greece, *Monthly Statistical Bulletins*, 1953.

It is important to note that private holdings of gold, aside from being significant in magnitude, had deeper social implications as well. If speculators held the economic system hostage, the gold policy was the ransom payment. The British economic mission, which eventually came to disapprove of the gold policy because it was taking on a permanent character, candidly assessed its social meaning: "The facility of obtaining gold has driven a wedge between the Greek population generally, which has not the resources to acquire gold on any considerable scale, and the trading and business classes who are enabled, so long as gold continues to be available, to contract out of the evils to which the bulk of the population is exposed."[57] The class content of the gold policy could not be more clearly stated. This was a policy for the benefit of the merchant-industrial bourgeoisie. Sales of gold enabled members of this class to convert wealth acquired during the occupation into international specie. This was a "laundering operation" on a grand scale. Inasmuch as occupation wealth had been amassed in forms that revealed its origins, its conversion to gold created a glittering veil that obscured those origins and relieved its owners from social stigma. The conversion also insulated the bourgeoisie from the crisis of the Greek economy. In effect, the acquisition of international specie *denationalized* the forms of wealth and unlinked economic calculations and perspectives from opportunities taking shape within the country. In short, instead of strengthening the stake of the indigenous bourgeoisie in Greek development, the gold policy weakened it, subverting the long-term stability of domestic economic structures.

The Currency Committee was the obverse facet of the gold policy in an institutional sense. It was evident that unless control of the drachmae supply was achieved on a parallel track, the implementation of the gold policy could lead to the rapid collapse of the monetary system. Monetary stabilization in the presence of gold convertibility of the drachma required a tight hold on the money supply. The government itself lacked, for all the reasons we have noted, the collective will to exercise this control. Runaway budget expenditures could easily have arisen within the framework of governance as it existed in Greece during the 1940s, with its autonomous military establishment, frequent rotation of government personnel, ministerial squabbling, political infighting, and continuous attempts to build clientelist constituencies. The control the government could not supply became the mandate of the Currency Committee. The

57. *Interim British Mission Report*, 118.

unanimity rule for committee decisions gave the committee's two foreign members the power of the veto over successive Greek governments. Thus, the committee represented a form of international financial control upon Greece. In conjunction with the economic power conferred on the British and U.S. governments by their aid to Greece, the presence of foreign members endowed the committee with a level of authority that was unmatched by the collective authority of the Greek cabinet. At the same time, the committee was not accountable to the Greek parliament, nor was it subject to formal government sanctions.[58] In effect, the Currency Committee was a supergovernment in economic matters. It could, in the name of monetary stability, regulate the budget to restrain the deficit. Once the gold policy was implemented, the need for such regulation became paramount.

If the budget deficit was one mechanism for the dissemination of money that had to be controlled, the provision of bank credit was the other. Since bank deposits and monetary assets had been wiped out by hyperinflation, the monetary issue of the central bank was effectively the only source of renewal of domestic credit. (After 1947, this source would be supplemented by U.S. counterpart funds.) As a result, the Currency Committee had to become the controller of credit as well. On the recommendation of the Porter Report of the American economic mission, this aspect of the committee's powers was greatly extended.[59] This recommendation was rooted in the concern that bank credits would be leaked into the gold market. The resulting quantitative and qualitative regulations on credit formed a nexus of restrictions unprecedented in the interventionist traditions of the Greek state. As in the case of foreign trade, the impetus for this regulatory intervention was a practical one: grave embarrassment could have resulted for the U.S. government if it turned out that taxpayer dollars devoted to aid were going instead to line the pockets of Greek wartime speculators with gold.

In formal terms, the institutional structures set up to handle monetary management entailed a contradiction. They combined extreme market liberalization with respect to currency and gold, and extreme regulation with respect to credit. The two sides of the contradiction fed each other.

---

58. For analysis and interpretation of the Currency Committee as a channel of foreign authority in Greece, see A. A. Fatouros, "Building Formal Structures of Penetration: The United States in Greece, 1947–1948," in *Greece in the 1940s,* 250–52.

59. Porter Report, chap. 2, p. 8.

The flight to gold created a capital shortage and imposed the need for credit rationing and tight regulation of the uses of credit. On the other side, strict credit regulation prevented the flow of capital into financial forms and reinforced the flight to gold. Thus, the extreme free-market policy on currency made necessary the negation of free-market functions in credit allocation. This "dualism" of institutional structures in the monetary sphere reflected, as it did in the area of foreign trade, the point of compromise between the goals of "external" economic authority and the aspirations of the indigenous bourgeoisie. It created a type of institutional equilibrium that was necessary for the legitimation of government economic authority vis-à-vis the two important poles of strength—foreign aid providers and domestic merchant-industrial interests.

Once the antispeculative versions were abandoned with the resignation of Varvaressos, stabilization policy was essentially reduced to two instrumentalities: monetary control and wage policy. Although these policies were not crowned with success in the 1940s, they maintained a precarious economic balance, which was nevertheless heavily dependent on large flows of outside aid. The challenge of the 1950s would be to preserve this balance after outside aid had stopped. The institutional structures that were formed in the 1940s in the areas of monetary management and wage policy would persist for a long time and would form the basis of the links between the state and the economy, and therefore also become the mediating mechanisms for economic policy in the ensuing decades. The dualism of monetary institutional arrangements would foster within the context of Greek social formation a permanent reproduction of parallel subsystems. To use present-day terminology, the origins of the modern "underground economy" are to be found in those distant resolutions of a tragic social conflict.

Reflections on Stability and Instability

The limited success of stabilization policies in the 1940s, and the highly regulatory arrangements that emanated from those policies, is a clear indication that the indigenous bourgeoisie did not exhibit the degree of compliance necessary for the rapid reconstitution of the national economic system. Their characteristic behavior was hoarding and speculation, and these activities constantly threatened the fragile economic structures that were slowly emerging. For example, in the 1940s the government was never able to issue an internal loan to finance the extraordinary expenditures of civil war. In many previous crises during the hundred-year history of the Greek state, internal loans had been a mechanism through which the Greek bourgeoisie had offered decisive support to a financially beleaguered government. In the 1940s, however, the government squandered its meager resources to endow the bourgeoisie with hard currency through the gold policy. This historical antinomy poses an important question. If the government was fighting a civil war for the ultimate preservation of the bourgeois social order, why did the members of the bourgeoisie refuse to comply with the economic requirements of that course? Why was it necessary for the fundamental impulses toward stabilization to come from British and American overseers rather than from the internal logic of bourgeois interests?

The Americans serving in the U.S. mission were acutely aware of these questions, and they formulated a plausible but simplistic answer: the Greek bourgeoisie was gripped by a fear that led to shortsighted reflexes. A typical statement of this theory was furnished by ECA in early 1949. "Private Greek capital, paralyzed by fear of guerrillas and invasion from the north, will not risk investment in industry. Fearful of inflation, capital takes refuge in gold or merchandise or, escaping the net of the exchange controller, is invested abroad."[60] This "theory of fear" is *not* sufficient to explain the *consistent* behavior of the bourgeoisie throughout the 1940s in the face of changing political conditions, both before and after the civil war broke out, and both before and after the large American commitment to support the anticommunist struggle of the Greek government had been announced. Nor does it explain the financial crises that continued to mar the economy for several years *after* the civil war had ended. There must have been other, more fundamental, reasons for the dissonance between the political interests and economic behavior of the Greek bourgeoisie.

To take a longer perspective for a moment, it is important to remember that in the prewar era the Greek bourgeoisie had not distinguished itself by undertaking great industrial initiatives. Interwar industrialization was undoubtedly remarkable compared to earlier times, but it was to a great extent conjunctural: limited to light industry, it was bolstered both by the breakdown of international trade and protectionism, and by a sudden

---

60. *ECA Greece,* 2.

abundance of "cheap labor" after the Asia Minor disaster. The postwar period promised to be one of free trade in the Western bloc. Furthermore, postwar circumstances in Greece meant that there would be no pliant pools of "cheap labor" so long as the Left continued to wield influence in the labor movement. Clearly, these were not conditions under which the Greek bourgeoisie would be prompted to suddenly develop an industrial ethos, of which it had precious little to start with.

From a shorter perspective, we must again recall that the period of occupation had offered opportunities for a new round of enrichment through speculation. The sections of the prewar bourgeoisie that survived economically through that period undoubtedly took part in this process. This method of enrichment had perhaps served to reinforce speculative habits, but its chief significance lay elsewhere: a grave social stigma attached to it. The owners of the resulting wealth were obviously reluctant to reveal its magnitude or form. They certainly resisted any mechanisms that would register their wealth for public view, including the tax rolls and the commitment of funds to industrial investment projects under a scheme of government supervision. They preferred instead liquid forms of wealth, such as gold or commodities, with which they could maintain their capital in a state of social anonymity. Government policies in monetary and trade matters facilitated the realization of that preference. In a sense, this reflected the *defensive* nature of the strategy of the merchant-industrial class, which sought to protect *previously* accumulated wealth from the threat of social appropriation under conditions of urgent need for public funds.

More important perhaps, there was also an *offensive* element in the strategy of private capital. After liberation, Greece would resume foreign trade. Furthermore, this trade would certainly consist initially of imports and be secured through foreign aid. This predictable eventuality would open up new and very large economic opportunities. *The merchant-industrial bourgeoisie had to recapture its position as the mediator of foreign trade.* Investment in stocks and gold were the obvious tools for realizing that goal, since control by private interests had to be established over commodities, as well as over international money. Once control over commodities and international money had been entrenched in the hands of the merchant-industrial bourgeoisie, domestic inflation became a profitable way of enlarging the value of their capital, so long as local prices exceeded international prices at the prevailing exchange rates. The creation of artificial shortages by hoarding within Greece ensured the latter condition. Indeed, in terms of local price inflation, the drachma remained overvalued for considerable intervals vis-à-vis the dollar and the pound sterling throughout the late 1940s. Thus, what appeared to be domestic speculation in response to fear was in effect a rational strategy. This would explain its persistence. In this sense, the incipient instability of Greece's monetary system was a simple outgrowth of rational behavior.

Questions still remain, however: Could the bourgeoisie have been so shortsighted that it sacrificed its long-term interests to the acquisition of immediate economic gains? Was it not understood that speculation could not sustain the social system over the long term? It is natural to assume that the Greek bourgeoisie was suffering from extreme social myopia at the time. Yet, it does not seem plausible. Its long history, its political dexterity, and its cosmopolitan traditions do not make the diagnosis credible. On the contrary, they suggest an alternate interpretation: *the indispensable underpinning of the strategy that manifested itself as speculative behavior was the institutionalization of a mechanism of foreign aid.* So long as a flow of resources from abroad could be maintained, the indigenous bourgeoisie could reproduce and expand its wealth through trade and monetary speculation. It could, by the same token, capture positions of strength within the emergent "open" economy that seemed to be becoming the dominant model as a result of the international initiatives of the United States since the end of the war, implemented forcefully through the European Recovery Program.

The institutionalization of a mechanism of foreign aid was fostered by internal political intransigence and the prolongation of the domestic social crisis. Thus, along with the dictates of British policy, the hardening anticommunist precepts of U.S. world strategy, and the aspirations of traditional Greek politicians, the refusal to reach a political accommodation with the Greek Left also held out the promise of economic gain, since it ensured large flows of foreign aid. A side benefit of such aid was that the expenses of normalization of the domestic economic system would be borne by outsiders rather than by the indigenous owners of wealth. It was not by coincidence that at various points in the mid- and late 1940s the British and the U.S. missions both supported the formation of centrist governments in order to moderate somewhat (without of course yielding substantive ground to the KKE) the extreme internal tensions that multiplied the costs of their intervention. In every case, these governments proved weak because they failed to gain essential support from the bourgeoisie. Right-wing governments, on the other hand, were more durable and followed a consistent recipe: increase internal tension and demand more vociferously increases in foreign assistance.

It is also necessary to note another antinomy. By holding out the prospect of aid, the British and U.S. governments in fact reinforced the strategy of domestic capital, thereby strengthening behavior they would subsequently deplore or explain with "theories of fear." As aid providers—and this holds especially for the United States—they sought to achieve a "self-supporting" economy in Greece as soon as possible. Hence, they exercised constant pressure for stabilization policies and internal regulation, using aid monies as the lever. The same aid monies, however, induced a prolongation of the "unruly" behavior of indigenous merchants and industrialists. The antipathies and conflicts between American mission personnel and local businessmen that one encounters at the interstices of documentary evidence can be clearly traced to this fundamental divergence in incentives between aid suppliers and aid beneficiaries.

Finally, it is also important to note that as U.S. aid from public funds dried up, the bourgeoisie discovered other ways to ensure the continuation of foreign resource flows. The invitation for direct foreign investment and the creation of preconditions for the expanded flow of "invisible" receipts, such as tourist and shipping revenues, would constitute the cornerstones of Greek policies in the 1950s and beyond.

8

Soviet Policy in Areas of Limited Control

The Case of Greece, 1944–1949

Peter J. Stavrakis

The analysis of Soviet policy in Greece during the immediate postwar years stands as a lamentable exception to the otherwise successful efforts of scholars to produce a more balanced appraisal of the 1940s and 1950s. The central problem in the Soviet case appears to be the tendency, manifest in scholars of the "traditional" as well as "revisionist" interpretations, to ascribe, a priori, a degree of constancy and immutability to Soviet behavior that actual events fail to support. Neither the presumption of a sustained Soviet drive to "communize" Greece through the agency of the Greek Communist Party (KKE), nor the argument that Stalin remained completely uninterested in Greek affairs, can produce an explanation with sufficient texture to capture the complexity of developments in the Balkans and the Near East in the postwar era. But if Soviet policy cannot be conveniently described by either of these extremes, how did Greece figure into Stalin's plans? Available evidence indicates that, following the successful conclusion of the war against Germany, Stalin sought to eliminate (or at a minimum reduce) the Western presence in the eastern Mediterranean and the Near East.

The countries within this region were accorded different treatment at the hands of the Soviets, reflecting Stalin's effort to capitalize on the resources provided by a variety of domestic conditions. In this respect, Greece was in a unique position compared with other states in the region. First, unlike Turkey and Iran, Greece possessed a strong Communist party organization; even after its defeat in December 1944, the KKE demonstrated a significant capacity for regeneration. Second, the initially tentative and ambiguous Western commitment to the defense of Greece stood in marked contrast to the West's support of Greece's Near Eastern neighbors: the United States and Britain had early on demonstrated strong support for the status of Iran and Turkey.

The anomalous position of Greece dictated that a strategy different from that directed toward other areas in the Near East was required to achieve the elimination of the Western presence. Consequently, from 1945 through the summer of 1946, the Soviets used the Greek Communist Party to pursue a policy of political gradualism in the region by urging the KKE to strive to meet its objectives in Greece through political means, while holding its military forces in reserve. In the near term, Stalin sought to establish a strong KKE political presence that would coexist with a weak yet minimally stable Greek government, which itself would remain within the Western sphere of influence. The goal was to create a "soft" Western state with pro-Soviet elements powerful enough to veto any anti-Soviet initiatives. This, in turn, would create favorable long-term conditions in which the Communists' military forces could be employed in a more aggressive policy. As British influence waned and the Americans proved reluctant to take up the burdens of a strategic commitment, the KKE military forces would inevitably play an increasingly influential role in Greek politics. Stalin's actions appear to reflect an opportunistic, two-stage policy. In the first phase, the Western commitment to Greece would be permitted to taper off while the KKE refurbished itself and prevented the formation of an anti-Soviet regime. The likely direction of Soviet policy in the second phase remains unclear, but given Stalin's advice to the KKE to retain its military forces, and his unwillingness to write off the military option entirely, it appears this was to be a much more aggressive phase than the first.

The striking feature of this ideal Soviet scenario is that it was largely unfulfilled: by the end of 1946, Stalin's cautious and gradualist strategy collapsed as Greek political rivalries deteriorated into civil war. The war convinced the Americans of the militaristic intentions of the Soviet Union and crystallized the strategic commitment the Soviet dictator had tried to avoid. After 1946, Stalin was compelled to concentrate on containing the Yugoslavs and regaining the initiative in Balkan Communist affairs.

The dramatic collapse of Soviet policy demonstrates the need to view foreign policy as a process in which actors must continuously respond to events that are beyond their control. Indeed, in view of the transformation of the international system that took place in the years following the Second World War, the limited degree to which the Soviets were actually able to influence events, and the internal instability in Greece, an analytical approach that focuses on the mutability of Soviet policy holds out the best prospect of yielding a plausible explanation of Soviet conduct.[1]

This analysis proceeds from the assumption that the shifting importance of strategic, regional, and local factors in the external environment profoundly affected the extent to which Stalin succeeded in advancing the interests of the Soviet Union in postwar Greece. As the Soviet leader pursued his long-term and short-term objectives, tension between policy goals combined with external pressures and constraints to create a policy characterized by pronounced shifts and turns. With respect to Greece, Soviet policy is shown to have been divided into several fairly distinct phases: (1) wartime collaboration with the West, with the primary objective being the defeat of Nazi Germany; (2) KKE political gradualism immediately following the war, which was designed to create a weak Greek government and a strong Communist political presence; (3) a "dual" strategy of political activity and simultaneous gradual preparations for war in response to the inexorable movement toward civil war; (4) civil war; and (5) a partial and brief effort to return to the pre–civil war strategy of gradualism.

The revelation that Soviet policy in Greece was highly textured and complex is significant, but this analysis also illustrates other basic aspects of Soviet conduct, several of which should be noted at the outset. A major factor in the evolution of Soviet conduct through the last half of the decade was Stalin's attention to strategic concerns and simultaneous inability to control local developments; only in areas secured through Red Army occupation did Stalin's efforts meet with success.[2] His preference

---

1. This chapter is a revised version of chapters 3 and 4 of my book-length study, *Moscow and Greek Communism, 1944–1949* (Ithaca, N.Y.: Cornell University Press, 1989).

2. Even in Iran, a key area of Soviet interest in the immediate postwar period, the degree of success achieved rested largely on the presence of Soviet forces.

for operating at the strategic level is related to a second, crucial aspect of Soviet policy: its cautious nature. In fact, Stalin was so cautious that his policies were ultimately overtaken by events. Despite the eventual deterioration of their Greek policy, however, the case demonstrates the high degree of sophistication and skill with which the Soviets were able to employ a wide variety of instruments in conditions of limited control in pursuit of their objectives. In particular, the manipulation of the tempo of developments indicates an astute leadership. Finally, this analysis makes it possible to begin assessing the impact of Soviet action (or inaction) on the outcome of events in Greece. Had Stalin preferred, for example, to pursue Soviet objectives at the regional or local level, his response to developments in Greece would have been dramatically different. In particular, Stalin's actions crucially affected KKE policy during the civil war, largely by contributing to the incoherence in Greek Communist policy.

This chapter is limited to the period following the end of the Second World War, primarily because Soviet conduct during the closing stages of the World War is well-traveled territory, while the postwar period has remained largely unexamined. Furthermore, the complexity of Soviet policy, as well as its sensitivity to the external environment, is best reflected in the latter stages of the civil war. The most reasonable starting place is therefore the signing of the Varkiza Agreement in February 1945, which formally ended the "second round" of the Greek civil war. The agreement failed, however, to remedy the basic antagonism within Greek society between the forces of the Right and those of the Left, leaving Soviet policy to deal with a national drama that had yet to reach its conclusion.

In early 1945, Soviet policy departed from its earlier emphasis on maintaining Allied unity at the expense of Greek Communist interests. At this time, Stalin switched to a policy of gradual political infiltration in Greece in order to capitalize on the collapse of British influence and the initial American reluctance to assume Britain's role.[3] The policy was intention-

---

3. Several scholars from various perspectives have come to a similar conclusion. Bruce Kuniholm stresses that U.S. policy emerged gradually during the period 1945–46. There was therefore a period immediately following the war in which American policy still had not crystallized decisively against the Soviet Union (*The Origins of the Cold War in the Near East: Great Power Conflict and Diplomacy in Iran, Turkey, and Greece* [Princeton: Princeton University Press, 1980], 298–303). Paolo Spriano reaches a similar conclusion regarding the Soviet Union, arguing that the period 1945–47 was one in which the East-West division had not yet solidified,

ally gradual, to avoid activating a strong American response, and focused on the use of the Greek Communist Party and other organizations and individuals sympathetic to Communist interests in a political campaign to shift the Greek government further to the left on the political spectrum.[4] This strategy, which continued into the spring of 1946, permitted Stalin to concentrate his energies on the more pressing objectives of consolidating gains in Europe and initiating the reconstruction of the Soviet Union while minimizing the possibility of threatening actions from the West. Despite encountering some success toward the end of 1945, the Soviet-inspired policy of political gradualism began to deteriorate in the early months of 1946, as chaotic conditions in Greece produced an escalation of violence, convincing large segments of the KKE that the only viable solution was a resort to arms. General Secretary Nikos Zahariadis succeeded in imposing on the party a compromise policy of the gradual development of armed struggle, a move that received Stalin's endorsement in April 1946. Zahariadis' strategy was in line with Stalin's desire to expand the KKE's political influence in the near term while holding Greek Communist military forces in reserve for longer-term objectives. But the subtle distinction between "gradual" preparation for armed struggle and an immediate resort to arms proved too difficult to convey to the KKE's military forces scattered throughout Greece. Consequently, KKE policy increasingly became marked by incoherence. By early autumn 1946, the KKE was drifting toward civil war and the original Soviet policy of political gradualism had all but vanished.

During the first months of 1945, the Soviet attitude toward the Greek government also changed significantly. Diplomatic relations with Greece had been interrupted in the summer of 1944 with the abrupt (and still unexplained) departure of Soviet Ambassador Nikolai Novikov from Cairo. Initially, the announcement in December 1944 of the appointment of Mikhail Sergeiev as ambassador to Greece appeared to indicate a Soviet desire to restore normal diplomatic relations. But, in an obvious

---

allowing for a degree of autonomous activity in Europe (*Stalin and the European Communists* [London: Verso Press, 1985], 235, 236). Spriano also argues that the international balance of forces in 1945 favored the Soviet Union (pp. 272–73) and that it was to the Soviets' advantage to avoid civil war in 1945 (p. 289).

4. Other examples of the Soviet policy of gradual political penetration combined with pressure on the British can be found in Iran and Java, both of which were developing at the same time events in Greece were reaching a critical stage. If the Soviet pressure on Turkey is included as well, one gets the clear impression of Soviet pressure against states along its southern border and simultaneous diplomatic efforts to diminish the British presence.

rebuff to the government of Nikolaos Plastiras, Sergeiev never reached Athens, and his appointment was soon recalled.[5] It is possible that the Soviets were attempting by this action to use their limited diplomatic contacts to register their disapproval of the new Greek government. According to the Soviets, the appointment was held up because they did not wish to complicate matters for the British in Greece. Instead of Sergeiev, Adm. Konstantin Rodionov was to be the new Soviet ambassador, but he was delayed due to his attendance at the founding meeting of the United Nations in San Francisco.[6] When Foreign Minister John Sophianopoulos met with Reginald Leeper in early March, he informed the British ambassador that the Soviets did not intend to appoint an ambassador until the Greek Communists entered the government.[7]

Following the Varkiza Agreement, the KKE was forced to turn to the reconstruction of its shattered party organs. Contact with the Soviets was minimal, most likely because Stalin was more concerned with ending the war and consolidating his control over Romania.[8] Even so, the KKE-dom-inated National Liberation Front (EAM) was apparently aware of Stalin's dislike of the Plastiras government. Euripides Bakirtzis, former Vice President of the Political Committe for National Liberation (PEEA), reported that in early March he had a conversation with Lt. Col. Nikolai P. Chernichev (the Red Army officer who was formally second in command of the Soviet military mission that had been dropped into Greece in 1944 and later First Secretary of the Soviet embassy in Athens) in which the Soviet revealed that all Soviet missions were being withdrawn from Greece because of disapproval of the Greek government.[9]

5. U.S. National Archives (hereafter cited as NARS), Department of State Records (hereafter cited as DSR), Record Group 59, 868.00/6-145, no. 1114.

6. Records of the British Foreign Office (hereafter cited as FO), 371-48294 R7276, 13 April 1945.

7. FO 371-48294 R4304, 6 March 1945.

8. According to Dimitris Partsalidis, a telegram from Bulgarian leader Georgi Dimitrov arrived in mid-December advising the KKE to preserve its forces as much as possible and wait for a more auspicious moment for the realization of its "democratic program." In the interim, the KKE was counseled to use its popular organizations in enlightening world public opinion and organizations regarding the aims of the KKE (Avgi, 29 February 1976). The advice to preserve forces is difficult to interpret from the Soviet standpoint, however, because the degree of control the Soviets had over Dimitrov at this time is unclear.

9. NARS, Office of Strategic Services document (hereafter OSS) L55474, 6 April 1945. This document also recounts a discussion with the EAM Secretary for Macedonia, Nikos Dilaveris, who claimed that the Soviet Union had no diplomatic representatives in Greece because it did not recognize the present government. Col. Grigorii Popov of the Russian military mission

This meshed with the demands of the KKE during this period, which was principally agitating for a representative government, an inter-Allied commission (whose function was never clearly specified), and an end to the abuses perpetrated by the Right. Consequently, during the early part of 1945, the Greek Communists were not in a position to affect events in Greece significantly; the fall of the Plastiras government had more to do with British motives and anticommunist pressure than any overt KKE policy. However, as the KKE regained its strength in the coming months, this would change. And given that this reconstruction would take place within the context of a Soviet strategy in which certain objectives had already begun to be articulated, KKE policy would have to take Soviet interests into account.

Sophianopoulos's activities also reflect an accommodation to Soviet interests. The Greek Foreign Minister was drawn toward Soviet policy primarily because of his own political concerns. As the young and ambitious leader of the small Peasant Party, he could not hope to accede to the premiership solely on the basis of his popular following. On the other hand, given the sensitive position of Greece in Great Power relations following the war, it was possible to improve his political standing by presenting himself as acceptable to all three Great Powers. While some politicians threw their lot in with the British, and some (as the KKE) with the Soviets, Sophianopoulos sought to distinguish himself by advocating the harmonious presence of both Britain and the Soviet Union in Greece.[10] Sophianopoulos would prove useful to the Soviets in a number of ways, among which his performance as a messenger during the San Francisco Conference is but one illustration.

The Soviet press, which had remained quiet during the fighting in Athens the previous December, increasingly began to reflect the demands of the KKE and EAM. This was accompanied by a rise in the number of articles concentrating on the chaotic and terroristic conditions prevailing in Greece. By March, the demands of the Soviet government closely reflected those of the KKE, which was calling for an end to the terror, the replacement of Plastiras, and the installation of a representative govern-

---

disappeared some days after the signing of the Varkiza Agreement, and his place was taken by TASS correspondent N. Velichonskii (DSR 868.00/6-145, no. 1114).

10. It does not appear that Sophianopoulos was subservient to Soviet interests, although by early 1947 U.S. Ambassador Lincoln MacVeagh had concluded that he was a "fellow traveler" (DSR 868.00/1-2847).

ment; only with respect to the KKE's desire for an inter-Allied commission were the Soviets silent. Soviet and KKE policy picked up momentum following the fall of Plastiras and his replacement by Adm. Petros Voulgaris. Diplomatic developments in the Near East during the summer of 1945, the return of Nikos Zahariadis to Greece, and the victory of the Labour Party in the July 1945 British elections strongly affected the evolution of KKE strategy.

The Soviets were particularly active on the diplomatic front during this period. In June 1945, they raised territorial demands against the Turkish provinces of Kars and Ardahan while pushing for a revision of the Montreux Convention, which would have allowed the Soviet Union to establish a stronger presence in the eastern Mediterranean. Against the claims of the Greek government for Northern Epirus (southern Albania), the Soviet press argued that Albania was a "factor of stabilization" in the Balkans.[11] In July, the Soviet government rejected an offer of Four Power supervision of the Greek elections on the grounds that this would constitute a violation of sovereignty—despite persistent KKE demands for "Allied supervision."[12] Yet, at the Potsdam Conference less than a week later, Soviet Foreign Minister Vyacheslav Molotov circulated a proposal urging the Great Powers to recommend to the regent immediate measures for creating "a government in the spirit of the agreement reached at Varkiza . . . between representatives of the then existing government of Greece and the representatives of Greek democracy."[13] Clearly, this reflected a Soviet desire to become involved in the internal affairs of Greece, but of even greater importance is the fact that Molotov cited the Varkiza Agreement, not the Yalta Agreement, as the legal basis for the proposal. If the proposal had been adopted, subsequent criticism of Soviet policy in Eastern Europe would have had no juridical basis, as the Soviets could always have pointed to the "exceptional" character of the Varkiza Agreement, which applied only to Greece.

In the wake of the Labour Party's victory in Britain in late July, Soviet policy became more aggressive, especially with respect to the British military presence in Greece. Raphael Raphael, the Greek ambassador to Turkey, had a conversation with his Soviet counterpart, Sergei Vinogradov,

---

11. *Krasnaia Zvezda*, 17 September 1945.

12. DSR 868.00/7-1445, no. 452, Secretary of State to U.S. Embassy, Athens.

13. Stephen G. Xydis, *Greece and the Great Powers, 1944–1947* (Thessaloniki: Institute for Balkan Studies, 1963), 110.

in which the Soviet ambassador was strongly critical of the Greek government. According to Raphael,

> Vinogradov . . . launched into a vigorous enunciation of "the scandalous internal situation and Rightist terror in Greece." The Ambassador said that in all parts of Europe occupied by Soviet troops there was peace and unity and only in Greece was there a backward government and tyranny. This state of affairs could not . . . be continued after the change in the British Government. The Labour success would be extended also to Greece. . . . The British Army must evacuate Greece as the USSR was evacuating its troops from the other European countries.[14]

Sophianopoulos's activities were vital to the Soviets in their efforts to bring about a change in the Greek government. Earlier in the year, the Greek Foreign Minister had caused great consternation at the San Francisco meeting of the United Nations by voting with the Soviets against the admission of Argentina. This maneuver on Sophianopoulos's part revealed his pro-Soviet leanings: when some officials considered removing him, Ambassador Leeper argued this was impossible because it would be interpreted by the Soviets as an unfriendly act.[15]

Several months later, on the eve of the British elections, Sophianopoulos returned to Athens from San Francisco and tendered his resignation as Foreign Minister, which served to undermine the already weakened Voulgaris government. In a statement that coincided remarkably with Greek Communist demands, the Greek Foreign Minister told the American ambassador, Lincoln MacVeagh, that he was convinced after talking with Molotov that the only hope of achieving the desired relations with the Soviet Union would be through the establishment of a political government representative of all parties. According to Mac-Veagh, Sophianopoulos believed that he would be the next Prime Minister in such a government.[16]

---

14. DSR 868.00/8-1445, Memorandum of Conversation. The participants were the Greek ambassador to the United States, and State Department officials Foy D. Kohler and Loy H. Henderson.

15. OSS L56331, 24 May 1945.

16. In a telegram to the State Department, MacVeagh commented that Sophianopoulos "appeared very cocky and on my remarking that one of the royalist leaders had just told me a political govt is 'impossible,' replied 'that depends on who would be its chief,' apparently meaning himself" (DSR 868.00/7-2445, no. 746). While Sophianopoulos did not get the premiership he apparently desired, in late December 1945, when it appeared that the Sophoulis government

Greek Communist policy during this period corresponded to a high degree with Soviet policy. With regard to Turkey, elements in EAM and the KKE were aware that Greece might be used by the Soviets as an additional pressure point against the vital straits linking the Black Sea to the Aegean. At San Francisco, the Soviet delegation had warned Sophianopoulos against any Greek effort to unite with Turkey against Moscow's efforts to "keep the Straits open."[17] After a conversation with Zahariadis on 10 July 1945, Bakirtzis told OSS agents in Athens that "Russia will take positive action to obtain [a] stronger hold over Turkey regardless of what Britain does."[18]

The return of Nikos Zahariadis coincided with a change in KKE policy regarding territorial claims. While in Paris, on 25 May, Zahariadis reportedly asserted that the Greek claim to Northern Epirus constituted a threat to peace and cooperation between the Balkan nations,[19] leading one to believe that the KKE leader was serving Soviet purposes. *Eleftheri Ellada,* the EAM organ, took the territorial issue a step further in the Soviet direction by opening a campaign for the inclusion of Eastern Thrace among Greek territorial claims.[20] Zahariadis later insisted he was misrepresented in his statements regarding Northern Epirus, but EAM persisted in its claim to Eastern Thrace throughout the summer.

Zahariadis increased the verbal offensive against the British presence in Greece as well, explicitly linking it to the chaotic situation in the country. The KKE's General Secretary also endeavored to pressure the Voulgaris government, declaring on 16 June that the KKE would consider abstaining from the planned elections if the free expression of the people's will could not be guaranteed.[21] This stand gained support from Center groups, all of whom were concerned about the prospect of rightist terror affecting the elections.

Yet another significant aspect of KKE policy was its role in bringing about the resignation of Kyriakos Varvaressos, Vice Premier and Minister of Supply in the Voulgaris government. The British, believing Varvar-

---

would fall, he was considered the logical choice to succeed Sophoulis (OSS XL32200, 20 December 1945).

17. Laird Archer, *Balkan Tragedy* (Manhattan, Kans.: MA/AH Publishing, 1983), 279. On Soviet hostility to the formation of a Greek-Turkish bloc, see DSR 868.00/7-2845, no. 1252.

18. DSR 868.00/7-1745, no. 708.

19. DSR 868.00/6-145, no. 1114.

20. *Eleftheri Ellada,* 3 June 1945.

21. DSR 868.00/7-1745, no. 1332.

essos to be capable of resuscitating the Greek economy, providing them with a much-needed victory for their policies, had invested a great deal of their prestige in his appointment.[22] Varvaressos believed that his program of taxing profits and rigid control of prices and available supplies could turn the economic situation around. More important, however, he believed that Greece's economic problems should be attacked without resorting to foreign aid, and he was opposed to utilizing external assistance to enlarge the Greek armed forces.[23]

This policy was bound to create resistance from the wealthier and conservative strata of society. In the end, however, Varvaressos's initiatives were undermined by the coalescence of a constellation of opposing elements, including the KKE. Independently of the Right, the Communists actively encouraged the fears of those worried that the Varvaressos program would unfairly burden them. Orders were given to party members working in the Taxation Department to take every opportunity to lay the heaviest taxes on members of the small-shopkeeper and employee class in order to drive them into an alliance with the proletariat. Other directives called for public demonstrations and the formation of strike treasuries in support of strikes directed at the Varvaressos program.[24]

The KKE's strategy reflected its commitment to a policy of political gradualism aimed at increasing the influence of the Communists. The Greek Communists had always used to good effect the argument that Greece was becoming a dependency of Britain, effectively losing its independence. If Varvaressos's program had succeeded, however, it would have fulfilled many of the KKE's demands without allowing it into the government. Ultimately, Varvaressos, under attack from both Left and Right, resigned on 1 September 1945. This represented yet another defection from the Voulgaris government.

The reconstruction of military and paramilitary organizations was also on the agenda of the KKE. Initially, the focus was on the development of self-defense organs (*Aftoamina*), ostensibly aimed at protecting party members from extermination by the Right. The development of these units began in early 1945 and continued throughout the year. With their emphasis on defensive militancy and the use of weapons,

22. DSR 868.00/9-1145, no. 1295.
23. John O. Iatrides, ed., *Ambassador MacVeagh Reports: Greece, 1933–1947* (Princeton: Princeton University Press, 1980), 684.
24. OSS XL21021, 14 September 1945.

Aftoamina units could easily be seen as the basic units in a policy designed to lead gradually to civil war.[25]

The evidence shows that the efforts at restoring the military arm of the KKE were quite extensive and may even have been overseen in part by Soviet agents. Communist penetration of the Greek armed forces occurred through the Organization of the Army and Security Forces (KOSSA),[26] which appears to have played a much more significant role in KKE planning in 1946. In addition, Zahariadis apparently was actively engaged in reestablishing contact with the various military leaders who had been out of touch with the Central Committee as a consequence of the December 1944 fighting. In mid-June 1945, Zahariadis met with senior officers to discuss the reorganization of ELAS. This meeting was followed a short time later by the order for the formation of "Veterans' Associations."[27] On 17–18 September 1945, British sources reported another secret meeting between Zahariadis and military leaders regarding ELAS.[28] The Soviets were apparently aware of the KKE general secretary's activities through their agents in northern Greece. According to an OSS report:

> A third and independent sub-source has informed source that fourteen Russians have been living in Salonika at the houses of . . . three Greeks for some weeks previous to 18th September. On this date four of these Russians left for Kilkis, two left for Kalamaria and four more went to Ekaterini.
>
> . . . These Russians accompanied certain KKE officials who about 20th September were visiting various KKE offices in Macedonia. The object of these visits was to check up on the activities of these offices since the visit of Zachariades to Macedonia. Each official was to present a progress report on the work done by the particular office he visited. This inspection tour . . . was camouflaged as a visit of EAM political enlighteners to various towns on the pretext of arranging celebrations for the 4th anniversary of EAM.[29]

25. Foivos Oikonomidis interview with Alekos Papapanagiotou, *Anti,* no. 178, 1981, 40.
26. OSS XL46486, February 1946. Additional information regarding the formation of various covert paramilitary organizations can be found in DSR 868.00/9-1845, no. 1538.
27. DSR 868.00/9-1845, no. 1538.
28. DSR 868.00/10-1745, no. 1714.
29. OSS XL29925, 16 November 1945. British Intelligence also reported that Soviets in civilian clothing were operating with the Communists in northern Greece (FO 371-48718, R18233, 19 December 1946).

The Soviet presence was not limited merely to a clandestine operation (although this in itself is significant); from the time the Soviet military mission arrived in July 1944, to the restoration of full diplomatic relations in December 1945, the Soviets managed to maintain a substantial official presence, ostensibly under the aegis of the Allied powers. In October 1944, the Soviets requested, and subsequently received, the right to establish a "repatriation" mission in Greece formally attached to the Allied High Command in the Mediterranean.[30] The remnants of the earlier mission were incorporated into the new mission, which proceeded to engage in wide-ranging travels throughout the Greek countryside, presumably in search of Russians eager to return to the Soviet Union. The mission, which regularly exceeded its mandate and was treated by the British with distrust, was complemented by numerous efforts on the part of Red Army officers to enter northern Greece. On several occasions the Soviets succeeded; in one instance it took the British a full week to locate Soviet officers who had crossed into Greece without permission. Upon being intercepted, at least one of the officers, who argued that he was attached to the "repatriation" mission, was permitted to remain. Hence, contrary to earlier assessments of a limited presence in Greece, the Soviets were well situated for gathering information on events and overseeing the development of KKE policy.

This strengthens the conclusion that the Greek Communists pursued a strategy in harmony with Soviet policy in 1945, acquiring greater purpose and direction in several key areas. First, as we have seen, the British presence was challenged, reflecting the basic Soviet objective of eliminating Western influence in the eastern Mediterranean. Second, the KKE also pursued policies that, combined with Soviet diplomatic moves, helped bring about the defection or resignation of several key ministers, thereby weakening the Voulgaris government. Meanwhile, the chaotic and terroristic conditions prevailing in Greece drove popular opinion away from the Right, as some Center parties shared the KKE's reservations about the possibility of unbiased elections. This further undermined the Greek government. Under Zachariadis' leadership (and apparently with Soviet knowledge and consent), the reconstruction of Greek Communist armed forces began to gain momentum at this time. Significantly, all of these events, except the last, fell in line with the Soviet preference for a strategy of gradualism. At the time, how the KKE's armed

---

30. The subject of Soviet contacts in Greece during 1945–46 and the "repatriation" mission are discussed in greater detail in Stavrakis, *Moscow and Greek Communism*, 58, 116–18.

forces—for the moment restricted to self-defense—figured in Soviet calculations remained ambiguous.

Under pressure from a variety of forces, the Voulgaris government collapsed on 8 September 1945. There followed a period of leaderless drift in the Greek government. British diplomats became convinced of the need to establish a government with greater representation from the Left. This was the conclusion British Ambassador Reginald Leeper reached in a conversation with MacVeagh on 15 October.[31] Ultimately, Under-Secretary of the Foreign Office Hector McNeill was sent by the British government to Greece to assist in forming a new government. The result was the formation of a government under Themistocles Sophoulis on 21 November 1945, which was the furthest to the Left of any yet appointed. That the appointment of the Sophoulis government was considered by the Soviets and the KKE to be a significant victory is obvious from their reaction. This was the high point of harmony between the Soviets and the KKE, however. In the following months, the growing divergence between Soviet policy and the actual conditions in which the KKE had to operate would be revealed.

The Soviets were obviously satisfied with the appointment of Sophoulis. A weak, Center-Left government was precisely what was needed to tax the British commitment to Greece further. Ambassador Vinogradov, who earlier had been sharply critical of Greek and British policy, changed his tune. In a conversation with the Soviet ambassador on 28 November 1945, Ambassador Raphael noted that Vinogradov was friendly and had remarked that he was glad to see Greece "was beginning to see the light."[32] One day later, the Soviet government announced the long-delayed appointment of Ambassador Rodionov (who was the first official Soviet representative to Greece since Novikov left Cairo in August 1944).[33] Relations continued to improve through the end of the year. Stalin and Dimitrii Manuilskii, the Ukrainian representative to the United Nations, sent greetings to the "Gr[ee]k gov[ernmen]t and people" to correspond with Rodionov's arrival in Athens on 30 December 1945.[34] Several days later, the regent, Sophoulis, and Foreign Minister Sophianopoulos (the latter having regained his position with the new

31. DSR 868.00/10-1645, no. 1169; see also DSR 868.00/10-3045.
32. DSR 868.00/11-2945, no. 1501.
33. DSR 868.00/11-3045, no. 1380.
34. DSR 868.00/12-3045, no. 1492.

government) received New Year's messages from Stalin, Molotov, and Soviet Politburo member Mikhail Kalinin.[35]

In contrast to the improvement in Greek-Soviet relations, Soviet attitudes toward the British became markedly more hostile. On 21 January 1946, Andrei Vyshinskii, the Soviet delegate to the United Nations, launched an attack against the British military presence in Greece and Indonesia. During the debate that followed (1–6 February 1946), Vyshinskii relied on copious EAM documents to further the Soviet argument that British forces posed a threat to peace in Greece and must be removed. The Soviets, long aware of Britain's declining global position,[36] were only too happy to use the delicate situation in Greece to put further pressure on the British.

Yet, by the time of the Greek elections (31 March 1946), the Soviet gains in Greece were beginning to deteriorate. Not only had the KKE abstained from the elections (which went ahead as scheduled despite an intense effort by the KKE to get them postponed)—thereby shutting itself out of the political system—but the increasing unrest and violence in Greece evoked concern among the Western allies regarding Soviet intentions. The careful Soviet effort to eliminate the British without alarming the Americans had failed, a result that can be explained largely by the internal problems the KKE was experiencing in its attempt to accommodate itself to Soviet policy.

The Greek Communists' initial reaction to the new Sophoulis government was, like Moscow's reaction, also positive. The KKE officially announced its support of all government measures aimed at restoring political equality and tranquility, and demands for amnesty, recognition of the resistance movement, and the need for a representative government were noticeably absent from the Communist press.[37] According to KKE politburo member Dimitris Partsalidis, the Communist-led EAM was willing to give the new government a chance to prove itself by restraining strike activities (scheduled for 24 November) on the grounds that a gov-

35. DSR 868.00/1-1346, no. 69.

36. Xydis, *Greece and the Great Powers,* 153–54, refers to the findings of the Ethridge Commission, which investigated conditions in the Balkans where, according to various Soviet military commanders and political commissars, Britain was "through" as a world power and somebody had to move into the areas from which the British were withdrawing. Gabriel Gorodetsky related in conversation with the author (26 March 1987) that Stalin was well aware of Britain's diminished global role as early as 1943.

37. DSR 868.00/11-2345, no. 1342.

ernment of the democratic Center had just been formed and a strike might give the Right an opportunity to create an abnormal situation.[38]

This benevolent attitude did not last long, however, and the KKE soon returned to pressing its familiar demands. On 1 December 1945, *Rizospastis* published an article by Zahariadis again demanding the government be broadened to include EAM. By 7 December, the KKE was openly threatening to "reconsider" its support of the Sophoulis government.[39] The reconsideration was not long in coming, and EAM announced its withdrawal of support for Sophoulis in mid-December, charging that no real change had occurred. This was soon followed in January by KKE support for the anti-British position the Soviet Union was taking in the United Nations.

However, as Zahariadis became more aggressive in his policies, the Soviets continued to counsel caution. An EAM delegation arrived in Moscow on 15 January 1946 and had the opportunity to determine the Soviet attitude toward events in Greece. When Partsalidis presented his case to members of the International Department of the Communist Party of the Soviet Union (CPSU) on 17 January, the EAM General Secretary emphasized that, due to the growing terror against leftists, an armed conflict would be hard to avoid.[40] In response, P. Petrov, the CPSU's Balkan specialist, informed Partsalidis that it was the advice of the party leadership that the KKE should take part in the elections scheduled for March and then adopt a "wait-and-see" attitude. The KKE was also advised to strengthen its paramilitary "popular self-defense."[41]

The rapidly deteriorating situation in northern Greece contributed to the appearance of an increased willingness on the part of the Greek Communists to resort to force. In reality, Zahariadis had never succeeded in establishing full control over all military units in Macedonia. The northern detachments, unaffected by the previous fighting in Athens and possibly influenced by the militancy of Tito, were acting more or less inde-

38. Dimitris (Mitsos) Partsalidis, *Dipli Apokatastasi tis Ethnikis Antistasis* (Double rehabilitation of the national resistance) (Athens: Themelio, 1978), 184.

39. DSR 868.00/12-1045, no. 1435.

40. Partsalidis, *Dipli Apokatastasi,* 199.

41. Ibid. On the advice to strengthen the *Aftoamina,* see Partsalidis' interview in *Tachidromos,* no. 25 (1977), and the interview with Alekos Papapanagiotou in *Anti,* no. 178 (1981), 40. In a later interview (*To Vima,* 6 January 1980), Partsalidis recalls that while in Moscow in January 1946 he met with Deputy Minister of Foreign Affairs Lavrentiev to discuss the situation in Greece. Following this, he received an order from the KKE to meet with Petrov in the International Department, where the order to participate in the elections was given.

pendently. The impact of unrest in the north and an aggressive KKE policy were now beginning to have an adverse effect on Soviet objectives, as Washington was becoming increasingly convinced that the presence of British troops in Greece was essential to prevent a revolutionary outbreak.[42]

In retrospect, as the KKE approached its crucial Second Plenum in February, Soviet policy appeared to be unraveling in view of the Western powers' alarm at the deteriorating situation in Greece. Furthermore, the Soviet advice—to participate in the elections and then wait and see—left the KKE to wonder what it was supposed to wait for. More important, the paramilitary *Aftoamina* was given no specific task, leaving Zahariadis in the position of having to anticipate the future interests of the Soviets.

The results of the Second Plenum of the KKE are still a matter of debate, but this analysis tends to support the argument that a decision was reached to pursue a "dual" strategy of simultaneous political activity and preparations for the gradual development of the armed forces of the KKE.[43] Zahariadis was no doubt operating under several constraints at the time of the plenum. There was a significant faction in the Central Committee that argued for the immediate development of an armed struggle, reflecting not only a desire to respond to rightist excess, but also a sense that the KKE had to act before the momentum swung in favor of the government's forces.[44] But a second factor may also have been important with respect to the final outcome: the Soviets apparently still had not provided any specific advice as to the future purpose of the KKE's armed forces. In order to formulate a policy that would take Soviet interests into account, Zahariadis needed to know more than that he should wait and see. Since the Soviets were evidently not forthcoming, Zahariadis was compelled to extrapolate. The resulting "dual" policy is interesting in that it tried to take into account the Soviet desire to eliminate the Western presence from Greece. According to Zahariadis, the

42. DSR 868.00/1-2346, no. 121.

43. This is the substance of Ole Smith's argument in "The Problems of the Second Plenum of the Central Committee of the KKE, 1946," *Journal of the Hellenic Diaspora* 12 (Summer 1985). Another view is presented by Heinz Richter, who argues that no decision was made at the Second Plenum regarding the armed struggle and that, as a consequence, the KKE drifted into civil war without a coherent policy (*British Intervention in Greece: From Varkiza to the Civil War* [London: Merlin Press, 1985], 482–95).

44. Vasilis Bartziotas, *O Agonas tou Dimokratikou Stratou Elladas* (The struggle of the Democratic Army of Greece) (Athens: Sychroni Epochi, 1982), 26–28.

gradual development of armed forces constituted "an additional, force-ful means of pressure on the adversary for . . . peaceful, smooth, develop-ment."[45] Thus, the plenum had decided on a "progressive development of the movement, with the strengthening of the groups of the persecuted, for the gradual passing into partisan struggle, into armed resistance."[46] The KKE General Secretary also justified this policy by referring to its impact on the position of the British: the armed struggle had to be devel-oped "in such a way as to avoid the direct, armed military intervention of the English forces that were in Greece."[47] Zahariadis also noted that this policy was directed at isolating the British.[48]

It is possible, therefore, that the source of the incoherence in KKE policy during the crucial period 1945–46 was a growing divergence be-tween Stalin and the Greek Communists in interpreting the dual strategy. The Soviets viewed the KKE strategy as a means of expanding the Greek Communists' political influence in the short term while preserving their military forces for some future, unspecified activity. Greek Communist leaders, on the other hand, tended to view the dual strategy as a prelude to civil war. This disparity reflected the radically different contexts within which the two Communist leaderships operated. To Stalin, since the developments in Greece presented no immediate threat to Soviet war-time gains, a cautious strategy held out the greatest potential for expan-sion at the expense of Western power. Furthermore, since there was no immediate necessity for military forces, the rather vague advice to wait and see made perfect sense as the logical consequence of an opportunistic policy; Stalin was content with a strategy that maximized resources for future use.

The KKE, on the other hand, did not have the luxury of viewing events in the same manner, and under the increasingly aggressive actions of Greek rightists, who were unrestrained by an ineffective government, the

---

45. Ibid., 28.
46. Panos Dimitriou, ed., *I Diaspasi tou KKE* (The splitting of the KKE), vol. 1 (Athens: Themelio, 1978), 92–94.
47. *Voithima gia tin Istoria tou KKE* (Aid on the history of the KKE) (KKE, 1952), 260, as cited in Ole Smith, "On the Beginning of the Greek Civil War," *Scandinavian Studies in Modern Greek* 1 (1977): 25.
48. Dimitriou, *I Diaspasi tou KKE*, 92–94. According to Bartziotas, Zahariadis also tried to support his policy by implying that his view was in concert with that of other Communist parties. It is not specified which parties, however (Bartziotas, *O Agonas,* 30). Giorgis Blanas says that Yiannis Ioannidis did essentially the same thing (*Emfilios Polemos, 1946–1949: Opos ta Ezisa* [Civil war, 1946–1949: As I experienced it] [Athens: n.p., 1976], 71).

Greek Communists concluded that action was essential. The longer the Communists waited for decisive action, the more their advantage would be reduced, as the arms caches hidden at the time of the Varkiza Agreement were uncovered and the government forces were purged of Communist supporters. Torn between acceding to the Soviet desire for gradualism and the KKE's demand for action, Zahariadis was compelled to adopt the dual strategy, which amounted to a compromise between political action and preparing for war.[49] In the chaotic and volatile Greek context, in which the KKE's control over its military detachments was still not secure, such a strategy was bound to create incoherence in Greek Communist policy.

Zahariadis nonetheless persisted in this line of policy, as shown by his proposal in early March to the weakened Sophoulis government for a fifty-fifty division of parliamentary seats between the centrists and the KKE in the upcoming elections.[50] But as the elections approached, the KKE's efforts to pursue a policy of gradualism met with diminishing success. Ultimately, the KKE leader took the remarkable step of committing the Communists to abstention, despite the explicit Soviet advice to the contrary two months earlier.

Zahariadis' decision to abstain has never been satisfactorily explained.[51] Vasilis Bartziotas (and later Zahariadis himself) argued that the abstention was simply a tactical error and not of decisive importance.[52] But Bartziotas believed an armed clash was inevitable, so the question of elections was secondary. A refinement of this explanation may be somewhat closer to the truth. At the time that the Soviets advised the Greek Communists to adopt a wait-and-see attitude, Zahariadis was under pressure from his party, in light of the conditions in Greece, to opt for military action. In this situation, the KKE leader may well have seen

49. In addition, plans for a coup to be carried out by the KKE on the eve of elections were also discussed (Blanas, *Emfilios Polemos*, 51, 58; and Dimos Votsikas, *I Ipeiros Xanazonetai T'Armata* [Epirus takes up arms again] [Athens: n.p., 1983], 83–84). Given that the coup was an undertaking separate from the gradual preparation of military forces for armed resistance, it must have been impossible to avoid confusion and misunderstanding.

50. *Rizospastis*, 7 March 1946.

51. In a piece written some years later, Zahariadis denied that there had been advice from an outside party, and he attempted to lay the blame for the failure to register in the elections on Partsalidis and George Siantos (*Provlimata tis Krisis tou KKE* [Problems of the crisis of the KKE] [Athens: Laikis Exousias, n.d.], 20–21). His interpretation must be greeted with some degree of skepticism, since at the time he wrote this Zahariadis was having to defend his position against attack by the majority of the KKE.

52. Bartziotas, *O Agonas*, 38.

abstention from the elections as an opportunity to present Stalin with a fait accompli when he met with the Soviet leader in early April after the elections.[53] With the KKE removed from the political process, Zahariadis could argue that he had no option but to focus on preparations for war. Since the Soviets apparently had not forbidden the KKE from expanding its military forces, this was not an inconsistent position; moreover, it had the virtue of finally forcing the Soviets to make their intentions clear. This interpretation is strengthened when one considers the difference it would have made to the KKE if it had had Stalin's consent to such a plan prior to the Second Plenum.[54]

Support for this interpretation comes from Zahariadis' activities following the Second Plenum and the Greek elections. According to Lefteris Eleftheriou, the KKE General Secretary traveled to Belgrade, Prague, and Moscow in an effort to gain support for his new policy. Zahariadis met with the Soviet leadership in Moscow in early April 1946, at which time Stalin reportedly agreed to the dual strategy of the KKE, arguing that the Greek Communists should "proceed gradually from the villages to the cities, in order to avoid an untimely British intervention, and with the objective of finding a compromise."[55] Not only does this faithfully reflect Stalin's commitment to a policy of political gradualism in the near term, it also illustrates the extent to which the Soviet leader was constrained by his lack of effective control over the KKE. The timing of these meetings correlates almost exactly with the KKE's abstention from the Greek elections, bolstering the argument that Zahariadis decided to abstain in part to present Stalin with a situation in which a resort to mili-

53. The evidence for this meeting is scant. Philippos Iliou refers to it without documentation in his series in *Avgi*, which presented excerpts from the KKE archives (*Avgi*, no. 1, 2 December 1979; no. 9, 12 December 1979). In December 1979, the Greek Communist (Interior) newspaper, *Avgi*, ran a series of excerpts from the archives of the KKE. Although the material contains a great many gaps, there is still enough information in it to make fascinating reading. Since the series was numbered and continued through January 1980, each citation to the archives will bear the name of the paper, the number in the series, and the date. Unless otherwise noted, citations refer to the actual archival material, not to editorial comment. The only account of this meeting is in Lefteris P. Eleftheriou, *Synomilies Me Ton Niko Zahariadi* (Conversations with Nikos Zahariadis) (Athens: Kentavros, 1986), 32–35, discussed below.

54. According to Alekos Papapanagiotou, "Zahariadis knew something, which no one else knew, and because of this until the end of his life insisted that the abstention from the elections was a tactical mistake and not of a strategic nature" (*Anti*, no. 178, 1981, 40). Unfortunately, Papapanagiotou does not tell us what it is that Zahariadis knew, leaving this interesting piece of information to await further elaboration.

55. Eleftheriou, *Synomilies Me Ton Niko Zahariadi*, 35.

tary force was the only logical alternative. There was little Stalin could do: by abstaining from the elections, the KKE had effectively closed the parliamentary route, and Communist parties elsewhere had enthusiastically endorsed the Greek Communist strategy. Under the circumstances, Stalin's response to Zahariadis was the furthest the Soviet leader could go in sanctioning military force while still trying to hold Greek Communist forces in reserve.

Despite Zahariadis' success in eliciting Stalin's support for the dual strategy, KKE policy began to deteriorate rapidly following the elections. The Greek Communist leader's policy represented a masterful effort to reach a compromise between external and internal pressures, but the need to structure policy within the ambiguous confines of Stalin's long-term plans for the eastern Mediterranean created a fatally incoherent and unrealistic policy: to have expected the British and the Americans to tolerate any Communist buildup in Greece, gradual or otherwise, was simply asking too much. Similarly, given the internal pressures on the KKE for military action, any step in the direction of armed activity would be interpreted by KKE military leaders as an official sanctioning of civil war.

Soviet policy in the Near East was also eroding. From its high point in November 1945, the Soviet policy of gradualism had been transformed into a dual strategy of political activity and simultaneous gradual military preparations. With the KKE out of the political process, and Stalin in no position to exert effective control over the Balkans, the inevitable shift toward civil war was interpreted by the West as a clear manifestation of Soviet expansionism, galvanizing American resolve (although it was still some time before the United States would take action). More important, Soviet prudence and subsequent efforts to restrain the Greek Communist insurgency gave the ideologically exuberant Yugoslavs the opportunity to take the lead in Balkan Communist affairs. Stalin now found himself in the dangerous position of following events in Greece rather than leading them, entailing another shift in Soviet policy. The remainder of the civil war would be dedicated to Stalin regaining the momentum without the loss of Soviet wartime gains.

The focus of Soviet policy following the elections was to hold the KKE to the dual strategy. This was accomplished through the denial of much-needed resources for the expansion of partisan forces and diplomatic activity designed to prevent civil war. But the movement toward civil war had now reached a point where the KKE found it increasingly difficult to pursue its objectives, let alone protect itself. Hence, while the Soviets tried to restrain a growing insurgency, the KKE felt compelled to reach for more militant alternatives. This eventually led the KKE to look toward the Yugoslav Communists for support. By the end of the year, the KKE had become dependent on Yugoslav assistance. The collapse of Stalin's policy necessitated yet another shift on the part of the Soviets, since they now had to confront the loss of control in Greece to Tito. Consequently, for the remainder of the civil war, Stalin was preoccupied with the problem of containing Tito and retaining the allegiance of the KKE under conditions in which his ability to control events was limited. Stalin effectively neutralized the militancy of the Greek and Yugoslav Communists by choosing skillfully when and when not to act. This was to affect crucially the tempo of developments in Greece, contributing to the defeat of the Greek Communists and the containment of Tito.

The situation throughout the Balkans in the period 1946–48 was initially unfavorable to the Soviets, primarily because Tito's influence had begun to imperil important Soviet objectives. In addition to civil war in Greece, Albania appeared about to be incorporated into Yugoslavia, and Bulgarian leader Georgi Dimitrov was exhibiting a disconcerting tendency toward autonomous behavior. Most important, the aggressiveness of Tito threatened Soviet strategic interests; Greece was therefore part of a larger problem of the loss of influence throughout the Balkan peninsula.

In the months following his meeting with Stalin in April 1946, Zahariadis engaged in an earnest effort to implement the dual strategy. It soon became apparent, however, that the KKE leader was seeking a more rapid development of the military option. In July 1946, even as the KKE leader was urging "national reconciliation" (*symfiliosis*), he was meeting with Markos Vaphiadis and instructing him to begin to develop a partisan army. But, as Ole L. Smith points out, Zahariadis' directives to Vaphiadis reveal that the mobilization of armed forces was to take place within the larger context of a strategy oriented toward eventual negotiation and compromise.[56]

56. The references to *symfiliosis* are numerous, as it was a theme that appeared repeatedly in the Communist press during the summer of 1946. For a representative sample, see *Rizospastis*, 13 July 1946. The discussion of the orders for mobilization, as well as the relevant document, are taken from Ole L. Smith, "A Turning Point in the Greek Civil War, 1945–1949?" *Scandinavian Studies in Modern Greek* 3 (1979): 38.

The central problem with the dual strategy was that it simply could not work in the conditions that existed in Greece; Greek society was collapsing under the increasing violence and terror, and appeals for reconciliation fell on deaf ears. The KKE was forced toward the military option, but this entailed the disadvantage of relying on Tito, whose desire to acquire Macedonia was a sensitive issue for the Greek Communists. The resulting situation was an uncomfortable one: the KKE depended for immediate physical survival on the Yugoslav Communists, yet its long-term political survival rested with the Soviets. Stalin must have been aware of this tension through his contacts in Greece, which might explain his initial willingness to tolerate Yugoslav dominance in Greek Communist affairs. The KKE's distrust of Tito would serve as a brake on the developing insurgency.

The Soviets tried to use diplomatic initiatives to contain the drift toward civil war and enhance the prospects (which they still apparently felt were good) for a compromise. In September 1946, Soviet representative Andrei Gromyko vetoed a U.N. proposal to send a commission of investigation to the Greek border. In a surprising reversal, however, the Soviets accepted the proposal when it was brought up again in December. It is tempting to conclude, as some scholars have argued,[57] that this represented a Soviet attempt to impede the Greek insurgency and the independent initiatives of the Yugoslavs. The decision not only left Yugoslavia in an exposed position, it would also lead to the obstruction of vital supply lines to the Greek Communists.

The Greek Communists were aware, through their contacts with other Balkan Communist parties, of the Soviet effort to contain the developing insurgency and direct it toward the bargaining table. In September 1946, politburo members Yiannis Ioannidis and Petros Roussos arrived in Belgrade at the start of a longer journey that would ultimately take them to Moscow. The purpose of their trip (besides constituting the first step of the transfer of leading politburo members to Belgrade) was to present a "report" to the leaders of other Communist parties on the situation in Greece and the future plans of the KKE. The basic points of the report continued to reflect a commitment to the dual policy, but with a greatly increased military component. Zahariadis proposed (1) that Greece be declared a neutral power under the guarantee of the Great Powers; (2)

57. Lawrence S. Wittner, *American Intervention in Greece, 1943–1949* (New York: Columbia University Press, 1982), 59.

that the Soviet Union provide material assistance in order to increase the number of *andartes* to between 15,000 and 20,000; and (3) that financial assistance be provided to the KKE and EAM.[58] Although word came that the trip to Moscow was canceled, the KKE delegates submitted the report to Dimitrov on 12 September 1946, and he passed it on to Moscow. The Soviet reply was disappointing. Once again, the Soviets insisted that the focus of KKE policy should be the "mass popular political struggle" and that because of the international situation and poor weather conditions, extensive measures in the armed struggle should not be taken.[59] The Soviets also appear to have reacted negatively to the idea of Greek neutrality, while Dimitrov agreed with the KKE's representatives.[60]

In February 1947, the KKE's dual policy deteriorated further. In a message to Stalin, Zahariadis pointed out: "The Politburo of the Central Committee of the Communist Party of Greece in its conference in February 1947 . . . arrived at the conclusion that the democratic movement . . . must consider that the armed struggle has become dominant."[61] This was not an official decision, however, and the task confronting Zahariadis was to gain support for this new orientation so that it could be adopted as official policy. On 17 April 1947, Zahariadis sent a letter to Markos charging him with the duty of drawing up a plan of action for the Democratic Army of Greece (DAG) with the fundamental objective of liberating a region of Greece with Thessaloniki at its center.[62] Several days later, Zahariadis traveled to Belgrade for talks with Tito. Tito apparently approved of the new policy, although the scant evidence on this meeting does not mention the crucial manpower problem that plagued the KKE.[63]

The interesting point is that only *after* putting plans for the insurgency in motion did Zahariadis meet with Stalin. This in effect gave the KKE

58. *Avgi*, no. 1, 2 December 1979.
59. Ibid. See also the State Department report that pertains to the efforts of the KKE to obtain material assistance: "Significantly, nothing is said of rumors . . . to the effect that Soviet orders for cessation of outside support of the bandit movement in Greece have caused consternation in local communist ranks. (The King told me [MacVeagh] the other day that he has heard that Mr. Zachariades is practically hysterical at being thus let down by Moscow)" (DSR 868.00/1-2847, no. 3579).
60. *Avgi*, no. 1, 2 December 1979.
61. *Avgi*, no. 7, 9 December 1979, and no. 11, 14 December 1979.
62. *Avgi*, no. 8, 11 December 1979.
63. *Avgi*, no. 7, 9 December 1979.

leader an advantage in arguing for his policy: it was senseless to talk about preventing a civil war, because one was already in progress. No records of the meeting with Stalin in May 1947 have yet surfaced, but there are indications that the talks were favorable for the KKE. When Ioannidis relayed information about Zahariadis' trip to his counterparts in Athens, he wrote that "these last few weeks Koukos [Zahariadis] met with grandfather [Stalin] where our matters were effectively discussed. From the results of these meetings we must be completely satisfied."[64] For Stalin to have refused assistance at this point would have been dangerous, since this would have entailed handing the initiative over to Tito.

The problem now confronting Stalin throughout the Balkans was how to regain the initiative and control over policy that had been usurped by the Balkan Communist parties. With respect to Greece, the Soviet leader dealt with this problem at two levels. First, in order to neutralize the escalating insurgency, he sought to control the tempo of developments by consenting to supply the Democratic Army, yet delivering on his promises so slowly (and in such small amounts) that it effectively compromised DAG's effectiveness. Stalin apparently agreed to provide support in May, but the first Soviet aid did not materialize until August.[65] Initially, KKE leaders were optimistic about the promised aid, but as time passed they realized that the aid was not only late but woefully inadequate as well. The impact of the delayed delivery was to give the impression that the KKE was making policy in an illogical manner. Its decision, in February 1947, to pursue the military option was based on conditions in Greece as of that date, but when the KKE announced its intention to create a separate state, it had not officially endorsed a plan of action or made sure that its cadres were not in exposed positions. A comprehensive plan was not developed until the Third Plenum in September 1947, but it was reflective of conditions that no longer held, and the KKE was still struggling to acquire desperately needed materials. Consequently, the formation of the Provisional Democratic Government on 24 December 1947 had the appearance of a hasty action, and the campaign to capture Konitsa that followed ended in defeat.

At the same time, Soviet policy with respect to Greece was a manifestation of a much broader policy designed to reestablish control in the Balkans. The formation of the Cominform was part of this plan, intended,

64. *Avgi*, no. 9, 12 December 1979.
65. *Avgi*, no. 20, 25 December 1979.

as Paolo Spriano has argued,[66] to get the Yugoslavs to commit to an ultracritical line, thereby alienating them from the other major West European Communist parties. This interpretation allows for a plausible explanation of the failure to invite the Greek Communists to participate, since the Yugoslavs would have wholeheartedly endorsed KKE policy at the time, which in turn would have contributed to the legitimacy of Tito's stand. The situation was also critical for the Stalinists among the Albanian leadership. Similarly, it was only in early 1948 that Stalin was able to block and criticize the federation proposals of Dimitrov. The end of 1947 was a crucial time throughout the Balkans for Stalin. The failure of the Greek Communist military effort provided Stalin with a powerful argument against Tito's aggressive, pro-Yugoslav policy. Now the Soviet leader was credibly able to castigate the Yugoslavs for thinking they could defeat the U.S.-supported government in Greece. His ability to manipulate the pace of developments in Greece meant that although the Soviet leader might have lost Yugoslavia he would succeed in retaining control over the rest of the Balkans at a time when his ability to control events directly was limited.

Another aspect of Soviet policy was also manifested in the persistent efforts to reintroduce the possibility of a compromise solution in Greece that would allow the KKE to retain at least a minimal presence in the country. In February 1947, for example, former Prime Minister Nikolaos Plastiras was invited to the Soviet embassy by Ambassador Rodionov, at which time Rodionov offered to lead a "great anti-British campaign" to get rid of the British and prevent Greece from doom.[67] Less than a month later, the Soviet representative on the U.N. Balkan Commission expressed his government's interest in finding a diplomatic solution to the crisis in Greece when he met with an EAM delegation. According to Mihalis Kirkos, the Soviet delegate, A. A. Lavrishchev, "told us only that understanding and compromise is always better and that the steadfast policy of the Soviet Union in every international political matter is the . . . promotion of agreements . . . in order to attain a compromise solution."[68]

Stalin felt secure enough in his position by June 1948 to excommuni-

---

66. Spriano, *Stalin and the European Communists,* 301. His case is based on the analyses of Tito's lieutenants Eduard Kardelj and Milovan Djilas.

67. DSR 868.00B/2-2447, no. 268.

68. *Avgi,* no. 38, 20 January 1980.

cate Yugoslavia from the Communist bloc. The impact on developments in Greece was considerable, since DAG depended on Yugoslav material support to sustain its activities. Consequently, the KKE distinguished itself in the Communist world by being the only national party not to condemn Tito openly, preferring instead to maintain a discreet silence. The dilemma presented by its dependence on the Yugoslavs for its immediate survival continued to temper the KKE's willingness to align itself decisively with Stalin.

In order to minimize the KKE's reliance on Tito, Stalin continued the basic policy of material support (through Albania), combined with efforts to achieve a compromise settlement. The fact that, following the battles of Grammos and Vitsi in late summer 1948, the prospects for Communist success appeared remote was not a bad thing from Moscow's viewpoint, since it obviated the need to be concerned with the consequences of a KKE victory.

In September 1948, after the summer campaigns, Zahariadis went to Moscow again. Giorgis Vontitsos-Gousias maintains that these meetings resulted in Stalin's reaffirming his commitment to provide material support to DAG.[69] But the amount of aid Gousias said was promised appears to have been too good to be true. Vasilis Bartziotas criticized Gousias for making "imaginary" claims, but Bartziotas does not deny that Zahariadis went to Moscow, nor does he deny that some form of aid was provided.[70]

The Soviets, and to a limited extent the KKE, continued their efforts to bring about a negotiated end to the civil war. On 7 April 1948, the KKE approached former Prime Minister Emmanuel Tsouderos and presented proposals for negotiations;[71] this was accompanied by a series of peace proposals broadcast on Democratic Army radio. American officials rejected these overtures, believing them to be a "peace offensive." When the Soviets secretly approached Foreign Minister Constantine Tsaldaris in early July, however, the Americans reacted differently. In this instance, a Soviet embassy official proposed initiating conversations between the Soviet and Greek governments for the settlement of outstanding differences. The offer intrigued American officials but was eventually

---

69. Giorgis Vontitsos-Gousias, *Oi Aities gia tis Ittes, ti Diaspasi tou KKE kai tis Ellinikis Aristeras* (The causes of the defeats, the splitting of the KKE and of the Greek Left), vol. 1 (Athens: Na Iperetoume to Lao, 1978), 440.

70. Bartziotas, *O Agonas*, 47.

71. Wittner, *American Intervention in Greece*, 264.

rejected on the grounds that the Soviets wanted the talks to be held exclusively with Tsaldaris and in secret.[72] Despite the failure of this move, the Soviets continued to seek an informal means of gaining a diplomatic foothold in Greece.

When the initiatives for a negotiated solution produced little result, Zahariadis was summoned to Moscow on 11 April 1949, where he received orders to terminate all Democratic Army operations. The reason given was that the Soviets now feared that Albania would be invaded by Greek government forces if the civil war dragged on.[73] This must have been a disappointment to the KKE, but it complied. On 20 April 1949, the Provisional Democratic Government announced that it was ready to make the heaviest sacrifices so that peace could triumph. Apparently, the Greek civil war was finally nearing its conclusion. But on 4 May, Democratic Army officers were stunned to receive a telegram from Zahariadis declaring that, in view of a new situation, vigorous offensive activity rather than retreat was required.[74]

What occurred between 20 April and 4 May to change Zahariadis' mind? The explanation has its roots in the diplomatic maneuvering between the United States and the Soviet Union. The threat of an invasion of Albania had apparently succeeded in compelling the Soviets to terminate their limited support operations to the KKE via Abania. But at a dinner with U.N. Secretary General Trygvye Lie on 26 April 1949, Assistant Secretary of State Dean Rusk inquired of Soviet representative Andrei Gromyko whether their respective governments and the British could do something to bring about a settlement of the Greek situation.[75] Gromyko probably sensed the shift on Washington's part implicit in this question from support for a military solution to a political one,[76] in which case Stalin could hope to salvage a degree of political influence

72. DSR 761.68/7-748, Marshall to U.S. Embassy, 16 July 1948.

73. Gousias, *Oi Aities gia tis Ittes,* 501–3.

74. Ibid., 506.

75. DSR 868.00/5-549, Memorandum of Conversation, as cited in Basil Kondis, *I Angloamerikaniki Politiki kai to Elliniko Provlima, 1945–1949* (Anglo-American policy and the Greek problem, 1945–1949) (Thessaloniki: Paratiritis, 1984), 465–72. See also Dimitris Gousidis, ed., *Markos Vafeiades: Martyries* (Markos Vaphiadis: Testimonies) (Athens: Epikairotita, 1983), 51.

76. By his own admission, Gromyko says he reported the matter to Moscow (DSR 868.00/5-549, Memorandum of Conversation, as cited in Kondis, *Angloamerikaniki Politiki,* 437–38). Gousias later recounted that Zahariadis, in order to justify the return to civil war, stated that Gromyko had made a serious peace proposal at the United Nations in May (Gousias, *Oi Aities gia tis Ittes,* 516).

after the war—if he could demonstrate that the KKE was in a position of some strength.

The Soviets evidently miscalculated American intentions on this occasion, as U.S. officials were not about to allow the Greek Communist Party any permanent presence in Greece. Stalin also may have overestimated the military potential of the Democratic Army's forces, for by mid-1949 they were no longer in a position to sustain a credible bargaining position. Consequently, when Tito chose to progressively close the border between Yugoslavia and Greece in July 1949, the end was not far off. Stalin had succeeded in the sense that he had wrested initiative and control of the Balkans from Tito, but on balance Soviet policy during the civil war must be judged a failure: its initially promising prospects had come to naught, and the Soviets had to settle for preserving their wartime gains. Even the final effort to bring the civil war to a negotiated end in order to retain at least a residual pro-Soviet presence in Greece ended in failure.

The Soviet Union's foreign policy in Greece during the civil war has emerged as an example of policymaking in an environment in which Soviet control over developments was limited. In such situations, the Soviets adopted a policy that favored the consideration of strategic factors above all else and was characterized by caution and gradualism. This is reflected in Stalin's constant efforts to pursue diplomatic options in order to preserve the limited bases of influence he possessed. But this focus on strategic considerations produced a policy that failed to account for the reality of the local political environment. Consequently, conflict between Soviet strategic interests and local interests emerged. Despite its initial success, Soviet policy in postwar Greece was ultimately overtaken by events. Ironically, Stalin's approach was so cautious that it undermined the basis of his own policy.

Stalin also exhibited a marked preference for political activity as opposed to military action. A major outcome of this analysis is the revelation that Stalin's policy was to be implemented in an evolutionary manner. In the near term, he called for political activity to solidify the Communist presence in Greece; simultaneously, however, military preparations were to be carried out to provide the basis for a more aggressive future strategy. The tantalizing question that remains unanswered is what specific plans the Soviet dictator might have had in mind for the KKE military forces he continuously counseled should be held in reserve.

No evidence exists on this point, but if the Soviets had been successful in displacing Western influence in the eastern Mediterranean, they certainly had at their disposal the basis for an expansionist policy. This was not to be, however, as the regional ambitions of the Yugoslavs, combined with domestic deterioration in Greece, diverted Stalin from his long-term ambitions, compelling him to act quickly to preserve his influence among the Balkan Communist states.

The impact of the Soviet-inspired dual strategy on KKE policy also seriously affected the activities of the party. The Greek Communists are often criticized for their (apparent) inability to implement a policy that made effective use of their armed forces. But it is clear that at bottom the KKE's inability to formulate a coherent military strategy was due to Stalin's unwillingness to specify in a manner relevant to Greek conditions the precise role of Communist military forces. The Soviet desire to maintain maximum tactical flexibility profoundly affected the KKE's own prospects for success. Stalin successfully manipulated the tempo of developments, but the impact of this was to make it increasingly difficult for the KKE to develop a policy that corresponded to prevailing conditions.

Another point that deserves to be mentioned is the degree to which Zahariadis was able to capitalize on the Soviets' lack of control to elicit their support for policies they otherwise would not have endorsed. In April 1946, and again in May 1947, Zahariadis traveled to Moscow to present the Soviet leader with a picture of events in which the die had already been cast. Just as the KKE's abstention committed the Communists to a military option, so the orders to Markos to create a partisan army the following year left Stalin little choice but to go along. KKE-Soviet relations during the civil war thus reflect the same kind of dynamic tension that existed in Yugoslav-Soviet relations: in each case, Stalin had to deal with the efforts of local Communist leaders to gain for themselves a greater degree of autonomy within the sphere of Communist affairs. Ironically, the Western presence that Stalin sought initially to eliminate in the end proved useful as a restraint on the growth of Communist autonomist activity in the Balkans.

One advantage of this type of analysis is its ability to assess the impact of Soviet policy on the evolution of events in Greece. The question now need no longer be phrased in terms of whether or not the Soviets were involved in the civil war, since it is clear that even through inaction the Soviets affected the war's outcome. If Stalin had chosen to operate through regional actors, including Yugoslavia, the outcome of the war would have been quite different, because the Balkan Communist forces would have had carte blanche to follow an aggressive policy. When it appeared that the KKE was turning toward Tito, Stalin skillfully allowed inaction to work to his advantage, acceding to KKE requests for material support, yet delivering so slowly and in such small quantities that he disrupted the Democratic Army's offensive plans. The behavior of the Soviet Union was unquestionably a major factor in the final outcome. However, this conclusion should not be confused with the argument that Soviet policy in Greece was an absolute success. Relative to initial Soviet objectives, the Greek civil war was a failure, since Stalin was left with less than he started with in 1945. When viewed from the perspective of 1947, however, Soviet policy represents a qualified success. At the time of the Truman Doctrine, Stalin had actually lost control over Balkan Communist developments, and it is a testament to the Soviet dictator's political skills that he succeeded in containing Tito and regaining the initiative in the peninsula while avoiding even greater losses. The cost of an effective policy for the Greek Communists was a small price to pay if in exchange Stalin succeeded in reestablishing his dominance in the Balkans.

9

The Tito-Stalin Split
and the Greek Civil War

Ivo Banac

In the course of the Second World War, the Komunistička partija Jugoslavije (KPJ, Communist Party of Yugoslavia) pursued a revolutionary policy that was sharply at odds with the Soviet line of "Anglo-Soviet-American coalition." Despite Soviet fears that Tito's policy would upset Roosevelt and Churchill, the Western allies embraced Tito in 1943, extracting, to Stalin's surprise, only chimerical political concessions in return. Without once mentioning the term "socialist revolution," the KPJ had effectively won state power, making Yugoslavia the only Communist-dominated country in Eastern Europe (besides Albania) to have done so without direct Soviet assistance. This peculiarity, along with the ultraleftist stance of the KPJ politburo, was bound to create tensions with Stalin, who was only reluctantly abandoning his coalitionist wartime position. The Yugoslav-Soviet clash, which reached its culmi-

This article represents selected and specially drafted excerpts from my book *With Stalin Against Tito: Cominformist Splits in Yugoslav Communism* (Ithaca, N.Y.: Cornell University Press, 1988). Used by permission of the publisher, Cornell University Press. I am most grateful to John O. Iatrides, as well as to Ole L. Smith and Lars Baerentzen, for their valuable comments and suggestions, which greatly improved this work.

nation in 1948, was indeed a Left-Right split, but the Right was represented by a cautious and conservative Stalin in his imperial twilight.

One of the focal points of the growing tension between Belgrade and Moscow was Tito's aggressive Balkan policy, which in 1945 prompted an early clash with Stalin over Yugoslavia's push in Carinthia, Trieste, and Venezia Giulia. Fearing that the Yugoslavs were endangering the Soviet-sponsored government of Karl Renner in Vienna, Stalin ordered the Yugoslavs out of Austrian Carinthia. And in the crisis over Trieste, Stalin supported the British demand that the Yugoslavs quit the city and its immediate environs (the future Zone A): "Within 48 hours you must withdraw your troops from Trieste," Stalin ordered Tito in early June, "because I do not wish to begin the Third World War on account of the Trieste question."[1] The Yugoslav posture in the southeast was equally alarming to Stalin, perhaps most so in Greece, where the Yugoslavs clearly fanned the revolutionary aspirations of Greek Communists. Moreover, in Greece, as well as in Albania and Bulgaria, Tito was vying with the Soviets for influence over the local Communist parties.[2]

On 23 February 1948, at the Red Army Day reception given by the Soviet embassy in Tirana, Albania, Soviet Chargé Gagarinov lifted his glass before the assembled Albanian leadership and Yugoslav diplomats and made an odd toast "in honor of Marshal Tito, insofar as his work strengthens the democratic front in the world."[3] Since this first deliberate utterance in the Soviet-Yugoslav rift took place in Albania some five months after the founding conference of the Cominform in Poland, it is clear that the Yugoslav Balkan policy was increasingly becoming an obstacle to Soviet international strategy. Indeed, the dramatic denouement of 1948 was related most directly to Stalin's proximate fear that Yugoslavia was beginning to assume the role of a regional Communist center, with all the possibilities for mischief in the relations with the West that the role implied. The Soviets must have been aware that in Western capitals they, not the Yugoslavs, were being blamed for Belgrade's anti-

1. Cited in Vladimir Dedijer, *Novi prilozi za biografiju Josipa Broza Tita* (New contributions to the biography of Josip Broz Tito) (Rijeka, 1981), 2:917.

2. This is not to suggest that Tito's policy in Greece was always bold. On 12 December 1944, during the fighting in Athens, Tito ordered the main staff of his partisan units in Macedonia not to permit an Aegean Macedonian brigade to reenter Greece, because "that would be an international scandal at this time" (*Zbornik dokumenata i podataka o narodnooslobodilačkom ratu naroda Jugosalvije* [Collection of documents and facts about the national liberation war of peoples of Yugoslavia], tome 2, vol. 14 [Belgrade, 1981] 421).

3. Vladimir Dedijer, ed., *Dokumenti 1948* (Belgrade, 1980), 1:170.

Western excesses, such as the shooting down of an American military transport plane over Yugoslav territory in August 1946 and the mining of Albanian waters off Corfu to which two British warships succumbed in October 1946; and so they had all the more reason to worry that the West viewed Tito as Stalin's cat's paw in Balkan affairs, especially in troubled Greece and Albania.

As early as the late spring of 1943, one of the leading Yugoslav Communists—Svetozar Vukmanović-Tempo, the delegate of the KPJ Central Committee and Tito's supreme staff to the partisans of Macedonia and Kosovo—had held that the establishment of the Balkan staff, in which the Yugoslavs would map out the course of military, hence political, behavior of the Communist movement in Albania, Bulgaria, and Greece, was the KPJ's natural appointment. The proposal, as expressed in the conclusions reached by Tempo and the leadership of Albanian Communists in June 1943, called for the establishment of a permanent supreme staff of Balkan national-liberation armies, made up of the "most respected military and political representatives appointed independently by each Balkan country."[4] The staff was to lead the "struggle of the Balkan peoples for their national liberation and the securing of popular democratic power in all Balkan countries," but its immediate operational scope was restricted to a zone of some fifty miles on both sides of the pre-1941 Albanian-Yugoslav, Albanian-Greek, and Yugoslav-Greek frontiers.[5]

The Albanian party, which was under considerable Yugoslav influence, accepted Tempo's proposal,[6] but the Bulgarians as a whole, and the majority of Greek Communist leadership, procrastinated. Far from the tension between the KPJ and Moscow, their wartime strategies were not at odds with the Soviet position. The Greek Communists, advancing the slogan of liberation "under the British flag," kept their party under conspiratorial wraps in the ranks of the British-directed resistance. The Bul-

---

4. Svetozar Vukmanović-Tempo, *Borba za Balkan* (Struggle for the Balkans) (Zagreb, 1981), 90.

5. Ibid., 90, 93.

6. In his memoirs on Albania's relations with Yugoslavia, Enver Hoxha, the leader of Albanian Communists, presented himself as being opposed to Tempo's overtures on the Balkan staff. According to Hoxha, his signature next to Tempo's on the joint document indicated only a willingness to discuss the matter, though the Albanians hardly suspected that "behind the idea of the Balkan 'staff' hid the megalomaniacal and hegemonistic intentions of the KPJ leadership to rule the Balkans" (Enver Hoxha, *Titistët: Shënime historike* [The Titoites: Historical notes] [Tirana, 1982], 47–55).

garians held to the Soviet strategy of strikes and sabotage, linking the liberation of Bulgaria to the prowess of Soviet arms. Both feared the Yugoslav intentions in Macedonia, whose unification within Yugoslavia—at the expense of Bulgarian and Greek territory and claims—was being popularized, however indirectly, by the Yugoslavs.[7] Both also feared the predominance of Yugoslavia in Balkan affairs. During the meeting with Tempo at the end of August 1943 in a village near Larisa in Thessaly, George Siantos, the acting General Secretary of the Kommounistikon Komma Elladas (KKE, Communist Party of Greece), observed that not enough time had elapsed since the dissolution of the Comintern (May 1943) to start thinking about a staff that could be considered a type of a "new Balkan International."[8] But in September 1943, Tito ordered Tempo to abandon all plans for the Balkan staff as "politically incorrect."[9] Quite unlike the other Balkan Communist leaders, Tito evidently believed that Tempo went too far with his Balkan staff, not because it enhanced the Yugoslavs but because it could diminish the importance of the Yugoslav partisan movement among the Balkan Communists.[10] In his explanatory note to Tempo, Tito included the claim that the abandonment of the Balkan staff underscored Yugoslav primacy in the Balkans: "In every regard, Yugoslavia holds the leading role in the Balkans, both from the standpoint of military might of the [Yugoslav]

7. C. M. Woodhouse, *The Struggle for Greece, 1941–1949* (London, 1976), 67. In 1943, Tito was indeed in favor of the unification of the whole of Macedonia within Yugoslavia. He wrote to Tempo on 6 December 1943: "As far as Macedonia is concerned . . . neither you nor the comrades over there [Greeks and Bulgarians] have approached this question correctly. The Macedonian people have the right to self-determination, and even to secession. . . . Sovereign in its [sic] rights, the Macedonian people have the right to join the federal community of other peoples. This is what they, in fact, should be doing today by joining the common struggle of the other peoples of Yugoslavia against the German conquerors and Bulgarian occupiers. This is the only guarantee that a genuinely democratic national movement will develop in Macedonia—the guarantee of the better future of the Macedonian people" (Josip Broz Tito, *Sabrana djela* [Collected works] [Belgrade, 1977–84], 18:19).

8. Tempo, *Borba za Balkan,* 119.

9. Tito, *Sabrana djela,* 16:225. For a discussion of the possibility that the Soviets (or Georgi Dimitrov, the Bulgarian Communist leader) had a hand in Tito's decision to end Tempo's action, see Elisabeth Barker, *British Policy in South-East Europe in the Second World War* (London, 1976), 191.

10. "The Balkan staff," Tito wrote Tempo on 6 December 1943, "which, as we can see is nonsense—because it does not (nor can it) exist (with 4 commanders and 4 commissars)—would in fact serve to drive back our national liberation struggle, the supreme staff, and the ANNOJ with some sort of a Pan-Balkan movement, which is not even close to being crystallized in the course of struggle" (Tito, *Sabrana djela,* 18:18).

National Liberation Army and from its experience in the establishment of people's power through the national liberation committees and antifascist councils. Therefore, in our opinion, as well as in the opinion of Grandpa [Moscow], we must be the center of Balkan countries in military and political regard."[11]

It is more likely, however, that the Soviet opinion of October 1943 was no less guarded on the expansion of Tito's influence in the Balkans than it was one year later when Stalin pressed the framing of a Yugoslav-Bulgarian federation upon Tito during the September talks between the two leaders at Moscow. Stalin's insistence on this step—he also urged it upon Edvard Kardelj and Ivan Šubašić on 22 November 1944—suggests that he saw this project as an expedient method of controlling Tito's policies by way of more dependable Bulgaria. The Yugoslavs "wondered why Stalin forced the Yugoslav-Bulgarian federation, because in other circumstances . . . he was very circumspect in all matters that could lead to the sharpening of relations between the Soviet Union and the West."[12] But though Stalin's haste aroused their mistrust, they offered a response that could only strengthen their hand in the Balkans. Instead of a dualist union between Sofia and Belgrade, the Yugoslavs proposed a seven-member federation in which Bulgaria would be added to the six emerging Yugoslav republics. Moreover, Pirin Macedonia—that is, the portion of Macedonia that belonged to Bulgaria—was to be united to Vardar (or Yugoslav) Macedonia even if the unification with Bulgaria fell through.[13]

Some of the Bulgarian leaders opposed the federation (Trajčo Kostov), but others supported it on dualist terms (Georgi Dimitrov and Velko Červenko). After the failure of Kardelj's mission to Sofia in late December 1944, the representatives of the two countries were invited to Moscow in late January 1945 for Soviet arbitration. According the Moša Pijade, the leading Yugoslav delegate, Stalin initially spoke "in the spirit of the Bulgarian proposal, that is, for a dualist federation, explaining his stand with the argument that Bulgaria has been an independent country for a long time." Pijade countered this view by pointing out that "Serbia

---

11. Ibid., 17:36–37.
12. Edvard Kardelj, *Sećanja* (Memoirs) (Belgrade, 1980), 106.
13. This was certainly the argument that Kardelj used in his negotiations with the Bulgarian leaders at Sofia on 23 December 1944. See Moša Pijade, "Govor o balkanskoj federaciji na Osmom redovnom zasedanju Narodne skupštine FNRJ," in *Izabrani spisi* (Selected writings), tome 1, vol. 5, ed. Pero Morača (Belgrade, 1966), 748.

and Montenegro were independent a lot longer than Bulgaria" and that, "moreover, why should the Croats, who had their state a millennium ago, not be equal to the Bulgars?"[14] In a technical sense Pijade was right, but the prospect of being as independent as Montenegro could not arouse Bulgarian fervor. When, a day or so later, Stalin unexpectedly came around to Pijade's viewpoint, he was probably only soothing the Yugoslavs by empty compliance. By that time he was aware that the British government, on 26 January, had cautioned the Bulgarians, who had not yet signed the peace treaty with the Allies, against any plans for a federation with, or the cession of, Pirin Macedonia to Yugoslavia. For the time being, the Yugoslav-Bulgarian federation was as good as dead. "I must admit," recalled Kardelj, "that this did not make us feel unhappy."[15]

Although Stalin's phlegm had stopped Tito's parrying of the Bulgarian link, nothing, seemingly, could be done to check the Yugoslavification of Albania, where the Soviets had little to say until 1948. In Greece, on the other hand, Stalin aimed to live up to the Percentages Agreement negotiated with Churchill, through which 90 percent of political interest in Greece was allotted to Britain. But here, too, Tito's policy clashed with Stalin's. In November 1944, he encouraged the KKE's plans to seize Athens, even though this course would almost certainly lead to a clash with the British troops that had already disembarked in Greece for the purpose of disarming the Communist-led guerrillas and propping up the anticommunist forces.[16] After the failure of the Communist uprising in December, Georgi Dimitrov, the Bulgarian leader and the Comintern's former General Secretary, was reflecting Stalin's wishes when he informed the KKE in early 1945 that the Greeks in the future must do everything to avert a confrontation with the British, there being little advantage in this course for themselves, and a great deal of possible harm

14. Ibid., 751–52.
15. Kardelj, *Sećanja*, 105.
16. D. George Kousoulas, *Revolution and Defeat: The Story of the Greek Communist Party* (London, 1965), 201. I am grateful to Lars Baerentzen for bringing to my attention a very suggestive document from a British War Office file at the Public Record Office (WO 204/8903: Land Forces Greece, General Staff Intelligence Branch, Security Intelligence Middle East, political reports, no. 0747, December 15, 1944) that includes the following intercepted telegram, dated 30 November 1944, from Stergios Anastasiadis, a member of the KKE leadership on a fact-finding mission to Yugoslavia and Bulgaria, to Siantos: "Saw BULGARIANS and TITO: They advise we must insist on not rpt not being disarmed. No rpt no British interference."

to Yugoslavia and Bulgaria.[17] For their part, the Yugoslavs were still encouraging the KKE's resistance and promising the Greek Communists military support.[18]

Despite Yugoslav assurances, the Greek party leadership convinced itself that it could not count on significant support from the north. At Varkiza in February 1945, at a conference between the Communists and Greek nationalists, the KKE underwrote the disarming of its powerful guerrilla army in exchange for a limited amnesty and the party attaining legal status. And at the Yalta Conference, which took place that same month, Stalin placed no obstacles in the path of British intervention in Greece, expressing his confidence in British policy. There followed a period of intensive repression of Communist and resistance activists, who were hounded by the police and rightist thugs, though the legality of the KKE leadership in Athens was itself never violated.

Nikos Zahariadis, General Secretary of the KKE, who resumed his post after his return from Nazi captivity in late May 1945, soon developed the theory of "two poles," whereby Greek foreign policy was to be equidistant from the Soviet Balkans and the British Mediterranean. His strategy was to pressure the British government and Greek nationalists to restore the balance that had been tipped in favor of London. Failing that, he did not exclude the possibility of armed resistance, which was the strategy favored by the Yugoslavs. Despite Soviet advice to the contrary (as well as that of the Italian and French Communists), Zahariadis ordered the KKE to boycott the parliamentary elections of March 1946. When the elected nationalist majority intensified the persecution of the KKE, Zahariadis and the party leadership agreed upon armed resistance.[19]

The KKE's "third round," or third bout of armed struggle since the beginning of the war, also received a major boost from the Yugoslavs. Zahariadis still pursued limited goals, designed to moderate the policies of the Greek cabinet. He had purposely instructed the guerrillas to wage

17. Dominique Eudes, *The Kapetanios: Partisans and Civil War in Greece, 1943–1949* (New York, 1972), 226.

18. Evangelos Kofos, *Nationalism and Communism in Macedonia* (Thessaloniki, 1964), 146–67.

19. For Zahariadis' main political and strategic concepts in 1945 and 1946, see Heinz Richter, *British Intervention in Greece: From Varkiza to Civil War (February 1945 to August 1946)* (London, 1985), 246–87, 477–517. Richter's interpretation is convincingly challenged by Ole L. Smith in "The Problems of the Second Plenum of the Central Committee of the KKE, 1946," *Journal of the Hellenic Diaspora* 12 (1985): 43–62.

only defensive operations, and only against the nationalist bands, not against the regular Greek army.[20] The militant wing of the KKE, however, had never quite accepted the Varkiza Agreement. Under the leadership of the *kapetanioi,* or guerrilla chieftains, the *andartes,* or insurgents, were increasingly organized for the offensive. The leading *kapetanios,* Markos Vaphiadis, the former party leader in Thessaloniki, was making preparations to confront the regular army.[21] Charged by Zahariadis, in October 1946 Markos united the local insurgent bands, which operated from Macedonia to the Gulf of Corinth, into the Democratic Army of Greece (DAG), with himself as its supreme commander. The KPJ clearly favored the offensive policy that was identified with General Markos.[22]

Yugoslav aid was crucial for the Greek rebellion. The indoctrination camp at Buljkes, near Backa Palanka (Vojvodina), was the school for the KKE cadres and became the rear base of DAG.[23] Transmissions of Radio Free Greece originated in Yugoslavia, as did most of DAG's food and supplies. According to Slobodan Krstić-Uča, who was, in 1946, the Chief Secretary of Serbia of the Uprava državne bezbednosti (UBD-a, Administration of State Security), the Yugoslav security police, Markos was escorted to Greece from Yugoslav territory in September 1946, obviously after prior consultations with the KPJ leaders. The Yugoslavs furnished Markos with medical supplies and light weapons—rifles, machine guns, and submachine guns—which had to be Wehrmacht issue so as not to incriminate Greece's northern neighbors. The aid in weapons from Albania and Bulgaria was also of Yugoslav origin: "We gave it to the Albanians and Bulgarians, and they to the Greeks."[24]

The supply network for Greece was in the firm hands of Aleksandar Ranković, the number-three man in the Yugoslav politburo, who was responsible for the security apparatus. Within the UDB-a the Greek line

20. Eudes, *Kapetanios,* 269.

21. Dragan Kljakić, *General Markos* (Zagred, 1979), 124.

22. For an excellent summary of the Yugoslav role in the Greek civil war, see Nicholas Pappas, "The Soviet-Yugoslav Conflict and the Greek Civil War," in *At the Brink of War and Peace: The Tito-Stalin Split in a Historic Perspective,* ed. Wayne S. Vucinich (Brooklyn, N.Y., 1982), 219–37, 324–32. See also John O. Iatrides, "Civil War, 1945–1949: National and International Aspects," in *Greece in the 1940s: A Nation in Crisis,* ed. John O. Iatrides (Hanover, N.H.: University Press of New England, 1981), 195–219, 385–92; and Woodhouse, *Struggle for Greece,* 169–258.

23. Pappas, "The Soviet-Yugoslav Conflict," 222.

24. D. Golubović, "Zašto Markos ne kaže sve" (Why is Markos not telling everything), *Duga,* 17 July 1982, 28.

was administered by Generals Jovo Kapičić and Jovo Biljanović, as well as by Krstić. In the summer of 1947, the Yugoslavs started sending large shipments of arms to Greece, faster and more generously than the Soviet Union and the rest of its East European allies. All told, according to Krstić, until the break with the Soviet Union, the Yugoslavs sent 35,000 rifles, 3,500 machine guns, 2,000 German bazookas, 7,000 antitank guns, 10,000 field mines, clothing for 12,000 men, and 30 wagons of food to Greece. They furnished all the supplies and equipment for the First DAG division, including 500 draft horses, and operated three field hospitals, at Mount Osogovo, Katlanovska Banja, and Jasenovo (at the foot of Mount Babuna), all in Yugoslav Macedonia, for the wounded *andartes*.[25] Yugoslavia became a ready sanctuary for the DAG fighters as well as for refugees (by early 1948, 8,000 refugees from Greece were settled in the former German villages of Gakovo and Kruševlje, near Sombor, in Vojvodina). In addition, Yugoslav influence over DAG was exercised through the Slavo-Macedonians of northern Greece and their organization, the National Liberation Front (NOF).

Although NOF had been formed in April 1945, before the "third round," it became a constituent part of DAG. It commanded the allegiance of almost half of DAG's fighters (Markos himself admitted later that 45 percent of the Democratic Army's fighting force consisted of Macedonians).[26] The founders of NOF included Slavo-Macedonians from Greece who were former Yugoslav-trained officers in the Yugoslav army.[27] NOF ostensibly fought for the national rights of the Macedonians "within the framework of democratic Greece," but its underlying goal was the unification of Macedonia within the Yugoslav federation. NOF's autonomy within DAG was manifested by special units and the running of separate "agitprop" and educational networks that promoted Macedonian schools, press, and cultural-educational institutions.[28]

In comparison with Yugoslavia and its client Albania, Bulgaria played a relatively limited role in the Greek civil war, perhaps because Yugosla-

25. Golubović, "Zašto Markos," 29–30. Cf. Dedijer, *Novi prilozi,* 3:266–67.

26. Jovan Popovski, *General Markos: Zašto me Staljin nije streljao?* (General Markos: Why did Stalin not shoot me?) (Belgrade, 1982), 9, 76. According to R. V. Burks, 11,000 Macedonian *andartes* in early 1948 constituted "somewhat less than half the strength of the army at that time" (*The Dynamics of Communism in Eastern Europe* [Princeton: Princeton University Press, 1961], 102).

27. Kofos, *Nationalism and Communism,* 167.

28. Ibid., 170–71.

via's Macedonian policy, notwithstanding Sofia's official acceptance of Macedonian national individuality, still went against the grain of Bulgarian national aspirations.[29] After the promulgation of the Truman Doctrine in March 1947, when Washington assumed the burden of British policy against the Greek insurgents, American military and economic aid started flowing into Greece and Turkey. The American policy of containment did not at the time differentiate among the Communist parties, which were all seen as unqualified agencies of Soviet policy. Nevertheless, the growing American presence in the Aegean necessarily had a direct effect on Yugoslavia and Bulgaria, in that it brought about a cohesion of their Communist leaders to a degree that far exceeded the limits preferred by Stalin.

In late July 1947, at the Yugoslav resort of Bled (Slovenia), Tito and a Bulgarian government and party delegation led by Georgi Dimitrov reached a series of agreements that affected the future of Yugoslav-Bulgarian relations. The two sides agreed to conclude a treaty of friendship and detailed a series of measures on economic relations, imposts, and legal arrangements aimed at establishing the closest possible alliance between the two states. Yugoslavia waived its right to any war reparations incurred by Bulgaria,[30] and in a series of measures affecting the status of Macedonians in Bulgaria, Dimitrov concurred with the Yugoslav demands for a new policy in Pirin Macedonia. Beginning in September 1947, Bulgaria imported some ninety teachers from Yugoslav Macedonia, introduced new, de-Bulgarized textbooks in Pirin schools, and started promoting Macedonian language, culture, and contacts among the Macedonians on both sides of the frontier. Portraits of Tito and Lazar Kolishevski, Premier and KPJ Secretary of Yugoslav Macedonia, were introduced to the Pirin region alongside those of Dimitrov and Stalin.[31] In a reference to the Balkan situation, the delegations at Bled, as a result of the "provocations of Greek monarchofascists," pointedly recommended close contacts and coordinated work between the two governments in all important international affairs that concerned the two countries.[32]

From the Western standpoint, the Bled Agreement was clearly aimed

29. Ibid., 169.
30. Slobodan Nešović, *Bledski sporazumi: Tito-Dimitrov, 1947* (The Bled agreements: Tito-Dimitrov, 1947) (Zagreb, 1979), 49–73.
31. Ibid., 136–34.
32. Ibid., 63.

against Greece, the full Bulgarian accession to the Yugoslav tenets on Macedonian affairs being seen as subservient to the Yugoslav plan of pushing into Aegean—or Greek—Macedonia.[33] But whereas the worried Turks, for example, believed that the final liquidation of the Yugoslav-Bulgarian dispute over Macedonia prefigured the "Slavic expansion" in the Balkans,[34] the leadership of the KKE breathed a sigh of relief, convinced that Bled was a result of Stalin's signal for an offensive in Greece. Zahariadis now abandoned the privilege of legality and in mid-September ordered the full mobilization of the KKE. Though his aim was to take charge of the Mountain—the partisan base areas—Zahariadis' military strategy was no better than his sources of information. In the field by late November, he ordered Markos to drop guerrilla tactics in favor of positional war—this at the moment when the government's military effort was showing the effects of lavish American aid and expert assistance.[35] Also at the end of November, as the Greek authorities stepped up the execution of imprisoned Communists, Tito and Dimitrov met at Evksinograd near Varna to sign the Yugoslav-Bulgarian friendship treaty. One month later, Yugoslav-operated Radio Free Greece announced that the Provisional Greek Democratic Government had been formed on Mount Grammos, the liberated territory close to the Albanian frontier city of Korcë. The Greek civil war could no longer be reversed.

Zahariadis was laboring under the misapprehension that Stalin backed a Balkan offensive. On the contrary, the Soviet government and press ignored the Bled and Evksinograd agreements.[36] Soviet annoyance became evident on 29 November, after the second meeting between Tito and Dimitrov, when Stalin saluted the Yugoslav state holiday in his most stiffly precise manner. In addition to Tito's gambling action in Greece, but in close connection with it, the Soviets were evidently especially upset by Belgrade's policies in Albania. On 20 November, Nako Spiru, a twenty-eight-year-old member of the Albanian politburo, who was responsible for economic policy, committed suicide. Despite his long as-

33. According to a noted Greek conservative who, however, offers no proof for his claim, during that same summer Markos himself negotiated a new agreement with the Yugoslav and Albanian staffs at Bled. Moreover, these agreements, which significantly increased military aid to DAG and placed its officers under the supervision of a joint Balkan Communist staff, were underwritten by the Soviets. See Evangelos Averoff-Tossizza, *Le feu et la hache: Grèce 46–49* (Paris, 1973), 190–91.

34. Nešović, *Bledski sporazumi,* 113.

35. Eudes, *Kapetanios,* 302–7.

36. Nešović, *Bledski sporazumi,* 120–22, 164–65.

sociation with the Yugoslavs, Spiru had opposed the Yugoslav measures for the control of Albanian economy, and he felt isolated and destitute of allies among his comrades, who either supported the Yugoslavs or dared not oppose them openly. A year earlier, upon his return from Belgrade, where he had signed a series of unequal economic deals with Yugoslavia, he had commented in his dry, sarcastic style about some of his intimates: "So, are the people saying that Nako Spiru sold Albania to Yugoslavia just as [ex-King] Ahmet Zogu sold it to Italy?"[37] Spiru's desperate protest was all the more poignant since he had the ear of Enver Hoxha, the party leader and Premier, and had developed close ties with the Soviets, "who did not conceal their sorrow over his loss."[38]

In the months preceding Spiru's suicide, the Albanian politburo had become the arena of a battle between the pro- and anti-Yugoslav forces. The pro-Yugoslavs were Koçi Xoxe, Pandi Kristo, and Kristo Themelko, the latter a Slavo-Macedonian, and they had the tacit support of Tuk Jakova and Bedri Spahiu. Through Xoxe, the Minister of the Interior and Organizational Secretary of the Partia Komuniste e Shqipërisë (PKSH, Communist Party of Albania), the KPJ exercised almost total control over the Albanian party and state administration. Spiru tried to offset the Yugoslav influence by relying on the Soviets and on the behind-the-scenes support of Premier Hoxha and two of Hoxha's supporters, Hysni Kapo and Gogo Nushi. Yugoslavia's extensive economic investment and aid in Albania, as well as its tutelage in Albanian party, military, and security affairs, proceeded from the premise that Albania was hardly different from any of Yugoslavia's own underdeveloped republics. In fact, Albania's unification with Yugoslavia had been taken for granted by the leaders of the KPJ since the end of the war. For example, Moša Pijade proposed that the plans for the new federal hall in Belgrade include seven cabinets, for Yugoslavia's six republics and Albania.[39] But Belgrade had no hope of bringing this curious assumption to pass against Soviet opposition.

Remote hints of Soviet displeasure merely hastened Tito's designs. After Spiru's suicide, according to Milovan Djilas, "Tito became increasingly nervous and started to hurry the unification with Albania. In his circle of intimates, he did not hide his fears, nor could he, that the

---

37. Hoxha, *Titistët*, 292.
38. Ibid., 356.
39. Dedijer, *Novi prilozi*, 2:902.

'Russians' will beat us to it and 'grab' Albania."[40] In December, his emissaries imposed on Albania a Yugoslav-controlled joint coordinating commission, which was to oversee the integration of the two economies. A similar mechanism was proposed for the unified command of the Yugoslav, Albanian, and Bulgarian armies, as the first step toward the unification of Balkan Communist armed forces. When Gen. Mehmet Shehu, the chief of Albanian general staff, opposed this idea, he was dismissed at the instigation of Koçi Xoxe.[41] Moreover, "without any real cause, that is under the pretext that Albania was threatened by 'Greek reaction' and the 'imperialists' stationed in Greece, Tito ordered that two complete and completely equipped divisions be readied for stationing in Albania."[42] A regiment of the Yugoslav air force was already on its way to Albania.

Stalin's reaction was swift. He undoubtedly linked the Yugoslav moves with the proclamation of the Greek provisional government at Grammos, and at the end of December he summoned a Yugoslav party delegation to Moscow. He specifically requested Djilas's participation in the mission, hoping perhaps to win this key politburo member away from Tito.[43] Upon his arrival in Moscow in early January 1948, Djilas was stunned by the show of Stalin's provocative favor for Yugoslavia's "swallowing" of Albania.[44] The point was to arouse the Yugoslavs to an unvarnished expression of their plans for Albania, while simultaneously lulling them into a false sense of security.

The effect of the baited snare was to overturn the Yugoslav Balkan policy by enticing it into overdrive. On 26 January, Tito formally requested from Hoxha a base for the Yugoslav divisions at Korçë, opposite Grammos, so that the Yugoslav units would be able to intervene more quickly in case of Greek nationalist provocation. Convinced that the Yugoslav occupation of Albania was imminent, Hoxha secretly, on his own authority, appealed to Stalin for protection.[45] At practically the same time, in Bucharest, Dimitrov spoke to the press about the inevitability of a federation that would unite all of the Eastern European people's democracies, including Greece, whose participation he pointedly stressed.[46] His statement, just as pointedly, was disavowed by *Pravda* on

40. Milovan Djilas, *Vlast* (Power) (London, 1983), 121.
41. Hoxha, *Titistët,* 387–403.
42. Djilas, *Vlast,* 121.
43. Ibid., 123.
44. Milovan Djilas, *Conversations with Stalin* (New York, 1962), 143–46.
45. Hoxha, *Titistët,* 405–10.
46. Dedijer, *Dokumenti 1948,* 1:167.

29 January. While, behind the scenes, Molotov threatened the Yugoslav leadership with a public rift over the divisions, Stalin summoned Tito and Dimitrov to Moscow. In an affront to the Soviet leader, Tito sent Kardelj instead.

It is nowadays generally agreed that, as Tito put it, the "first conflict [between Moscow and Belgrade] broke out on account of Albania."[47] Indeed, the sensitivity over the Yugoslav forces in Albania and Belgrade's military aid to DAG obliged Kardelj, as late as 1953, to forbid any references to these subjects in Tito's official biography.[48] But it was the larger issue of Yugoslavia's independent—and combative—foreign policy, as well as Belgrade's readiness to assert its militant alternative to the Soviet Union in Eastern Europe, especially among the Balkan Communist parties, that dominated the dramatic meeting with Stalin on 10 February. Stalin charged the Bulgarians and Yugoslavs with ignoring the Soviet Union. He insisted, over Kardelj's objections, that the Bled Agreement had been signed without consultation with Moscow, the disinclination to consult being a policy—not just an error—on the part of Yugoslavia. Dimitrov's federalist schemes and the projected entry of the Yugoslav divisions into Albania, too, were initiated without Soviet approval. The latter could still lead to serious international complications, as it "would give the Americans the excuse to attack."[49] The phrase in the treaty of Evksinograd that committed the Balkan partners to all "initiatives that were directed against the hotbeds of aggression" was tantamount to preventive war. Stalin also believed that the reference was to Greece. Given his nervousness over DAG's general offensive, which commenced on 5 February, and the shelling of Thessaloniki by Markos's forces a day before the Moscow conclave, he was unwilling to excuse such zeal. In Stalin's view, the phrase from Evksinograd was the commonest excess, worthy of an inexperienced Komsomol activist but unforgivable in Tito and Dimitrov.

47. "Zapisnik sa sednice CK KPJ of 12. i 13. aprila 1948," in Dedijer, *Novi prilozi*, 3:370. See also Djilas, *Vlast*, 118.

48. Dedijer, *Novi prilozi*, 3:318. For his part, as late as 1961 Djilas considered it prudent to omit Kardelj's blaming of Tito for the precipitate stationing of two divisions in Albania. Djilas had been in Moscow since mid-January 1948 and welcomed Kardelj's delegation there on 8 February. When asked why such a tense period was chosen to press for the divisions in Albania, "Kardelj responded with resignation, 'The Old Man (Tito) is pushing this. You know yourself. . . .'" Djilas excluded the "Moscow whisperings with Kardelj from his *Conversations with Stalin*, so as not to give arguments to the Soviet-Albanian propaganda at the time when the whole matter was still of current interest" (Djilas, *Vlast*, 131).

49. "Zapisnik sa sednice CK KPJ od 1. marta 1948, godine," in Dedijer, *Novi prilozi*, 3:304.

The point was that the Greek uprising had to fold immediately. "What do you think," Stalin lectured to Kardelj, "that Great Britain and the United States—the United States, the most powerful state in the world—will permit you to break their line of communication in the Mediterranean Sea! Nonsense. And we have no navy."[50] Stalin insisted that the federation between Bulgaria and Yugoslavia be effected immediately. And in the early hours of 12 February, Molotov summoned Kardelj to the Kremlin and ordered him to sign a treaty that obliged Yugoslavia to consult the Soviet Union on all foreign policy matters.

The meeting with Stalin changed nothing. Stalin's insistence on a Yugoslav-Bulgarian federation, which would initially exclude Albania, was no more than a delaying tactic. Nor, given Dimitrov's mood, was this the most reliable way of exercising more control over Belgrade. At his dacha near Moscow, Dimitrov tried to convince Kardelj that the federation would make the South Slavs strong and independent of Stalin. "Together," Dimitrov argued, "we shall build a more democratic socialism."[51] On 22 February, Moscow rejected new Yugoslav economic requests. The time for surgical action was at hand.

The question of socialism came up again at the meeting of the KPJ Central Committee on 1 March. In a statement that alluded to the Soviet doctrine of people's democracy, Kardelj noted that the ideological differences between Moscow and Belgrade had to do with the question of socialist development in Eastern Europe, the Soviets not wishing to see the "establishment among these countries of a certain formation, which would permit the development of these countries toward socialism." Tito agreed, noting that Yugoslavia confirmed its path to socialism despite the limiting Soviet notion of encirclement. He stressed that if Yugoslavia was to remain independent it had to withstand Soviet economic pressure. Under the circumstances, the federation with Bulgaria could only introduce a Trojan horse inside the KPJ. As for Albania, Kardelj intimated that Moscow wished to edge the Yugoslavs out of Hoxha's army: "We

50. Almost identical accounts of the meeting can be found in Djilas's memoirs. See *Conversations with Stalin*, 173–84; and *Vlast*, 131–36. Kardelj's version is considerably different. Some of its peculiarities, as on the nature of federation with Bulgaria, are probably a result of confusion between this and earlier meetings, but in some particulars—for example, on the importance and relevance of the stationing of Yugoslav troops in Albania—Kardelj's account is dissembling and unreliable. Moreover, it is contradicted by the extant minutes of the KPJ Central Committee meeting of 1 March 1948. See Kardelj, *Sećanja*, 111–17.

51. Kardelj, *Sećanja*, 118.

must maintain a tight grip on Albania, because we invested a great deal there and the country is important for us. We should continue our policy in all questions of political and economic cooperation as before. We should demand that the Soviet advisers in Albania be within our group. (Their number according to our appraisal.) Our division is near Ohrid. It would not go alone, but with still greater forces; let each grab his own."[52] And indeed, the KPJ had already engineered a turnabout in Albania. During the marathon Eighth Plenum of the PKSH Central Committee (26 February–8 March), Koçi Xoxe carried out the purge of anti-Yugoslavs, forcing Hoxha into self-critical retreat. On 18 March, the Soviets withdrew all their military advisers from Yugoslavia. And on 27 March, the seventh anniversary of the military coup against the Yugoslav government that acceded to the Axis, Stalin sent his famous First Letter, the first of the secret letters that opened the rift between the Soviet Union and Yugoslavia, to the KPJ Central Committee. Two days earlier, the Communists had staged their coup d'état in Czechoslovakia. Within a month, as the neologism "cold war" gained rapid currency, five Western European countries concluded a treaty of self-defense, the Brussels Treaty, which was the forerunner of NATO. The time had come for the Soviets to try to shake the leadership of the KPJ.

There was a political eon between Oskar Davičo's propaganda poem "I Grammos biće spomenik" (Grammos too will be a monument [1947]) and the signing of the military part of the Balkan Alliance (Yugoslavia, Greece, and Turkey) at Bled on 9 August 1954. Still, before a lapse of only seven years, Bled was the scene of an entirely different agreement that was hardly conducive to any type of alliance between Belgrade and Athens. The passage of time marked a total change in Yugoslavia's state interest and, with it, the abandonment of Yugoslav regional militancy. As for the Soviets, the dialectic of their relations with Yugoslav leftism bears out the deradicalizing influence of the imperial Soviet Union in the international Communist movement. The circle was completed when the Stalinist doctrine of "socialism in one country" was rendered invalid in the absence of Soviet military participation. And since Soviet troops were not committed to Greece, Stalin metamorphosed the Greek revolution into a counterrevolutionary impediment to Soviet state interest.

52. "Zapisnik sa sednice CK KPJ od 1. marta 1948, godine," in Dedijer, *Novi prilozi*, 305.

10

The Impact of the Macedonian Question on Civil Conflict in Greece, 1943–1949

Evangelos Kofos

No other issue had such diverse repercussions on the inception, planning, conduct, and perceptions of the Greek civil war as the Macedonian question. Imbued with the legacy of conflicting nineteenth-century national visions and destabilizing interwar revisionist schemes, the Macedonian question persisted in the wartime whirlpool of revolutionary change, activating forces—and passions—that affected developments in three Balkan states.[1]

An examination of the impact of the Macedonian question on the civil war therefore cannot be restricted to the years 1946–49. Its ramifications in Greek domestic conflicts were discernible even in the early phases of the Axis occupation and throughout the period of the resistance; they continued unabated to December 1944 and, despite the Varkiza settlement, were consequential during the interlude of 1945–46.[2]

1. William H. McNeill reflected a commonly shared perception of the time when, during the heat of the civil war, he wrote: "The future history of the Greek state and people may depend in large part on the development of the Macedonian issue" (*The Greek Dilemma: War and Aftermath* [Philadelphia, 1947], 261).

2. The war years are covered, with a related bibliography, in my study "I Valkaniki Diastasi tou Makedonikou stin Katochi kai tin Antistasi" (The Balkan dimension of the Macedonian

Perceptions and realities in Macedonian affairs rarely coincided during these years. Contemporaries lacked dependable information on the aims and policies of adversaries and allies alike. Preconceived notions frequently substituted for intelligent analysis. As a result, deep-rooted fears and suspicions persisted, creating a permanent sense of insecurity that was exacerbated by psychological warfare operatives who played on this sensitive national issue for political ends. Dogmatic approaches to rapidly changing situations blurred the vision of leaders and disoriented public opinion. In the end, actors on the Macedonian stage found themselves performing in a theater of the absurd.

During the occupation, civil strife in Greek Macedonia between resistance groups was not limited to a contest for postwar political predominance. In certain cases it grew into a struggle for national survival. Contenders sought to discredit each other with accusations of "antinational" or "treacherous" behavior. Followers of Communist-led EAM/ELAS were labeled "Slavo-Communists" (even though most were neither Slavs nor Communists); they, in turn, summarily categorized their opponents as "collaborationists" (even though most of them opposed the German, Italian, and Bulgarian occupiers, as well as their ideological foes).

The same tactics continued throughout the civil war. Slogans and labels of antinational behavior hardened adversaries' perceptions of each other, fomented fanaticism, and distorted issues. Both sides turned to foreign ideological relatives to help them fight their own kin, and as a result their respective causes and activities were frequently identified with those of their patrons.

The international aspects of the Macedonian problem were also decisive in influencing domestic developments. It is possible in this context to speak of "micro" and "macro" Macedonian questions. On the micro level were the internal social, political, and racial issues that existed in each of the three parts of Macedonia; on the macro level were the international elements of the problem. The latter included conflicting Great Power objectives in the Balkan subregion as well as the policies of each of the three Balkan states relating to the Macedonian issue. The recurring

question during the occupation and the resistance), in *I Ellada to 1936–1944: Diktatoria, Katochi, Antistasti. Praktika, A'Diethnes Synedrio Sychronis Istorias* (Greece from 1936 to 1944: Dictatorship, occupation, resistance. Annals, first international conference on contemporary history), ed. H. Fleischer and N. Svoronos (Athens, 1989), 418–71 (hereafter cited as "Valkaniki Diastasi"). See also my earlier *Nationalism and Communism in Macedonia* (Thessaloniki, 1964).

crises in Macedonia can therefore be attributed to the interaction of the macro and micro elements of the problem.

Decades after the termination of hostilities, confusion over the Macedonian issue persists. Polemical literature, the published memoirs of warriors and politicians, and many monographs on the resistance and the civil war perpetuate wartime distortions, when they do not evade the issue altogether.[3] In recent years, the availability of new documentary sources—although they are fragmentary and unbalanced in terms of their provenance—offers the opportunity for a new attempt at assessing the impact of the Macedonian question during the 1940s.[4]

3. A notable exception is Philippos Iliou's serialization of KKE documents, "Ta Archeia tou KKE" (The archives of the KKE), in *Avgi*, December 1979–January 1980. Useful references to the Macedonian question may be found in the following memoirs of KKE protagonists: Petros Roussos, *I Megali Pentaetia, 1940–1945* (The great five years), 3rd ed. (Athens, 1982); Yiannis Ioannidis, *Anamniseis* (Memoirs), ed. Alekos Papapanagiotou (Athens, 1979); Thanasis Hatzis, *I Nikifora Epanastasi pou Chathike* (The victorious revolution that was lost), 3 vols. (Athens, 1977–79), the latter with questionable interpretations of documentary KKE sources of Skopje provenance. For an example of the distorted phraseology and systematic omissions on the Macedonian question, see Markos Vaphiadis, *Apomnimonevmata* (Memoirs), 3 vols. (Athens, 1984–85). Compare his oral (taped) reminiscences with the writings of Yugoslav authors Jovan Popovski, *Zašto me Staljin Nije Streljano?* (Why did Stalin not shoot me?) (Ljubljana, 1982); and Dragan Kljakić, *General Markos* (Zagreb, 1979). From the progovernment side, recent books by journalist Nikos Mertzos, *Svarnout: To Prodomeno Antartiko* (Svarnut: The betrayed resistance), 5th ed. (Thessaloniki, 1983), and *Emeis, Oi Makedones* (We, the Macedonians) (Thessaloniki, 1986) offer critical appraisals of the KKE's Macedonian policy as seen through pro-KKE publications. Yugoslav Macedonian authors are more critical of KKE historiography on the Macedonian issue. See, for example, Petar Galabov, "Inforbirovski Diskriminacii i Frankolevantinski Insinuacii" (Cominform's discriminations and Francolevantistic insinuations), *Iselenicki Kalendar*, Skopje, 1982, 79–85. Galabov writes: "As defeated 'generals' they have come to realize that they believed one thing as 'romantic revolutionaries,' and now, in their old age, after losing two revolutions, they believe in another. What is more tragic with these people is that they think they are passing exams as 'more loyal' Greeks, [to prove] that they have always struggled for the national fulfillment of their country (which no one has questioned), and that the Macedonian national question was a cancer caused by others. Vlandas and Gousias, Roussos and Katsoulis, Bartzotas and Blanas, P. Nefeloudis, and many others distort facts in their books in a pharisaic, greater-Greek and anti-Marxist way and struggle to give an entirely different direction and dimension to the political situation in Greece, blaming each other for errors committed. But when the question refers to the Macedonian national question, as in a chorus, they reject or ignore anything Macedonian. There is not a single word in their books about the Macedonians." Giorgis Katsoulis, *Istoria tou KKE* (History of the KKE), vol. 5: *1940–1945* (Athens, 1977), comes under particularly sharp attack for treating the Macedonian question from the viewpoint of "greater-Greek chauvinists and nationalists." For the best bibliographical guide, consult H. Fleischer and S. Bowman, eds., *I Ellada sti Dekaetia 1940–1950* (Greece in the decade 1940–1950) (Athens, 1984), which is a revised Greek edition of John O. Iatrides, ed., *Greece in the 1940s: A Bibliographic Companion* (Hanover, N.H.: University Press of New England, 1981).

4. Archiv na Makedonija, *Egejska Makedonija vo NOB* (Aegean Macedonia in the national liberation war), 7 vols., 1941–49 (Skopje, 1971–85) (hereafter cited as *Eg.M.*). See also *KPG i*

The origins of wartime and postwar policies and attitudes in Macedonia can be traced to events that occurred long before 1940. The legacy of the armed clashes of the first decade of the twentieth century (known as *Makedonikos Agonas*), the peace settlements of the second decade, and the mass population movements of the third decade influenced policies (particularly in Bulgaria) and determined the attitudes of large population groups in Bulgaria, Yugoslavia, and Greece. Bulgarian-Macedonian organizations, on both the right and the left, had created strong pressure groups—mainly in Bulgaria and southern Yugoslavia—that sustained revolutionary fervor.[5] In Greece, despite a large-scale exodus of Slavs during and after the First World War, Slav-speakers continued to live in certain border communities of western Macedonia. By the 1930s, there were two opposing factions, a Greek-oriented Slavophone faction and a Slav-oriented faction (the latter with a pro-Bulgarian tilt), nurturing vendettas that stemmed from the years of the *Makedonikos Agonas*.[6] The juxtaposition of Greek-, Vlach-, and Slav-speaking indigenous inhabitants and hundreds of thousands of Greek-, Vlach-, and Turkish-speaking Christian Orthodox refugees from Asia Minor, the Pontus, Bulgaria, and Yugoslavia had created a Greek national character in Greek Macedonia. At the same time, however, this population movement gave rise to a whole range of social and economic problems requiring adjustments.

Another factor affecting policies and attitudes grew out of Bulgaria's revisionist stand toward the peace settlements after the First World War.

Makedonskoto Prašanje, 1918–1974 (Skopje, 1982) (hereafter cited as *KPG*). Both contain selected documents of EAM/ELAS, the KKE, and NOF in the possession of Archiv na Makedonija, Skopje. There are additional documents in the Institute for National History in *Izvori na Osloboditelnata Vojna i Revolucijata vo Makedonija, 1941–1945* (Sources of the liberation war and the revolution in Macedonia), vol. 1 (6 books) (Skopje, 1968–79). See also two books by Svetozar Vukmanović-Tempo, *Revolucija koja teče: Memoari* (The running revolution: Memoirs) (Zagreb, 1981), and *Borba za Balkan* (Struggle for the Balkans) (Zagreb, 1981); and also Risto Kirjazovski, *Narodno Osloboditelniot Front i Drugite Organizacii na Makedoncite od Egejska Makedonija, 1945–1949* (The National Liberation Front and the other organizations of the Macedonians of Aegean Macedonia) (Skopje, 1985). To be used with care, on account of frequent distortions and inaccuracies, is Vangel Ajanovski, *Egejski Buri* (Aegean storms) (Skopje, 1975).

5. Elisabeth Barker, *Macedonia: Its Place in Balkan Power Politics* (London, 1950), 21–29. Kofos, *Nationalism and Communism*, 50–54.

6. Understandably, Yugoslav Macedonian writers tend to exaggerate interwar Slavo-Macedonian activity in Greek Macedonia. See, for example, Tošo Popovski, *Makedonskoto Nacionalno Malcinstvo vo Bugarija, Grcija i Albanija* (The Macedonian national minority in Bulgaria, Greece, and Albania) (Skopje, 1981), 64–80; and Ajanovski, *Egejski Buri*, 11–75.

This was the Greek perception of a threat from the north, which led to the construction of impressive defense works along the Greek-Bulgarian frontier. (These fortifications proved useless when Bulgaria joined the Axis and took possession of parts of Greek Macedonia and Thrace without having to fight for them.)

This perceived threat to Greek security was intensified by the revisionist policy of the Bulgarian Communist Party—a policy sanctioned by the Comintern—which called for a united independent Macedonia (and Thrace) within a Balkan Communist federation. When the Greek Communist Party (KKE) associated itself with the Comintern's Macedonian policy in 1924, the move provoked serious objections even within the party, although a major split was avoided. Outside the party, however, the outcry was general, and the KKE's image suffered from accusations of "national treachery." In the minds of Greeks, the status quo in Macedonia was being challenged not merely by a single Balkan country but by a world political alliance headed by the Soviet Union. This meant that Greek Macedonia could be severed from the Greek state by social revolution as well as by war. As a result, official legislation equating communism with sedition was introduced in parliament.[7]

As pressure from outside and from within its ranks mounted, the leadership of the Greek Communist Party finally gathered sufficient courage to bypass Comintern directives and, in 1935, adopted a new resolution. This new position changed the KKE's slogan for "a united and independent Macedonia" to one calling for "complete equality for the minorities." At the same time, the Marxist principle of "self-determination" for national minorities was reaffirmed, and the door was left open for a "definite" brotherly solution to the Macedonian question "after the victory of the Soviet power in the Balkans."[8] This new Macedonian platform carried the party into the 1940s and up to 1949. However, the Metaxas dictatorship gave the Greek Communists little chance to popularize the new "equality" principle over the old "independence" line,

7. George Th. Mavrogordatos, *Stillborn Republic: Social Coalitions and Party Strategies in Greece, 1922–1936* (Berkeley and Los Angeles: University of California Press, 1983); N. C. Alivizatos, *Les institutions politiques de la Grèce à travers les crises, 1922–1974* (Paris: R. Pichon and R. Durand-Auzias, 1979); Eleftherios Stavridis, *Ta Paraskinia tou KKE* (Behind the scenes of the KKE) (Athens, 1953), 285–91, 300–302, 432–47, 459–62.

8. Alekos Papapanagiotou interview in *Anti* (Athens), 19 June 1981, 35; Pavlos Nefeloudis, *Stis Piges tis Kakodaimonias* (At the sources of misfortune), 2nd ed. (Athens, 1974), 93–97. Documents in KKE, *Deka Chronia Agones, 1935–1945* (Ten years of struggle) (Athens, 1945), 45, 75–76; Kofos, *Nationalism and Communism*, 90–92.

and government propaganda continued to accuse the party of sedition. During this period, certain dissatisfied Slavo-Macedonian Communist cadres also chose to place more emphasis on the party's nebulous "self-determination" principle than on the specific "equality" platform.[9] On the eve of the war, confusion reigned among disoriented Greek- and Slav-speaking groups in Greek Macedonia.

Greece, like other Eastern European countries, had pursued a policy of assimilation of ethnic groups during the interwar period. After the First World War—with some hesitation in the early 1920s—it had decided to treat the remaining Slav-speakers as Slavophone Greeks. Their numbers, according to Greek statistics, never exceeded 100,000.[10] They were concentrated mainly in the prefectures of Kastoria, Florina, and Pella, although certain dispersed Slavophone or mixed villages could also be found in other Macedonian prefectures. The Metaxas regime, haunted by the specters of Slavism and communism, initiated a policy of accelerated assimilation. Applied by incompetent and shortsighted civil servants, this policy antagonized even Slavophones of the Greek faction.[11] To peasants of Bulgarian orientation, it served as proof that the Greek state could not offer them a national shelter. In 1941, with the occupation of Greece by the Germans and the entrance of Bulgarian troops into eastern Macedonia and Thrace, accumulated bitterness reached maturity.

Meanwhile, in Yugoslav Macedonia a more vigorous Serbianization campaign had come up against insurmountable difficulties. Local Slavs either remained stubbornly attached to Bulgarian nationalism or, more prudently, avoided making a choice by seeking refuge in the regional Macedonian name.[12]

The war and the cession by the Germans to Bulgarian occupation authorities of large parts of Greek—and Yugoslav—Macedonia, reversed the situation. A part of the Slavophone population exhibited its pro-

9. This is alleged, a posteriori, by Slavo-Macedonian writers. See Ajanovski, *Egejski Buri,* 55.

10. Barker, *Macedonia,* 31; Kofos, *Nationalism and Communism,* 47–48.

11. Kofos, *Nationalism and Communism,* 50. Similar conclusions are reached in a secret service report dated 17 December 1949, which was submitted to the commander in chief, Gen. Alexander Papagos. The text of the report is in the Archives of the Greek Ministry of Foreign Affairs, A/59179/Aut. Mac./G5Ba/1949.

12. Stephen Palmer and Robert King, *Yugoslav Communism and the Macedonian Question* (Hamden, Conn., 1971), 14–15, 56. Evangelos Kofos, *I Makedonia sti Giougoslaviki Istoriografia* (Macedonia in Yugoslav historiography) (Thessaloniki, 1974), 6, n. 2.

Bulgarian sympathies by taking revenge on its Greek neighbors, particularly those who had settled in Macedonia after their eviction from Turkey. In their zone of occupation the Bulgarians resorted to practices of genocidal dimensions, including the eviction of Greeks and the settlement of Bulgarians.[13]

Among Greeks, opposition to the Bulgarian occupation of eastern Macedonia and Thrace and to the efforts to extend Bulgarian influence to central and western Macedonia was unanimous. Prior to the development of mass resistance organizations, local community leaders, professionals, and intellectuals took it upon themselves to organize Greek opposition to Bulgarian schemes. Even the collaborationist government in Athens found it expedient to ride the popular bandwagon, dispatching to Macedonian prefectures former army officers enjoying a wider political acceptance. The initiative gradually passed, first to nationalist resistance organizations—such as the Yperaspistai Voreiou Ellados (Defenders of Northern Greece) (YVE), later renamed Panellinia Apeleftherotiki Organosis (Panhellenic Liberation Organization) (PAO)—and subsequently to ELAS. Nationalists proceeded from the traditional assumption that the Slavophones were divided between Greek and Slav factions and sought to protect and strengthen the resistance of the Greek faction. Slavophones who had fallen prey to Bulgarian propaganda—frequently in exchange for food rations in famine-stricken Macedonia—or who distanced themselves from Hellenism as Slavo-Macedonians were considered to be enemies of the Greek nation.[14]

Meanwhile, a smaller group of Slavophones began to surface within EAM/ELAS as Slavo-Macedonians. EAM, having endorsed in practice the KKE's post-1935 position on the equality of rights of minorities, accepted into its ranks not only Slavophones of the Greek faction but also those who distanced themselves from both the Greek and Bulgarian factions.[15] Although this movement held little attraction until the beginning of 1944, it was apparent that the traditional dichotomy of Slavophones was growing into a trichotomy.

Thus, on the key issue of the Slavophones, Greek political and resistance groups in Macedonia—particularly prior to the dissolution of the

---

13. Kofos, *Nationalism and Communism*, 100–102. Hagen Fleischer, *Im Kreuzschatten der Mächte: Griechenland, 1941–1944* (Frankfurt, 1986), 69–72.

14. Details in Kofos, "Valkaniki Diastasi."

15. Ibid., quoting EAM and KKE sources published in *Eg.M.*, vol. 1.

military units of PAO by ELAS in 1943—differed significantly. During the formative years of these groups during 1941–43, crossing fences from one faction to the other was common practice. Crossovers were frequently prompted by neither ideology nor national inclination, but by sheer opportunism or to ensure self-preservation. This constant movement and the shifting allegiances bewildered spectators and local actors even during the early stages of the internal Greek struggle for postwar predominance. Unable to follow the radically changing situation, they fell back on their traditional perceptions—a misleading yardstick for assessing developments in occupied Macedonia.

To Greek nationalists, the acceptance of Slavo-Macedonians (who were by definition non-Greek and possibly anti-Greek Slavophones) signified that EAM/ELAS was pursuing the prewar "antinational" Macedonian policy of the KKE. On the other hand, the KKE, working through EAM/ELAS, considered its policy to be in accordance with its declared principles and believed that it could effectively undermine Bulgarian proselytism among the Slavophones. Although it was not widely known at the time, there was considerable opposition even within EAM/ELAS to accepting nationalist-minded Slavo-Macedonians into the Greek resistance.[16]

In their part of Macedonia, the Yugoslavs had to cope with an even more acute problem of Bulgarian nationalism. The local Communist organization had severed its ties with the Yugoslav Communist Party and joined the still illegal Bulgarian party. Faced with the dual challenge presented by pro-Bulgarian nationalists and Communists in Macedonia, the Yugoslav partisan leaders decided not only to reassert control in their own region of Macedonia but also to seek a permanent solution to the wider problem that had repeatedly threatened the sovereignty and territorial integrity of their country. Their main thesis was that Slav-speakers in the three Macedonian provinces were all ethnic "Macedonians"—a Slavic people different from the Bulgarians and the Serbs—who consequently had the right to self-determination and state unification within the Yugoslav federation.[17]

When, in August 1941, Tito succeeded in gaining Stalin's endorse-

16. Ibid.

17. Palmer and King, *Yugoslav Communism,* 54–55. For a Bulgarian author's detailed review of the CPY's policy on the Macedonian question, see Konstantin Palešutski, *Jugoslavskata Komunisticeska Partija i Makedonskijat Văpros, 1919–1945* (The Yugoslav Communist Party and the Macedonian question) (Sofia, 1985).

ment,[18] it became evident that the center of gravity of the Macedonian question had shifted from Bulgaria to Yugoslavia. But the Greeks, engaged in their own internal struggles in Greek Macedonia, had no idea of these developments. They continued to operate and fight on the basis of their prewar perceptions, having no control over the sweeping changes that were taking place in Macedonia and that soon would reach their own land.

Svetozar Vukmanović-Tempo, Tito's emissary to Kosovo and Macedonia, was the man who, in the summer of 1943, outlined to the leaders of the KKE and ELAS the Yugoslav plans for wartime collaboration of Balkan Communist-controlled partisan armies in Yugoslavia, Albania, Greece, and even Bulgaria. He also briefed them on the postwar settlement of the Macedonian question, as seen by the Yugoslav Communists.[19] The essence of his proposals called for a Balkan general staff to coordinate the activities of the four partisan organizations, not only against the occupying forces but also against the nationalist—"reactionary," in his words—organizations, and thus to secure a new postwar social order and possibly a Balkan federation. There would be a cooperative effort aimed at curtailing Bulgarian nationalist influences among the Macedonian Slavs. Free movement of partisan bands across the borders would be allowed, while Yugoslav Macedonian political instructors would be given a free hand in presenting to Slavophones in Greece the Yugoslav model for the solution of the Macedonian *national* question. This would entail complete freedom to propagate—apparently among all three factions of Slavophones—the idea of the "Macedonian" nation and language and to give assurances that the right of self-determination, including the right of secession, would be extended to the Slavo-Macedonians. Moreover, Slavo-Macedonians would be permitted to form their own political organization and armed units. Tempo avoided any explicit reference to postwar territorial changes in Macedonia. To judge, however, from frequent contemporary Yugoslav Macedonian pro-

18. "Macedonia should be attached to Yugoslavia for practical reasons and for the sake of expediency. . . . The two parties should take up the stand of the self-determination of the Macedonian people" (Comintern directive to the Bulgarian and Yugoslav Communists via radiogram, August 1941, quoted in Tsola Dragoycheva, *Macedonia: Not a Cause of Discord but a Factor of Good Neighborliness and Cooperation* [a rather euphemistic title for a work on such a divisive issue] [Sofia, 1979], 57–58).

19. Tempo, *Borba za Balkan,* 79–138; idem, *Revolucija,* 3:7–106; Dragoycheva, *Macedonia,* 77–79; Ioannidis, *Anamniseis,* 131–35 (particularly the comments by Papapanagiotou, 516–20). For a general appraisal of these sources, see Kofos, "Valkaniki Diastasi."

nouncements, the Yugoslavs were aiming—as a maximum objective—at a greater Macedonian state that would incorporate those parts of Macedonia granted to Bulgaria by the treaty of San Stefano. Its boundaries were appropriately renamed for the occasion "Macedonian ethnological boundaries." As a minimum objective, they sought the annexation of Greek Macedonian districts adjacent to Yugloslavia, including—for strategic reasons—the port city of Thessaloniki.[20] Tempo's key argument in putting forward his proposals centered on the necessity of luring the Bulgarian-oriented Slavophones in all three parts of Macedonia away from the grip of the Bulgarian nationalists and including them, as Slavo-Macedonians, in the common struggle.

Tempo's proposals opened entirely new perspectives, not only for the Greek resistance but also for the future of Greece. The leaders of the KKE sensed, for the first time, that they had an alternative to British tutelage. For political reasons, however, they rejected the idea of a Balkan general staff, although they accepted the concept of transfrontier cooperation of partisan units. An initial order from ELAS General Headquarters provided for the formation of joint Greek-Yugoslav partisan detachments to operate on both sides of the frontier in order to attract to their ranks both the Slavo-Macedonians of Greece and the Greeks of Yugoslavia. Similarly, Yugoslav partisan units were given permission to cross into Greek territory, and Yugoslav Macedonian political instructors were allowed to move freely in Greek Macedonian villages to acquaint Slavophones with the idea of the "Macedonian" nation.[21] More important was the decision to allow the formation of an independent political organization of the Slavo-Macedonians—the Slovenomakedonski Narodno Osloboditelen Front (SNOF)—as well as special Slavo-Macedonian armed units. KKE leaders, however, shelved Yugoslav proposals for a postwar renegotiation of the Macedonian question. Pointing to its tremendous cost to their own cause, they appeared determined to adhere to their 1935 position. Their postwar aims were couched in rather vague terms: they would seek solutions to problems between the Balkan peoples in a spirit of brotherly cooperation and in accordance with the principle of the self-determination of peoples.[22]

20. Quoted in Kofos, "Valkaniki Diastasi."

21. The order, dated 9 July 1943, was signed by Saraphis, Velouhiotis, and Tzimas (published in *KPG*, 177–78).

22. Yugoslav writers, Tempo in particular, have claimed since the war that in 1943–44 EAM/ELAS consented to the ultimate right of self-determination of the Slavo-Macedonians, including

In the field, some of the decisions (such as to create joint Greek-Yugoslav detachments or independent Slavo-Macedonian units) were not acted upon, apparently because of dissenting voices within EAM/ELAS. Furthermore, certain of the arrangements reached with Tempo were extended in ways that had not been initially envisaged. Such was the case with the free-roaming Yugoslav-Macedonian activists within Greece, who did not limit themselves to luring Bulgarian-oriented Slavophones into SNOF, but openly propagated the idea of Macedonian unification. As a result, for a full year—from the end of 1943 to the end of 1944—Greek western Macedonia became a battleground of antagonistic social forces, opposing ideologies, and national hatreds. This created a confused situation, the like of which was not to be found in any other region of occupied Greece.[23]

This insufficiently researched aspect of the Macedonian "civil war" bore the weight of all prewar evils. Its most important components were the contest for ideological dominance—generally, but not accurately portrayed as communism versus anticommunism—and the struggle to fill the political vacuum at the moment of liberation. In Macedonia, this dual contest was fought by the anticommunist forces on the basis of national loyalties.

Seditious Slavo-Macedonian propaganda in EAM-controlled regions fueled suspicions that the KKE had once again "sold" Macedonia to the Slavs. Given the prevailing climate, it is no wonder that texts of alleged agreements of the KKE with the Bulgarian and the Yugoslav Communists found their way into circulation. Despite detectable discrepancies, these "agreements" were widely accepted as authentic by nationalist Greeks.[24]

---

the right of secession, but they subsequently did not honor their commitments. See Fitzroy MacLean's report, Foreign Office circ. D217, 5 February 1945. Contemporary KKE documents, now in the possession of the Yugoslavs, do not support the allegation about secession. Particularly revealing is Siantos's telegram of 14 July 1944 to Tzimas, then in Belgrade, which outlines the KKE's policy as follows: The Macedonian question is raising problems with the Yugoslavs. The KKE's position is that after victory all peoples will have the right to determine by themselves their position. The brotherly parties (Yugoslav and Bulgarian) are pursuing an ambiguous line, but the KKE's position is correct on the basis of the present ethnological composition of Greek Macedonia. The telegram concludes: "Beware of this delicate issue. Lack of understanding will help Greek reaction in its struggle against the Party and the liberation movement" (copy in the "Relations with Greece, 1941–1945" file, Archives of the Central Committee of the Communist Party of Yugoslavia, Belgrade [hereafter cited as A/CC/CPY]).

23. Numerous documents of KKE and EAM/ELAS provenance in *Eg.M.*

24. Kofos, *Nationalism and Communism*, 128–34.

In the military arena, by 1944 EAM/ELAS had gained supremacy over its adversaries, with a few notable exceptions in southern and east-central Macedonia. As EAM's opponents could no longer oppose their ideological adversary, they found themselves leaning more and more heavily for assistance and even guidance either on the Greek government in exile and the British secret agencies or on the local administrative and security services of the collaborationist government in Athens. The concern that the latter association carried the risk of indirectly—and at times directly—collaborating with the Germans was dismissed on the ground that the risk for Greece of losing Macedonia to the Slavs in the event of a Communist takeover of the country was of greater import than an ephemeral accommodation with the occupier.[25] Perceptions of Slav and Communist menaces in Macedonia certainly blurred vision in this instance.

Despite ELAS's military successes over its political opponents, internal dissension over KKE-directed Macedonian policy could be detected within EAM and ELAS, particularly on the local levels in Macedonia, where political and military leaders maintained serious reservations. These reservations led, in certain cases, to the reversal of party orders and the extermination of dissidents. Even prior to the summer of 1943, ELAS officers in western Macedonia had led their units against Slavophone partisans and villagers who were suspected of being "Bulgarians." Nonetheless, party functionaries stood firm on their dogmatic interpretations of the party's "equality" policy, to the point of encouraging Slavo-Macedonian nationalism. They were encouraged in this view by Slavo-Macedonian Communist cadres who argued that a more liberal attitude toward the Slavophones, including the pro-Bulgarian collaborationists, would bring the Slavophone peasants to EAM. As, however, the allegiance of these cadres was in itself questionable, the KKE leaders found themselves receiving mixed signals from the Macedonian front. Torn between the strategic requirements of collaborating with the Yugoslav partisans and the political necessity of building a patriotic image at home, they frequently reversed decisions and sent contradictory instructions to the field. As a result, confusion and dissension among the rank and file

25. This is the view expounded in Athanasios Chrysochoou's six-volume study, *I Katochi en Makedonia* (Occupation in Macedonia) (Thessaloniki, 1949–52). For a sociological approach, see Giorgos Margaritis, "Oi Emfylies Diamaches stin Katochi, 1941–1944" (Civil conflicts during the occupation, 1941–1944), in *Dekapenthimeros Politis* (Athens, 5 October 1984, 30–33). See also Fleischer, *Kreuzschatten*, 285–94.

increased. It is interesting to note that late in the spring of 1944, SNOF was dissolved by party orders. Some of its influential leaders escaped into Yugoslavia. In less than three months, however, the party once again reversed itself, allowing the return of irredentist-prone Slavo-Macedonian cadres, with Naum Pejov at their head, and authorizing the formation of pure Slavo-Macedonian armed units within ELAS. In the end, faced with open rebellion by these units, ELAS military leaders—both locally and at General Headquarters—overcame the hesitancy and even open resistance of party functionaries and attacked these units, forcefully evicting them from Greek Macedonia in October 1944. The termination of the Axis occupation in Greece probably prevented a major internal crisis within EAM/ELAS on this issue. A number of ELAS officers and men under their command who had played a leading role in subduing the Slavo-Macedonian units subsequently ended up in the ranks of the national army; this was a direct consequence of the wartime dissension within EAM/ELAS over Macedonian policy.[26]

Meanwhile, the admittance of Slavophones, as "Slavo-Macedonians," into the ranks of the resistance had accentuated traditional antagonisms and even "racial" hatreds in certain areas between autochthons (*gigeneis*) and Greek Pontic and Asia Minor refugees (*prosfyges*). Although more research is required on the social underpinnings of the wartime attitude of the Turcophone refugee groups that took up arms to resist ELAS, their fear of Slav-Macedonian vengeance in a postwar Communist-ruled Greece is certainly detectable.[27]

Fratricidal conflicts also developed within the trichotomized Slavophone community. The Bulgarian-oriented Slavophone bands that had appeared early on the scene, armed and commanded by Bulgarian officers, concentrated their vengeance primarily on members of the Greek Slavophone faction. Carrying on vendettas that went back to the exarchist-patriarchist feuds of the *Makedonikos Agonas,* they labeled their opponents "Grecomans"—maniac Greeks—and set out to exterminate their leaders and terrorize the masses into submission.[28] Throughout the occupation, this persecuted sector of the population either sought refuge

26. Documents in *Eg.M.*, vol. 1, and *KPG*, as cited in Kofos, "Valkaniki Diastasi." Renos Michaleas in Kastoria and "Panos" Evripidis in Edessa are two examples of KKE cadres who pursued a pro-Yugoslav line on the question of the Slavophones.

27. Margaritis, "Oi Emfylies Diamaches," 32–33.

28. Documents in *Eg.M.*, 1:350, 388–90, reveal that Slavo-Macedonian activists within the ranks of EAM/ELAS sought to exterminate the leaders of the pro-Greek faction of the Slavophones. Also cited in Kofos, "Valkaniki Diastasi."

in PAO and ELAS or sought the protection of the civil authorities and gendarmerie of the puppet government in Athens. Others escaped to Thessaloniki and other urban centers. In the Kastoria prefecture of the Italian zone of occupation, where the establishment of Greek civil and gendarmerie authorities was delayed, persecution of the Greek Slavophone faction became widespread. The pendulum of violence in Macedonia had swung against the Greeks.

The relations (which took the form of antagonisms, feuds, and alliances) between the initially strong Bulgarian faction and the emerging Slavo-Macedonian faction were more intricate. Both drew from the same pool of anti-Greek (or non-Greek) Slavophones. This made identification difficult and led to erroneous impressions. There had been instances when Slavo-Macedonians within the ranks of EAM/ELAS clashed openly with the so-called Bulgarian *comitadjis*. Generally, however, these Slavo-Macedonians operated as a lobby within the KKE and EAM for the adoption of a lenient attitude toward pro-Bulgarian collaborationists. They were well aware that to secure a popular base for their claims to Greek Macedonian territories they needed to augment their numbers by the transformation of Bulgarian Slavophones into Slavo-Macedonians. Despite the occasional concessions by the KKE and mass indoctrination efforts by local Slavo-Macedonian instructors and agents from Yugoslav Macedonia, however, progress was slow. As late as the spring of 1944, there was a resurgence of Bulgarian activity in the Edessa region, where whole villages were armed by Bulgarian officers. It was only in the closing months of 1944, when the departure of the Germans appeared imminent, that most Bulgarophiles became eager to exchange the Bulgarian crown for the Slavo-Macedonian red star.[29]

In yet another side of this triangular relationship, the disposition of Slavo-Macedonians toward the Greek Slavophones was not much better than that of the Bulgarophiles. Although both factions could be found in the ranks of EAM/ELAS, it was evident that a collision was unavoidable, as Greek Slavophones could hardly condone the steadily growing orientation of Slavo-Macedonians toward a united Macedonian state within Yugoslavia. Thus, in the closing months of 1944, another fratricidal war was brewing on the local Macedonian level. It exploded immediately after liberation and was carried on during the civil war.

Trying to maneuver among the Macedonian Symplegades, the KKE

---

29. *Eg.M.*, 1:477, 488, 491–94; *KPG*, 243–45, 255–63, 268, 276–80. See also Kofos, *Nationalism and Communism*, 125–26.

issued contradictory instructions and reversed decisions. This neither advanced its cause nor helped it meet its short-term and long-term objectives. KKE leaders appeared to be acutely conscious of the propaganda cost to the party of being implicated directly or indirectly in Yugoslav Macedonian aims and activities. They tried to minimize criticism and calm even their own followers in EAM/ELAS by appealing directly to Tito to restrain the extremist Yugoslav Macedonians. There is also evidence that they went so far as to appeal to Dimitrov to restrain Tito.[30] Such frantic efforts could have no lasting effects so long as the party refrained from adopting the iron-fist policy toward Slavo-Macedonian secessionists that it had reserved for its ideological foes. To opponents, both within and outside EAM, it mattered little whether KKE leaders could justify their concessions on the Macedonian issue, namely that adherence to ideological orthodoxy on the nationality question was mandatory; that drawing the Slavophones away from the grip of the Bulgarian nationalists strengthened the resistance; and that appeasing Tito and securing his support as a counterpoise to British intervention served the long-term interests of the Communist revolution in Greece.

Thus, the image of the party had been tarnished after all. The stain of treason was certainly unfair to the extent that it was caused by allegations of nonexistent wartime agreements ceding Greek Macedonia and Thrace to the Slavs. But it was unavoidable once the party leadership yielded to Yugoslav pressures and let Yugoslav Macedonians meddle in internal Greek Macedonian affairs, particularly since, by 1944, Yugoslav hegemonic and expansionist designs in the Balkans could hardly be concealed.[31] In sum, the KKE's wartime Macedonian policy should be held accountable for turning an ideological contest and even civil strife in Macedonia into a struggle for racial and national survival. Its immediate and long-term repercussions became apparent during the post-Varkiza interlude and the civil war.

On 30 October 1944, Thessaloniki was liberated. Four days later, Euripides Bakirtzis, ELAS's military commander for northern Greece, issued an order to units under his command to man the Greek-Yugoslav frontier with "loyal" troops free of Slavo-Macedonian infiltration.[32] Both

30. A/CC/CPY, Kiro Milievski (Sofia) to Tempo and Kolishevski, October 1944, "Greece IX-29-IV/2."

31. See Tempo's report to the Central Committee of the Communist Party of Yugoslavia, 8 August 1943, in *Revolucija*, 71. See also Tempo, *Borba za Balkan*, 88, 98, 133; and Ioannidis, *Anamniseis*, 127.

32. *Eg.M.*, 1:520–21.

developments underlined the fact that central and western Macedonia were once again firmly in Greek hands. Soon thereafter, the elimination of the last vestiges of the nationalist forces of Anton Tsaous in eastern Macedonia established the indisputable authority of EAM from one end of Macedonia to the other. Macedonian Cassandras had failed in their prognostications: Greek Macedonia had not been "sold to the Slavs" by the KKE. As for the Slavo-Macedonian activists, they had failed to retain even a strip of Greek Macedonian borderland.

As Macedonian micro politics appeared to recede into the background, Macedonian macro politics, involving the Great Powers and Greece's northern neighbors, entered the picture. A new phase of the Macedonian question was unfolding outside Greece, even as the Greeks themselves were moving into position in the south, ready to commence their "second round."

Long-standing global security perceptions had led the British government to formulate a geopolitical approach to the war and postwar arrangements that aimed at blocking a Soviet presence in the Straits and the northern Aegean. Despite the failure to open a Balkan front in 1943, Churchill had succeeded in obtaining Stalin's consent to a free hand in Greece, a tacit understanding that was formalized in the well-known Percentages Agreement. In the concluding months of 1944, developments in Macedonia posed an indirect though still very serious challenge to the British position in Greece, which had been gained after painful bargaining.[33] Despite the ascension to power in Bulgaria of the Fatherland Front (on 9 September), Bulgarian authorities and troops in Greek Macedonia and Thrace had been reluctant to withdraw. They had concluded separate agreements with both Anton Tsaous and EAM/ELAS for gradually turning over authority to one or the other, hoping to gain time. This was a desperate move, made on the chance that the Allies might consider

33. The Greek government in exile, unaware of British-Soviet agreements, showed increased nervousness at British-Yugoslav contacts, fearing possible concessions in Macedonia detrimental to Greek interests (U.K. Secretary of State for Dominion Affairs to Secretary of State for External Affairs, Canada, 12 April 1944, D554, Canadian Archives [hereafter cited as CA]). A 26 August 1944 study of the British Foreign Office Research Department rejected as "not practical" proposed plans for the independence, autonomy, or federation of Macedonia. It favored the prewar status, with a proposal for free port facilities in Thessaloniki and Kavala for Yugoslav Macedonia and Bulgarian Macedonia, respectively. Commenting on this study in November 1944, Ambassador Leeper suggested the transfer of "perhaps 120,000 Slav Macedonians north of the Greek frontiers of 1941" (FO 371/43649/97481, British Embassy [Athens], 57, 24 November 1944).

allowing them to retain possession of lands ceded to them by Hitler.[34] For his part, however, Marshal Tolbukhin upheld Great Power understandings. He refused to cross the border into Greece, even though he was invited to do so by local Greek Communist chiefs.[35] In the end, it was British (and U.S.) démarches to Moscow that compelled the Bulgarians to withdraw. Despite its happy conclusion, the incident indicated to the British that the possibility of a Soviet descent, by proxy, to the Aegean shores was very much alive.[36]

Soon, however, a second and more complicated problem began to emerge, with direct implications for Macedonia. In the Pirin Macedonian district of Bulgaria, Yugoslav Macedonian infiltration had come into the open after the takeover of the government by the Fatherland Front. For almost three months—until the end of November—"Macedonian" national agitation for the immediate incorporation of the Pirin region into the new Yugoslav Macedonian republic developed into a grass-roots campaign, the aim of which was to create a fait accompli. To judge by the writings of Yugoslav and Bulgarian authors, the activity of emissaries from Skopje and their local supporters in Pirin bears a surprising resemblance to similar activities in Greek Slavophone border areas throughout 1944. In Pirin, the local Bulgarian Communist cadres appeared to render full support to the idea of unification, whereas in Greek Macedonia secessionist-prone Slavo-Macedonians came into open conflict with EAM/ELAS and finally were driven out of the country.[37]

Meanwhile, on the diplomatic level, Belgrade and Sofia had initiated negotiations for a South Slav federation, featuring a unified Macedonian federative state. It was not known at the time that Stalin himself had encouraged the federation project,[38] apparently in order to secure his

34. Details in Kofos, "Valkaniki Diastasi."

35. On the initiatives of the eastern Macedonia KKE leaders to invite the Soviet army in and allow the Bulgarian army to remain, see G. Erythriadis's report to the Central Committee of the KKE, in *7 Olomeleia tis KE tou KKE, 14–16 Maiou 1950* (The 7th plenum of the CC of the KKE), September 1950, 73. See also his report to the Macedonian Bureau, KKE, 15 October 1944 (published in *KPG*, 263–64).

36. The Churchill-Stalin Percentages Agreement was concluded in Moscow on 9 October 1944. On British pressures on the Bulgarians to withdraw, see Stoyan Rachev, *Anglo-Bulgarian Relations During the Second World War, 1939–1944* (Sofia, 1981), 189–204.

37. Dragoycheva, *Macedonia,* 84–85. This is also supported by such Yugoslav writers as Kolishevski, Tempo, and Apostolski.

38. CA, Canadian Legation (Belgrade), no. 210, 13 May 1950, quoting Tito's speech of 27 April 1950 to the National Assembly in which he revealed that it was the Soviet Union that envisaged a Yugoslav-Bulgarian federation.

hold on the two Balkan states. Despite disclaimers by Yugoslav and Soviet officials, from November 1944 to February 1945, evidence mounted that a Yugoslav-Bulgarian agreement was imminent. As a result, the British had not much difficulty persuading the Americans to join them in putting pressure on the two Balkan capitals—and the Soviet Union—to annul their federation plans. Apart from considerations of principle (Bulgaria, being a former enemy state, could not undertake any commitments prior to signing a peace treaty), the proposed federation threatened to upset the meticulously knit British security planning in the area. The loss of Greek Macedonia—and possibly Thrace—could destroy British strategic aims, much as could the loss of Greece as a whole.[39]

For Tito, the project certainly fit his ambitious wartime vision of a predominant role for Yugoslavia in the Balkans. Georgi Dimitrov, still in Moscow, was in agreement for different reasons. He advised his comrades in Sofia to conclude a military, economic, and political alliance with Yugoslavia, as a first step toward unification of the two countries in a federal state of the southern Slavs. In his view, such an arrangement would place a protective umbrella over Bulgaria, ensure control of the country by the Communist party, and absolve the Bulgarian people of the wartime alliance with Germany.[40]

Tito, having received repeated British warnings, should have been convinced that the British meant to hold on to Greece, including Greek Macedonia—their last remaining piece of real estate in the Balkans. The Soviet Union, furthermore, had proved unwilling to challenge the British in three important cases involving Greece: on the Bulgarian withdrawal from Macedonia and Thrace; on the British intervention in Athens in December 1944; and on the Yugoslav-Bulgarian federation scheme. Being a realist, Tito gave assurances that he would wait for the termination of the war to stake his claims for a united Macedonia "in an orderly fashion," probably at the peace conference.[41]

The leaders of the KKE, who were deeply involved in Greek internal developments and had only a superficial knowledge of rapidly changing

39. The British legation in Sofia had learned "from a most reliable source" that the inclusion of Thessaloniki in the proposed federation "would enjoy Soviet support" (FO 371/48181/8533, Report no. 108, 21 January 1945).

40. Letter by Georgi Dimitrov to Trajko Kostov, 1 December 1944, cited in Dragoycheva, *Macedonia*, 86.

41. CA, U.K. Secretary of State for Dominion Affairs (London) to Secretary of State for External Affairs (Canada), no. 1, 1 January 1945.

Balkan alignments, sought to appraise Tito's and Dimitrov's views on an armed bid for power. It is still difficult to assess—given the fragmentary data available—whether the Macedonian question had any direct or indirect influence in determining Yugoslavia's inconsistent reaction to the KKE's decision to meet with military action the dual challenge of the Papandreou government and the British.

Secret correspondence reveals that the KKE had repeatedly requested military equipment from the Yugoslav partisans during the concluding months of the war.[42] As late as 28 August 1944, George Siantos sent a dispatch to Andreas Tzimas at Tito's headquarters, to ask for weapons from the Yugoslav leader in order to equip a new division. He stressed that "now as never before we have need of war supplies."[43] In October, just a few days after the eviction of the armed Slavo-Macedonians by ELAS, Aleksandar Ranković gave the order to Tempo, who was still in Yugoslav Macedonia, that *"for the time being* you should not send our own units into Greece."[44] As these directives indicate, the KKE was preparing itself for a confrontation after the withdrawal of the Germans, while at the same time the Yugoslav Macedonian partisans were being alerted to the possibility of a border crossing into Greek Macedonia. What cannot be established on the basis of the available documentation is the connection, if any, between these two things. There are other pieces of information concerning the fate of Greek Macedonia that require careful scrutiny as well.

At about the same time (October 1944), Vlado Poptomov, a leading Bulgarian Communist and a native of Macedonia, on returning from Moscow, communicated Dimitrov's views to the Yugoslavs. The Bulgarian leader was in favor of the unification of Macedonia but preferred to commence with the South Slav federation while preparing the ground for public acceptance of the idea. He believed that the accession of Greek Macedonia to a unified Macedonian state was "a little more difficult" to achieve because the inclusion of Thessaloniki would be viewed by the British as a threat to their Mediterranean routes. Therefore it was neces-

---

42. Polycronis Enepekidis, *I Elliniki Antistasis, 1941–1944* (The Greek resistance) (Athens, 1964), 90, quoting German sources on the dispatch of military equipment from Yugoslav partisans to ELAS.

43. A/CC/CPY, Radiogram, Siantos to Tzimas, 28 August 1944, "Relations with Greece, 1941–1945."

44. A/CC/CPY, Ranković to Tempo, no. 3, 5 October 1944, "Relations with Greece, 1941–1945" (emphasis added).

sary to build a case by collecting economic, geographical, and national data that would support the claim to Greek Macedonia in a postwar peace conference. In his view, emphasis should have been placed on projecting the argument that the expulsion of the Slavs from Greek Macedonia after World War I had been unjust.[45] It apparently mattered little to him what kind of government would be in power in Greece at the time of the peace conference.

Since Dimitrov was still in Moscow, this conveyed the impression that such views had the endorsement of the Soviets. The Yugoslav Communists certainly were not opposed to the approach proposed. Successive public speeches by such leading figures as Milovan Djilas, Tempo, and Dimitar Vlahov reaffirmed Yugoslav attachment to the idea of the unification of Macedonia, including Greek Macedonia. In the event, the arguments suggested by Dimitrov were also found in Yugoslav statements.[46]

It was apparent that during the critical weeks between the liberation of Greece and the commencement of the "second round" Yugoslavs and Bulgarians were in agreement on detaching, in one way or another, Greek Macedonia from the Greek state. What was still uncertain was whether the Yugoslavs would try to force a solution. Public pronouncements at the time and subsequent writings by Yugoslav authors indicate that at least certain leaders in Yugoslav Macedonia and in the Central Committee of the Yugoslav Communist Party favored some kind of military action.[47]

It will be recalled that after the withdrawal early in October of the armed Slavo-Macedonians from Greece, ELAS had sealed the border in order to prevent their return. Meanwhile, the stream of refugees crossing over to Yugoslav Macedonia grew steadily. Among them were persons associated with the Bulgarian occupiers who judged it safer to emerge as "Macedonians" in the newly formed Macedonian state. In the enthusiastic atmosphere prevailing at the time in the border towns of Yugoslavia, particularly in Bitola (Monastir), Slavo-Macedonian refugees were inducted into the "1st Aegean Macedonian Brigade" and began training for eventual duty in Greek Macedonia. Rumors flew and expectations were high that two Yugoslav divisions were about to enter Greece, along

45. A/CC/CPY, Kiro Milievski to Tempo and Kolishevski, October 1944, "Greece IX-29-IV/2."

46. Kofos, *Nationalism and Communism,* 136, and "Valkaniki Diastasi."

47. FO 371/48181, Brigadier Maclean to the Foreign Office, 1 February 1945. See also Ajanovski, *Egejski Buri,* 139–45.

with the Aegean Macedonian Brigade, allegedly to assist ELAS in facing the British.[48]

This was the situation when the KKE decided to make its bid to Tito for assistance. Tito was favorably disposed toward the KKE, but there is no concrete evidence to show whether his promise of support entailed anything more than military supplies.[49] Similarly, there are no data to support the idea that the fate or the role of Slavo-Macedonian fighters, then in Yugoslav Macedonia, was discussed. Probably it was not. This is inferred from the refusal of the KKE, early in December, to accept an offer by these Slavo-Macedonians to enter Greece and join in the ELAS operation against EDES. This offer was accompanied by a request for a free indoctrination of Slavophones in the spirit of the "Macedonian nation."[50] Years later, a Greek partisan leader revealed that ELAS attacked EDES in order to prevent an attack by Yugoslav partisans against Zervas.[51] Although the reasons for Aris Velouhiotis' action against EDES are certainly broader than the ones hinted at above, the evidence nevertheless reveals that the possibility of the entry of Yugoslav partisans into Greece preoccupied the leaders of the KKE during the critical days prior to and during the December 1944 events.

As the fighting in Athens intensified, KKE leaders instructed Tzimas to renew the plea to Tito for support. This time Tito's reply was negative.[52] Moreover, he sent orders to divert Slavo-Macedonian troops from the

48. The author has it from a reliable source that in November 1944 two KKE emissaries, Stergios Anastasiadis and Barbalexis, sought Tito's views on an armed bid for power and that the Yugoslav leader returned a favorable answer, promising full support. When the shooting started in Athens, however, Tito went back on his promise. In an interview with Vasos Mathiopoulos, Yugoslav historian Vojmir Kljaković confirmed that the KKE had obtained Tito's views prior to the December events, but he evaded saying what Tito's response was. He added, however, that when the shooting started, Tito decided to keep his distance, not wanting to offer the British a pretext for intervention in Yugoslavia. Vasos Mathiopoulos, *I Elliniki Antistasi (1941–1944) kia oi "Symmachoi"* (The Greek resistance [1941–1944] and the "Allies") (Athens, 1976), xvi.

49. Zahariadis revealed later that the KKE asked Tito for military aid for the December events, but that Tito turned down the request and instead prepared partisan units to invade Greek Macedonia. See Zahariadis' report to the Central Committee of the KKE in 7 *Olomeleia,* 182, 275, and also the speech by Ioannidis, 124. See also Stringos to Tzimas (Belgrade), 14 November 1944, in *KPG,* 317.

50. Ajanovski, *Egejski Buri,* 140–45.

51. Andreas Mountrichas ("Orestis") told Kousoulas that Siantos gave him this explanation. D. George Kousoulas, *Revolution and Defeat: The Story of the Greek Communist Party* (New York, 1969), 211.

52. See note 49 above.

Greek border. Thus, instead of liberating Thessaloniki—already in the firm control of EAM/ELAS—Slavo-Macedonian activists found themselves chasing nationalist Albanians in Kosovo.[53]

Even though the lack of data prevents a fully accurate interpretation of Tito's reversal of his earlier promise, Dimitrov's similarly negative response to a subsequent KKE inquiry[54] indicates that the two Balkan leaders were recipients of counsel (or directives) from the same central authority. This is corroborated by the fact that toward the end of December Tito gave assurances to the British that he did not intend to use force to further his plans for the annexation of Greek Macedonia but that he would raise the issue at the peace conference.[55] Thus, although for a short time they toyed with the idea of some kind of involvement in Greek Macedonia, the Yugoslav Communists quickly backed down when the shooting started in Athens. Safeguarding the revolution at home was their first priority. Ambitious plans for Greek Macedonia could wait for a more opportune moment.

The rather quick and unexpected capitulation of KKE/ELAS at Varkiza on 12 February 1945 upset Tito's plans for the future of a unified Macedonia. The only means left for keeping the flames of the Macedonian question alive in Greece while the war against Germany continued were the Slavo-Macedonian fugitives, who had found refuge in Yugoslav Macedonia. The first step in that direction was the formation of a new National Liberation Front (NOF) for Greek Macedonia under the control of the Communist Party of Macedonia (CPM).[56] By December 1944, Slavo-Macedonian agitators had already infiltrated border regions of Greek Macedonia. Working clandestinely, they had succeeded in forming the small Secret Macedonian Liberation Organization (TOMO) in the Edessa district to work, ostensibly, for the liberation of Macedonia,

---

53. Ajanovski writes of 4,000 Slavo-Macedonians from Greek Macedonia who were inducted into the Yugoslav army to take part in operations in Kossovo and other parts of Yugoslavia (*Egejski Buri*, 145).

54. V. Kontis, *I Angloamerikaniki Politiki kai to Elliniko Provlima, 1945–1949* (Anglo-American policy and the Greek problem) (Thessaloniki, 1984), 44–46.

55. Ibid., 44–45, 107–8.

56. Ajanovski, *Egejski Buri*, 118–32; Risto Poplazarov, "The National Liberation Movement of Macedonians in Southern Macedonia," reprinted in *Makedonija*, Melbourne, 9 November 1982; Kole Mangov, "Pred 35 godini: Otporot na Makedoncite od Solunske" (Thirty-five years ago: The resistance of the Macedonians from the Thessaloniki region), *Makedonija*, Skopje, October 1981, 14; and Risto Kirjazovski, *Narodno Osloboditelniot Front*, 106–45. NARS, 760H.68/7.2445, report by W. H. MacNeill, Athens, 24 July 1945.

which ironically had just been liberated from German and Bulgarian occupation and was administered by EAM.[57]

When the Varkiza Agreement was signed, the Slavo-Macedonians refused to abide by it. NOF proceeded to form armed bands, dispatched them across the border, and commenced a small-scale, local guerrilla war. The key objective was to conduct underground agitation throughout western Macedonia for the eventual "liberation" of Greek Macedonia and its incorporation into Yugoslav Macedonia. Publicly, emphasis was placed on the social and political status of the Slavo-Macedonians within Greece. New data reveal that NOF functioned at the time as the Aegean Macedonian Committee of the CPM.[58]

Such activity had its victims. The KKE and the whole of the EAM/ELAS movement were the first to suffer. Its opponents in Macedonia would not accept as sincere the KKE's disclaimers of connivance with the former ELAS Slavophone fighters who were ambushing government and British troops, reaching the border regions in the early months of 1945. Throughout 1945, the KKE stepped up its open condemnation of NOF's activities as being "provocatory," "chauvinistic," and "autonomist."[59] But this was to no avail. At the same time, the KKE resorted to nationalistic rhetoric on Greek national claims, which included Northern Epirus—but no longer the rectification of the Greek-Bulgarian frontier—apparently in an effort to dispel accusations of wartime "antinational" behavior on the Macedonian question.[60]

The second victim was the Slavophone population itself. NOF's initiatives, which involved armed activity, offered government forces and irregulars a pretext for taking revenge on Slavophones suspected of having collaborated with the Bulgarian occupation authorities or the pro-

57. Ajanovski, *Egejski Buri,* 159–60; and Kirjazovski, *Narodno Osloboditelniot Front,* 101–5.

58. Keramitziev and Gotse to the Central Committee of the KKE, 2 June 1949, published in Slavomacedonian, in *Eg.M.,* 6 (1949), 311–31 (hereafter cited as Keramitziev-Gotse letter). This was known to the KKE. See Zahariadis' report in 7 *Olomeleia,* 275, stating that the NOF-ites belonged not to the KKE but to "Kolishevski's Party of Skopje."

59. The pro-KKE Florina newspaper *Agonas,* 5 October 1945, following the official line, attacked NOF followers as traitors, to which NOF responded by threatening to slaughter pro-EAM/KKE villagers (NARS 76OH.68/12.1845, Athens report 2019, 18 December 1945; details in Kirjazovski, *Narodno Osloboditelniot Front,* 147–55).

60. On the Northern Epirus question, see *Apofasi tis 12is Olomeleias tis KE tou KKE* (Decision of the 12th plenum of the CC of KKE) (Athens, 1945), 48. After the end of the civil war, that decision came under sharp criticism from all KKE leaders. Details in Kofos, *Nationalism and Communism,* 165–66.

Yugoslav, Slav-Macedonian organizations. Personal vendettas also played their part. Although there is no evidence of a specific government plan for the eviction of the Slavophone population from the country, it is difficult to ascertain the intentions of local officials and nationalist army officers in the field. There was no doubt that the pendulum of violence had swung once again, this time against the Bulgarian and Slavo-Macedonian factions of the Slavophones. Certainly, the situation in Greek Macedonia in 1945–46 was not dissimilar to that in other countries emerging from foreign occupation, where for one reason or other minorities had collaborated with the occupiers only to find themselves, after the war, the target of vengeful nationalists. Although in Greek Macedonia persecution never reached the level of the genocidal practices perpetrated, for example, in Yugoslavia against the Germanophone minorities,[61] the climate was hardly tolerable for persons associated directly or indirectly with either the Bulgarian or the Slavo-Macedonian "Slavic menaces." As a result, the number of Slavophones crossing into Yugoslavia in 1945–46 increased to 15,000–20,000.[62]

If we accept the thesis of the pivotal role of Yugoslavia in Zahariadis' decision to initiate the "third round," it is logical to assume that a normalization of relations between the KKE and NOF would have had top priority. There are now reports available of secret meetings between Zahariadis and other members of the Central Committee of the KKE and NOF leaders in Thessaloniki as early as December 1945. These encounters eventually led to Zahariadis' complete reversal on the KKE's assessment of NOF's activities and its future role. The Greek Communist leader, speaking to party cadres in Thessaloniki in March 1946, instead of openly condemning NOF referred to NOF as a "democratic," "anti-

61. Following the annihilation, persecution, and eviction of the Germanophone minorities, the new Yugoslav government made it absolutely clear to the British and the Americans that it had no intention of readmitting these former Yugoslav citizens. See Yugoslav note no. 2183 to the U.S. embassy, dated 27 July 1945, stating that the German minorities, after cooperating with the occupation authorities, left the country "of their own will" and "through their option, renounced their Yugoslav citizenship" (NARS, 740.6OH114/8-345, U.S. embassy dispatch from Belgrade, A-105, 3 August 1945). Note also the 17 May 1946 Yugoslav request of the Allies for help in transferring to Germany the remaining 110,000 members of the German minority (NARS, 840.4016/5-2346, U.S. embassy [Belgrade] report no. 361, 23 May 1946).

62. NARS, 800.4016DP/11-1445, U.S. embassy (Belgrade) report no. 165, 14 November 1945. As a permanent solution, the British considered, late in 1944, the transfer of approximately 120,000 Macedonian Slavs north of the Greek frontiers (FO 371/43649/97481, Leeper to Eden, no. 57, 24 November 1944).

fascist" organization working for the common cause.[63] The new position on this crucial issue cleared the road for the talks late in March with Tito, who endorsed Zahariadis' decision to commence the armed struggle and promised his support.[64]

By May 1946, the first Greek Communist armed bands began to co-operate with NOF bands already in the field, while KKE cadres in the border prefectures of Macedonia entered into discussions with local NOF leaders on matters of common interest. Nonetheless, both organizations maintained their organizational and operational autonomy.[65]

From May to November 1946, high-level negotiations were conducted between the KKE, on the one hand, and NOF, the CPM, and the CPY, on the other. Details are fragmentary, but sufficient to draw a picture.[66] There were many obstacles to be surmounted, and certain misunder-standings to be cleared up, before a final agreement could be reached. It is interesting to note that as late as 7 September 1946, Lazar Kolishevski, head of the CPM, found it necessary to report to Tito that in "Aegean Macedonia," the leaders of the Greek *andartes* "are not willing to carry out decisions in the spirit of the discussions held with Zahariadis, but they try, with every means at their disposal, to disorganize and dissolve the Macedonian units." He added that in Greek Macedonia there were only 70 Greek, compared with more than 500 "Macedonian," *andartes* operating under the orders of NOF. Again, on 24 September, Kolishev-ski, reporting on Markos Vaphiadis' arrival in Skopje, informed the Cen-tral Committee of the CPY of Vaphiadis' request to Slavo-Macedonian leaders to go to Greece. Vaphiadis' instructions to NOF, however—ac-cording to Kolishevski—were not in the spirit of a previous meeting at-tended by Vaphiadis, Tito, Djilas, and himself. Therefore, Kolishevski

63. Ajanovski, *Egejski Buri,* 198–200; Kirjazovski, *Narodno Osloboditelniot Front,* 151–52.

64. Late in March 1946, Zahariadis went to Eastern Europe. He secured Gotwald's and subsequently Tito's promise for military assistance, and then traveled to the Crimea, where he met with Stalin and Molotov, probably between 3 April and 5 April. The decision for armed insurrection was made then and there, and the Greek leader was sent back to Tito to arrange the details, which he did. These facts, according to the author's privileged knowledge, were intimated by Zahariadis himself to close colleagues.

65. Kirjazovski offers details from the Yugoslav and KKE archives, *Narodno Osloboditel-niot Front,* 155–69.

66. Details in Keramitziev-Gotse letter; Kirjazovski, *Narodno Osloboditelniot Front; Eg.M.,* vol. 3; *KPG.*

wished to know from his superiors in Belgrade whether any changes were made "to the work in Aegean Macedonia."[67]

Tito's reply, cabled on 7 October, clearly sets out the ground rules of co-operation between the CPY and the KKE concerning the role and position of the Slavo-Macedonians in the Greek armed struggle. Tito, pleading ignorance—no doubt to Kolishevski's shocked surprise—asks the CPM to explain what units in Aegean Macedonia "you consider as ours." He then delineates Yugoslav policy as follows: "We consider that in this situation all units in the territory of Greece should be under the unified direction of Greek commands, with which you should now be in touch. Your people should not be mixed now with the organization and direction of the armed struggle in Greece. You should limit your activity in Aegean Macedonia only to offering specific assistance, as with the press, etc."[68]

The spirit of this document was reflected in the KKE-NOF agreement that was finally reached in November 1946. NOF undertook to sever its organizational links with the CPM, dissolve its political organization and armed bands, and fuse with the KKE and the Democratic Army of Greece (DAG). It must be inferred that NOF assumed the obligation to desist from conducting any irredentist activity inside Greece.[69]

---

67. A/CC/CPY, Kolishevski to the Central Committee of the CPY, 7 September 1946, "Relations with Greece, 1945–1955." For October, the same sources put the figure of *andartes* at 2,000 Slavo-Macedonians and 700 Greeks.

68. A/CC/CPY, Tito to Kolishevski, 7 October 1946, "Relations with Greece, 1945–1955."

69. Apart from documents cited in Kirjazovski, *Narodno Osloboditelniot Front*, 155–69, Keramitziev and Gotse, in their letter to the Central Committee of the KKE of 2 June 1949, give details of the agreement, signed on 24 November 1946. In June 1949, Zahariadis denied the existence of a written agreement, but there is the text of an agreement between Ioannidis and Karaivanov (on behalf of the KKE and the Communist Party of Macedonia, respectively), dated 15 October 1946, in A/CC/CPY, "Relations with Greece, 1945–1955." This text contains most but not all of the terms quoted by Keramitziev and Gotse, indicating that it was an earlier text. Its substance, however, remains the same. Its most important points are:

a. NOF will be incorporated into the KKE and, more particularly, into its Regional Committee for Macedonia and Thrace, severing its links with the CPM.

b. NOF will set up a central organ under Keramitziev and Mitrovski that will report to the Regional Committee of the KKE for Macedonia and Thrace. NOF will have its own youth organization and press.

c. The *andartes* in Aegean Macedonia [*sic*] and Greece will have complete organizational and political unity and action. No special "Macedonian" units will function.

d. Dzodze Urdarov, a member of the Aegean Committee of the CPM, will be assigned the task of supervising compliance with the [Yugoslav] party line in the partisan movement in "Aegean Macedonia."

The decision of the leadership of the KKE to put aside its reservations about NOF—despite the latter's behavior during 1945, its irredentist pronouncements, and its dependence on the CPM—was apparently influenced by several assessments. First, the great number of Slavo-Macedonians who had taken refuge in Yugoslavia represented a convenient reservoir of manpower. Second, NOF's clandestine network in the urban and rural districts of Kastoria, Florina, and Edessa could be turned to the benefit of the struggle and facilitate a quick takeover of the important border triangle adjacent to Yugoslavia and Albania. Furthermore, cooperation with the local CPM and the agencies of the People's (later) Socialist Republic of Macedonia would be rendered smoother, particularly for the flow of men and supplies across the border. On the other hand, failure to reach an understanding with NOF could raise a series of problems with the People's Republic of Macedonia's authorities and make it extremely difficult to elicit the meaningful cooperation and support of Yugoslavia. No one could possibly have denied that to foment a full-scale uprising in Greece without Yugoslav support would be problematic, to say the least.[70]

There were two major drawbacks in reaching an agreement with NOF. On the one hand, the KKE exposed itself, for a third time, to its adversaries on the sensitive issue of collaboration with the Slavs. On the other hand, it ran the risk of a recurrence of Slavo-Macedonian secessionist activity along the lines of 1944. To counter the first, the KKE launched its own campaign against "monarcho-fascism" and "Anglo-American imperialism." To meet the second, it endeavored to maintain a firm grip on Slavo-Macedonian activists without, however, causing rupture or defections.

Recently released data from the Yugoslav side[71] indicate that the KKE proceeded, at least on paper, to accord the Slavo-Macedonians full equality within the party, with proportional representation in KKE organs and DAG units of various echelons. In prefectures in which a sizeable proportion of the population was Slavophone, NOF cadres would have a leading role in regional party organizations, while dissemination of the

---

70. After the end of the hostilities, Zahariadis revealed that in his initial agreement with Tito he had also settled the issue of the Slavo-Macedonians, that the CPY had agreed that the Slavo-Macedonians would struggle alongside the KKE, and that the "erosion of the Macedonian people [apparently from Skopje] would cease" (Zahariadis' speech, 7 *Olomeleia*, 181–82).

71. Mainly in *Eg.M.*, vols. 3–6; *KPG;* and Kirjazovski, *Narodno Osloboditelniot Front*.

"Macedonian" national idea—but not secessionism—would not be ob-structed. Although not identified as such, these concessions appeared to lead to a form of self-rule in the three border prefectures under the aegis of the KKE. However, neither special Slavo-Macedonian armed units nor a separate Slavo-Macedonian party organization would be allowed to function inside Greece.

It is difficult to ascertain the role of the Slavo-Macedonians within DAG. NOF sources tend to classify—erroneously—all Slavophones as Slavo-Macedonians, and thus exaggerate their participation and impor-tance in the armed struggle. There have been claims that 50 percent of the DAG fighters and its casualties and of the refugees were Slavo-Macedonians. By July 1947, there were about 6,000 Slavo-Macedonian *andartes;* by the end of 1948 there were 14,000, compared with the total DAG force of approximately 40,000.[72] Even if these figures were inflated, it is a fact that from the end of 1946 to the end of 1948 Slavophones furnished the KKE with much-needed manpower disproportionate to their numbers. Inhabiting border regions that frequently passed under DAG control, they were more easily exposed to voluntary or compulsory conscription. Their importance, moreover, increased during the last year of the civil war, when most large-scale military operations took place in western Macedonia and adjacent Epirus.[73]

Nevertheless, the induction of Slavo-Macedonians into DAG units aroused mutual suspicions and was a cause of internal friction. When battle-ready Slavo-Macedonian bands (estimated at approximately 1,000 men) joined the newly formed KKE-sponsored units in December 1946, they were immediately sent for duty to central Greece. There they were disbanded, and the men were allocated to new mixed units under trusted KKE commanders. Most of the Slavo-Macedonian cadres found themselves demoted or given secondary posts.[74] Such treatment became

---

72. Keramitziev-Gotse letter.

73. In assessing the causes of military defeat and answering the criticism leveled at him for the change of the Macedonian line of the party, Zahariadis defended his policy mainly on the basis of the need to keep the Slavo-Macedonians loyal to the KKE, since in the concluding months of the struggle they provided the main source of reserves. Although he admitted that the new line did not correspond to the wider interests of the party at the time, what counted was a victory in the battle of Vitsi. Zahariadis' reports in *6 Olomeleia tis KE tou KKE (9 Ochtovri 1949* (Sixth Plenum of the CC of the KKE [9 October 1949]) (April 1951), 82, 92, and in *7 Olomeleia,* 175.

74. Keramitziev-Gotse letter.

a major irritant during the next two years. NOF complained that, despite the original agreement, no Slavo-Macedonian cadres reached top positions. Moreover, the Slavo-Macedonians of all ranks who had either been associated in wartime with NOF and the pro-Bulgarian nationalist bands (and later apparently repented) or had taken refuge in Yugoslav Macedonia after 1944 were suspected of "Macedonian" nationalism. Following the KKE's split with the CPY, pro-Tito Slavo-Macedonians, who deserted DAG and the KKE, accused the KKE of having promoted within the party and DAG commands Slavophones who had no connection with NOF, simply because their "Macedonian" national orientation was "dormant," or worse yet because they were "Grecomans." In his long letter to the Central Committee of the KKE of 2 June 1949, NOF leader M. Keramitziev complained: "We had to struggle against the Great Idea chauvinism of many Greek cadres . . . who were united with *the most fanatic anti-Macedonian elements, i.e. Macedonians from villages who said they were Greeks.*"[75]

For its part, the KKE leadership, in its tirades against the pro-Tito faction of NOF, revealed that throughout the two-year (1947–48) struggle Slavo-Macedonian activists had continued to conduct propaganda within Greece for the unification of Greek Macedonia to the People's Republic of Macedonia, undermine the unity of Greeks and Slavo-Macedonian fugitives in the People's Republic of Macedonia, and even organize defections from DAG.[76]

In assessing the Slavo-Macedonian factor in the KKE's armed struggle, it becomes apparent that until the Tito-Stalin split in mid-1948 the party leadership successfully exploited the Slavo-Macedonians to its own benefit. In contrast to what had happened in 1943–46, when the Slavo-Macedonians of Greece were under the guidance and patronage of the Yugoslav Macedonian partisans, after 1946 the KKE-CPY agreement allowed the KKE to exercise its authority over the Slavo-Macedonians free of irritating interventions by emissaries or commissars from Skopje. However, the KKE apparently underestimated the extent of NOF's ability to spread the idea of Slavo-Macedonian nationalism among Slavophone villagers. NOF took advantage of the opportunities afforded it by its

75. Ibid. (emphasis added). For similar complaints by Slavo-Macedonian protagonists turned authors, see Ajanovski, *Egejski Buri*, 191–231; Naum Pejov, *Makedoncite i Gradjanskata Vojna vo Grcija* (The Macedonians and the civil war in Greece) (Skopje, 1968), 145–51; and Hristo Antonovski in *Glas na Egejskite*, Skopje, 10 February 1952.

76. 6 *Olomeleia*, 42, 86, 92; 7 *Olomeleia*, 125.

control of the administration of certain villages and its role in teaching the language and printing Slavo-Macedonian publications. Its efforts were also aided by the KKE's classification of all Slavophones as "Slavo-Macedonians"—and later as "Makedones"—a fact that ignored the Greek faction of the Slavophones. At the time, the party was mainly concerned with classifying Slavophones as either loyal to the KKE or as suspected of Yugoslav Macedonian orientation.

The Greek Slavophones, who found themselves on the government side in the civil strife, must have been aware of this situation. Armed by the national army, they fought their own "national" war. In certain cases, entire Slavophone villages—which have been appropriately called "village-fortresses of Macedonia"[77]—organized their own defense units and, for the duration of the war, stood firm against their national, as well as their ideological, foes. In those regions, fratricidal conflict meant exactly that: brother fought brother, as by choice or coercion members of the same family frequently found themselves in opposite camps.

To the government camp, much of what is now known about the Macedonian situation was either unknown or appeared in a fragmentary and distorted form at the time. Government agencies had to depend on public pronouncements by the Yugoslavs, NOF, and the KKE, as well as on information of questionable worth provided by captured *andartes*. Led by its own preconceived notions, and ignorant of the nuances of the Macedonian policy of its adversaries, the government camp tended to lump the aims of the KKE, Slavo-Macedonians, Yugoslavs, Bulgarians, and the Soviet Union into one carefully orchestrated conspiracy for the detachment of Macedonia from Greece.[78] Although this simplistic view ignored the intricacies of the problem, there was ample justification for the government's perception of a threat. The Yugoslav-supported secessionist activities of the Slavo-Macedonians, which had occurred during the war and continued in the post-Varkiza interlude, were fresh in the minds of the policymakers and the public. Throughout 1945–47, repeated Yugoslav references to the unification of three parts of Macedonia kept the sense of imminent threat from the north alive. Bulgarian claims to Greek Thrace, which were presented at the Paris Peace Conference

77. Georgios Modis, *Choria Frouria tis Makedonias* (Village fortresses of Macedonia) (Athens, 1964).

78. Such an assessment is reflected in numerous contemporary publications. See, for example, Dimitrios Zafeiropoulos, *To KKE kai i Makedonia* (The KKE and Macedonia) (Athens, 1948), and *O Antisymmoriakos Agon* (The antibandit struggle) (Athens, 1956).

and supported by the Soviet Union and Yugoslavia, added insult to injury and increased apprehensions. Furthermore, the Tito-Dimitrov Bled Agreement concluded in the summer of 1947 revealed a thinly veiled plan for a unified Macedonian federative state within a South Slav federation.

The conviction that a Communist victory in the civil war would lead to the detachment of Macedonia from Greece was more or less shared by the entire political spectrum of the government camp.[79] As had been the case in Macedonia during the war years, the KKE was placed on the defensive as its opponents shifted the ideological battle from "bourgeois democracy versus a proletarian Communist state" to "the nation versus its enemies."[80] The KKE was identified with Soviet expansionism; consequently, the government camp argued, all good patriots should join the struggle against the KKE and the Slavic menace. The fate of Macedonia thus became the rallying point for government supporters. It matters little whether this policy was the product of a cool assessment of all the parameters of the question (which would have been a rather difficult exercise under the circumstances) or the result of the government's calculated psychological warfare technique. What counted at the time was that in the propaganda contest between the government and the KKE the government was scoring points. The KKE was only too conscious of the consequences of this contest, but unable to react.[81]

In addition to the propaganda strategy, legal measures that were taken in order to suppress the rebellion also focused on the threat to the northern provinces. Thus the Third Constitutional "Resolution," enacted in June 1946, initially provided for courts-martial only in northern Greece. Even when these judicial proceedings were extended to the whole of Greece, persons were prosecuted and sentenced to life imprisonment or death on two major counts: the violent overthrow of the existing political

79. Prior to the Fifth Plenum decision (1949) on the Macedonian question, there were certain dissenting voices (John Sophianopoulos, Ilias Tsirimokos, Alexander Svolos). Nikolaos Plastiras appeared to believe that the rebellion did not endanger Greece's territorial integrity, which could be threatened only by war (NARS, 868.00/11-948, Letter of "friends" of Plastiras to King Paul, U.S. embassy [Athens], report no. 1096, 9 November 1948).

80. K. Tsoukalas, "I Ideologiki Epidrasi tou Emfyliou Polemou" (The ideological impact of the civil war), in *I Ellada sti Dekaetia, 1940–1950, 575.*

81. In an October 1946 memorandum to the Communist Party of the Soviet Union, requesting assistance in its armed struggle, the KKE referred to the Macedonian question as "one of the most delicate issues which stirs the masses of Greece" (the text of the memorandum appeared in *Avgi,* 5 December 1979). This concern with the psychological impact of the problem is reflected in the memoirs of such KKE leaders as Petros Roussos and Yiannis Ioannidis.

system, and the detachment of part or the whole of the state (Compulsory Law 509).[82] The KKE was held by the government camp to be guilty of secessionist ("autonomist") activities in Macedonia. Prior to 1949, however, no convincing legal proof could be brought against it directly implicating the KKE in the annexationist schemes of Greece's northern neighbors.

On the international level, the Macedonian question was a major point in the Greek government's case. Greece, it was argued, was fighting not an internal civil war but an international conspiracy aimed at turning it into a Communist state or, at the very least, at detaching Macedonia. The government provided the U.N. Commission of Investigation Concerning Greek Frontier Incidents and its successor, the U.N. Special Committee on the Balkans, with all available evidence on the subject, including forged KKE wartime agreements with neighboring Communist parties for the cession of Macedonia to a Balkan Communist federation. There was, of course, ample documentation of the material support provided to the Greek Communist insurgents by Yugoslavia and Bulgaria and of statements by the leaders of these states regarding the future unification of Macedonia. But until August 1947, when the Bled Agreement was concluded, it was difficult to build a thoroughly convincing case, particularly for third parties.[83]

What counted most, however, was whether the Greek government's perceptions were shared in London and in Washington.[84] The British government, having already committed itself to keeping Greece in the Western fold, needed little convincing. It frequently spearheaded anti-Soviet bloc polemics, pointing to the threat posed to Greece's territorial integrity by Yugoslav aspirations concerning Macedonia. Similarly, the United States, which was becoming more and more involved in Greek affairs, found in the Macedonian question a justification for its policy.[85]

82. Nicos Alivizatos, "Kathestos Ektaktis Anangis" (State of emergency), in *I Elladia sti Dekaetia, 1940–1950,* 397, 388–89, 391.

83. Harry Howard, "The U.N. Commission of Investigation Concerning Greek Frontier Incidents," *Department of State Bulletin* 17 (6 July 1987): 14–25. The U.N. Ethridge Report, May 1947, found little evidence to support Greek allegations (NARS, 501.BC-Greece/4-847). Furthermore, a U.S. intelligence agent in Greece, Thomas Karamesinis, reported late in 1946 that "proofs" gathered thus far by the Greek government could not be regarded as "conclusive" (NARS, 868.00/8-1046, U.S. embassy [Athens] report no. 3010, 8 October 1946).

84. G. M. Alexander, *The Prelude to the Truman Doctrine: British Policy in Greece, 1944–1947* (Oxford, 1982), 200, 216, 223–24, 230–31.

85. A State and War Departments memorandum forwarded to President Truman, 10 October 1946, stressed the need to safeguard Greece's *territorial* and political integrity (NARS, 868.00/10-1546). A State Department assessment of 6 December 1946 of Soviet objectives vis-

Yet, at times, more reserved assessments were voiced. Labour Foreign Minister Ernest Bevin, for instance, held the view in late 1946 that Yugoslav public statements for the unification of Macedonia were for domestic consumption and in no way constituted an imminent threat to Greece's territorial integrity. Later, however, when a Soviet threat to the Straits began to develop, the Foreign Office, and subsequently the State Department, assumed that gaining control of Macedonia and Thrace, along with the Straits, constituted part of a well-designed Soviet plan, the ultimate objective of which was control of the Aegean. Only the timing of the Soviet initiative was in doubt. Thus, the Macedonian question gradually emerged as a pawn in the global contest between East and West.[86] It is interesting to note that the Turks also expressed deep concern over rumors about the establishment of a unified Macedonian state that would include Greek Macedonia. In the words of a Turkish diplomat, a Slavo-Macedonian state, with Thessaloniki included, would reduce Greece to impotence and cut Turkey off from Europe. In such a case, he concluded, "if there were no Greece, there would be no Turkey."[87]

The State Department took the view that the crux of the Macedonian problem was nothing less than the maintenance of the territorial integrity of Greece itself. Although the United States could have no say over the unification of the Bulgarian and Yugoslav parts of Macedonia, the preservation of Greece's frontiers against irredentist claims by its northern neighbors justified "all possible and appropriate steps" by the U.S. government.[88]

Such concern was not without some basis. The Macedonian unification scheme that had emerged in the last months of 1944 in the abortive

---

à-vis Greece included among those objectives the overthrow of the Greek government *and* the detachment of Greek Macedonia (NARS, 760H.68/12-646). This theme recurs in many State Department assessments throughout 1947–48.

86. NARS, 868.00/7-2147, aide-mémoire, Bevin to Marshall, 21 July 1946; FO 371/72241 X/02621, British embassy (Athens), 139/11/48, 12 March 1948; FO 371/72241 X/PO2621, British embassy (Belgrade), 217/2/48, 15 March 1948; FO 371/72192 X/PO2727, British embassy (Belgrade), 195/28.8.1948, 28 August 1948.

87. NARS, 868.00/7-2147, Ambassador of Turkey to France Menemencioglu, in conversation with his British colleague Duff (British Embassy [Washington] to U.S. State Department, aide-mémoire G58/47, 21 July 1947). For more on Turkish apprehensions about the prospect of a Communist Slav Macedonian state, see NARS, 868.00/11-2946, U.S. embassy (Ankara), dispatch A 296, 29 November 1946.

88. NARS, 868.00/7-2147, aide-mémoire, 28 July 1947.

Yugoslav-Bulgarian negotiations for a South Slav federation, resurfaced with the conclusion of the Tito-Dimitrov agreements at Bled and Evxinograd (1 August and 27 November 1947, respectively).[89] Despite certain nuances as to the timing and sequence of steps for implementing the agreements, the fact remained that the leader of Bulgaria had committed his country to the cession of Pirin Macedonia to Yugoslavia. In making these agreements, Dimitrov relinquished all future interest in Macedonian affairs, along with the last portion of Macedonian land, in exchange for a federation arrangement with Yugoslavia and the return of the "Western Bulgarian regions" annexed by Yugoslavia after the First World War.

There is no doubt that at Bled an agreement was reached on the fate of Greek Macedonia as well. No concrete details were revealed at the time, nor have any become known since. Two years later, however, in 1949, Tito stated publicly that the case of Greek Macedonia had been examined and that the two leaders had decided to "definitely solve the Macedonian question *as a whole;* the Macedonian people not only in the Vardar, but in Pirin, *and Aegean Macedonia,* would receive their rights and they alone will decide on their future."[90]

Despite the fate of the South Slav federation, the signing of the agreement was a turning point in the history of the Macedonian question. Yugoslavia had finally secured a contractual agreement from Bulgaria that it was to be the master of the coveted land. But what was the position of the KKE leaders on this triangular question? There was an inexplicable silence at the time that has been maintained to this day. Was Zahariadis aware of the Yugoslav-Bulgarian deliberations throughout 1947? Was he consulted by Tito or Dimitrov? And if so, what were his reactions or his commitments, if any? His opponents suspected the

89. Kofos, *Nationalism and Communism,* 161–63. Texts of the Yugoslav-Bulgarian agreements, signed at Bled and Evxinograd, were published by Slobodan Nešović, *Bledski Sporazumi: Tito-Dimitrov, 1947* (The Bled agreements: Tito-Dimitrov, 1947) (Ljubljana, 1979). Nešović claims to have published "all" the agreements, although this author has privileged information of Bulgarian provenance about a secret protocol concerning Greek Macedonia.

90. *Borba,* 3 August 1949 (emphasis added). Two months prior to the agreements, Dimitrov told two Western journalists that in due course all three parts of Macedonia would be united within the framework of Yugoslavia (FO 371/72192/ X/PO2727, British embassy [Belgrade], no. 217/22/48, 28 August 1948). During the Tenth Plenum of the Central Committee of the Communist Party of Bulgaria in August 1946, Dimitrov had declared: "It is not right to use the phrases 'Vardarska Makedonija,' 'Pirinska Makedonija,' and 'Egejska Makedonija.' There are not three Macedonias. There is only one Macedonia" (quoted in Nešović, *Bledski Sporazumi,* 55).

worst—that he had tacitly consented to the arrangements—but have produced no proof to support their suspicions. The question resurfaced after the publication of certain documents from the KKE archives in the Athenian daily *Avgi* in 1979.[91]

On 14 April 1947, Zahariadis, who was in Yugoslavia, along with part of the politburo of the KKE, sent Vaphiadis his instructions outlining the strategic objective of the struggle:

> Events show that the region which constitutes the weakest and the most important point for the enemy, which offers the people's democratic movement the most favorable politico-social prerequisites, is Macedonia and Thrace, with Thessaloniki at the center. Thus, under these conditions, a basic objective of DAG today is the occupation of Thessaloniki, which would bring a decisive change in the situation and would solve our entire problem.[92]

Zahariadis presented the same views in the memorandum he sent to Tito following their talks on 22 April. He added that "northern Greece for 'monarcho-fascism' was its weakest—and the most important—point from a social, economic, political, *national,* military and geographical viewpoint." Consequently, DAG was planning to concentrate its main strike in this region. The final objective was to secure a territorial base for the establishment of a nucleus for a "Free Greece."[93]

The plan was approved by Tito and subsequently by the Soviet leadership. It was endorsed by the Third Plenum of the Central Committee of the KKE in October 1947. The plan was discussed extensively with the leadership of the CPY, which would bear most of the burden for its logistical support. Whether it corresponded to Tito's wishes for a South Slav federation and a unified Macedonian state is still a matter for speculation. The timing of the discussions between Zahariadis and the Yugoslav leaders, however, coincided with the Yugoslav-Bulgarian negotiations that led to the Bled Agreement. Furthermore, Zahariadis' reference, in his memorandum to Tito, to the *national* factor as a point of weakness in the Greek government's hold on northern Greece—a reference missing in the instructions he sent to Vaphiadis—should be interpreted as refer-

91. *Avgi*, December 1979–January 1980.
92. *Avgi*, 11 December 1979.
93. *Avgi*, 9 December 1979 (emphasis added).

ring to the question of national minorities. To speculate further, without more concrete evidence, is precarious. Nevertheless, the coincidence in the timing of the discussions of the two disparate plans—one for the establishment of a "free Greek state" in northern Greece, the other for a unified Macedonian state in the context of a South Slav federation—leads to the assumption that Zahariadis could have had at least some knowledge of the aims of the two Balkan leaders.

Meanwhile, the rapid deterioration of Soviet-Yugoslav relations did not augur well for the revolution in Greece. When those relations reached the point of crisis in late June 1948, Zahariadis sided with the Soviet Union. A side effect of these developments was that Yugoslav Macedonia became the focal point of the Macedonian question. Bulgaria lost no time in profiting from the Stalin-Tito split. Statements by Bulgarian leaders were carefully phrased at first. They denied neither the existence of "Macedonians" nor the ideal of a "united Macedonian state." But now, as in the past, these terms meant different things to those who were working toward different and at times contradictory political ends. The "Macedonians" were now linked by Sofia propagandists to the Bulgarian nation. Continued references to a "united Macedonian state" within a South Slav federation certainly was not the concept envisaged at Bled; instead, they brought forth recollections of the 1924 Comintern scheme for a Bulgarian-oriented independent Macedonia. In the late months of 1948, however, a long-term solution to the Macedonian question was not the major preoccupation of the Bulgarian leaders, who were hard at work trying to eradicate four years of "Macedonian" infiltration of Bulgarian Macedonia before counterattacking by reintroducing Bulgarian nationalism among the population of the People's Republic of Macedonia.[94]

Such was the situation in his immediate vicinity when Zahariadis sought to seize full control of NOF and the Slavo-Macedonians at home. New documents reveal that in the second half of 1948 the KKE, having already sided with the Cominform, lost no time in removing the pro-Tito Slavo-Macedonians from the leadership of NOF and from important posts in regional KKE organizations. In a single stroke, the KKE leadership freed itself not only of avowed Titoists but also of extremist Slavo-Macedonians, who maintained close relations with the People's Republic of Macedonia. Nevertheless, instead of attempting to stamp out "Mace-

94. Kofos, *Nationalism and Communism*, 188–91.

donian" nationalism and consolidate the Slavophone element within the Greek revolutionary movement, Zahariadis revealed his weakness by going in the opposite direction. Having placed trusted Slavophones at the head of NOF, he initiated a series of measures aimed at raising the level of indoctrination and education of Slavophone peasants and *andartes* in the concept of the "Macedonian" nation.[95] This was a policy full of contradictions, dictated by international developments and the specific requirements of the armed struggle. Imitating the Bulgarian Communists, Zahariadis tried to profit—or at least not to lose—from the turn of Macedonian politics. His own gamble came late in January 1949.

The announcement of the KKE's Fifth Plenum resolution, passed on 31 January 1949, and particularly its reference to the Macedonian question, sent shock waves through the world's chanceries, forced the fence-sitters among Greek politicians and the Greek public to reappraise their attitudes toward the KKE, and hardened the Greek government's policy toward the KKE, an effect that survived the end of the civil war by decades. Worse yet, it made collaboration with Tito's Yugoslavia almost impossible. Internal criticism of the KKE's policy came into the open immediately after the defeat in August 1949 and continued until Zahariadis' expulsion from the leadership of the party.[96]

Briefly stated, the new party line, as presented in a series of documents and public statements, was the reintroduction of the 1924 platform for an independent Macedonian state probably within a Balkan Communist federation. But whereas the 1924 decision could be taken merely as a statement of intent, its reintroduction in 1949 appeared to be an action program for a revolution in full swing. Certainly, the full extent of this major policy shift could not have been and is not reflected in the carefully worded Central Committee resolution. To understand the policy behind it, the historian would have to examine all official statements made at the time (including those of the KKE-controlled NOF), know the measures taken by the KKE leadership to implement the party's decision, and be cognizant of the criticism voiced from within the party hierarchy after the end of the armed struggle and while Zahariadis was still at the helm. Undoubtedly, the detailed accounts and documents released in recent years by pro-Tito Slavo-Macedonians give us a better perspective, although caution is needed for points of omission.

95. Keramitziev-Gotse letter.
96. See 6 *Olomeleia* and 7 *Olomeleia*.

The basic, much-quoted texts are the resolution of the Fifth Plenum of the Central Committee of the KKE (31 January), the decision of the Executive Council of NOF (4 February), KKE and NOF "disclaimers" (broadcast by Radio Free Greece on 8 and 9 March), and the resolution of the Second Congress of NOF (end of March).[97] These texts clearly indicate that after the successful conclusion of the revolution, the Slavo-Macedonians were to be allowed to establish their own Macedonian state within a Balkan Communist federation. The fact that, in Zahariadis' presence, the Second Plenum of the Executive Council of NOF stated that the Second NOF Congress would announce "the union of Macedonia into a complete, independent and equal Macedonian state within the People's Democratic Federation of the Balkan Peoples," gave the Fifth Plenum's resolution a sense of immediacy. It was this expectation of an immediate declaration of the establishment of a Macedonian state that caused anxiety in Western capitals and alarm in Athens. Once again, the interaction of perceptions and realities came into play, confusing contemporaries.

Western diplomats saw the KKE resolution in terms of a wider Soviet move aimed primarily at undermining Tito. The reference by the KKE to a Balkan federation, hitherto a popular theme among Bulgarian and Yugoslav leaders only, led Western diplomats to think that there was a plan to encircle Tito's Yugoslavia from the south. What was difficult to ascertain was whether this scheme, to which many Western observers gave credence, was merely a theoretical policy objective or was meant for immediate application. If the latter was the case, there was an imminent threat of direct involvement by the Soviet Union in Balkan affairs.[98] Certainly, there were also more sober appraisals that suggested that the international situation offered no indication to justify such a Soviet initiative. It is more probable that the Soviets thought that the psychological

97. Kofos, *Nationalism and Communism*, 177–84. Texts of the Fifth Plenum resolution and relevant discussion in the Central Committee of the KKE in *5 Olomeleia tis KE tou KKE, 30–31 Genari 1949* (Fifth Plenum of the CC of the KKE, 30–31 January 1949) (June 1949), specifically page 16 of the document; Zahariadis' report, 29–31, 37–38; Porphyroyenis' qualified approval, 58–59. Most of the documents and extensive commentary were published in the newspaper *Pros ti Niki* from March to August 1949.

98. Typical of British concern was a Foreign Office minute: "The creation of an autonomous/independent Macedonian state would solve Soviet problems. Salonica would be offered to Tito's successors, and Bulgaria would get E. Macedonia and W. Thrace. It is clear, therefore, that we must do all possible to prevent Macedonian autonomy" (FO 371/78396/18, 17 March 1949).

impact on internal Yugoslav politics would be sufficient to cause Tito's overthrow.

The Greek government and media resorted to alarmist assessments. The KKE announcement signified to them the public acknowledgment of what the government camp had suspected all along, namely that the KKE was prepared to cede Greek Macedonia to a Slav-dominated Macedonian state. They believed that, in order for the KKE to have reached this decision, Zahariadis must have secured solid assurances of increased support from the Soviet Union, which was not the case. Faced with this imminent threat to Macedonia, it was no wonder that the Greek media interpreted the government's anxieties in a sensational way. This served the government objectives in two ways: by projecting an image of the KKE as antinational and by strengthening its argument for increased economic and military aid from the Allies.[99]

On the Yugoslav side, understandably, there was deep concern about the KKE's pronounced intentions. As early as July 1948, the Yugoslav Communists had been aware of the KKE's decision to place the Slavo-Macedonians under its firm control. But they had kept quiet. Even when the pro-Tito leadership of NOF was removed, there were no public recriminations. Moreover, the decision of the Fifth Plenum was commented upon favorably for acknowledging the Slavo-Macedonians' right of self-determination. The only criticism it evoked was that it was untimely, since it was linked to the Cominform-inspired Balkan federation. Thus, although the Yugoslavs restrained themselves from publicly condemning the KKE's position on the Macedonian question, they also saw it as part of the orchestrated Cominform drive against their party leadership.[100]

Meanwhile, the Bulgarian government-controlled media gave limited coverage to the KKE's decision. They showed considerable self-restraint, moreover, in identifying Greek and Bulgarian views with a more general

99. This is clearly depicted in the report of the Chief of the Imperial Staff, Gen. William Slim, after his visit to Greece (9–10 March): "It may be part of the 1949 Cominform policy in Greece to resurrect the idea of an 'Independent Macedonia,' comprising . . . a large part of Northern Greece including Salonica." That would result in "an increased movement of Communist trained forces across the frontier from Bulgaria." The need to offer additional aid to the Greek national army was the logical conclusion (FO 371/7834/26, "Report on Greece," 16 March 1949).

100. Moje Pijade, "On the Question of a Balkan Federation," quoted in Kofos, *Nationalism and Communism,* 180–81. This article was originally published in *Borba,* 6 March 1949.

Soviet plan. Certainly, the Bulgarians viewed the KKE's position positively, insofar as it offered support for their own interpretation of a solution to the Macedonian question.[101]

On the issue of Soviet involvement in the formulation of the KKE's new Macedonian policy, there was little doubt in the West—and certainly not in Yugoslavia—that Moscow was the real instigator of the decision. What was not known at the time was that there had been an encounter in Bucharest in March 1949 between Baranov, Cominform's liaison officer with the KKE, and the KKE troika, Ioannidis, Roussos, and Partsalidis. Baranov expressed surprise and questioned the wisdom of the KKE in raising the Macedonian question at such an inopportune moment. Partsalidis confronted Zahariadis with Baranov's remarks during the Seventh Plenum of the Central Committee of the KKE meeting in exile in 1950. Zahariadis did not dispute Partsalidis' revelations but sought to defend *his* decision, as a tactical move intended to keep the Slavo-Macedonians on his side. This debate between the two KKE leaders certainly placed the alleged Soviet participation in the decisions of the Fifth Plenum in a different light. But it was not made public, remaining a privileged communication for members of the Central Committee only.[102]

The worldwide interest in the KKE/NOF declarations created a climate that party leaders most likely had not anticipated. To judge by subsequent statements, it appears that there was consensus among KKE leaders that Zahariadis had overextended himself in his public pronouncement of the new policy. It is probably for this reason that the Second NOF Congress avoided any specific reference to an independent Macedonian state, reverting to traditional declarations of principle that, with a stretch of the imagination, could be interpreted either way.[103]

This "retraction" misled no one at the time. The KKE continued to popularize the idea of eventual self-determination for the Slavo-Macedonians among party cadres and the Slavo-Macedonians at large. Inquisitive Greek party cadres were told that self-determination (including the right of cessation) was a Marxist-Leninist principle, but they were

---

101. The Bulgarians were extremely reserved in their commentary on the KKE's Macedonian decision (Kofos, *Nationalism and Communism*, 180).

102. Statement by Partsalidis, 7 *Olomeleia*, 38.

103. Kofos, *Nationalism and Communism*, 182.

also assured that the final form and extent of an independent Macedonian state would depend on circumstances and the outcome of a plebiscite.[104]

Meanwhile, a series of specific measures was introduced. Slavo-Macedonians loyal to the KKE leadership assumed high posts in the provisional government and commands in DAG and the regional Macedonian organizations. More important, however, was the fact that by the spring of 1949 the Communist Organization for Aegean Macedonia had been formed, ostensibly to operate within the KKE but, in fact, to function as a separate party organization for the Slavo-Macedonians. There was no explanation for this decision other than that it was a first step toward creating an autonomous Slavo-Macedonian party organization.[105]

The British and Americans were relieved by the KKE's disclaimers, which alleviated their sense of crisis. They saw this as an indication that the Soviet Union was not contemplating a major new initiative in the Balkans, which would have required a reappraisal of their own strategic requirements. Freed from the fear that the Soviets and the KKE intended to move immediately, the Americans and the British shifted their attention to the creation of a climate in which to seek a rapproachment with Tito. Such a rapprochement would have indirectly relieved the pressure on the Greek government to crush the revolution.[106]

The Greek government did not share their views, however. The KKE's verbal "whitewashing" of the initial KKE/NOF declaration was hardly taken into consideration by the authorities in Athens. The incident had created both widespread anguish and exultation. Both, if properly exploited, could be beneficial to the government's aims. On the domestic front, condemnation of the KKE's policy by former supporters or sympathizers—as, for example, Alexander Svolos—added cogency to the gov-

---

104. The party's policy was popularized in the pages of *Pros ti Niki* (March–August 1949). In his strong criticism of Zahariadis' Macedonian policy, Partsalidis revealed that, following the Fifth Plenum, the Slavo-Macedonians disseminated rumors that "the borders of the independent Macedonian state would start from Mount Olympus, with Thessaloniki as capital, while we remained silent, thus increasing confusion" (7 *Olomeleia*, 38).

105. Kofos, *Nationalism and Communism*, 182; Ajanovski, *Egejski Buri*, 378–89; Kirjazovski, *Narodno Oslododitelniot Front*, 303–12.

106. Elisabeth Barker, "Yugoslav Policy Towards Greece, 1947–1949"; and Jože Pirjevec, "The Tito-Stalin Split and the End of the Civil War in Greece," in *Studies in the History of the Greek Civil War, 1945–1949*, ed. Lars Baerentzen, John O. Iatrides, and Ole L. Smith (Copenhagen: Museum Tusculanum, 1987), 286–94, 312–15.

ernment's appeal to all Greeks to rally around to safeguard the country's territorial integrity, not merely its social system. It was a call for a pan-Hellenic *jihad*. Under the circumstances, even the most severe measures against opponents could be justified. In practice, the government made it a capital offense for any person to so much as identify himself with the KKE, which was regarded as tantamount to approving of the Fifth Plenum resolution. The mandatory penalty for this was death.[107]

On the international level, the Greek government sought to magnify the potential threat not only to its own territory but to the entire Balkan area. Early in April, the Coordinating Council of Ministers, presided over by King Paul, drew up a detailed memorandum of the government's assessments in the presence of Gen. Alexander Papagos. According to this scenario, it was the avowed intention of the Soviet Union to step up support for Greek and Slavo-Macedonian guerrillas in Greece and Yugoslav Macedonia in order to place Greece and Yugoslavia under its control. With the Balkans under Soviet domination, the threat to Turkey and Italy would increase significantly. The Greek government proposed that the West, in the event of a Soviet attack on Yugoslavia, should consider occupying Albania in order to hold it as a hostage for exchange; that it should encourage Turkey to contribute more actively to averting the Soviet threat; and that it should provide aid to Greece not only for military purposes but also to facilitate its rapid reconstruction.[108]

It should be added that similar assessments were made at the time by British and American officials, who reached the conclusion that the Greek government and army should be bolstered materially in order to face a growing and potentially grave threat. In the event, this threat did not materialize. Nonetheless, augmented aid was supplied to the Greek national army in time for its final drive against DAG in the summer of 1949.[109]

As for Yugoslavia, even though Tito tried to keep his bridges open, the KKE's handling of the Macedonian question and, more important, its efforts to turn the Slavo-Macedonians onto an anti-Tito course, finally

107. FO 371/7834/35, "Brighter Prospects for Greece," report dated 29 March 1949; NARS, 868.00/3.3049, U.S. embassy (Athens) report, 30 March 1949. On the reaction of northern Greeks, see FO 371/78366/36, British consulate (Thessaloniki) report, March–April 1949. On the reaction of the Greek press, see FO 371/78396/10. For Minister of Public Order Rendis' statement, see FO 371/78398/4, 3 April 1949.
108. The full text is in Kontis, *I Angloamerikaniki Politiki*, 465–72.
109. Ibid., 389–90.

raised a clear security problem for the Yugoslavs in their southern province. This was a matter that required drastic measures, even if this meant going against ideological principles and comradely *solidarnost*. That it was difficult for the Yugoslavs to end their support of the Greek Communists is evidenced by the fact that for almost a year, despite certain feelers from Western capitals and even from Athens, they had refrained from reaching any understanding with the Greek government.[110] Finally, however, in July, the border was closed to the *andartes*. What Zahariadis said about the *pisoplato chtypima* (stab in the back) by the Yugoslavs against DAG units has now been shown to have been entirely inaccurate and unfair.[111]

The military battles of the civil war ended in the Vitsi and Grammos mountains in August 1949. From the beginning, the Macedonian question, in both its macro and micro aspects, had influenced the course of the Communist revolution in Greece. At times, it had been advantageous to the Communist side. In the end, however, it proved to be a catalyst for disaster.

Nearly five decades after the critical 1940s, there are still significant blank spots in our knowledge of events connected with the Macedonian question, gaps that prevent us from making a complete assessment of this important issue on civil-war developments. In recent years, however, certain confusing aspects of the question have been clarified: the wartime Yugoslav policy objectives toward Greek Macedonia; the role of the Slavo-Macedonians; and the attitudes and policies of the KKE toward Yugoslav objectives and the Slavo-Macedonians. Some progress has been made in understanding Tito's behavior prior to and during the *Dekemvriana,* but information is still inconclusive on Yugoslav policymaking concerning a possible military intervention in Greek Macedonia during October-November 1944, which was ostensibly in support of ELAS but more probably aimed at creating conditions favorable to a future Yugoslav claim on the region.

110. On the initial Yugoslav reaction, see Pijade, as quoted in Kofos, *Nationalism and Communism,* 180–81.

111. The Sixth Plenum adopted Zahariadis' contention that Yugoslav troops, along with Greek army units, attacked DAG units during the Kaimaktsalan operations early in August 1949. See N. Zahariadis, "To Stileto tou Tito Chypta Pisoplata ti Laiki Dimokratiki Ellada" (Tito's dagger stabs the People's Democratic Greece in the back), *Syllogi Ergon,* April 1953, reprinted from Cominform's *For a Lasting Peace for a People's Democracy,* 1 August 1949.

New data have now revealed, beyond reasonable doubt, NOF's relationship as an appendage of the Communist Party of Macedonia for nearly two years, 1945–46. The terms regulating the collaboration of the Slavo-Macedonians and the KKE and DAG until the split between the KKE and the CPY are now fairly well established. What remains uncertain, however, are Zahariadis' obligations to Tito, at the time of the KKE-NOF agreement, on the future settlement of the Macedonian question.

Similarly, there is uncertainty in connection with the Tito-Dimitrov Bled Agreement. There is no doubt that Greek Macedonia was the subject of an arrangement reached between the two leaders. But no information has been revealed concerning the steps by which it was to have become part of a unified Macedonian state. And, more important, it remains uncertain whether Zahariadis had been consulted or was aware of the plans of the two Balkan leaders. There was a strange silence on the part of the KKE on this subject at the time the agreement was concluded. This silence continued even after the split with Tito and has been kept by all sides. Although it matters little for general assessments, this particular moment in the history of the Macedonian question remains a tantalizing enigma.

The most criticized turning point of the KKE's Macedonian policy—the decision of the Fifth Plenum of the Central Committee in January 1949—has been reviewed and anathematized by all concerned, including, in subsequent years, by the KKE itself. Opponents saw in it the diktat of the Kremlin in the context of Soviet efforts to undermine Tito. Supporters, with Zahariadis in the lead, tried to explain it in terms of the armed struggle (attract the Slavo-Macedonians and stamp out Tito's subversive aims in Greek Macedonia); in other words, they presented it as their own initiative. No serious analyst of the period has put much credence in these weak explanations as the basis for such a major decision. Here again, there is no documentation on the actual Soviet role. Strangely, Greek Communist leaders critical of Stalin have given no convincing evidence either. On the contrary, there is now enough evidence that the importance of the Slavo-Macedonians within DAG had grown in the last year of the civil war to the point that their continued association and loyalty to the KKE's cause were sine qua non for the future course of the revolution. Was it possible that Zahariadis, in assessing the overall anti-Tito attitude of the Soviet bloc, the reversal of the Macedonian policy of the Communist Party of Bulgaria, and the fact that his own party had been condemned by its adversaries for "treason" on this sensitive issue, underestimated the psychological reverberations and took it upon himself—without having been requested by the Kremlin to do so—to introduce the new policy in the Central Committee plenum? This is still only an assumption. But the actions of the Soviet Union and Bulgaria during those two critical months—February and March 1949— tend to support the view that Zahariadis was not coerced into aligning his party with a general Soviet scheme for Macedonia. Unless further evidence is produced, the responsibility for the decision must be placed squarely on the KKE leaders who signed the Fifth Plenum resolution.

Even with such gaps in our knowledge, we have reached a point where our vision is clearer. We have come closer to the realities of this intricate and elusive problem, thanks to newly available data and to a less polemical approach to the events of the 1940s. What, then, is our present assessment of the Macedonian question as a factor in the civil war?

Throughout the 1940s, the Macedonian question was basically shaped by forces and interests outside Greece. Neither of the two protagonists in the Greek civil war—the KKE and the Greek government—had any interest in disrupting the status quo in Macedonia. But the Macedonian question had its own dynamism, which developed over time and was utilized by the Greek duelists. It was inevitable that the two issues—the fate of Macedonia and the course of the revolution in Greece—would converge, interact, and shape the destinies of both. Both sides tried to benefit from this situation militarily, politically, and psychologically.

The international aspects of the problem were no less intriguing. Given the fluidity of the situation in the Balkans during the last two years of the war against Germany, and the uncertainties that existed at the time of liberation and until the concretization of spheres of influence, it is no wonder that the Macedonian question seriously affected the strategic conceptions and tactical options of the Great Powers.

The real protagonist of the Macedonian question was Yugoslavia. The policies, and the power and security perceptions of its leaders, as well as the need to firmly entrench this new nation—which was christened in 1944 "Macedonian"—had a profound effect on wartime and postwar developments in Greece and in the Balkans as a whole. In sum, from 1943 to 1949, Yugoslavia's Macedonian interests and needs coincided perfectly with Yugoslav political options vis-à-vis the Communist movement in Greece.

GREECE, 1939–1952:
A Chronology of Political Events

1939

13 April
Following the Italian occupation of Albania, Britain and France offer Greece guarantees of territorial integrity.

September
At the outbreak of the Second World War, Greece remains neutral while maintaining close relations with Britain.

1940

1 July
Italian dictator Benito Mussolini accuses Greece of allowing the British navy to use Greek territorial waters to attack Italian ships and threatens to take military action.

15 August
The Greek cruiser *Helli,* in the port of Tinos during religious festivities, is sunk by an Italian submarine.

28 October
Following an ultimatum, which the Greek Prime Minister and dictator Ioannis Metaxas rejects on the spot, Italian forces in Albania attack Greece. By 8 November, the Greek army, commanded by Gen. Alexander Papagos, has driven the Italians out of Greece and is pursuing them deep into Albanian territory. Heavy winter and exhaustion produce a stalemate.

1941

29 January
Death of Metaxas. Alexander Koryzis, a prominent Athenian banker, is appointed Prime Minister by King George II.

February–March
About 50,000 British and allied troops land in Greece to reinforce the Greek forces in the north, in anticipation of a German spring offensive.

6 April
German mechanized forces, having crushed Yugoslavia's defenses, attack Greek positions in Macedonia (Metaxas Line) and advance toward Thessaloniki, while the bulk of the Greek troops continue to face the Italians in Albania.

21 April	Without authorization, elements of the Greek army under Gen. George Tsolakoglou surrender to the Germans. When Koryzis commits suicide (18 April), the new Prime Minister, Emmanuel Tsouderos, and his cabinet flee with the king and Crown Prince Paul to Crete and then to Egypt, where a government-in-exile is established.
27 April	German troops occupy Athens.
28 April	The first collaborationist government under General Tsolakoglou is established. Tsolakoglou is replaced in November 1942 by Prof. Constantine Logothetopoulos and, in April 1943, by John Rallis, a Metaxas protégé. The Rallis government forms "Security Battalions," which, armed by the Germans, hunt down resistance fighters, especially leftists. Proper punishment of collaborators thus emerges as a highly emotional issue under the occupation.
20–30 May	German parachutists defeat Greek and British troops defending Crete, completing the occupation of Greece. The Germans allow Italy and Bulgaria to have their own zones of occupation. Especially brutal is the Bulgarian administration of Greek Thrace, which is treated as annexed territory, forcing many Greeks to flee to other parts of the country. Although successful, the airborne operation against Crete costs the invaders their only airborne division, which is virtually destroyed. No such parachute operations are attempted by the Germans again. The resistance encountered by Hitler's Balkan campaign forces a delay in the launching of Germany's invasion of the Soviet Union and contributes to the Nazis' subsequent defeat on the eastern front.
5 July	First reported act of armed resistance: a group of demobilized soldiers fire on a German patrol outside Kozani. Other sporadic acts of spontaneous resistance follow. The German, Italian, and Bulgarian occupation authorities respond with mass arrests, executions, and the destruction of entire villages.
September	The Communist Party (KKE), joined by several small leftist groups, forms the National Liberation Front (EAM), which becomes the largest and most effective resistance organization. Its military arm, the National Popular Liberation Army (ELAS), fields its first bands in May 1942. By the end of the occupation, EAM boasts at least half a million supporters and ELAS has 40,000–50,000 men and women under arms.
October	Establishment of the National Republican Greek League (EDES), ostensibly under Nikolaos Plastiras but actually commanded by Col. Napoleon Zervas, who takes the field in June 1942 and operates almost entirely in Epirus. Gradually taking a pro-monarchy stand, EDES reaches a peak strength of 12,000–15,000.
Winter 1941–42	The disruption of farming and breakdown of transportation, the expropriation of food supplies by the occupation authorities, and the allied blockade of Greece as enemy-controlled territory produce severe famine conditions in urban centers, especially Athens, where tens of thousands die of starvation and malnutrition.

1942

29 September   A British Special Operations Executive (SOE) team under Col. E. C. W. Myers and his deputy, Col. C. M. Woodhouse, parachutes into Greece. Originally on a sabotage mission, the team remains in the Greek mountains and serves as liaison between Allied authorities in Cairo and the Greek resistance organizations. British military and political authorities seek to foster and control resistance activity in occupied Greece.

25 November   Destruction of the Gorgopotamos railroad bridge on the Athens-Thessaloniki line by Myers's SOE team supported by ELAS and EDES contingents.

1943

March   Greek army units, reconstituted in the Middle East and comprising three battalions, mutiny (there were also small naval formations). British authorities restore order, and senior Greek army and navy officers are replaced, as are several members of the Tsouderos cabinet. In a public message, King George announces that, following his return to Greece, he will "base himself on the will of the people and will follow the opinion which the people will express freely on all questions concerning them."

April–May   Systematic arrest and deportation of Greek Jews by the German authorities. By August, virtually all of Greece's Jews (approximately 75,000) have been sent to their death in extermination centers.

May   ELAS forces attack and dissolve a smaller resistance organization (EKKA) in an apparent move to neutralize groups hostile to KKE/EAM. Under British pressure, ELAS accepts the "National Bands Agreement," pledging to cooperate with other resistance organizations and to submit to Allied authority. ELAS assists in the execution of Operation Animals, intended to mislead the Germans into expecting major Allied landings in Greece.

21 June   Myers's SOE team destroys the Asopos viaduct as part of Operation Animals.

4 July   King George announces in a radio message that within six months after the country's liberation a new constituent assembly will decide all major national issues. While not explicit on the monarchy's future, this statement is viewed by most Greeks as a promise that the king would respect the popular will on the question of his return. Anti-monarchy sentiment continues to grow in occupied Greece and among the Greek armed forces in the Middle East.

August   Representatives of the major resistance groups are flown to Cairo for talks with the Tsouderos government that could bridge the gap between the leftist-dominated resistance and the bourgeois parties represented by the government. The talks collapse when Tsouderos refuses to discuss demands that he expand his government to include resistance groups and commit himself to a plebiscite on the monarchy's future. ELAS attacks on rival groups resume.

October

The Italian army division in northwestern Greece, which surrendered to the Greek resistance forces and British liaison officers when Rome's Fascist government capitulated, is disarmed by ELAS, and its heavy weapons are used in attacks on EDES. The fighting stops only when the German occupation forces launch a major operation directed primarily against ELAS.

1944

16 March

EAM announces the establishment of the "Political Committee of National Liberation" (PEEA) in the Greek mountains. This move is generally perceived as a challenge to the Tsouderos government.

April

Mutinies among the Greek armed forces in Egypt, which declare their support for PEEA, are crushed by British troops. After a sweeping purge of agitators and leftists, a new "Third" or "Mountain" Brigade is formed under strongly anticommunist leadership and distinguishes itself at the battle of Rimini (thus also "Rimini Brigade").

24 April

George Papandreou, the Liberal politician who recently escaped from occupied Greece, is named Prime Minister following a major cabinet crisis.

17–20 May

The Lebanon Conference, organized by Papandreou under British supervision, brings together representatives of political factions and resistance groups. It produces the *Lebanon Charter,* which calls for the creation of a broadly based "Government of National Unity," reorganization of the Greek armed forces, and unification of resistance bands under the new government. Although there is no specific agreement on the central issue of the monarchy's future, Papandreou declares on 12 June that the king will not return until a plebiscite has decided the matter.

26 July

A ten-man Soviet military mission under Col. Gregori Popov lands near ELAS headquarters in Thessaly. While probably an intelligence-gathering unit, it may also have brought political advice to the KKE leadership, which soon agrees to join the Papandreou government.

26 September

The Caserta Agreement places ELAS and EDES under the command of a British officer, Lt. Gen. Ronald Scobie, and strictly confines their operations to specified areas and tasks in anticipation of liberation.

9 October

The Churchill-Stalin "spheres-of-influence" agreement consigns

Greece to Britain's zone of responsibility. The result of prolonged discussions, and over American reservations, this understanding is already in effect when German and Bulgarian troops withdraw from Greece in September-October.

18 October — Papandreou's government and Allied representatives arrive in Athens escorted by a small British military contingent.

9 November — On orders from Papandreou and Scobie, and over the objections of the EAM ministers, the "Third Brigade" arrives in Athens from Italy in an apparent attempt to counterbalance ELAS's numerical superiority across the country.

17–18 November — At ELAS headquarters in Lamia, military commanders and KKE leaders discuss possible countermeasures in anticipation of government plans to demobilize and disarm all resistance groups. Although some participants speak in favor of opposing such plans by force, no decision is made.

2 December — The EAM ministers resign to protest Papandreou's plan to disarm and demobilize the resistance bands and replace them with a new national army. The disbanding of ELAS, which remained in control of much of the countryside, would have deprived EAM and the KKE of the powerful political leverage they enjoyed after liberation. When General Scobie announces that demobilization will go into effect on 10 December, EAM declares a general strike for 4 December and calls for a mass demonstration in Athens on 3 December.

3 December — The EAM-organized demonstration is fired upon by the police at Constitution Square, and scores are killed or wounded. The violence soon escalates into savage fighting in Athens, which rages all through December. It is finally suppressed by British troops rushed in from Italy.

25 December — Prime Minister Winston Churchill and Foreign Secretary Anthony Eden fly to Athens, where a conference brings together representatives of the warring factions. Although agreement on the key political issues proves impossible, the conference leads to a truce and to the acceptance of Archbishop Damaskinos as regent, pending resolution of the monarchy question.

1945

12 February — The Varkiza Agreement formally ends the violence and provides the framework for political compromise. It calls for an early plebiscite on the monarchy question, followed by elections for a constituent assembly, the immediate disbanding and disarming of ELAS (EDES had been attacked and destroyed by ELAS during the December crisis), a new national army, and amnesty for political crimes. A government of moderates and centrists, but no Communists, is formed by Nikolaos Plastiras, who is named Prime Minister on 4 January.

8 April   Attacked by the Right, and having failed to establish an effective government, Plastiras resigns. He is succeeded by Adm. Petros Voulgaris, a onetime republican with strong anticommunist credentials who is favored by the British.

29 May   Nikos Zahariadis, the Moscow-trained General Secretary of the KKE who had been imprisoned by the Metaxas regime and later sent to a German concentration camp, arrives in Athens and takes charge of the party.

Summer   Right-wing armed bands, which the authorities are unable or unwilling to suppress, intensify their attacks on EAM/ELAS veterans and on leftists and republicans.

19 September   At the urging of the regent, Damaskinos, the British, French, and American governments agree that the Greek elections will precede the plebiscite on the monarchy (thus reversing the order in the Varkiza Agreement) and will be held as soon as possible. The three governments had earlier agreed to send observers, which the Soviet Union refused to do. At the Foreign Ministers Council, the Soviet representative condemns unrest and violence in Greece, which he blames on the persecution of the Left and on Britain's support of "reactionary" elements.

22 November   Following Voulgaris' resignation, the octogenarian Liberal leader Themistocles Sophoulis forms a coalition government that is to prepare the country for elections. However, meager economic resources, ineffective government, and the rising level of political violence obstruct recovery and increase polarization and uncertainty.

1946

1 February   The Soviet delegate to the U.N. General Assembly blames political violence in Greece on British interference and demands that British troops leave Greece.

17 February   Following the Second Plenum of the KKE Central Committee, the party warns that unless conditions improve drastically the impending elections will not be free and fair and the Left will abstain, with "tragic consequences for the country." It is generally assumed that party leaders also discussed a possible resort to armed force.

21 February   The KKE announces its intention to boycott the upcoming elections and accuses Britain of propping up a reactionary regime whose tactics preclude fair elections.

31 March   Boycotted by the Left, the elections result in a clear victory for the conservative-monarchist Populist Party and its allies. The foreign observers pronounce the elections to have been basically fair. Par-

ticipation in the supervision of the 1946 elections is the first significant step in U.S. involvement in Greek political affairs.

31 March   Communist guerrillas attack and overpower the police station of Litohoro village, near Mount Olympus. Although there were similar incidents earlier in the year, the attack on Litohoro is often cited as the start of the civil war, with the level of violence rising rapidly afterward. British economic, military, police, and other missions assist the Athens government, but throughout 1946 and much of 1947 its security forces prove ineffective and inadequate.

18 April   A conservative government under the Populist leader Constantine Tsaldaris is established. Its punitive measures against the Left, combined with poor management of the nation's needs, result in further polarization and more violence.

27 June   The Foreign Ministers Council decides to transfer the Dodecanese islands (occupied by Italy since 1912) to Greece; the transfer is formally carried out in February 1947.

July   On instructions from the KKE, veteran ELAS leader Markos Vaphiadis leaves for the mountains to take charge of guerrilla bands already operating on their own.

27 August   Reversing his previous assessment, the U.S. ambassador to Greece, Lincoln MacVeagh, reports that the KKE is secretly controlled by the Soviet Union. This view, which Washington officials readily accept, convinces the Truman administration that the Soviet Union is responsible for the Greek civil war.

1 September   The plebiscite on the monarchy, from which leftists abstain in large numbers again, results in a 68 percent vote in favor of the king's return. King George arrives in Athens on 27 September. Upon his death, on 1 April 1947, he is succeeded by his younger brother Paul. Many Greeks, including lifelong republicans, see the monarchy as protection against a Communist takeover.

28 October   A KKE-convened conference of guerrilla leaders establishes a General Partisan Headquarters, and the following month the bands are renamed the "Democratic Army of Greece." At first a guerrilla force of less than 10,000, DAG grows to about 30,000 by May 1948, when its strength declines rapidly because of heavy casualties caused largely by a switch from guerrilla tactics to static warfare and by the growing size and firepower of the government troops.

3 December   Advised by Britain and the United States, the Greek government complains at the United Nations that its Balkan neighbors are supporting the Communist insurgents. In part, the Greek initiative is in response to Soviet criticism of the Athens government in the United Nations: in August, the Ukrainian delegate had charged that the conduct of the Greek government constituted a threat to peace and security in the Balkans. In response to the complaint from Greece, the U.N. Security Council establishes a Commission of Investigation, which travels to the Balkans in the

spring of 1947. The commission's report, and the United Nations' handling of it, reflects the East-West divisions of the cold war.

1947

12 January	In a long letter to Stalin signed by Zahariadis, the KKE appeals for extensive Soviet assistance in order to bring victory to the Communist insurgency in Greece. Stalin's response remains a matter of speculation.
24 January	In an attempt to broaden support for the government, Dimitrios Maximos replaces Tsaldaris as Prime Minister, and several prominent Liberals receive cabinet posts.
February	First major operation of government troops against DAG bands in the Vermion Mountains takes place. After suffering serious losses, the bands retreat, crossing into Albania and Yugoslavia. Once the government troops are withdrawn, the bands reinfiltrate the region.
21 February	Britain's Labour government notifies the United States that British aid to Greece and Turkey will end on 31 March and urges the Truman administration to assume the burden of supporting those two states.
3 March	In a formal note that was actually drafted by American officials, the Greek government requests that U.S. specialists assist in the distribution and management of the anticipated U.S. aid to Greece.
12 March	In a major policy statement before a joint session of Congress (the Truman Doctrine), President Truman requests economic and military assistance for Greece and Turkey. The legislation, which provides $400 million to be administered by U.S. civilian and military missions, is signed on 22 May 1947. The U.S. Army Group Greece (USAGG) and U.S. Navy Group Greece (USNGG) are established to provide logistical support.
20 June	Greece and the United States sign a formal agreement defining the terms of American assistance: American officials in key posts in Athens are to have a controlling influence over most sectors of Greek state activity.
28 June–25 July	Government troops attack a large DAG formation in the Grammos Mountains and inflict heavy casualties. In the first large-scale static warfare battle, DAG units counterattack toward the town of Konitsa but eventually retreat.
29 August	Tsaldaris returns to the premiership in an all-conservative government.
7 September	Under extreme pressure from American officials, Tsaldaris yields the premiership to Sophoulis and becomes Deputy Prime Minister and Foreign Minister. Restructured several times, the So-

phoulis coalition government lasts until the Liberal leader's death in June 1949.

31 October   The Joint U.S. Military Advisory and Planning Group (JUSMAPG) is established to provide overall support and advice to the Greek government forces in their effort to defeat the insurgency.

24 December   The formation of a Provisional Democratiç Government in the mountains under "General" Markos is announced. The insurgents' desperate attempts to seize and control several towns (Florina, Grevena, Konitsa) and to establish a capital for Markos's government, which might have induced Soviet bloc states to extend recognition, are defeated by government troops in bloody battles. Although effective as a guerrilla force, DAG cannot prevail in protracted static warfare.

25 December   DAG opens a major attack on Konitsa in an apparent attempt to acquire a capital for the Provisional Democratic Government. After two weeks of fierce fighting, DAG retreats with very heavy losses.

27 December   Under Emergency Law 509, the KKE and its affiliates are outlawed and all "Communist activity" is subjected to harsh punishment, including the death penalty.

1948

8 February   At a Moscow meeting, Stalin berates Yugoslav leaders for supporting the Greek insurgents and demands that assistance to the Greeks be terminated. The Stalin-Tito split, and Yugoslavia's expulsion from the Cominform, are major setbacks for the Greek insurgents. When the KKE sides with Stalin against Tito, the Yugoslavs close their border with Greece, thus depriving the insurgents of valuable supply and training bases, as well as of some of their reserves.

27 February   The Greek government formally charges that the insurgents are abducting Greek children and removing them to Eastern European countries. This *paidomazoma,* which the Athens authorities characterize as "genocide" and "dehellenization," emerges as possibly the most contentious and emotional issue of the civil war. Perhaps as many as 28,000 children are taken across the Greek border. International investigations, while inconclusive, suggest that in many but not all cases the children are taken against their parents' wishes.

31 May   Markos's Provisional Democratic Government announces its intention to accept and encourage initiatives from any quarter that might end the civil war and guarantee the country's independence and democratic institutions. With the government troops ready to launch major sweeping operations, Markos's feeler produces no results.

30 July

In a bold move aimed at public morale, the insurgents' modest artillery fires on Thessaloniki, but the Communist unit and its gun are captured and paraded through the city.

November

In a series of decrees, martial law is proclaimed throughout the country.

1949

10 January

With the support of American officials, Marshal Alexander Papagos becomes commander in chief of the armed forces, with the authority to bypass civilian government in prosecuting the war against the insurgents.

31 January

Markos, who is blamed for DAG's failures during the previous year, is removed and crosses into Albania on his way to the Soviet Union. Zahariadis takes personal command of DAG, which will soon fight its final battles on the Grammos and Vitsi mountain ranges.

3 April

A reconstituted Provisional Democratic Government under Dimitris Partsalidis, veteran leader of the wartime EAM, is announced.

30 April

The Provisional Democratic Government appeals to the United Nations to help end the violence in Greece and declares itself "ready to make the greatest concessions."

May

Soviet feelers to the U.S. and British governments for ending the civil war in Greece are unproductive.

30 June

Following the death of Sophoulis (on 24 June), a new coalition government is formed under Alexander Diomidis.

July-August

After fierce battles on the Grammos and Vitsi mountain ranges, government forces defeat and scatter the main body of DAG, remnants of which escape to Albania. Although minor clashes continue for several months, the civil war is over.

1950

February

Martial law is lifted but special security measures remain.

5 March

National elections take place, contested by more than forty parties grouped into blocs. Although no party wins a clear victory, the parties of the Center receive the largest number of votes, and a weak coalition government is formed under the ailing Plastiras (15 April). A new coalition government is formed on 21 August under Sophocles Venizelos.

1951

11 February	Responding to growing agitation among Greek Cypriots, Venizelos publicly calls for the union of Cyprus with Greece. Britain and, increasingly, the United States pressure the Greek government not to raise "the Cyprus issue."
31 May	Following friction with the palace, where his political ambitions are viewed with apprehension, Papagos resigns from active military service. His new conservative Greek Rally, which replaces the virtually defunct Populist Party, will dominate Greek politics for years to come.
31 May	Coup by military officers devoted to Papagos is aborted when Papagos orders them to disperse.
9 September	New elections, under a system of "reinforced" proportional representation, result in another political deadlock. A weak coalition government under Plastiras faces strong opposition from Papagos's conservatives and from the United Democratic Left. There are clear indications that unless a stable conservative government can be formed the United States will drastically reduce its aid to Greece.
22 October	Greece and Turkey are formally invited to join NATO, which they do on 18 February 1952. Both states send combat troops to fight in the Korean conflict.

1952

1 January	A new constitution replaces that of 1911. While basically a democratic and even liberal document, it allows repressive "emergency" laws to remain in effect and to be employed in persecuting the Left.
March	In the midst of public debate concerning new elections, U.S. Ambassador John Peurifoy declares that the proportional electoral system can produce only weak and unstable governments, which in turn will have "destructive results upon the effective utilization of American aid to Greece." Although the statement is widely denounced as interference in Greek domestic affairs, the new electoral law, which goes into effect in October 1952, is based on the simple majority system favored by the Americans, the palace, and Papagos.
16 November	National elections produce a decisive victory for Papagos's Greek Rally and a strong if repressive government, ushering in a decade of conservative rule.

Contributors

Nicos C. Alivizatos studied law in Athens and received his doctorate from the University of Paris (Paris II) in 1977. He is professor of constitutional law at the University of Athens, where he also teaches constitutional history. His publications include *Les institutions politiques de la Grèce a travers les crises, 1922–1974* (1979), *Introduction to the Constitutional History of Modern Greece, 1821–1940* (in Greek, 1981), *State, Radio, and Television: The Institutional Dimension* (in Greek, 1986), *The Constitutional Status of the Armed Forces* (in Greek, vol. 1, 1987; vol. 2, 1992). He is currently working on the role of the judiciary and judicial review in a comparative perspective.

Ivo Banac is professor of history and master of Pierson College at Yale University. He received his M.A. and Ph.D. degrees from Stanford University and is the author of *The National Question in Yugoslavia: Origins, History, Politics* (1984), which was awarded the Wayne S. Vucinich Prize of the American Association for the Advancement of Slavic Studies; and *With Stalin Against Tito: Cominformist Splits in Yugoslav Communism* (1988), which was awarded the Josip Juraj Strossmayer Award by the Zagreb Book Fair, as well as numerous reviews, articles, and collections, including most recently *Dubrovacki eseji* (Dubrovnik essays) (1992). He has edited six additional books and is a corresponding member of the Croatian Academy of Sciences and Arts, the editor of *East European Politics and Societies,* and a member of several editorial boards.

David H. Close holds undergraduate and doctoral degrees from Oxford University and is currently senior lecturer in history in the Faculty of Social Sciences at the Flinders University of South Australia. He has written articles or chapters on the modern political history of Britain and of Greece and has edited *Revolution: A History of the Idea* (Croom Helm, 1985), and *The Greek Civil War, 1943–1950: Studies of Polarization* (Routledge, 1993). He is also the author of *The Character of the Metaxas Dictatorship: An International Perspective* (Centre of Contemporary Greek Studies, King's College, London, 1990). He is preparing a book for Longmans on the origins of the Greek civil war.

Hagen Fleischer received his Ph.D. in history and communications studies from the Free University, Berlin, and is professor of modern history at the University of Athens. He is the author of *Im Kreuzschatten der Mächte: Griechenland, 1941–1944* (1986; Greek version: *Stemma kai swastika,* vol. 1, 1988; vol. 2, 1994) and of numerous articles on Greece in the twentieth century, particularly in the 1940s and 1950s. He was the permanent expert adviser of the "International Commission of Historians Designated to Establish the Military Service of Lieutenant Kurt Waldheim" and is co-author of the report, recently published in an updated English version: *The Waldheim Report* (Museum Tusculanum Press, 1993). He has edited (with Nikos Svoronos) *I Ellada, 1936–1944: Diktatoria—Katochi—Antistasi* (1989). He is at work on a larger study of Greece's relations with the two German states from 1949 to 1989, as well as on a monograph on German reparations.

John O. Iatrides received his education in Greece, the Netherlands, and the United States (Ph.D. in international politics, Clark University, 1962). He served with the Hellenic National Defense General Staff (1955–56) and the Prime Minister's Press Office (1956–58) and is professor of international politics at Southern Connecticut State University. He has taught courses on contemporary Greece at Harvard, Yale, Princeton, and New York universities. His publications include *Balkan Triangle: Birth and Decline of an Alliance Across Ideological Boundaries* (1968), *Revolt in Athens: The Greek Communist "Second Round," 1944–1945* (1972), *Ambassador MacVeagh Reports: Greece, 1933–1947* (1980), and numerous essays on the Greek civil war and Greek foreign policy. He is the editor of *Greece in the 1940s: A Nation in Crisis* (1981); editor with Theodore A. Couloumbis of *Greek-American Relations: A Critical Review* (1980); and editor with Lars Baerentzen and Ole L. Smith of *Studies in the History of the Greek Civil War* (1987).

Evangelos Kofos pursued undergraduate and graduate studies in the United States and received his Ph.D. in history from the University of London (1973). He is the author of *Nationalism and Communism in Macedonia* (1964), *I Epanastasis tis Makedonias kata to 1878* (1969), *Greece and the Eastern Crisis, 1875–1878* (1975, Athens Academy Award), *O Ellinismos stin Periodo 1869–1881* (1981), and numerous articles on Greek and Balkan history. His most recent papers in print include: "The Balkan Dimension of the Macedonian Question in Wartime and the Resistance" and "Greece and the Balkans in the '70s and '80s." At present, he serves as special counsellor on Balkan affairs in the Greek Ministry of Foreign Affairs.

George Th. Mavrogordatos received his Ph.D. from the University of California at Berkeley in 1979. He is associate professor of political science at the University of Athens. His publications include *Rise of the Green Sun: The Greek Election of 1981* (London: Centre of Contemporary Greek Studies, King's College, 1983) and *Stillborn Republic: Social Coalitions and Party Strategies in Greece, 1922–1936* (Berkeley and Los Angeles: University of California Press, 1983), for which he received the Woodrow Wilson Foundation Award of the American Political Science Association in 1984. In Greek, he has published *Between Pityocamptes and Procrustes,* a book on interest groups in contemporary Greece and has edited, with C. Hadziiossif, a volume on Venizelism and bourgeois modernization.

Ole L. Smith was educated in classical philology at the University of Aarhus, Denmark, and received a Dr.Phil. degree in 1978. He was professor of Greek in the Department of Classics of the University of Gothenburg, Sweden. His major publications include *Studies in the Scholia on Aeschylus,* vol. 1 (Leiden: Brill, 1976) and *Scholia in Aeschylum,* vols. 1 and 2 (Leipzig: Teubner, 1975–82). He also published (in Danish) *From Military Dictatorship to Socialism: Greece, 1974–1983* (Copenhagen: n.p., 1984). At the time of his sudden death in early February 1995 he was doing research on the history of the Greek Communist Party and on prewar *rebetika*.

Peter J. Stavrakis is associate professor of political science at the University of Vermont and author of *Moscow and Greek Communism, 1944–1949* (Ithaca, N.Y.: Cornell University Press, 1989) and several other essays on the Greek civil war. In 1990, he received a John M. Olin Foundation Faculty Fellowship to study Soviet-European Community relations and subsequently published several articles on this subject. In 1992–93, he was a research fellow at the Kennan Institute for Advanced Russian Studies of the Woodrow Wilson International Center for Scholars, working on a book-length study of statebuilding and the bureaucratic transformation of the Soviet successor states.

Stavros B. Thomadakis is a graduate of Yale University and earned his Ph.D. in financial economics from M.I.T. in 1974. He is professor of economics and finance at Baruch College, C.U.N.Y, and has held professorships at the University of Athens and the Sloan School of Management at M.I.T. He has served on the Greek Council of Economic Advisers, the European Community's Monetary Committee, and the board of directors of the European Investment Bank. In 1990, he served as a member of the "Angelopoulos Commission" on the Stabilization and Development of the Greek Economy. He has published extensively in the fields of financial theory, empirical financial and industrial economics, Greek economic structures and policies, and Greek economic history (nineteenth and twentieth centuries). He has recently edited, with Harry Psomiades, *Greece, Europe, and the Changing International Order* (New York: Pella, 1993).

Linda Wrigley is associate editor of *World Policy Journal* and a freelance editor specializing in international affairs. She was formerly associate director of the Lehrman Institute. She is a graduate of Gettysburg College and holds a master's degree in history from Trinity College (Connecticut).

Index